Themis
Bar Review

Multistate Bar Exam
Lecture Handouts

MBE Workshops

Civil Procedure

Constitutional Law

Contracts & Sales

Criminal Law

Criminal Procedure

Evidence

Real Property

Torts

Themis
Bar Review

MBE Workshops

MBE WORKSHOP: CIVIL PROCEDURE
PROFESSOR LISA TUCKER
DREXEL UNIVERSITY SCHOOL OF LAW

CHAPTER 1: **INTRODUCTION**

- Most testable areas: Jurisdiction, _____, service and venue, _____ motions

Question 1 | 5137 | MBE CIVIL PROCEDURE | SUBJECT MATTER JURISDICTION | Diversity Jurisdiction

The distracted driver of a powerboat struck and seriously injured two water skiers who, at time of the accident, were performing a stunt in which one was on the shoulders of the other. The unrelated skiers, who each suffered damages in excess of $100,000, filed a joint complaint based on negligence in a federal court located in the district in which the accident occurred. One of the skiers was a citizen of the forum state. The driver-defendant and the other skier were citizens of a neighboring state. The forum state has a long-arm statute that permits the exercise of jurisdiction to the extent permissible under the Due Process Clause of the Fourteenth Amendment.

Upon which of the following grounds can the driver most likely successfully move for dismissal of the claim asserted by the skier who is not a citizen of the forum state?

(A) Improper joinder

(B) Lack of subject matter jurisdiction

(C) Lack of personal jurisdiction

(D) Lack of venue

_____
_____
_____
_____
_____
_____
_____
_____
_____

A plaintiff, a resident of State A, filed a complaint against two defendants in a state court in State B, where a car accident between the parties took place. The claims were based solely on state law. One defendant resides in State B, where the accident occurred, and another resides in State C, a neighboring state. The complaint alleged $100,000 in damages. The defendant who resides in State B was personally served with a complaint and summons while he was walking to work. The defendant who resides in State C was served by a process server in the forum state after attending a business meeting in that state. Shortly thereafter, both defendants filed a motion to remove the case to the federal district court in the district where the case was filed. The federal district court denied the motion.

What is the most likely reason that the motion was denied?

(A) One of the defendants is a citizen of the state in which the action was filed.

(B) The federal court could not exercise personal jurisdiction over both defendants.

(C) The federal court lacked subject-matter jurisdiction over the claims.

(D) Venue would be improper in the federal district court.

_____
_____
_____
_____
_____
_____
_____
_____
_____
_____
_____
_____
_____
_____
_____
_____

A plaintiff was severely injured when her car collided with the defendant's truck on a highway in State A. The plaintiff was a citizen of State B and the defendant was a citizen of State A. The defendant had no contacts with State B. The plaintiff filed suit in federal district court in State B under diversity jurisdiction, asserting a state law claim for damages resulting from the defendant's alleged negligence. The defendant filed an answer, specifically denying each of the plaintiff's claims. Three months later, after discovery concluded and just before trial, the defendant filed a motion to dismiss the action for lack of personal jurisdiction.

Should the court dismiss the action for lack of personal jurisdiction over the defendant?

(A) No, because dismissal would prejudice the plaintiff, since discovery has already occurred in the case.

(B) No, because the defendant has waived the objection to the court's jurisdiction.

(C) Yes, because the defendant had no contacts with State B.

(D) Yes, because the court may dismiss an action for lack of personal jurisdiction at any time prior to final judgment.

During the defendant's cross-country road trip, he was involved in a car accident with the plaintiff in the state where the plaintiff lived. Following the accident, the plaintiff sued the defendant in federal court located in the state where the accident occurred. Prior to the accident, the defendant had never been to the forum state. The defendant flew home from the forum state directly following the accident, and has not been back to the forum state since that time. Before filing a responsive pleading, the defendant filed a motion to dismiss, arguing that the court lacked personal jurisdiction. The court denied the defendant's motion.

What is the most likely basis for the exercise of jurisdiction over the defendant in this case?

(A) General jurisdiction.

(B) In rem jurisdiction.

(C) Quasi in rem jurisdiction.

(D) Specific jurisdiction.

A plaintiff filed a complaint in federal district court under diversity jurisdiction seeking damages for injuries arising out of a car accident with the defendant. The following day, the plaintiff's spouse served the complaint together with the summons on the defendant. Twenty days later, the defendant learned that the plaintiff's spouse had not submitted proof of service to the court. The defendant then filed a motion to dismiss for insufficient service of process.

Should the court grant the defendant's motion to dismiss?

(A) No, because the failure to file proof of service does not affect the validity of the service.

(B) No, because the time for filing a motion to dismiss for insufficient service of process has expired

(C) Yes, because the time for filing proof of service has expired.

(D) Yes, because the plaintiff's spouse served the summons and complaint.

The plaintiff resides in a city in the Southern District of State C. The plaintiff credibly alleges that her federal legal rights were violated in a city in the Western District of State D by two defendants. The first defendant resides in a city in the Northern District of State C. The second defendant resides in a town in the Central District of State C, where the plaintiff's employer is located.

In which of the following districts would venue be proper as to all the parties?

(A) The Western District of State D, the Northern District of State C, or the Southern District of State C.

(B) The Western District of State D, the Central District of State C, or the Southern District of State C.

(C) The Western District of State D, the Northern District of State C, or the Central District of State C.

(D) The Western District of State D, the Northern District of State C, the Central District of State C, or the Southern District of State C.

Question 7 | 5163 | MBE CIVIL PROCEDURE | PLEADINGS | Answer

A bakery negotiated with a supplier regarding a long-term commitment to supply flour. They agreed to specific terms to be memorialized in a written contract. Due to an oversight, the supplier never signed the written contract, although it began providing flour to the bakery under the terms of their agreement. Six months later, the price of flour rose dramatically following a nationwide drought. The supplier, realizing that it had never signed the contract, told the bakery that it would have to charge a higher price for the flour. The bakery properly filed a complaint in federal district court, alleging that the flour supplier had breached their contract. The flour supplier filed an answer in which it denied the factual allegations in the complaint regarding the price and duration of the contract, but did not raise any affirmative defenses. The following day, the flour supplier filed a motion to dismiss, asserting that the oral contract between the parties violated the Statute of Frauds.

Can the court grant the defendant's motion to dismiss?

(A) Yes, because the answer denied the factual allegations regarding the terms of the contract.

(B) Yes, because the complaint failed to state a claim upon which relief could be granted.

(C) No, because the defendant waived any objection on the pleadings by filing an answer.

(D) No, because the defendant did not assert a defense based on the Statute of Frauds in its answer.

_____

_____

_____

_____

_____

_____

_____

_____

_____

_____

_____

_____

A defendant filed a complaint against a third-party defendant for contribution permitted under federal law for any environmental damages for which the defendant was found liable. The third-party defendant and the defendant were domiciled in the same state. The third-party defendant filed a motion to dismiss for failure to state a claim upon which relief could be granted. The third-party defendant submitted affidavits in support of its position, but the court refused to consider them. After taking all well-pleaded facts in the complaint as true and resolving all doubts and inferences in the defendant's favor, the court denied the motion to dismiss.

Has the court acted properly in making its ruling?

(A) No, because the court lacked subject-matter jurisdiction over the complaint against the third-party defendant.

(B) No, because the court failed to consider the third-party defendant's affidavits.

(C) Yes, because the court took all well-pleaded facts in the complaint as true and resolved all doubts and inferences in the defendant's favor.

(D) Yes, because a third-party defendant cannot file a motion to dismiss for failure to state a claim upon which relief can be granted.

_____
_____
_____
_____
_____
_____
_____
_____
_____
_____
_____
_____

Two unrelated passengers on a small plane sued the pilot of the plane for injuries suffered during a rough landing after a sightseeing trip. They filed a negligence action in federal district court with the younger passenger, who had only minor injuries, claiming $5,000 in damages and the older passenger, whose injuries were life threatening, claiming $95,000. The two passengers are citizens of the same state. The pilot is a citizen of another state. The pilot moved to dismiss the younger passenger's claim for lack of subject matter jurisdiction.

Should the court dismiss the younger passenger's claim?

(A) No, because the total damages sought exceed the amount-in-controversy requirement.

(B) No, because the court can exercise supplemental jurisdiction over the claim.

(C) Yes, because this claim fails to satisfy the amount-in-controversy requirement.

(D) Yes, because the younger passenger is a citizen of the same state as the older passenger.

A plaintiff filed an action against a defendant in federal district court. The complaint alleged that the defendant had infringed upon a trademark held by the plaintiff under federal law and sought $55,000 in damages. In addition, the plaintiff claimed damages of $30,000 allegedly attributable to the defendant's negligence in causing an auto accident involving the two parties. The plaintiff and the defendant are citizens of different states. The defendant moved to dismiss the negligence claim for lack of subject matter jurisdiction. The court denied the motion.

Is the court's ruling correct?

(A)   Yes, because the court can exercise supplemental jurisdiction over the negligence claim.

(B)   Yes, because the court has diversity jurisdiction over the negligence claim.

(C)   No, because neither diversity nor supplemental jurisdiction exists with respect to the negligence claim.

(D)   No, because a state law based claim may not be joined with a claim over which the court has federal question jurisdiction.

_____
_____
_____
_____
_____
_____
_____
_____
_____
_____
_____
_____

Three shareholders brought an action in federal district court for a violation of federal securities law against a corporation. The shareholders sought certification of a class of all persons who had purchased stock during a two-year period. The members of the class suffered damages that ranged from $75 to $65,000, with the total damages sought just exceeding $3 million. Some members of the class are citizens of the same state as the corporation but none of the three representative shareholders is a citizen of the same state as the corporation.

Does the court have subject matter jurisdiction over this action?

(A) Yes, because none of the three representative shareholders is a citizen of the same state as the corporation.

(B) Yes, because the action is based on a violation of federal securities law.

(C) No, because no member of the class has suffered damages in excess of $75,000.

(D) No, because some members of the class are citizens of the same state as the corporation.

_____
_____
_____
_____
_____
_____
_____
_____
_____
_____
_____
_____
_____
_____
_____

The plaintiff, a State N citizen, properly invokes a State M federal court's diversity jurisdiction in a tort suit against the defendant, an airplane manufacturer based in State M. The plaintiff credibly alleges that he was severely injured when the defendant's airplane crashed as a result of an improperly installed engine part. During discovery, the plaintiff learns that an employee of the defendant who installed engine parts at the time the plane was manufactured was an alcoholic whose drinking may have impaired his work. The defendant fired the employee before the plane crash that injured the plaintiff.

What discovery device may the plaintiff use to obtain more information from the former employee?

(A) An oral deposition.

(B) An interrogatory.

(C) A physical examination.

(D) A request for admission.

Question 13 | 5029 | MBE CIVIL PROCEDURE | PRETRIAL PROCEDURE AND DISCOVERY | Adjudication Without Trial

A tenant properly filed a complaint under state law against his landlord in federal district court under diversity jurisdiction, alleging that the landlord's negligence in failing to repair the stairs in a common area of the apartment building resulted in the tenant falling and sustaining significant injuries. After the landlord served his answer, the tenant moved for summary judgment. In support of his motion, the tenant submitted affidavits from three other tenants in which each stated that she had told the landlord prior to the accident that the stairs needed to be fixed. In opposition to the motion, the landlord submitted an affidavit from the maintenance worker employed by the landlord, stating that the stairs were in good condition on the day of the tenant's accident.

How should the court rule on the motion for summary judgment?

(A) Grant the motion, because in viewing the evidence in the light most favorable to the tenant, the tenant is entitled to judgment as a matter of law.

(B) Grant the motion, because the tenant presented more evidence in support of the motion.

(C) Deny the motion, because the tenant did not meet the burden of production.

(D) Deny the motion, because a reasonable jury could return a verdict in favor of the landlord.

_____
_____
_____
_____
_____
_____
_____
_____
_____

A mayor sued a blogger for defamation in federal district court under diversity jurisdiction. The mayor alleged in her complaint that the blogger had published defamatory statements about her that suggested she was having an adulterous relationship. The mayor's entire case rested on her own testimony establishing the prima facie elements of her claim and a properly authenticated and admitted copy of the allegedly defamatory publication. At the end of the mayor's presentation of evidence to the jury, the blogger filed a motion for judgment as a matter of law. Finding that the mayor's meager evidence was insufficient for a jury reasonably to find that the publication was false, as was required by state law, the judge granted the blogger's motion and directed a judgment in favor of the blogger. The mayor immediately appealed the judgment, contending that the trial judge applied the wrong legal standard in granting the motion.

On these facts, should the judgment be set aside on appeal?

(A) No, because the district court's ruling was not clearly erroneous.

(B) No, because the mayor failed to meet her burden of establishing a prima facie case as a matter of law.

(C) Yes, because a motion for judgment as a matter of law cannot be granted until both parties have presented their cases.

(D) Yes, because the district court improperly evaluated the weight of the evidence.

_____
_____
_____
_____
_____
_____
_____
_____
_____
_____
_____
_____

In a civil action properly brought in federal district court based on diversity jurisdiction, a jury of seven persons was empanelled. During the trial, the court excused a juror for good cause. After the case was submitted to the jury for deliberation, the court excused a second juror, also for good cause. The remaining jurors returned a unanimous verdict for the plaintiff.

Can the defendant successfully challenge this verdict?

(A) No, because the jury verdict was unanimous.

(B) No, because the court excused both jurors for good cause.

(C) Yes, because fewer than six jurors returned the verdict.

(D) Yes, because the court may not excuse a juror once deliberations have begun.

_____
_____
_____
_____
_____
_____
_____
_____
_____
_____
_____
_____
_____
_____

A consumer filed a products liability action against a manufacturer in federal district court based on diversity jurisdiction. Prior to trial, the manufacturer filed a motion in limine to exclude testimony by an expert on the consumer's witness list on the grounds that it was based on subjective belief and unsupported speculation. After holding a hearing, the judge granted the manufacturer's motion. Because of this ruling and the consumer's inability to produce other evidence in support of her case, the judge granted the manufacturer's subsequent motion for summary judgment. The consumer appealed the judgment, contending that the district court judge had erroneously excluded the testimony of the consumer's expert.

In reviewing this challenge to the trial court's ruling, what standard should the appellate court apply?

(A) Abuse of discretion, because the judge had made an evidentiary ruling.

(B) Absence of a genuine dispute and entitlement to judgment as a matter of law, because the ruling affected the summary judgment motion.

(C) A preponderance of the evidence, because the ruling was outcome determinative.

(D) Clearly erroneous, because the ruling was made by the judge.

_____
_____
_____
_____
_____
_____
_____
_____
_____
_____
_____
_____
_____

A mother bought reusable snack bags from a company. The company uses an antibacterial agent called triclosan in its snack bags to help prevent mold from growing in the reusable bags. Triclosan is a known toxin that may, if used in a sufficient amount, weaken the immune system, especially when used in a moist environment, such as with reusable snack bags containing fruit or other damp foods. The mother who purchased the snack bags sued the company in federal court because she believed that the toxins in the company's snack bags caused her son to contract an illness due to his weakened immune system. At a trial without a jury, the judge, despite finding that the amount of triclosan used by the company in its snack bags was sufficient to cause the weakening of a child's immune system, held for the company because the plaintiff failed to prove that the boy would not have suffered from this particular illness unless his immune system had been weakened. In an unrelated action also filed against the company in the same federal court, a father sought damages from the company on behalf of his daughter, who contracted an illness after using the company's snack bags. During the trial, the father moved, on the basis of collateral estoppel, to prevent the company from contending that the amount of triclosan it used in its snack bags was insufficient to cause the weakening of a child's immune system.

Can the court grant this motion?

(A) Yes, because offensive use of collateral estoppel is permitted.

(B) Yes, because the facts involved are related in time, space, origin, or motivation.

(C) No, because a jury did not render a final judgment on the merits.

(D) No, because the daughter was not a party in the prior case.

_____
_____
_____
_____
_____
_____
_____
_____
_____

[END OF HANDOUT]

MBE WORKSHOP: CONSTITUTIONAL LAW
PROFESSOR LISA TUCKER
DREXEL UNIVERSITY SCHOOL OF LAW

CHAPTER 1:   INTRODUCTION

- The MBE will only test black and white rules

- Most testable areas:

  - Federal _____

    - Standing, mootness, ripeness, etc.

  - Balance of Powers

    - _____ and _____
      branches and their powers

      - Pardons, commerce, spending

    - Federalism (power of the States)

  - Individual Rights

    - Due process
    - Equal _____
    - Free speech
    - Freedom of religion

A potential candidate for city council publicly expresses his opinion to the media that although he has not yet officially declared his candidacy, he is not optimistic about his chances of winning if he were to run for a city council position within a particular political party. Because he has an interest in both running and winning, he therefore publicly declares that he would like to be placed on the ballot as a member of "every party possible" in order to increase his chances. The elections commissioner publicly declares that if the potential candidate attempts to "spread his luck around the ballot," he will be prohibited from being placed on the ballot at all. The potential candidate sues in federal court, stating that such a prohibition is unfair.

How should the court proceed?

(A) Dismiss the case, because the commissioner has not prohibited the potential candidate's inclusion on the ballot.

(B) Dismiss the case, because the city has the right to regulate ballot access in any way it sees fit.

(C) Dismiss the case, because the question is a political one that the court has no standing to hear.

(D) Rule in favor of the potential candidate because a candidate may appear on the ballot as a member of multiple parties.

The President created an office to encourage the improvement of local communities through faith-based organizations. The office was funded from monies appropriated by Congress for the general discretionary use of the President. The office provided support only to religious organizations. A taxpayer brought suit in federal court challenging the constitutionality of this office. The federal government has moved to dismiss this suit.

Should the court allow the taxpayer's suit to proceed?

(A) Yes, because the funding of the office violates the First Amendment Establishment of Religion Clause.

(B) Yes, because the source of the funds for the office is a congressional appropriation.

(C) No, because the plaintiff as a taxpayer lacks standing.

(D) No, because the First Amendment Establishment of Religion Clause does not apply to the executive branch.

_____
_____
_____
_____
_____
_____
_____
_____
_____
_____
_____
_____

In response to growing concerns about the overcrowding of landfills with scrap metal, Congress passed a statute requiring all unwanted vehicles to be disposed of at federally licensed auto-recycling facilities. These facilities were able to recycle more components of vehicles than most other recycling facilities. However, due to the high operating costs of these facilities, the cost of disposing the vehicles was much higher than the cost of disposing them at general purpose recycling facilities. A state wants to dispose of its fleet of decommissioned trucks at a state-operated recycling facility. However, this facility is not federally licensed.

Is the state permitted to dispose of its decommissioned trucks at the state-operated facility?

(A) No, because the federal statute was passed pursuant to Congress's power to legislate for the general welfare.

(B) No, because the federal statute regulates interstate commerce.

(C) Yes, because the market-participant exception applies.

(D) Yes, because there is a presumption against preemption in an area governed by the state's police power.

_____
_____
_____
_____
_____
_____
_____
_____
_____
_____
_____
_____
_____

Question 4 | 7048 | MBE CONSTITUTIONAL LAW | THE POWERS OF CONGRESS | Taxation and Spending

Due to the rising cost of water, Congress enacted a statute that allocated $20 million to fund a consortium of independent non-profit water organizations. The purpose of the consortium was to address the various issues causing a rise in the cost of water and water shortages across the United States, and to fund research into solutions. The statute provided clear guidelines about what the consortium should research and what it could spend, and specified that the remaining funds would be allocated for infrastructure improvements. In addition, the statute delegated to the Department of the Interior the power to select the water organizations to participate in the consortium.

Is the statute constitutional?

(A) No, because Congress is delegating its authority to the executive branch of the government.

(B) No, because the statute exceeds the scope of Congress's investigative power.

(C) Yes, because Congress has the power to enact this legislation under the Necessary and Proper Clause.

(D) Yes, because Congress has the power to spend for the general welfare of the public.

Question 5 | 3204 | MBE CONSTITUTIONAL LAW | PRIVILEGES AND IMMUNITIES | Article IV

A state anticipates a possible reduction of its native oyster population due to a variety of factors, including non-customary weather patterns and polluted waters. To discourage excessive fishing until oyster numbers are confirmed for the season, the state enacts a statute raising the cost of oyster-fishing licenses for all out-of-state residents to twenty times that of in-state residents. The statute does not distinguish between commercial and recreational oyster fishing. An out-of-state commercial oyster fisherman files suit in federal court to have the statute struck down.

Is the statute constitutional?

(A) No, because the statute violates the Privileges and Immunities Clause of Article IV.

(B) No, because the statute violates the Privileges or Immunities Clause of the Fourteenth Amendment.

(C) Yes, because the statute does not discriminate against out-of-state commerce.

(D) Yes, because the statute also applies to recreational oyster fishing.

_____
_____
_____
_____
_____
_____
_____
_____
_____
_____
_____
_____
_____
_____

In response to recent unusual earthquake activity, a large city has enacted an ordinance requiring the permanent placement of seismographic equipment in the basement of 20 randomly selected commercial buildings throughout the city as part of the creation of an early warning network. Although the owners of the buildings will not be compensated, the cost of the purchase and installation of the equipment is to be borne by a private university that will operate the early warning network. The owner of one building that has been randomly selected as a site for this equipment has challenged this law as unconstitutional.

Should the court rule in favor of the owner?

(A)   No, because the economic impact on the owner would be slight.

(B)   No, because the owner's building was randomly selected.

(C)   Yes, because the city will not operate the network.

(D)   Yes, because the equipment will reside permanently in the building.

A state with heavy snowfall each winter sough to prevent injuries and accidents on the road caused by snow falling off of the roofs of large trucks. To further this interest, the state enacted a statute that requires state-employed road maintenance crews to set up random checkpoints at highway on-ramps and state border crossings during the winter months. At these checkpoints, every truck above a certain size is required to stop so the maintenance crews can make sure any snow on its roof is brushed off. The statute has caused significant traffic delays, but the effect on the rate of accidents on highways in the winter has been minimal. An out-of-state company that ships its goods across the state has started losing business because this program has made it nearly impossible to estimate delivery times due to the delays. As a result, the out-of-state company has brought an action challenging the constitutionality of the state statute.

Is the company likely to succeed in its constitutional challenge to the state statute?

(A) No, because the state statute does not discriminate against out-of-state commerce.

(B) No, because the state statute serves an important state interest.

(C) Yes, because the state statute imposes an unreasonable burden on interstate commerce.

(D) Yes, because the state statute is not rationally related to a legitimate state interest.

_____
_____
_____
_____
_____
_____
_____
_____
_____
_____
_____
_____
_____

The Judiciary Committee of the U.S. House of Representatives initiated impeachment proceedings against a federal district court judge. The President, a lifelong friend of the judge, considered the grounds for impeachment that were being discussed to be politically motivated and without substantial merit. Prior to any hearing on matter by the House committee, the president pardoned the judge.

What effect does this pardon have on the impeachment proceedings against the judge?

(A) The proceedings must stop, because the President's power to pardon is plenary.

(B) The proceedings must stop, because the President acted in good faith in granting the pardon.

(C) The pardon has no effect on the proceedings because a President's power to pardon does not extend to impeachment.

(D) The pardon has no effect on the proceedings because a President may not pardon a person until that person has been convicted.

_____
_____
_____
_____
_____
_____
_____
_____
_____
_____
_____
_____
_____
_____

A municipality that owned a public swimming pool normally uses government funds to hire lifeguards and other staff and to maintain the pool. During hours when the pool closed, the municipality rents the pool out to any private group with appropriate liability insurance that also provides their own lifeguards and other staff. A private group rented the public pool in order to host an "All-American" swim competition to raise funds for veterans. The competition was open to the general public. However, because the group wanted to promote patriotism, all participants in the competition were required to be U.S. citizens. A resident alien wanted to participate in the swim competition, but was refused entry. The man has sued the group in the appropriate court for violating his rights to equal treatment under the Fourteenth Amendment.

Is the man likely to prevail in his action?

(A) No, because the group is not a state actor and is therefore not subject to the Fourteenth Amendment.

(B) No, because resident aliens are not a protected class under the Fourteenth Amendment.

(C) Yes, because the Fourteenth Amendment prohibits the group from discriminating against members of the public based upon their alienage.

(D) Yes, because using a public swimming pool owned and run by the municipality subjects the group to the Fourteenth Amendment.

_____
_____
_____
_____
_____
_____
_____
_____
_____
_____
_____
_____
_____
_____

A federal law provides that all employees of the federal library system whose job descriptions include cataloging or disseminating materials will be required to take a reading comprehension test. The law provides that employees who do not meet a minimum standard of reading comprehension will either be fired or reassigned to a different position. The law does not provide for a hearing process for these employees, who are not at-will employees. An employee whose job description included cataloging materials failed to meet the minimum standard and was reassigned to a different position at a lower grade. The government denied his request for a hearing. He sued to enjoin the government from reassigning him, arguing that his constitutional rights were violated.

Which of the following constitutional provisions provides the best support for the employee's suit?

(A)   The Privileges and Immunities Clause of Article IV.

(B)   The Due Process Clause of the Fifth Amendment.

(C)   The Takings Clause of the Fifth Amendment.

(D)   The Contract Clause of Article I, Section 10.

Question 11 | 5948 | MBE CONSTITUTIONAL LAW | SUBSTANTIVE DUE PROCESS | Standard of Review

In response to a highly publicized incident involving a local sonographer who failed to correctly read a sonogram, and at the urging of a state association of medical technicians, the state legislature enacted a bill that lengthened the period of education required to receive a license to be employed as a sonographer from one year to two years.   Prior to the enactment of this law, an obstetrician with a private practice had promised a clerk who worked in her office that she would employ him as sonographer if he obtained the necessary state license.   Three months before the passage of the law, the clerk had begun his coursework in order to satisfy the then one-year educational requirement to become a sonographer.   Although discussed at the hearing that the legislative committee had held on this legislation, the statute did not contain a provision that delayed its effective date for those already enrolled in an educational program to become a sonographer.   The clerk has filed suit challenging the constitutionality of the state statute as applied to him due to its failure to grant him an exemption from the two-year educational requirement.

How is the court likely to rule?

(A)   For the clerk, because employment is a fundamental right and the state cannot satisfy the strict scrutiny test.

(B)   For the clerk, because the statute violates the Contract Clause of Article I, Section 10.

(C)   For the state, because the legislation is a regulatory taking of intangible personal property, and therefore the Takings Clause of the Fifth Amendment does not apply.

(D)   For the state, because the state legislature could rationally believe that the statute, as passed, was in the best interest of the public.

_____
_____
_____
_____
_____
_____
_____
_____
_____
_____
_____
_____

Concerned over the increasing frequency of livestock theft, the legislature of a state with a sizable number of ranches passed legislation, which the governor signed into law, creating the position of livestock identity inspector within the state Department of Agriculture. The inspector is tasked with enforcing the state laws regarding branding of livestock. The state statute confined this position to U.S. citizens. A longtime resident of the state who was a citizen of a foreign country applied for the position and was rejected. He wants to seek injunctive relief against the state Secretary of Agriculture to prevent her from enforcing this requirement as it applies to him.

Of the following, which is the best federal constitutional ground upon which the plaintiff can base this action?

(A) The Equal Protection Clause of the Fourteenth Amendment

(B) The Privileges or Immunities Clause of the Fourteenth Amendment

(C) The Contract Clause of Article I, Section 10 of the U.S. Constitution

(D) The Comity Clause of Article IV, Section 2 of the U.S. Constitution

A small, struggling, formerly industrial city in one state was only 30 miles from the border of the neighboring state, and only 40 miles from a booming city in the neighboring state. In an effort to entice more citizens of the neighboring state to come to the small city to shop, dine, and otherwise spend money, the small city passed an ordinance relieving out-of-state citizens from paying the city's sales tax. A group of small-city citizens properly brought a suit against the city, challenging the ordinance.

Of the following constitutional provisions, which would be the basis on which the citizens could most effectively challenge the ordinance?

(A) The Due Process Clause of the Fifth Amendment.

(B) The Equal Protection Clause of the Fourteenth Amendment.

(C) The Privileges and Immunities Clause of Article IV, Section 2.

(D) The Privileges or Immunities Clause of the Fourteenth Amendment.

_____
_____
_____
_____
_____
_____
_____
_____
_____
_____
_____
_____
_____
_____

A state enacted an intestacy statute that provided full inheritance rights for marital children from both parents. Under the statute, nonmarital children were permitted to inherit only through their mothers. The underlying purposes of the statute were to promote family relations and establish an accurate and efficient method of disposing property at death. The father of a nonmarital child recently died intestate. The nonmarital child brought suit challenging the constitutionality of the statute.

Which of the following most accurately states the appropriate standard of review for the court?

(A) The court must determine whether the statute is the least restrictive means of achieving an important government interest.

(B) The court must determine whether the statute is rationally related to a legitimate government interest.

(C) The court must determine whether the statute is substantially related to an important government interest.

(D) The court must determine whether the statute is narrowly tailored to achieve a compelling government interest.

Faced with poorly performing public schools in a city, the state instituted a state-funded voucher program for parents with school age children who lived in the city. The state gave parents a voucher for each school-aged child that could be used either towards tuition for the child to attend a private school in the child's school district, whether parochial or not, or be presented to the child's public school, which would receive the same amount in additional funding. The choice of whether to attend a private or public school was solely left up to the parents and their child. Over 95 percent of the vouchers were used by parents towards tuition payments to parochial schools. The program contained no restrictions as to how the schools used the funds.

Is this program constitutional?

(A) No, because the primary effect of the voucher program is to provide state aid to parochial schools.

(B) No, because the program contained no provisions to prevent the use of state aid to fund religious instruction at the parochial schools.

(C) Yes, because governmental financial assistance that benefits religious educational institutions is constitutional so long as it does not result in excessive government entanglement with religion.

(D) Yes, because the program is neutral with respect to religion and provides financial assistance directly to citizens who have a choice as to whether to use the voucher at a parochial or nonparochial school.

_____
_____
_____
_____
_____
_____
_____
_____
_____
_____
_____
_____
_____
_____
_____

A state highway administration, acting pursuant to statutory authorization by the state legislature, has promulgated rules for large electronic billboards located along roads maintained by the state. These rules are concerned with the potential for driver distraction and the ensuing adverse consequences for highway safety. Among the rules is one that bans the graphic display of violence. The producer of a movie wants to promote the movie through a short clip from the movie on billboards subject to this rule. The clip contains a graphic display of violence. The producer has filed an action in the appropriate federal court challenging the state highway administration's rule as a violation of the First Amendment as applicable to the states through the Fourteenth Amendment.

Of the following standards, by which should the state highway administration's rule be judged?

(A) As a rule that deals with a matter traditionally subject to regulation, it must be upheld unless it is arbitrary or irrational.

(B) As a regulation of commercial speech, there must be a reasonable fit between the government's ends and the means chosen to accomplish those ends.

(C) As a time, place, or manner restriction, it must be narrowly tailored to serve a significant governmental interest.

(D) As a content regulation, it must be necessary to achieve a compelling governmental interest.

Concerned with the proliferation of signs about upcoming events and the failure to remove those signs after the event, a city enacted an ordinance that limited the number of such signs that could be displayed on public property and set a time period before and after an event during which signs about that event could be displayed. A social organization wants to display signs about its monthly dinner, which is held to attract new members, in greater number and for a longer period than permitted by the ordinance. The organization has filed a lawsuit, challenging the constitutionality of the ordinance.

Of the following, by which standard will this ordinance be judged?

(A) It must be narrowly tailored to further a significant government interest, and leave open alternative channels of communication.

(B) It must be the least restrictive means for accomplishing a compelling governmental interest.

(C) It must be rationally related to a legitimate government interest.

(D) It must not have a negative impact on the organization's freedom of assembly.

_____
_____
_____
_____
_____
_____
_____
_____
_____

- Pluses with Con Law:
  - It's easy to cross out _____,
  - The same areas are tested over and over, and
  - There can be no gray areas on the MBE; everything is black and white.

[END OF HANDOUT]

MBE WORKSHOP: CONTRACTS
PROFESSOR LISA TUCKER
DREXEL UNIVERSITY SCHOOL OF LAW

CHAPTER 1:   INTRODUCTION

- Your first step in any Contracts question is to figure out which law applies: the
  _____ or the _____

- Do lots of practice questions and be sure to carefully read the

  _____

- Most testable areas:

  o _____ of contracts

      ▪ _____, _____,
         _____

      ▪ Modification
      ▪ Unilateral contracts
      ▪ Assignment and delegation

  o Statute of Frauds and Parol Evidence

  o When Contracts Fail:

      ▪ Remedies
      ▪ Damages

A homeowner entered into a contract with a landscaper. The contract specified that the homeowner would pay the landscaper $10,000 upon completion of a list of projects. The landscaper performed the work while the homeowner was away on vacation. When the landscaper sought payment, the homeowner refused, noting that a tree had not been trimmed as required by the contract. The landscaper responded that, since he would now have to forego other work in order to trim the tree, he would do it but only if the homeowner agreed to pay him a total of $10,500 for his services. The homeowner, desperate to have the work completed, agreed. Once the work was completed, however, the homeowner gave the landscaper a check for $10,000, and refused to pay more. The landscaper sued for breach of contract.

Is the landscaper likely to succeed in his claim?

(A) No, because an enforceable contract cannot be renegotiated.

(B) No, because there was no consideration for the promise to pay $10,500 and no unanticipated circumstances arose.

(C) Yes, because there was a valid modification of the contract.

(D) Yes, because the landscaper suffered a detriment by foregoing other work.

_____
_____
_____
_____
_____
_____
_____
_____
_____
_____
_____
_____
_____
_____
_____

A wholesaler of bicycle chains sent a retailer the following fax on December 1: "Because of your continued loyalty as a customer, I am prepared to sell you up to 1,000 units of Bicycle Chain Model D at $7.50 per unit, a 25% discount off our original $10.00 price. This offer will remain open for 7 days." The fax was not signed, but was on the wholesaler's letterhead and had been initialed by the wholesaler's head of sales. On December 4, the wholesaler's head of sales called the retailer and informed the retailer that he had decided to revoke his December 1 offer. On December 5, the retailer placed an order for 1,000 bicycle chains, stating that he would pay the discounted price of $7.50 per unit.

What is the correct value of the order placed by the retailer?

(A) $7,500, because the wholesaler's revocation was not in writing.

(B) $7,500, because the wholesaler was bound to keep the offer open for 7 days.

(C) $10,000, because the offer was not signed by the wholesaler.

(D) $10,000, because the retailer did not provide consideration to hold the offer open.

_____
_____
_____
_____
_____
_____
_____
_____
_____
_____
_____
_____
_____
_____
_____

A retailer received a written firm offer signed by a supplier. The offer committed the supplier to providing the retailer with up to 10,000 tubes of toothpaste over the next 45 days at $1 a tube. Thirty days later, the supplier informed the retailer that the price per tube of toothpaste would be $1.10. The next day the retailer ordered 6,000 tubes of toothpaste from the supplier, which the supplier promptly shipped. Sixty days after the receipt of the offer, the retailer ordered another 4,000 tubes of toothpaste, which the supplier also promptly shipped.

What price is the retailer permitted to charge the supplier for the toothpaste?

(A) $10,000 (10,000 * $1), because the supplier's firm offer was effective for three months regardless of its terms.

(B) $10,400 ((6,000 * $1) + (4,000 * $1.10)), because the supplier's firm offer was effective for only 45 days.

(C) $11,000 (10,000 * $1.10), because the firm offer rule does not apply where the buyer is a merchant.

(D) $11,000 (10,000 * $1.10), because the supplier informed the retailer that the price was increased to $1.10 before the retailer's placement of either order.

_____
_____
_____
_____
_____
_____
_____
_____
_____
_____
_____
_____
_____
_____

Question 4 | 6011 | MBE CONTRACTS & SALES | FORMATION OF CONTRACTS | Mutual Assent

On May 10, the coach of a youth league baseball team sent a letter to a supplier asking the supplier to promptly ship 20 red jerseys to him. On May 15, the supplier received this letter and sent the coach a reply letter accepting the offer. On May 16, the supplier realized that he had no red jerseys with which to fill the order, and sends the coach 20 blue jerseys with a note that the blue jerseys were tendered as an accommodation. The coach received the jerseys and accommodation note on May 18, and received the supplier's acceptance letter on May 19.

On May 20, which of the following is a correct statement of the parties' legal rights and duties?

(A) The coach can either accept or reject the blue jerseys and, in either event, recover damages, if any, for breach of contract.

(B) The coach can either accept or reject the blue jerseys, but if he rejects them, he will thereby waive any remedy for breach of contract.

(C) The supplier's shipment of nonconforming goods constituted an acceptance of the coach's offer, thereby creating a contract for the sale of the blue jerseys.

(D) The supplier's shipment of the blue jerseys constituted a counteroffer.

Question 5 | 7073 | MBE CONTRACTS & SALES | FORMATION OF CONTRACTS | Consideration

A maker of hand-woven rugs contracted with a supplier to provide yarn made from sheep's wool. The written contract specified that, for four years, the supplier would provide the rug maker with 2,000 spools of yarn made from 100% sheep's wool per month, at $10 per spool, for a total of $20,000. Two years into the contract, the supplier sent 2,000 spools of yarn to the rug maker made from 90% sheep's wool and 10% synthetic fiber. The rug maker sent a check to the supplier for $15,000 for the shipment, and added a clear note on the check stating that the payment was in full for the shipment, but was $5,000 less due to the synthetic fiber in the yarn. The supplier promptly deposited the check, and then four months later filed suit against the rug maker for the remaining $5,000. The supplier has submitted evidence of the written contract, and the rug maker has submitted evidence of the deposited check.

What is the rug maker's best defense in this situation?

(A) The rug maker's and supplier's good faith dispute over the yarn composition suspended the rug maker's obligation to pay the remaining $5,000.

(B) The act of knowingly depositing the check for $15,000 by the supplier was a novation that relieved the rug maker from any further liability.

(C) The supplier deposited the check for $5,000 less than the contract price, thereby discharging the rug maker of any further duty to pay the remaining amount for that month's shipment.

(D) By depositing the check, the supplier was estopped from claiming that the rug maker owed him an additional $5,000.

_____
_____
_____
_____
_____
_____
_____
_____
_____
_____
_____
_____
_____

The owner of a restaurant who highlighted local ingredients when creating his menu bought cheese and other dairy products from a local dairy farmer. The owner and the farmer had entered into written requirements contracts each spring for the past ten years. In the winter of the tenth year, the farmer purchased a substantial amount of new dairy cows and expanded his farming capabilities. He notified all customers that he would have a much higher amount of available products the following spring, and would adjust his deliveries accordingly. The owner responded with a date he wished for the products to be delivered, as per custom, but said nothing else. On the agreed upon date, the farmer delivered substantially more products than he would customarily provide. The owner attempted to accept half of the shipment, as that was roughly his customary quantity, but the farmer stated that the products were already packaged and that the owner should have spoken up after receiving the notice from the farmer. The owner then rejected the shipment in its entirety.

Did the owner breach the contract with the farmer as to this shipment?

(A) No, because no contract existed, as the parties did not agree to a quantity.

(B) No, because the farmer made a nonconforming tender of goods.

(C) Yes, because the owner should have given the farmer time to cure the nonconformity.

(D) Yes, because the owner rejected the shipment in its entirety.

_____
_____
_____
_____
_____
_____
_____
_____
_____
_____
_____
_____
_____
_____

Question 7 | 6379 | MBE CONTRACTS & SALES | DISCHARGE | Impracticability

A homeowner entered into a written contract with a contractor to construct an elaborate tree house among the large trees located in the homeowner's backyard. After commencing construction of the tree house, the contractor discovered that one of the trees intended to be used as support for the tree house had a relatively common fungal infection in its core that would cause the strength of the tree's branches to falter if left untreated. Neither the homeowner nor the contractor had knowledge of the fungal infection when they entered into the contract, but the contractor knew that such infections were common in the area and did not request an inspection of the trees before entering the contract. The contractor also knew that treatment was available at a high cost, but even after treatment, he would need to create additional heavy-load bearing supports for the tree at a substantial cost. When the contractor informed the homeowner that he would not perform under the contract unless the homeowner provided at least 75% of the additional costs needed to make the structure safe, the homeowner refused to pay the additional amount. The homeowner then sued the contractor for breach of contract.

What is the likely result?

(A) The contractor wins, because his performance was discharged due to impracticability.

(B) The contractor wins, because neither party was aware of the fungal infection.

(C) The homeowner wins, because the contractor assumed the risk of the fungal infection.

(D) The homeowner wins, because the fungal infection did not render performance impossible.

_____
_____
_____
_____
_____
_____
_____
_____
_____
_____
_____
_____
_____

A sister convinced her brother that they should open a small coffee shop. Their friend, a guitarist, suggested bringing his band to play live music and attract customers. He did not request any payment, saying the publicity would be good for the band. The siblings agreed, and the band started playing at the shop weekly. The coffee shop became a success, in no small part due to the band's performances. When a businessperson offered to buy the coffee shop from the siblings, they orally agreed to each pay $10,000 out of their share of the sale proceeds to the guitarist for his help in making the shop popular. The sister told the guitarist about their agreement. He was so delighted with it that he put a down payment on a new car. By the time the sale of the business was finalized, the brother had encountered financial difficulties. After the sale, the siblings signed a written contract stating that the sister would pay the guitarist $10,000 and her brother would pay him $5,000.

If, after the sale, the brother pays the guitarist only $5,000, will he have a valid basis for action against the brother for another $5,000?

(A) No, because the guitarist was bound by the written modification of the contract made by the siblings.

(B) No, because the guitarist was only a donee beneficiary of the oral contract between the siblings.

(C) Yes, because the guitarist's reliance on the promised payment prevented the siblings from changing the obligations of their oral contract.

(D) Yes, because the oral promise to pay $10,000 to the guitarist was made binding by the guitarist's valuable and uncompensated contributions to the business.

_____
_____
_____
_____
_____
_____
_____
_____
_____
_____
_____
_____
_____
_____

While attending a rodeo on August 20, a hat maker entered into a valid, written agreement with the rodeo manager to make 500 leather cowboy hats for an upcoming rodeo event at a price of $75 per hat. Per the agreement, the rodeo manager agreed to pay one-fourth of the total purchase price to a tannery owner to whom the hat maker owed a debt for a previous leather order. On August 25, the hat maker changed his mind about paying one-fourth of the purchase price to the tannery owner. The hat maker and rodeo manager subsequently executed a valid modification of the original agreement. The rodeo manager's brother was also present on August 20 when the original agreement was executed, but he did not know about the August 25 modification of the agreement to no longer pay the tannery owner. On August 30, the brother, who was friends with the tannery owner, called and told him that his debt from the hat maker would finally be paid off. However, the rodeo manager refused to pay one-fourth of the purchase price to the tannery owner.

If the tannery owner sues the rodeo manager for one-fourth of the purchase price, will he recover?

(A) No, because the tannery owner did not rely on the August 20 agreement between the hat maker and the rodeo manager.

(B) No, because there was no consideration for the promise to pay the tannery owner by the hat maker and the rodeo manager.

(C) Yes, because the tannery owner had the right to sue the rodeo manager to enforce the contract between the rodeo manager and the hat maker.

(D) Yes, because the rodeo manager agreed to pay one-fourth of the purchase price to the tannery owner on August 20.

_____
_____
_____
_____
_____
_____
_____
_____
_____
_____
_____
_____
_____

Question 10 | 6392 | MBE CONTRACTS & SALES | ASSIGNMENT OF RIGHTS AND DELEGATION OF DUTIES | Delegation of Duties

A boutique hotel contracted with a seamstress to hand make 500 pillows. The signed contract specified that the pillows should be filled with down, and that the pillow covers be made with white, 1000 thread count cotton fabric. Before the seamstress began making the pillows for the boutique hotel, she secured another commission for work that would prevent her from making the hotel's pillows. As a result, the seamstress informed the boutique hotel that she was passing on the hotel's contract to her former business partner, who was comparable in talent and skill at making high-quality pillows. The boutique hotel agreed to the substitution. The former partner diligently worked on making the pillows, using white, 1000 thread count fabric to make the pillow covers. However, instead of using down to fill the pillows, she used a comparably priced synthetic microfiber. The boutique hotel subsequently filed a breach of contract action against the seamstress.

Will it succeed?

(A) No, because the former partner's use of a synthetic microfiber instead of down did not reduce the value of the pillows.

(B) No, because the boutique hotel agreed to the delegation of the seamstress's duties to her former partner.

(C) Yes, because the boutique hotel had not released the seamstress from liability under the contract.

(D) Yes, because the seamstress did not give consideration for delegating the contract to the former partner.

_____
_____
_____
_____
_____
_____
_____
_____
_____
_____
_____
_____

Question 11 | 7616 | MBE CONTRACTS & SALES | STATUTE OF FRAUDS | Types of Contracts Within the Statute of Frauds

A shoe manufacturer contends that the owner of a shoe store called and ordered 50 pairs of a type of shoe. The manufacturer promptly sent the owner a written acknowledgment of the alleged order that reflected the manufacturer as seller and the shoe store owner as buyer, as well as the number and type of shoes, but that did not indicate the price of the shoes. The owner admits to receiving the acknowledgement the following day. Two weeks later, the owner received a shipment of 25 pairs of the shoes along with an invoice that reflected the price of $100 per pair. The owner immediately called the manufacturer and asserted that he had never ordered the shoes.

Can the manufacturer enforce this contract against the owner?

(A) Yes, but only to the extent of $2,500, which is the price of the shoes shipped.

(B) Yes, because the owner did not respond to the written acknowledgement in a timely manner.

(C) No, because the acknowledgement did not indicate the price of the shoes.

(D) No, because of the Statute of Frauds.

_____
_____
_____
_____
_____
_____
_____
_____
_____
_____
_____
_____
_____
_____
_____
_____

A baker and a bride-to-be entered into a contract in which the baker agreed to bake the wedding cake for the bride's wedding at a cost of $2,500. The contract contained a clause that read: "An express condition of Bride's performance under the Contract is Baker's satisfaction of Bride's aesthetic expectations in the design of her wedding cake." In keeping with the wedding's butterfly theme, the baker constructed an elegant cake accented with colorful butterflies, flowers, and caterpillars. At the wedding reception, the guests were enthralled by the cake. The bride, however, upset over the inclusion of the caterpillars, to which she had a genuine aversion, refused to pay the baker. The baker sued the bride for $2,500.

Should the court require the bride to pay the baker?

(A) Yes, because the cake was aesthetically pleasing to the wedding guests.

(B) Yes, because the baker substantially performed.

(C) No, because the bride was personally and honestly dissatisfied with the cake.

(D) No, because no contract was formed between the parties.

_____
_____
_____
_____
_____
_____
_____
_____
_____
_____
_____
_____
_____
_____
_____

A nature magazine advertised a photography contest in its January issue, offering "$1,000 to any subscriber who sends us a photograph of the rare Florida Grasshopper Sparrow that we use for the cover of our May issue. Only submissions meeting our technical specifications and received by April 1 will be considered." The only subscriber to respond to the advertized contest sent the magazine a photograph of the sparrow that met the magazine's technical specifications. The photograph arrived on March 15. However, due to an ecological disaster that occurred in early April, the magazine used a different picture on the cover of its May issue. The magazine used the picture on the cover of its June issue, and has refused to pay $1,000 to the subscriber on the grounds that it was not used on the May cover.

Is the subscriber likely to prevail in a breach of contract action against the nature magazine?

(A) No, because the subscriber's photo was not used on the cover of the May issue.

(B) No, because the subscriber failed to adequately notify the magazine of his acceptance.

(C) Yes, because all of the express conditions of the offer have been satisfied.

(D) Yes, because the nature magazine prevented the publication of the photograph.

A homeowner called a septic cleaning company and made arrangements for the company to remove the waste from the septic tank on the homeowner's property. After completing the job, the company mailed the homeowner a bill for $500, the fair market value of the services rendered by the company. The bill indicated that payment was due in 60 days. Upon receiving the bill, the homeowner called the company and informed it that, since he had lost his job due to an accident, he would not be paying the company's bill. The following day the company filed suit for breach of contract. Ten days later, the homeowner moved to dismiss the suit. The court granted the motion, dismissing the suit without prejudice.

Is the court's dismissal proper?

(A) No, because the parties' dealings created an implied-in-fact contract.

(B) No, because the homeowner has repudiated the contract.

(C) Yes, because the vendor failed to demand assurances.

(D) Yes, because the vendor's complaint is premature.

_____
_____
_____
_____
_____
_____
_____
_____
_____
_____
_____
_____
_____
_____
_____
_____
_____
_____

Question 15 | 2790 | MBE CONTRACTS & SALES | BREACH OF CONTRACT AND REMEDIES | Remedies: Damages for Breach of Contract

A mining company contracted with a railroad to transport 10,000 tons of coal from the company's mines to a power company at a cost of $100,000. The railroad told the mining company that the coal would arrive at the power company on June 1st, but the contract contained a clause that the railroad would not be liable for any losses suffered by the mining company as a result of a late shipment. The railroad was aware that the mining company had contracted with the power company to deliver the coal on June 1st, and pursuant to standard industry custom, the price to be paid by the power company decreased by $1 per ton for each day that the coal was late. The shipment of coal did not reach the power company until June 10, and the railroad had no justification for the 10-day delay. Because of the delay, the mining company lost $100,000 in revenue from the sale. The mining company filed suit against the railroad for breach of contract, claiming $100,000 in damages.

Is the mining company likely to succeed in its claim?

(A) Yes, because the damages that the mining company would suffer from the railroad's delay were known to the railroad prior to shipment of the coal.

(B) Yes, because consequential damages cannot be excluded by a merchant.

(C) No, because the claimed damages are disproportionate to the original contract price between the railroad and the mining company.

(D) No, because the contract between the mining company and the railroad protected the railroad from losses suffered by the mining company due to a late shipment.

_____
_____
_____
_____
_____
_____
_____
_____
_____
_____
_____
_____
_____

A new florist placed a written order with a wholesaler for $15,000 worth of fresh flowers. Delivery was to be made to the florist via a national delivery service. Because the florist was a new customer, the wholesaler accepted the order on the condition that he pay $5,000 in advance, and the remaining $10,000 within 20 days of delivery. There was no discussion as to who bore the risk of loss. The wholesaler arranged with a national delivery service to pick up and deliver the flowers to the florist. The delivery service picked up the flowers, but, due to malfunction of the temperature controls on the transporting plane, the flowers were worthless upon arrival. The florist rejected the flowers and notified the wholesaler, who refused to ship other flowers. The wholesaler filed a claim against the florist for the remaining $10,000. The florist counterclaimed for the return of its $5,000 payment to the wholesaler.

How should the court rule on these claims?

(A) Grant the wholesaler's claim for $10,000 and deny the florist's claim for $5,000 because the risk of loss passed to the florist.

(B) Grant the florist's claim for $5,000 and deny the wholesaler's claim for $10,000 because the risk of loss remained with the wholesaler.

(C) Offset the two claims against each other and require the florist to pay the wholesaler $2,500 because, since neither party was at fault for the loss, each should bear the loss equally.

(D) Deny both claims because the florist accepted the risk of loss up to the amount he had paid for the goods.

_____
_____
_____
_____
_____
_____
_____
_____
_____
_____
_____
_____
_____

A collector agreed to sell his collection of authentic extras' costumes from a cult classic 80's show to a costume store for $10,000, payable one month after the collection was delivered to the store via a third-party carrier. Due to the time and expense that went into accumulating and repairing the costumes, the collector expected a $2,000 profit. The costumes suffered minor water damage in transit, and the store immediately notified the collector that it was rejecting the collection and would hold the collection until the collector picked them up. The collector told the store that he would look for a new buyer and would pick up the collection in a few weeks. The collector quickly found another buyer willing to pay the original contract price. However, before the collector retrieved the costume collection, the store sold and delivered the costumes to a theater company who knowingly accepted the costumes despite the water damage. The theater company paid the store $15,000 for the collection, which the store retained.

If the store's sale of the costumes was NOT an acceptance, what is highest value remedy available to the collector?

(A) $2,000, the collector's lost profit.

(B) $5,000, the difference between market price and contract price.

(C) $10,000, the collector-store contract price.

(D) $15,000, damages for conversion.

_____
_____
_____
_____
_____
_____
_____
_____
_____

- Final tips:
  - Make sure you know the common law and UCC version of every rule
  - Fact patterns can be long, but apply the rules methodically and the answer will be apparent
  - Lots of points to pick up in Contracts!

[END OF HANDOUT]

MBE WORKSHOP: CRIMINAL LAW
PROFESSOR LISA TUCKER
DREXEL UNIVERSITY SCHOOL OF LAW

CHAPTER 1:   INTRODUCTION

- Unless they tell you otherwise, you are dealing with the _____ definition of crimes

- Memorize the elements of every crime

- Most testable areas:

  o Murder and manslaughter

  o Property crimes

    ▪ Burglary, larceny, robbery

  o Inchoate crimes

    ▪ Attempt, conspiracy, and solicitation

By federal statute, it is unlawful to knowingly possess any endangered species of fish or wildlife. Any person who violates this statute is guilty of a misdemeanor and is subject to a fine of not more than $50,000 or imprisonment of not more than six months, or both. Congress indicated that the statute should be applied as broadly as possible in order to accord the endangered species maximum protection.

Which of the following is likely the minimum that the prosecution must establish in order to obtain a conviction of a defendant found in the possession of an endangered bird?

(A) The defendant knew that the bird in her possession was a member of an endangered species.

(B) The defendant knew that there was a federal statute that made possession of the bird a crime.

(C) The defendant knowingly possessed the bird.

(D) The defendant possessed the bird.

The mother of a 16-year-old girl found out that the girl and one of her teachers were selling the girl's prescription sedatives to other students. The mother confronted the teacher, and told him that she was reporting him to the school authorities and the police. To prevent her from doing so, the teacher pulled out a gun and shot at the mother, but missed the mother and instead hit the girl, who had just entered the room. The teacher then ran away from the scene of the shooting. Crying out in pain, the girl begged the mother to call for help. The mother, angry at the girl for her actions, told her "[t]hat's what you get for being a criminal."   The mother delayed summoning medical assistance. The girl died shortly thereafter, but would have lived had medical assistance been timely provided.

Can the police properly charge the teacher with the murder of the girl?

(A)   No, because the girl's death was caused by the mother's delay in calling for medical assistance.

(B)   No, because the teacher did not intend to kill the girl when he shot the gun.

(C)   Yes, under the felony murder rule.

(D)   Yes, because the teacher intended to harm the mother when he shot the gun.

A convenience store clerk was complaining about his financial troubles to his best friend. The friend said that the clerk's employer had been cheating him out of a decent salary for too many years, and that the employer owed the clerk. The friend suggested that if the clerk robbed the store during another clerk's shift, he would never get caught. The friend offered to loan the clerk his gun to use to scare the clerk on duty. Both men agreed that no one would get hurt in the process. The next day, the clerk carried out the plan to rob the store while the friend waited outside in the car. During the robbery, the clerk accidentally discharged the gun, and a customer was shot and died instantly. The clerk panicked and left the store empty handed. The friend drove the clerk back to his mother's house, told him to lay low, and then drove home. The clerk later decided that he needed to get out of town quickly. He stole his mother's car, which was more reliable than his own, to drive to a nearby state.

In a case against the friend, which of the following charges would most likely be successfully prosecuted?

(A) Attempted robbery, murder, and larceny.

(B) Felony murder.

(C) Attempted robbery only.

(D) Attempted robbery and murder only.

A mother with a terminal illness told her son that she was in a great deal of pain. She requested that he end her suffering by taking her life. After unsuccessfully attempting to dissuade his mother, the son, who had no medical training, researched the matter on the internet. Acting in compliance with his mother's request, the son injected his mother with drugs that resulted in her quick and painless death. He did not financially benefit from his mother's death in any way, as she had properly devised all of her property to a charity.

Of the following crimes listed in descending order of seriousness, which is the most serious crime of which the son may be convicted?

(A) Murder

(B) Voluntary manslaughter

(C) Involuntary manslaughter

(D) Assisted suicide

Question 5 | 6672 | MBE CRIMINAL LAW | HOMICIDE | Types of Homicide

A carpenter was using a nail gun in the construction of a small outdoor deck on a house. The carpenter knew that the nail gun could fire a nail with sufficient force to kill a human being at close range. Aware of the presence of three other carpenters on the other side of the nearly finished deck, one of whom the carpenter disliked, the carpenter fired the nail gun twice at a table located between himself and the other three carpenters. The first nail from the gun struck the table but the second nail, ricocheting off the table, struck and killed the disliked carpenter. At trial, a jury, based on this evidence, found the carpenter guilty of murder.

If the carpenter appeals his conviction on the grounds that the evidence was not sufficient to support his conviction, how should the appellate court rule?

(A) Affirm the conviction, because the evidence is sufficient to establish that the carpenter acted with criminal negligence.

(B) Affirm the conviction, because the evidence is sufficient to establish that the carpenter acted with malice.

(C) Overturn the conviction and remand for a new trial, because the evidence is not sufficient for murder but can support an involuntary manslaughter conviction.

(D) Overturn the conviction and remand for a new trial, because the evidence is not sufficient for murder but can support a voluntary manslaughter conviction.

The defendant, his brother, and his best friend formed a plan to rob a bank. On the day of the crime, the defendant and his brother entered the bank carrying guns, while the best friend stayed in the car to act as a getaway driver. After the defendant received one bag of money from a bank teller, he saw a security guard pull out a gun. The defendant tried to shoot the security guard but instead shot his brother. The defendant panicked and ran out of the building toward the getaway car. The security guard chased the defendant and fired a shot toward him as he approached the car. The shot hit the best friend, who was in the driver's seat of the car. Shortly thereafter, the police arrived and arrested the defendant. The brother and best friend later died as a result of their gunshot wounds.

For which of the following crimes is the defendant most likely to be convicted and punished?

(A)   Robbery and two counts of felony murder for the death of the brother and best friend.

(B)   Robbery and one count of felony murder for the death of the brother.

(C)   Two counts of felony murder for the death of the brother and best friend.

(D)   One count of felony murder for the death of the brother.

After a woman and her roommate got into a fight, the woman and her boyfriend formulated a plan to get back at the roommate. The woman planned to distract the roommate while the boyfriend snuck into the apartment through the open back door to steal her new camera, which was on the kitchen counter. The woman and her boyfriend headed back to the apartment and put their plan into action. The plan went awry when the roommate heard a noise and went into the kitchen to find the boyfriend with her camera in hand. Panicked, the boyfriend pushed the roommate to the floor and ran out of the apartment with the camera.

The boyfriend is most likely to be convicted of which of the following crimes?

(A) Burglary only.

(B) Burglary and battery.

(C) Robbery only.

(D) Robbery and battery.

_____
_____
_____
_____
_____
_____
_____
_____
_____
_____
_____
_____
_____
_____
_____

A woman broke into her former lover's house at night with the intent to take back various items of her clothing that the former lover had refused to return to her. After conducting a search and being unable to find the clothing, she came across another woman's clothing. Extremely angry, she took a cigarette lighter and lit the lover's bed on fire, destroying the bed.

With which of the following crimes can the woman be properly charged?

(A)   Arson.

(B)   Burglary.

(C)   Both arson and burglary.

(D)   Neither arson nor burglary.

An attorney represented a client in a legal battle over a valuable necklace that had belonged to the client's deceased grandmother. The attorney told the client, who had possession of the necklace, that the client was legally required to leave the necklace with the attorney until the legal issues were resolved. In fact, there was no such requirement. Rather, the lawyer intended to sell the necklace and retire on a small island where the lawyer believed she would never be found. After the client gave the necklace to the lawyer, the lawyer sold the necklace to a jeweler. The jeweler, who had known the grandmother, later recognized the necklace as the grandmother's, and he called the police. The attorney was arrested at the airport later that day.

The attorney is guilty of which of the following crimes?

(A) Embezzlement.

(B) False pretenses.

(C) Larceny.

(D) Larceny by trick.

Question 10 | 4334 | MBE CRIMINAL LAW | OTHER CRIMES | Crimes Against Property

A woman broke into her ex-husband's house late one night when she knew he was away on business, intending to take a sculpture that he had been awarded in their divorce settlement. She searched the entire house, but was unable to find the sculpture. She figured he had probably sold the sculpture, which made her furious because he knew how much she loved it. In a rage, she slashed a painting of his new girlfriend before leaving the house.

For which of the following crimes is the woman guilty?

(A) Attempted larceny only.

(B) Larceny only.

(C) Burglary only.

(D) Burglary and attempted larceny.

_____
_____
_____
_____
_____
_____
_____
_____
_____
_____
_____
_____
_____
_____

A dog sitter customarily went into her clients' homes, with keys they provided to her, to care for their pets. Over the years, she grew to especially love one particular dog. She would regularly enter the home of her client on days she was not scheduled to watch the dog and would take the dog to the park. One afternoon, the dog she loved wandered into her yard as she was doing yard work. She did not immediately call her client, but instead decided to keep the dog for a few days. A week later when she returned him to the client, the client stated that she so enjoyed having the house to herself that she was going to sell him. The dog sitter immediately purchased him and brought him back to her home.

Were the dog sitter's actions sufficient to meet the requirements of larceny?

(A) No, because she had a key to enter the home.

(B) No, because she was only going to keep the dog for a few days.

(C) Yes, because she kept the dog despite knowing who owned it.

(D) Yes, because she would enter the client's home regularly and take the dog to the park.

_____
_____
_____
_____
_____
_____
_____
_____
_____
_____
_____
_____
_____
_____

A woman searched on the internet for a hit man who would kill her husband in exchange for cash. She found a purported mercenary in a chat room who agreed to kill the husband in return for $50,000. The mercenary turned out to be an undercover police officer and the woman was arrested.

With which of the following crimes could the woman properly be charged?

(A) Conspiracy only.

(B) Solicitation only.

(C) Both conspiracy and solicitation.

(D) Neither conspiracy nor solicitation.

A gang member decided to rob a bank and approached a fellow member of his gang to invite him to participate. The other member, who was actually an undercover officer, agreed. The gang member purchased a toy gun, planning to use it to threaten the bank teller during the robbery. When the gang member went to meet the undercover officer the next day behind the bank they had planned to rob, he was immediately arrested.

The applicable jurisdiction has adopted the Model Penal Code's definition of conspiracy.

Can the gang member be convicted of conspiracy?

(A) No, because the overt act of purchasing a toy gun was not illegal.

(B) No, because the undercover officer lacked the necessary intent to agree to accomplish an unlawful purpose.

(C) Yes, because of the Wharton Rule.

(D) Yes, because the undercover officer's false agreement does not negate any required element of the crime.

_____
_____
_____
_____
_____
_____
_____
_____
_____
_____
_____
_____
_____
_____
_____
_____

A man planned to rob a city bank. Waiting until he saw the bank's security guard leave the building to take a walk around the perimeter, the man entered the bank and walked up to a teller with his hand pointed in his pocket, as if he had a gun. The teller had her back to the man and did not see him at all. Before the teller could turn around, the security guard re-entered the building. Seeing the guard, the man took his hand out of his pocket and ran out of the building. The man was arrested and charged with attempted robbery of the bank.

Should the man be found guilty?

(A) Yes, whether or not he abandoned his plan.

(B) Yes, because robbery is a specific intent crime.

(C) No, because he successfully withdrew from the robbery.

(D) No, because he used no actual force on the teller.

_____
_____
_____
_____
_____
_____
_____
_____
_____
_____
_____
_____
_____
_____
_____
_____
_____
_____
_____

A daughter was homeschooled by her bohemian parents for most of her life. The parents did not believe in mainstream medicine, so they taught the daughter about homeopathic remedies as part of her homeschooling. She helped her parents with their extensive garden as part of her daily chores. Unfortunately, the daughter was lonely, she did not believe in homeopathy, and she wanted to eat meat, so she resolved to kill her parents by poisoning them, but making it look like an accident. Amongst the plants she was growing was the castor oil plant, which her parents used to treat a variety of skin conditions and to stimulate the immune system. However, the seeds of the castor oil plant contain the toxin called ricin, which is deadly if ingested by humans. The daughter extracted the seeds from a castor oil plant, crushed them, and then added the ricin powder to her parents' oatmeal. Unbeknownst to the daughter, she had actually picked the wrong plant, known as the "false castor oil plant," which was similar in appearance, but did not produce poisonous seeds. After the parents ate the oatmeal laced with the harmless seeds, they suffered some gastric distress. They went to the garden to find an herbal remedy, and noticing that all of the false castor oil plants were missing, they suspected that someone untrained in plant species tried to poison them, so they called the police. The police were able to piece together what actually happened, and they arrested the daughter for attempted murder.

Could the daughter be found guilty of attempted murder?

(A) No, because factual impossibility is a defense to the crime of attempted murder.

(B) No, because it was legally impossible for the daughter to kill her parents.

(C) Yes, because mistake of fact is not a defense to the crime of attempted murder.

(D) Yes, because factual impossibility is not a defense to the crime of attempted murder.

A homeowner was selling illegal drugs out of his house, which was located in a well-heeled suburban neighborhood. A customer, knowing that the homeowner likely had a large amount of cash from selling drugs, knocked on the homeowner's door. When the homeowner opened the door upon recognizing the customer, the customer pulled out a toy pistol that looked like a real gun and demanded money. The customer followed the homeowner inside and over to a table in the entryway with a drawer in which the homeowner told the customer there was money. The homeowner instead pulled a gun out of the drawer and shot and killed the customer. The homeowner is arrested and charged with murder. The jurisdiction does not follow the "retreat doctrine."

Should the homeowner be convicted of the customer's murder?

(A) No, because it was reasonable for the homeowner to believe that his life was at risk.

(B) No, because the jurisdiction does not follow the retreat doctrine.

(C) Yes, because the customer was not armed with a deadly weapon.

(D) Yes, because the homeowner was committing a crime by selling the drugs and therefore was not privileged to use self-defense.

Three coworkers were employed at a jewelry store. They were always complaining to one another about the long hours, the paltry pay rate, and the lack of medical benefits. Two of the coworkers came up with a plan to steal a valuable collection of gems from the jewelry store, but it was a three-person job; they asked the third coworker to join in on their plan, but he refused. The two coworkers knew how devoted the third coworker was to his family, so they threatened to kill his wife and kids if he did not help them or if he tried to foil their plan by notifying the police. Believing that he had no other choice, the third coworker joined in on the plan. The three men entered the jewelry store that night, having received the permission of their boss in order to polish all of the jewelry in preparation for a jewelry show the next day. While the two coworkers broke into the wall safe where the gems were kept, the third coworker kept watch for the night guard on his hourly walk-through of the store premises. The night guard decided to do his walk-through ten minutes early, saw the men breaking into the safe, and pulled out his gun. The excitement of the event caused the night guard to have a heart attack, which was fatal. The police entered at that moment and arrested the three men for burglary and felony murder of the night guard.

What is the third coworker's best defense against the felony murder charge?

(A) He did not intend to kill the night guard.

(B) He was under duress to commit the burglary.

(C) He had permission to enter the jewelry store.

(D) He could not have foreseen the security guard's heart attack.

_____
_____
_____
_____
_____
_____
_____
_____
_____
_____

- Final tip: Memorize the elements, look at the crime charged, and walk yourself through the fact pattern, identifying each element.

[END OF HANDOUT]

MBE WORKSHOP: CRIMINAL PROCEDURE
PROFESSOR LISA TUCKER
DREXEL UNIVERSITY SCHOOL OF LAW

CHAPTER 1:   INTRODUCTION

- Remember that the questions are only as current as the test is

    o Don't worry about questions that test a brand new ruling (within the last six months); you don't need to know the new rule—just apply the rule as you learned it.

- Most testable areas:

    o Fourth Amendment

        ▪ Search and Seizure

        ▪ Automobiles

        ▪ Warrant requirements (or exigent circumstances)

    o Miranda

    o Sixth Amendment

    o Double Jeopardy

- Good guessing strategy: if you REALLY, TRULY can't answer a question, pick an answer choice that sides with the _____, not the _____.

    o Remember, this is just a last resort

A security guard at a popular appliance store reported the theft of a number of the store's televisions to the police. The police requested that the security guard contact them if he learned anything new about the theft. On a hunch that an employee was involved in the theft, the security guard befriended the employee and asked to watch a major sports event on television with the employee at the employee's home. When the employee stepped out of the room during the sports event, the security guard located the serial number on the television and discovered it was one of the stolen televisions. The security guard provided the information to the police. The employee was charged with larceny based on the information provided by the security guard.

If the employee files a motion to suppress, how should the court rule?

(A) Deny the motion, because the employee consented to the security guard coming into his home.

(B) Deny the motion, because the security guard is not a state actor.

(C) Grant the motion, because the security guard conducted a search of the employee's home.

(D) Grant the motion, because the security guard did not have a warrant.

The defendant was charged with conspiracy to distribute drugs for his alleged involvement in a major drug trafficking ring. The evidence tying the defendant to the drug trafficking ring was obtained from a warrantless search of the home of a business partner. The defendant had been living with his business partner, but recently moved out, leaving a bag filled with cocaine and his identification in the business partner's home. The bag was discovered by police during a search of the home with the business partner's consent. Prior to trial, the defendant filed a motion to suppress the cocaine.

How should the court rule on the defendant's motion to suppress?

(A) Deny the motion, because the business partner consented to the search of the home.

(B) Deny the motion, because the defendant does not have a privacy interest in the home.

(C) Grant the motion, because the defendant had a reasonable expectation of privacy in the home.

(D) Grant the motion, because the evidence was discovered as a result of a warrantless search.

_____
_____
_____
_____
_____
_____
_____
_____
_____
_____
_____
_____
_____
_____

Two officers went to a man's home to serve an arrest warrant, but no one answered the door. As they walked around the man's house, the officers looked into his next door neighbor's window and saw the man inside the neighbor's kitchen drinking coffee. The officers knocked on the neighbor's door, and when the neighbor answered, the officers informed the neighbor that they had a warrant to arrest the man. The officers pushed past the neighbor into the kitchen and arrested the man. While they were in the kitchen, the officers saw a bag of marijuana on the neighbor's counter. The officers arrested the neighbor, and he was subsequently charged with possession of narcotics. The neighbor moved to suppress evidence of the drugs, and the prosecution argued that the evidence was admissible under the plain view exception to the warrant requirement.

Are the drugs seized in the neighbor's kitchen likely to be admitted against the neighbor?

(A) No, because the officers could not lawfully enter the neighbor's home without his consent.

(B) No, because the officers did not knock and announce to the neighbor their intention to arrest the man.

(C) Yes, because the arrest warrant implicitly authorized the officers to take measures necessary to serve the warrant.

(D) Yes, because the officers entered the neighbor's home under exigent circumstances.

_____
_____
_____
_____
_____
_____
_____
_____
_____
_____
_____
_____
_____
_____
_____

A police officer received an anonymous tip that the defendant was manufacturing methamphetamine in his basement. Based solely on the tip, the officer obtained a warrant to search the defendant's basement for drugs and related manufacturing equipment. The officer and his partner went to the defendant's home to execute the warrant. Believing the defendant was not home, the officers did not knock on the door, but simply opened the unlocked door. In searching the defendant's basement, the officers found large quantities of methamphetamine, related manufacturing equipment, and a notebook that said "Ledger" across the cover. The notebook contained a ledger, with the names of the defendant's clients and statements of their accounts. The officers seized all these items. The defendant seeks to suppress the evidence seized by the officers.

What is the defendant's best argument in favor of suppressing the notebook?

(A) The notebook was not named in the warrant.

(B) The notebook was in the nature of a personal diary.

(C) The officers failed to "knock and announce" their presence.

(D) The warrant was invalid.

Two undercover police officers, with probable cause to believe that the defendant was a drug dealer, entered the living room of the defendant's apartment, at the defendant's invitation, to buy cocaine. Before the transaction could take place, the defendant shot and killed one of the officers. After a brief struggle, the defendant was subdued by the other officer and placed under arrest for murder. Responding to the officer's request for assistance, uniformed police officers came to the apartment, conducted a protective sweep, and took the defendant to jail. Then the uniformed officers conducted a thorough warrantless search of the apartment, during which they uncovered a large quantity of cocaine in the mattress in the defendant's bedroom. Based on the amount of cocaine seized, the defendant was charged with possession of cocaine with intent to deal in addition to murder. The defendant filed a motion to suppress the cocaine as having been unconstitutionally seized.

Should the court grant this motion?

(A) Yes, because the search was conducted without a warrant.

(B) Yes, because the defendant was arrested for murder not drug dealing.

(C) No, because the defendant had a lesser expectation of privacy once arrested.

(D) No, because the murder created exigent circumstances.

_____
_____
_____
_____
_____
_____
_____
_____
_____
_____
_____
_____
_____
_____
_____
_____

Question 6 | 6670 | MBE CRIMINAL PROCEDURE | FOURTH AMENDMENT: APPLICATION TO ARREST, SEARCH AND SEIZURE | Search and Seizure

While on patrol one night, two officers noticed the car of a known drug dealer in the drive-through lane of a fast-food restaurant. Based on prior discussions with informants, the officers had probable cause to believe that the drug dealer regularly made drug deliveries from his car. Noticing that the drug dealer's headlight was out, the officers pulled him over once he left the restaurant and searched his car. The officers did not find any evidence of drugs, but they did find several illegal weapons in the trunk.

Did the officers' seizure of the weapons violate the drug dealer's Fourth Amendment rights?

(A) Yes, because the stop was pretextual in nature.

(B) Yes, because the officers were searching for drugs, not weapons.

(C) Yes, because the drug dealer could not access the trunk from the passenger compartment.

(D) No, as a valid application of the automobile exception to the warrant requirement.

A corporation is being investigated for tax fraud and for several other offenses regarding insider trading. The prosecutor requested that the corporation turn over several types of corporate records, including emails from several of the corporation's officers and other business papers. The request was made of the corporation's Chief Operating Officer (COO), who acted as the custodian of the corporate records. The business papers would implicate several members of the corporation, including the COO, in criminal misconduct. Further, many of the emails written by the COO contained statements about the officers of some of the corporation's competitors; these statements were defamatory and would likely result in civil liability if they were released. The COO objects to producing this evidence, arguing that being forced to turn over these corporate records would violate his Fifth Amendment privilege against self-incrimination.

The court should:

(A) Grant his motion as to the emails, but deny his motion as to the business papers.

(B) Deny his motion as to the emails, but grant his motion as to the business papers.

(C) Grant his motion as to both the emails and the business papers.

(D) Deny his motion as to both the emails and the business papers.

Following the armed robbery of a local bank, the police identified the defendant as a suspect and brought him to the police station for questioning. As soon as they sat down in the interrogation room, the police read the defendant his Miranda rights. The defendant noted that "this seems like the kind of thing where you should have a lawyer." The police responded that the defendant had that right. The defendant noted that he "didn't even know a good lawyer," and dropped the issue. In response to each question, the defendant simply repeated, "I don't know anything about it." Frustrated, the police discontinued questioning after an hour and left the defendant in the interrogation room alone. Three hours later, the police returned and, without repeating the Miranda warnings, told the defendant that his best friend, who was also a suspect, had already told them all about the robbery and the defendant's involvement. In fact, the police were searching for the defendant's best friend to bring him in for questioning but had not been able to locate him. The defendant immediately blurted out, "It was all his idea. I didn't even want to rob that bank."

What is the defendant's best argument that his statement was taken in violation of his Fifth Amendment rights?

(A) The defendant did not receive fresh Miranda warnings after the break in questioning.

(B) The defendant did not sign a written waiver of his Miranda rights.

(C) The lie regarding his best friend's statement rendered the defendant's statement involuntary.

(D) The police continued to question the defendant after he invoked his right to counsel.

A defendant was arrested and charged with robbery. While he was awaiting trial, an inmate in the jail in which he was housed was assaulted, and the police suspected that the defendant was involved. They brought the defendant in for questioning about the assault and provided him with Miranda warnings. The defendant said that he was willing to talk, and did not ask for his attorney. He proceeded to tell the police that he had provided another inmate with information about how to obtain a weapon and believed that inmate had been involved in the assault. The defendant was later charged as a co-conspirator in the assault, and sought to suppress his statement to the police. He argued that his attorney should have been present during the interrogation.

Is the defendant's statement likely to be suppressed?

(A)   No, because the defendant did not specifically invoke his Fifth Amendment right to counsel.

(B)   No, because the defendant waived his Sixth Amendment right to counsel by failing to request his attorney.

(C)   Yes, because the defendant did not waive his Fifth Amendment right to counsel.

(D)   Yes, because the defendant did not provide a knowing, voluntary, and intelligent waiver of his Sixth Amendment right to counsel.

_____
_____
_____
_____
_____
_____
_____
_____
_____
_____
_____
_____
_____

A defendant was on trial for arson of an office building. During the trial, the police officers who initially arrested him began to suspect that the defendant was also responsible for a theft of several computers that took place in the office building on the same night as the arson. One evening during the arson trial, the police visited the defendant in jail, read him his Miranda rights, and began to question him about the theft. The defendant eventually confessed, and the police informed the prosecutor of his confession. The prosecutor later wants to charge the defendant with theft, using the statement that was obtained by the police in the jail. The defendant's attorney objects on the grounds that the defendant's Sixth Amendment rights were violated.

The court should:

(A) Allow the prosecutor to use the confession because the defendant was read his Miranda rights.

(B) Allow the prosecutor to use the confession because theft and arson each require proof of an additional element that the other does not.

(C) Prevent the prosecutor from using the confession because the arson and the theft took place during the same criminal transaction.

(D) Prevent the prosecutor from using the confession because the defendant was represented by counsel in connection with the arson case.

_____
_____
_____
_____
_____
_____
_____
_____
_____
_____
_____
_____
_____
_____

The defendant was the primary suspect in a string of robberies. At the request of the police, the defendant appeared in a line-up at the police station, and one of the victims identified him as the person who robbed him. The police then took the defendant into custody and interrogated him, after which the defendant was released without being charged. The following day, the defendant was arrested and appeared at an arraignment, where he entered a plea of not guilty. After the arraignment, the defendant was appointed an attorney. The defendant had not been represented by an attorney at any point before that time, nor had he requested an attorney. The defendant intends to argue that he was denied his Sixth Amendment right to counsel.

At what point did the defendant's Sixth Amendment right to counsel first attach?

(A)   The defendant was entitled to counsel at the line-up.

(B)   The defendant was entitled to counsel during the interrogation.

(C)   The defendant was entitled to counsel at the arraignment.

(D)   The defendant was entitled to counsel following the arraignment.

_____
_____
_____
_____
_____
_____
_____
_____
_____
_____
_____
_____
_____
_____

A defendant was indicted by a grand jury for attempted murder. When the prosecution put its evidence before the grand jury, the grand jurors asked if there was any other relevant evidence that they should consider, but the prosecution provided none. Before trial, the prosecutor provided the defendant with a statement made by the victim that she had a personal vendetta against the defendant and would do anything to harm him. The defendant's attorney filed a motion to dismiss the charges based on the prosecutor's failure to inform the grand jury of the victim's statement.

How should the court rule?

(A) Deny the motion, because the information does not prove the defendant is innocent.

(B) Deny the motion, because the prosecutor was not required to present the statement to the grand jury.

(C) Grant the motion, because the prosecutor acted improperly.

(D) Grant the motion, because the prosecutor withheld Brady material.

_____
_____
_____
_____
_____
_____
_____
_____
_____
_____
_____
_____
_____
_____
_____
_____
_____

Question 13 | 6989 | MBE CRIMINAL PROCEDURE | TRIAL | Jury Trial

A defendant on trial for burglary planned to raise in his defense that his arrest was a result of racial profiling. During voir dire, the prosecutor exercised his peremptory challenges to exclude all nonwhite jurors, not just those of the defendant's race, from the jury panel. When the defendant objected to these challenges as racially discriminating, the prosecutor responded that he was concerned that nonwhite jurors would unfairly side with the defense's argument that the police unjustly profiled the defendant.

Should the court sustain the defendant's objection?

(A) No, because the ultimate burden of persuasion regarding racial motivation rests with the opponent of the strike.

(B) No, because the prosecutor's challenges excluded all nonwhite jurors, not just those of the same race as the defendant.

(C) Yes, because race is "inextricably bound up" in a case involving allegations of racial profiling.

(D) Yes, because the prosecution failed to provide a race-neutral explanation for the peremptory strikes.

_____
_____
_____
_____
_____
_____
_____
_____
_____
_____
_____
_____

A contractor was indicted by a state grand jury for bribery of a public official. The suspect was tried and convicted of the crime. The contractor, who is a member of one racial group, sought to reverse her conviction on grounds that members of another racial group were intentionally excluded from service on the grand jury on the basis of their race. The appellate court found that the exclusion was harmless error with respect to the contractor's conviction.

Should the appellate court reverse the contractor's conviction?

(A) Yes, because there is a constitutional right to a grand jury indictment.

(B) Yes, because the rights of the members of the excluded racial group were violated under the Equal Protection Clause of the Fourteenth Amendment.

(C) No, because the exclusion of the racial group was harmless error with regard to the contractor's conviction.

(D) No, because the contractor lacks standing to challenge the exclusion of members of another race from the grand jury that indicted her.

_____
_____
_____
_____
_____
_____
_____
_____
_____
_____
_____
_____
_____
_____
_____
_____

Question 15 | 3107 | MBE CRIMINAL PROCEDURE | TRIAL | Due Process

A state's legislature imposed a "three-strike law" imposing a mandatory minimum sentence of 25 years for the conviction of a third felony. At the time the legislation passed, a citizen of the state had already been convicted of two such felonies, and was convicted of stealing a $1,500 set of golf clubs shortly thereafter.

If the citizen wishes to challenge the constitutionality of the law, what is the most likely result?

(A) The law will be overturned as a violation of double jeopardy.

(B) The law will be overturned as a violation of the prohibition against cruel and unusual punishment.

(C) The law will be overturned as an ex post facto law.

(D) The law will be upheld.

In a jury trial, an adult defendant was found guilty of first-degree premeditated murder, a capital offense. During the sentencing phase of the trial, the defense presented evidence of mitigating circumstances, while the prosecution presented evidence of aggravating circumstances. The jury rendered an advisory sentence of death without specifying the factual basis for its recommendation. The judge independently found the existence of two aggravating circumstances beyond a reasonable doubt, weighed the aggravating and mitigating circumstances, and, agreeing with the jury's advisory sentence, imposed the death sentence.

On appeal, the defendant has challenged the imposition of the death sentence as unconstitutional.

How should the appellate court rule?

(A) For the defendant, because the judge imposed the death sentence.

(B) For the defendant, because the jury did not find a specific aggravating circumstance that justified the impositon of the death penalty.

(C) Against the defendant, because jury and judge both concurred with imposing the death sentence.

(D) Against the defendant, because the judge found two aggravating circumstances beyond a reasonable doubt.

A defendant was charged with both battery and robbery of a victim. The defendant was found guilty of battery but acquitted of the robbery charge. Subsequently, the victim died from the injuries inflicted by the defendant. The defendant has been charged with felony murder of the victim. The defendant has moved for dismissal of this charge on double jeopardy grounds.

How is the court likely to rule on this motion?

(A) Grant the motion, because the defendant was convicted of battery.

(B) Grant the motion, because the defendant was acquitted of robbery.

(C) Deny the motion, because the victim's death took place after the defendant's first trial.

(D) Deny the motion, because of the collateral estoppel doctrine.

_____
_____
_____
_____
_____
_____
_____
_____
_____
_____
_____
_____

- Final tips:
  - Focus on the Fourth Amendment
  - Understand the difference between Fifth and Sixth Amendment rights to counsel
  - Don't neglect juries!

[END OF HANDOUT]

MBE WORKSHOP: EVIDENCE
PROFESSOR LISA TUCKER
DREXEL UNIVERSITY SCHOOL OF LAW

CHAPTER 1: INTRODUCTION

- Evidence on the MBE follows the Federal Rules of Evidence

- Most testable areas:

    ○ _____ and exceptions
    ○ _____ evidence
    ○ Impeachment

Question 1 | 6486 | MBE EVIDENCE | PRESENTATION OF EVIDENCE | Introduction of Evidence

In the prosecution of a defendant for murder, the state seeks to qualify a forensic analyst as an expert in order to have her testify as to her professional opinion of the crime scene. The defense has objected on the grounds of inadequate qualifications. The prosecution now seeks to introduce a letter written by the editor-in-chief of a well-respected academic journal of forensic science, stating that the forensic analyst has published a number of well-reviewed papers on the subject of crime-scene analysis and is generally acknowledged in her field as very qualified.

On the issue of the forensic analyst's qualifications, may the judge consider the editor's letter?

(A) Yes, because the letter is not hearsay.

(B) Yes, because the judge may consider the letter without regard for the hearsay rule.

(C) No, because the letter is hearsay not within any exception.

(D) No, because it is the role of the jury to determine the credibility of the evidence of the forensic analyst's qualifications.

_____
_____
_____
_____
_____
_____
_____

A jurisdiction defines receiving stolen property as (i) receiving control of stolen property, (ii) with the knowledge that the property is stolen, and (iii) with the intent to permanently deprive the owner of the property. A defendant, charged with receiving stolen property after the police found a stolen television in his home, denied that he knew it was stolen. On cross-examination, the prosecutor asked the defendant, "Didn't you also previously buy a stolen stereo from the same man who sold you this television?" The defendant's attorney immediately objected.

What is the strongest basis for the defense attorney's objection?

(A) The probative value of the prosecutor's question is substantially outweighed by the danger of unfair prejudice.

(B) The prosecutor's question was irrelevant because it does not establish an element that the prosecutor must prove.

(C) The relevance of the prosecutor's question depends upon whether the defendant knew the stereo was stolen, and the prosecutor has not offered sufficient proof to support that finding.

(D) The risk of unfair prejudice is not substantially outweighed by the probative value of the prosecutor's question.

_____
_____
_____
_____
_____
_____
_____
_____
_____
_____
_____
_____
_____
_____

In his criminal trial for battery, a defendant sought to admit evidence of his peaceful character. He met the leader of a local animal rights group once during a recent animal rights demonstration in front of the mayor's office, during which the man succeeded in calming down an angry group of protestors. The defendant planned to ask the group leader to testify about this incident to the jury. The prosecution objected to the introduction of this evidence.

How should the court rule on the objection?

(A) Sustain the objection, because this testimony constitutes an inappropriate use of character evidence.

(B) Sustain the objection, because the leader of the animal rights group only met the defendant once.

(C) Overrule the objection, because the defendant may introduce evidence of his good character if relevant to the crime charged.

(D) Overrule the objection, because specific acts are admissible in criminal cases if introduced by the defendant.

_____
_____
_____
_____
_____
_____
_____
_____
_____
_____
_____
_____
_____
_____
_____
_____
_____

A politician on trial for the misdemeanor assault and battery of a reporter asserts that the reporter started the altercation by shouting questions in his face and shoving him. At trial, the politician did not take the stand and did not introduce evidence of his own character, but did call the reporter's neighbor to testify that the reporter has a reputation among neighbors for violent outbursts. After the neighbor testified, the prosecution moved to introduce testimony by a community leader that the politician has a reputation for violence in the community as evidence that the politician started the altercation.

Is the prosecution's evidence regarding the politician's reputation admissible?

(A) No, because the politician did not "open the door" to the introduction of evidence of his bad character by introducing evidence of his own good character

(B) No, because the defendant's character is not at issue, as he did not testify.

(C) Yes, because the politician "opened the door" to the evidence of his bad character for violence by introducing evidence of the reporter's character for violence.

(D) Yes, because violence is an essential element of battery.

A defendant was charged with battery following a bar fight with his neighbor. At trial, the defendant asserted that he did not initiate the altercation, but instead acted in self-defense. In addition to testifying about the event in question, he also sought to testify that the preceding night, he and a co-worker had gone out for a drink at the same bar, and that the evening passed peacefully. Prior to his own testimony, the defendant sought to introduce testimony of a lifelong acquaintance of the neighbor that, in the opinion of the acquaintance, the neighbor had a violent streak. After his testimony, the defendant sought to introduce testimony of the pastor of the church that the defendant regularly attended that the defendant had a reputation among the members of the church as a nonviolent person. Following testimony introduced by the prosecution that impeached the defendant's truthfulness, the defendant sought to introduce testimony of his employer that, in his opinion, the defendant was a truthful individual.

Which of the proffered testimony is most likely to be successfully challenged by the prosecution?

(A)   The testimony of the lifelong acquaintance of the neighbor regarding the neighbor's violent streak.

(B)   The testimony of the defendant regarding his peaceful behavior on the night before the bar fight.

(C)   The testimony of the defendant's pastor as to the defendant's reputation as a nonviolent person.

(D)   The testimony of the defendant's employer that the defendant was a truthful individual.

Question 6 | 5842 | MBE EVIDENCE | RELEVANCE | Bad Acts

A defendant was charged with aggravated assault arising from an altercation following a car accident. The defendant called a witness who testified that, in his opinion, the defendant was a non-violent person. On cross-examination, the prosecutor asked the witness whether he was aware that the defendant had been involved in a bar fight during the past year. Although the defendant was actually involved in such a fight, the prosecutor herself was not aware of the incident, as the defendant had not been arrested or charged. However, the prosecutor had witnessed the defendant's short temper during her interactions with the defendant, and knew that he was a drinker. As it happened, the witness was aware of the defendant's involvement in the fight.

Should the court require the witness to answer the prosecutor's question?

(A)   Yes, because the witness's knowledge of defendant's past behavior goes to the witness's credibility.

(B)   Yes, as a specific instance of the defendant's conduct.

(C)   No, because the defendant was not arrested or charged in connection with the bar fight.

(D)   No, because the prosecution did not know the defendant had been involved in a bar fight.

_____
_____
_____
_____
_____
_____
_____
_____
_____
_____
_____
_____
_____
_____

A defendant was charged with burglary. One of the key pieces of evidence in the case was a note left by the burglar that read, "It's just 2 easy." At trial, the defendant testified in his defense, asserting that he did not commit the crime. On cross-examination, the prosecutor, having a proper factual basis, asked the defendant if he had been convicted of felony burglary five years ago after having left a note at the crime scene that read, "It's just 2 easy." The defendant's attorney, having received proper notice from the prosecutor regarding use of the prior conviction, objected to the prosecutor's question as seeking to elicit improper criminal propensity evidence. The court, after determining that the probative value of this evidence and its prejudicial effects were equal, overruled the objection and instructed the defendant to answer the question.

Has the court acted properly?

(A) No, because evidence of the defendant's prior conviction constitutes improper criminal propensity evidence.

(B) No, because the court did not find that the probative value of the conviction outweighed its prejudicial effects.

(C) Yes, because the defendant may be impeached by a prior conviction of burglary within the last ten years.

(D) Yes, because the prior conviction helps establish the defendant as the perpetrator of the burglary for which he is on trial.

_____
_____
_____
_____
_____
_____
_____
_____
_____
_____
_____
_____
_____
_____

A defendant was charged with assault. Upon learning that the defendant intended to testify in his own defense, the government gave the defense proper notice of its intent to introduce as impeachment evidence the defendant's conviction for embezzlement nine years prior. The defense filed a motion to exclude all evidence of the defendant's conviction, arguing that it would prejudice the defendant. In a pre-trial hearing, the judge noted that the conviction would likely have little prejudicial effect.

Is the judge likely to grant the defendant's motion?

(A) No, because the conviction relates to a crime involving dishonesty and occurred within the last 10 years.

(B) No, because the probative value of such a conviction outweighs its prejudicial effect.

(C) Yes, because a prior conviction may not be used to impeach a defendant who testifies in his own defense.

(D) Yes, because the conviction for embezzlement is not probative in determining whether the defendant committed an assault.

_____
_____
_____
_____
_____
_____
_____
_____
_____
_____
_____
_____
_____
_____
_____
_____
_____
_____

Question 9 | 6966 | MBE EVIDENCE | WITNESSES | Competence

While shopping in a busy grocery store, a five-year-old girl accidentally got separated from her mother. After a few minutes, a woman approached the girl and asked her if she was lost. When the girl replied that she was, the woman said, "Your mommy was in an accident and is in the hospital. She told me to take you there." The girl went with the woman in her car. After driving for a few minutes, the woman saw police cars approaching. The woman immediately pulled over and forced the girl to get out of her car before speeding away. Based upon eyewitness statements, the woman was apprehended and prosecuted for kidnapping the girl.

At trial, the prosecution called the girl to testify about the kidnapping.

(A) The testimony is not admissible, because the testimony of a five-year-old has little probative value.

(B) The testimony is not admissible, because a five-year-old is too young to understand the importance of telling the truth.

(C) The testimony is admissible if the prosecution offers evidence to convince the judge that a five-year-old is competent to testify.

(D) The testimony is admissible if the court determines that the girl has personal knowledge and understands the difference between the truth and falsehood.

A defendant is on trial for bank robbery. In seeking to prove that the defendant was the robber, the prosecution introduced a handwritten note given by the robber to the bank teller. The teller testified that the note presented to her on the witness stand was the note that she received from the robber. The prosecution also seeks to have the teller testify as a lay witness that the handwriting on the note is that of the robber based on her comparison of the note with ten customer signature cards presented to her by the prosecutor after the robbery.

Is the teller's testimony that the handwriting on the note matches that of the robber's customer signature card admissible?

(A) No, because a lay witness may not testify as to whether a document is in a person's handwriting.

(B) No, because the teller's familiarity with the defendant's handwriting arose from the actions of the prosecutor.

(C) Yes, because the process was not unduly suggestive as the prosecutor presented her with ten customer signature cards.

(D) Yes, because a lay witness may testify as to whether a document is in a person's handwriting.

_____
_____
_____
_____
_____
_____
_____
_____
_____
_____
_____
_____
_____
_____

A defendant was charged with fraud in connection with the sale of nutritional supplements. The prosecution alleged that the defendant verbally represented himself as a physician to convince elderly individuals to sign contracts authorizing the defendant to charge their credit cards monthly fees for deliveries of these supplements. In fact, the defendant had no medical training. The contracts did not identify the defendant as a physician, but the prosecution intended to introduce witness testimony that the defendant verbally represented himself as a physician. The sole issue in dispute is whether the defendant made such representations. At trial, the prosecution introduced a photocopy of a contract between the defendant and one of the alleged victims in order to lay a foundation that the alleged victim bought supplements from the defendant. The defendant did not deny that the alleged victim bought supplements from him, but objected to the introduction of the contract on the grounds that the prosecution was required to introduce an original contract under the best evidence rule. The court sustained the defendant's objection.

Did the court err in making its ruling?

(A) Yes, because the best evidence rule allows for the introduction of an original or duplicate document.

(B) Yes, because the best evidence rule is not implicated in this case.

(C) No, because the best evidence rule applies to a document that has a legal effect, such as a contract.

(D) No, because a photocopy is not admissible when the absence of the original is not explained.

Question 12 | 3011 | MBE EVIDENCE | PRIVILEGES AND OTHER POLICY EXCLUSIONS | Public Policy Exclusions

A boat owner initiated a products liability action against the manufacturer of the boat's engine. The owner alleged that the engine manufacturer failed to warn the owner about the proper operation of a switch on the engine, and that improper operation of the switch caused the owner's injuries. The boat owner offered evidence that the manufacturer had begun including a written warning for the switch for all boats manufactured beginning in the year after the owner's boat was manufactured. The owner had owned his boat for five years prior to his injury.

Is this evidence admissible?

(A) No, because evidence of the manufacturer's warning is inadmissible as a remedial measure.

(B) No, because the remedial measures exclusion is limited to negligence cases.

(C) Yes, because the manufacturer began providing the warning before the boat owner's accident.

(D) Yes, because evidence of the need for a warning is not subject to the remedial measures exclusion.

_____
_____
_____
_____
_____
_____
_____
_____
_____
_____
_____
_____
_____
_____
_____

Two officers, a veteran and a novice, brought an experienced drug-sniffing dog on patrol one evening. They properly pulled over a driver on a bridge for erratic driving, and the veteran waited in the car to let the novice handle the stop. As the novice officer questioned the driver through the driver's window, the dog circled the car and began barking and pawing desperately at the passenger-side door. The novice officer noticed that the driver had a package sitting on his passenger seat. When asked about the package, the driver responded that it was just meat from a butcher shop. As the novice officer stepped away from the window to write a ticket, the driver grabbed the package and threw it out the passenger window and over the railing of the bridge. The dog immediately stopped barking. The veteran officer saw the whole event.

Assuming that the parties stipulate that the veteran is an expert in the training and reactions of drug-sniffing dogs, is the veteran officer's testimony describing the dog's reactions to the package admissible in a trial of the driver for possession of illegal drugs?

(A) No, because the dog's behavior was assertive conduct, making it hearsay not within any exception.

(B) No, because the dog's presence at the stop resulted in an improper search.

(C) Yes, as evidence that the package contained illegal drugs.

(D) Yes, because evidence generated by a machine or animal falls under an exception to the hearsay rule.

_____
_____
_____
_____
_____
_____
_____
_____
_____
_____
_____
_____
_____
_____
_____
_____
_____

A witness to an armed robbery identified a suspect in a proper police lineup that was not attended by the suspect's attorney. Charges were brought against the suspect, but the witness, a tourist from out of the country, had returned to her home country before the trial began. At trial, the prosecutor seeks to introduce the witness's prior statement of identification into evidence. The defendant objects to the introduction of the evidence.

Should the court allow the prior statement of identification into evidence?

(A) Yes, it should be admissible as nonhearsay.

(B) Yes, because the witness is unavailable, so the statement of identification falls under a hearsay exception.

(C) No, because the defendant's attorney was not present at the identification.

(D) No, because the witness is unavailable.

_____
_____
_____
_____
_____
_____
_____
_____
_____
_____
_____
_____
_____
_____
_____
_____
_____
_____

A defendant is acquitted of murder. Subsequently, the family members of the victim bring a wrongful death action against the defendant. The defendant seeks to introduce a properly authenticated, certified copy of the final judgment to show that the defendant did not wrongfully kill the victim. The victim's family members object to the introduction of the judgment.

May the defendant introduce the copy of the final judgment from his criminal case?

(A) No, because a judgment in a criminal case is inadmissible in a subsequent civil action.

(B) No, because the judgment is inadmissible hearsay.

(C) Yes, because the copy of the judgment satisfies the original document rule.

(D) Yes, because the level of proof in a civil action is less than that in the murder case.

_____
_____
_____
_____
_____
_____
_____
_____
_____
_____
_____
_____
_____
_____
_____
_____
_____

In a criminal trial for arson, a prosecution witness testifies under oath that she saw the defendant set fire to the victim's home. The defendant's attorney does not cross-examine the witness, but seeks to admit testimony that the witness gave at a deposition several months before the trial. At the deposition, the witness testified under oath that she did not see the defendant set fire to the victim's home.

Should the court admit the deposition testimony?

(A) The court should admit the witness's deposition testimony for impeachment purposes, but not as substantive evidence.

(B) The court should admit the witness's deposition testimony for impeachment purposes and as substantive evidence.

(C) The court should not admit the witness's deposition testimony because the defendant's attorney did not allow the witness the chance to explain her inconsistent testimony.

(D) The court should not admit the witness's deposition testimony because it is hearsay.

_____
_____
_____
_____
_____
_____
_____
_____
_____
_____
_____
_____
_____
_____
_____
_____

A father and son are charged with burglary. Prior to the trial, the prosecutor approached the son and asked him if he would be willing to testify against his father in exchange for a reduced sentence. After discussing the son's role in the burglary and some negotiation, the prosecutor and the son's defense attorney reached a settlement agreement. The son pleaded guilty, and was called to testify against his father. On cross-examination of the son, the father's attorney brought up the fact that the son was also originally charged with the burglary, and asked whether it was true that he received a lesser sentence for agreeing to testify against his father. The prosecutor objected to this line of questioning.

How should the court rule on the prosecutor's objection?

(A) The objection should be sustained, because the response calls for hearsay.

(B) The objection should be sustained, because it is against public policy to introduce evidence of a plea agreement.

(C) The objection should be overruled, because the question concerns bias.

(D) The objection should be overruled, because the son's sentence is irrelevant to the father's guilt.

_____
_____
_____
_____
_____
_____
_____
_____
_____
_____
_____
_____
_____

- Final tips:
  - Character, Impeachment, Hearsay
  - Memorize the _____
  - Read the _____ very carefully

[END OF HANDOUT]

MBE WORKSHOP: REAL PROPERTY
PROFESSOR LISA TUCKER
DREXEL UNIVERSITY SCHOOL OF LAW

CHAPTER 1:   INTRODUCTION

- Methodically walk through Real Property questions

- Most testable areas:

  o Easements, equitable servitudes, covenants, licenses

  o Estates in land

    ▪ Future interests
    ▪ Life estates

  o Landlord/Tenant law

  o _____ and security interests

An owner conveyed one of his properties to his son for the son's life, remainder to his daughter. The son lived on the property without paying any rent, although the property could have been rented for $4,000 a month. The property was assessed annual property taxes of $10,000. The son did not pay the taxes on the property. Not wanting to have a lien on the property or otherwise have it foreclosed upon, the daughter paid the property taxes. The fair market value of the life estate was 10 percent of the fair market value of the property held in fee simple absolute.

How much can the daughter recover from the son for the tax payments?

(A) $10,000, because life tenants are responsible for paying the full amount of taxes assessed on the property.

(B) $10,000, based on the reasonable rental value of the property.

(C) $1,000, the amount of taxes owed based on the fair market value of the life estate.

(D) Nothing, because the property taxes are the responsibility of the holder of the remainder interest.

_____
_____
_____
_____
_____
_____
_____
_____
_____
_____
_____
_____
_____
_____
_____

Question 2 | 3138 | MBE REAL PROPERTY | OWNERSHIP | Concurrent Estates

Two brothers owned a pasture as joint tenants with the right of survivorship. The older brother had one child, a daughter. The younger brother was a bachelor. Together the brothers deeded a 20 percent interest in the land to the older brother's daughter. Recently, the older brother gave his daughter an additional 10 percent interest in the land.

Under a traditional joint-tenancy analysis, what are the current ownership interests in the land?

(A) The two brothers have a 70 percent interest, and the daughter has a 30 percent interest, each as joint tenants with the other two.

(B) The two brothers have a 70 percent interest as joint tenants, and the daughter has a 30 percent interest as a tenant in common with her father and uncle.

(C) The two brothers each have a 35 percent interest and the daughter has a 30 percent interest, each as a tenant in common with the other two.

(D) The younger brother has a 40 percent interest, the daughter has a 30 percent interest, and the older brother has a 30 percent interest, each as a tenant in common with the other two.

_____
_____
_____
_____
_____
_____
_____
_____
_____
_____
_____
_____
_____
_____
_____

An attorney was a sole practitioner specializing in family law. Her niece was a recent law school graduate, and her nephew was an attorney. The attorney decided to retire, and conveyed the historic building that housed her law practice "to my niece, but if she fails to pass the bar exam within a year of her law school graduation, to my nephew."

Which of the following is an accurate description of the property interests created?

(A) The niece has a fee simple subject to condition subsequent, the nephew has a right of re-entry, and the attorney has no interest.

(B) The niece has a fee simple subject to an executory interest, the nephew has an executory interest, and the attorney has no interest.

(C) The niece has a fee simple determinable, and the attorney and the nephew each have a possibility of reverter.

(D) The niece has a fee simple subject to condition subsequent, the attorney has a right of re-entry, and the nephew has an executory interest.

_____
_____
_____
_____
_____
_____
_____
_____
_____
_____
_____
_____
_____
_____
_____

The owner of a commercial building leased the premises at fair rental value to a civic organization for a 25-year term. The lease contained a reasonable right of first refusal provision granting the organization a right to purchase the building if the owner found a buyer who was ready, willing, and able to purchase the building at a price agreed to by the owner and the buyer. Fifteen years into the lease, the owner was approached by a friend who was ready, willing, and able to purchase the building. Because of the friendship, the owner agreed to a purchase price that was below the market price. The owner notified the civic organization of the proposed sale, and the organization invoked its right of first refusal. However, the owner refused to sell the building to the organization for less than its fair market value. The applicable jurisdiction has retained the common law with respect to the Rule Against Perpetuities.

May the civic organization compel the owner to sell the building to the organization at the price agreed upon by the owner and the friend?

(A) No, because the organization's right of first refusal violates the Rule Against Perpetuities.

(B) No, because the organization's right of first refusal constitutes an encumbrance on marketable title.

(C) Yes, because the right of first refusal was reasonable.

(D) Yes, because the right of first refusal was a valid covenant running with the land.

An adult college student entered into a written, one-year lease of a condominium unit owned by a professor who was taking a one year sabbatical in France. The lease, which began on September 1, called for a yearly rent of $12,000 to be paid in monthly installments of $1,000. The student, who attended classes during the fall semester at the college, lived in the unit for four months and paid rent to the professor for each of those four months. The student moved out of the unit in late December and has not made any rental payments since then. In a signed note, the student transferred all of his rights under the lease for the remaining eight months to an employee of the college. Nothing in the lease prohibited the student from making this transfer. The employee moved into the unit on January 1. She lived there for five months, and mailed the $1,000 monthly payments for those five months to the professor in France, but otherwise had no contact with the professor. At the end of May, the employee moved out and has not made any further rental payments. Despite making a good faith effort through friends at the college, the professor was unable to find anyone to rent the condominium unit for the remaining three months of the lease. Under the terms of the lease, the student is liable to the professor for any unpaid rent. However, upon his return from France in September, the professor sued the employee for the unpaid rent of $3,000.

Is the employee liable to the professor for the unpaid rent?

(A) No, because the employee did not enter into a lease agreement with the professor.

(B) No, because the student remained liable for the rent under the terms of the lease.

(C) Yes, because the employee was the person who vacated the condominium unit.

(D) Yes, because the employee was in privity of estate with the professor.

_____
_____
_____
_____
_____
_____
_____
_____
_____
_____
_____
_____
_____
_____

Pursuant to a written lease, the owner of a warehouse leased the premises to a manufacturer for a term of one year at a total rent of $60,000. The lease called for the rent to be paid in monthly installments of $5,000 at the beginning of each month. The lease contained no provisions regarding termination or extension. The manufacturer promptly made the required rental payment each month. At the end of the year, the owner did not provide notice to the manufacturer of the termination of the lease. The manufacturer tendered a rental payment of $5,000 for the following month to the owner, which the owner refused to accept.

In the absence of an applicable statute, how much advance notice must the owner give the manufacturer before seeking to evict the manufacturer?

(A) None, because the manufacturer is a tenant at sufferance.

(B) A reasonable time, because the manufacturer is a tenant at will.

(C) A month, because the manufacturer, by tendering a rental payment, has created a periodic tenancy.

(D) Six months, because the manufacturer, by tendering a rental payment, has created a tenancy for years.

Question 7 | 3123 | MBE REAL PROPERTY | TITLES | Adverse Possession

A woman and a man each owned tracts of adjacent farmland. The woman used her land as an active farm; the man maintained a large vegetable garden near his home, but otherwise used his farmland simply to enjoy the outdoors, taking leisurely walks around different parts of his property almost daily. Thirty years ago, the woman began planting crops on the man's property. As of twenty years ago, the woman had planted crops on approximately ten acres of the man's land. Because the man used the land only for his daily walks, he did not mind that the woman planted seasonal crops on his land. In fact, he enjoyed walking through them and watching them grow; approximately once a week, the man would visit the ten acres upon which the woman planted her crops. The woman recently died, leaving her farm to her son. Her son informed the man that the woman had acquired the ten acres on which the crops were planted by adverse possession, and that he planned to use the ten acres as his own. The jurisdiction in which the farms are located has a twenty-year period for adverse possession.

If the man and the son bring suit to quiet title to the ten acres and the man wins, what is the most likely reason?

(A)   The woman did acquire title by adverse possession, but the son is unable to tack his ownership to hers.

(B)   The woman never acquired titled to the land because she did not acquire possession of the entirety of the ten acres at once.

(C)   The woman never acquired title to the land because she planted the crops only seasonally, not continuously.

(D)   The woman never acquired title to the land because she was not in exclusive or hostile possession of it.

_____
_____
_____
_____
_____
_____
_____
_____
_____
_____
_____
_____

The owner of land donated it to a charity by quitclaim deed. The charity did not record the deed. The following month, the owner sold the same land by warranty deed to a woman who paid valuable consideration and did not know about the prior gift of the land to the charity. The woman promptly and properly recorded her warranty deed. A month later, the charity recorded its quitclaim deed. The following year, the woman gave the property to her son by quitclaim deed. Although the land had remained undeveloped at all relevant times, the son discovered the possible conflict with the charity's claim after the conveyance. The son then recorded his deed. The recording act of the jurisdiction provides: "No unrecorded conveyance or mortgage of real property shall be good against subsequent purchasers for value without notice, who shall first record."

Who owns the land?

(A) The charity, because the charity recorded its deed before the son recorded his deed.

(B) The charity, because the son was not a purchaser for value.

(C) The son, because the charity was not a purchaser for value.

(D) The son, because his mother's purchase and recording of her deed terminated the charity's right to the land.

_____
_____
_____
_____
_____
_____
_____
_____
_____
_____
_____
_____
_____
_____

Anticipating the death of his mother and needing money, the only child of a terminally ill widow represented himself as owner of the widow's residence to a couple. The couple paid the son $200,000 for the residence. Although the couple did not immediately move into the residence, they promptly recorded the warranty deed they received from the son in the land records for the county in which the residence was located. The couple was unaware of the mother's ownership of the residence, which was also reflected in those same land records. One week after the land sale, the mother died. Upon her death, the residence passed by the terms of the mother's will to her son. The son, claiming ownership of the residence, has moved into it. The son has offered to return the $200,000 to the couple and pay for any expenses they have incurred with regard to this matter. The recording act of the applicable jurisdiction reads: "No conveyance or mortgage of real property shall be good against subsequent purchasers for value and without notice unless the same be recorded according to law."

Of the following, which provides the best argument for the couple that they hold title to the residence?

(A) The son's rights to the residence have been lost through ademption.

(B) The couple's ownership of the residence is protected by the recording act.

(C) The son's ownership of the residence vests automatically in the couple under the shelter rule.

(D) The residence belongs to the couple by application of the estoppel by deed doctrine.

_____
_____
_____
_____
_____
_____
_____
_____
_____
_____
_____
_____
_____
_____
_____

A man owned a 25-acre tract of land. He conveyed 20 of the 25 acres to a developer by warranty deed and continues to live on the five-acre portion he retained. The deed to the 20-acre tract was promptly recorded and contained the following:

"It is a condition of this deed that all owners, their heirs and assigns, of any portion of the 20-acre tract shall use the land for single-family residences only."

The applicable zoning ordinance allows for single and multi-family homes in this area. The developer fully developed the tract into a residential subdivision consisting of 20 lots with a single-family home on each lot. The lots were subsequently sold and the deed to each lot referenced the quoted provision. A woman purchased one of the lots and decided to build an addition to the house. The woman plans to build an entirely separate apartment and rent it to college students. A nosy neighbor in an adjoining subdivision opposes this development because she does not want rowdy college students driving through the neighborhood.

Can the neighbor prevent the woman from building the apartment?

(A) Yes, because the original parties intended for the rights and duties to run with the land.

(B) Yes, because the restriction is valid under the common-law Rule Against Perpetuities.

(C) No, because the zoning ordinance allows for multi-family homes as well as single-family homes.

(D) No, because the neighbor does not have the right to enforce the restriction.

A brother and sister own parcels of adjacent property. Their father had owned the land in its entirety, and when the siblings graduated from college, he split his estate in two and gave each sibling a parcel. The brother's property was landlocked, so his sister granted him an easement over her property in order to access the sole public road. The easement was not recorded. Five years later, the brother, having never set foot on his parcel, sold it to his sister. The sister eventually resold this parcel to a stranger, after telling the stranger about the easement she had granted her brother. Shortly thereafter, she sold her own parcel to a colleague. The stranger seeks access over the colleague's parcel in order to reach the public road, but the colleague refuses.

Does the stranger have a right to an easement across the colleague's parcel?

(A) No, because the brother's easement was not recorded.

(B) No, because the brother's easement was extinguished upon the sister's acquisition of her brother's parcel.

(C) Yes, because the stranger requires an easement by necessity.

(D) Yes, because the colleague had notice of the brother's easement.

CHAPTER 3:   REAL PROPERTY, CONTINUED

Question 12 | 5879 | MBE REAL PROPERTY | DISPUTES ABOUT THE USE OF LAND | Easements

The owner of a house in a suburban neighborhood converted a driveway from rock to asphalt. The owner's neighbor did not have a driveway but instead parked on the street that ran in front of both of their homes. When asked by the neighbor, the owner told the neighbor that she could also use the driveway to access her house. For 11 years, the neighbor used the driveway on occasion when engaged in tasks such as bringing furniture and appliances into her house, or on days when it was raining heavily. Throughout these years, only the owner maintained the driveway. Recently, the owner sold his house to a couple. The owner informed the couple about the neighbor's use of the driveway when they first looked at the house, but neither the contract of sale nor the deed made reference to it. When the neighbor used the driveway on the first rainy day after the couple moved in, the couple told her that she could no longer use their driveway. The neighbor sued the couple, seeking a judgment that she has a right to use the driveway. In the applicable jurisdiction, the term for the creation of a prescriptive easement is 10 years.

Who is likely to succeed?

(A)   The couple, because a license, as a property interest, must be in writing.

(B)   The couple, because the neighbor's license to use the driveway has been revoked.

(C)   The neighbor, because her use of the driveway created a prescriptive easement.

(D)   The neighbor, because the couple had notice of her driveway use before buying the house.

A speculator and the original owner of a condominium unit entered into a contract for the sale of the unit. The contract, which contained no reference to the marketability of the title, called for the owner to transfer the unit to the speculator by quitclaim deed, which the owner did on the date called for in the contract. A year later, the speculator entered into a contact to sell the unit to a third party at a price significantly higher than the price paid by the speculator for the unit. The contract specifically required the speculator to provide the third party with title to the unit free from all defects. Upon investigation, the third party discovered that the unit was subject to a restrictive covenant that rendered the title to the unit unmarketable, and that the restrictive covenant had existed at the time that the speculator had purchased the unit. The third party refused to complete the transaction. The speculator subsequently sued the original owner of the condominium unit for breach of contract.

For whom is the court likely to rule?

(A) The speculator, because a covenant of marketable title was implied in the contract.

(B) The speculator, because of the warranty against encumbrances.

(C) The original owner, because the condominium unit was transferred by a quitclaim deed.

(D) The original owner, because of the merger doctrine.

_____
_____
_____
_____
_____
_____
_____
_____
_____
_____
_____
_____
_____
_____
_____
_____

A woman obtained ownership of a cottage after her grandmother died. The owner, who lived out of state, decided to sell the cottage to a buyer. The parties agree that closing would occur the following week. The owner has casualty insurance on the cottage, while the buyer did not obtain such insurance. On the evening before the closing was to take place, a fire caused by lightning destroyed the cottage. The jurisdiction has not adopted the Uniform Vendor and Purchaser Risk Act.

If the seller seeks specific performance, may the buyer rescind the contract for the sale of the cottage?

(A) No, because the buyer bears the risk of loss.

(B) No, but the owner must give the buyer credit against the purchase price in the amount of the insurance proceeds.

(C) Yes, because the owner has casualty insurance and can more easily bear the loss.

(D) Yes, but the buyer must reimburse the owner for the cost of the casualty insurance.

_____
_____
_____
_____
_____
_____
_____
_____
_____
_____
_____
_____
_____
_____
_____
_____
_____

A corporate officer purchased a house with the aid of a loan at a favorable interest rate from the corporation. The corporation required the officer to grant it a mortgage as security for the loan. The officer also signed a note promising to repay the loan over a period of ten years. The note contained a due-on-sale clause, which required, at the corporation's option, payment of the full outstanding amount of the loan if the officer sold the house without first obtaining the corporation's written consent. After making timely payments on the loan for three years, the officer sold the house to an unrelated buyer without obtaining the corporation's consent. The deed given by the officer acknowledged that the house was being transferred subject to the mortgage. After payment of the purchase price to the officer, the buyer promptly recorded the deed. Subsequently, neither the officer nor the buyer made any payments on the loan to the corporation. The corporation has sued the buyer for the outstanding amount of the loan.

Of the following, which is the buyer's best defense to this action?

(A)   The due-on-sale clause is void as an impermissible restraint on alienation.

(B)   The buyer is not personally liable for repayment of the outstanding amount of the loan.

(C)   The buyer is not in privity of estate with the corporation.

(D)   The officer remains personally liable for repayment of the outstanding amount of the loan.

_____
_____
_____
_____
_____
_____
_____
_____
_____
_____
_____
_____
_____
_____
_____
_____

A woman received a loan from a bank to purchase a new home. She secured the loan by a mortgage on the home. The woman made regular payments on the mortgage for 8 years. However, the woman fell into debt and eventually defaulted on the loan. The bank gave the woman proper notice of foreclosure proceedings. Before the foreclosure sale took place, the woman received an inheritance from a distant relative. The woman contacted the bank and offered to pay the remaining balance of the loan and any accrued interest in exchange for clear title to the property.

Is the bank required to accept the woman's offer?

(A) No, because the bank has already initiated foreclosure proceedings.

(B) No, because the bank can sell the property in a judicially supervised public sale.

(C) Yes, because the woman exercised her right under the equity of redemption.

(D) Yes, because the woman exercised her statutory right of redemption.

_____
_____
_____
_____
_____
_____
_____
_____
_____
_____
_____
_____
_____
_____
_____
_____
_____
_____
_____

A married couple bought a house to use as a residence. Their bank loan was secured by a mortgage on the house. The following year, the couple granted a second mortgage to a savings and loan association in exchange for a loan. The proceeds from this loan were used in the couple's business. Several years later, the couple defaulted on both loans. The couple offered their interest in the house to the bank by deed in lieu of foreclosure and the bank accepted.

What effect does this transaction have on the savings and loan association's mortgage?

(A) As an interest with priority over the bank's mortgage, the savings and loan association's mortgage is unaffected.

(B) As a junior interest to the bank's mortgage, the savings and loan association's mortgage is completely eliminated.

(C) The savings and loan association cannot foreclose on its mortgage, but must look to the personal liability of the couple, now that the bank owns the house.

(D) The house remains subject to the savings and loan association's mortgage.

_____
_____
_____
_____
_____
_____
_____
_____
_____
_____
_____
_____

- Final tips:
  - As you are practicing, take your time to walk through the questions
    - Make sure you can point out the relevant facts
    - Try to come up with an answer before you even see the choices
  - Practice, practice, practice!

[END OF HANDOUT]

MBE WORKSHOP: TORTS
PROFESSOR LISA TUCKER
DREXEL UNIVERSITY SCHOOL OF LAW

CHAPTER 1: **INTRODUCTION**

- Key for acing Torts: Learn the _____; have all the _____ of the tort been _____?

- Default rule for the MBE (unless told otherwise: assume _____ and _____

    o You may be told to apply a different rule

- The best defense: one of the elements _____

- Look for the _____ answer, not a perfect answer

- Breakdown of questions in Torts:

    o _____ – 50% of the questions in Torts
    o Intentional Torts
    o Strict and Products Liability
    o Nuisance, Defamation, Privacy Torts

Two pranksters threw ice from a soda cup over a shopping mall railing onto the heads of patrons two floors below. They intended to post videos of the ice hitting these patrons and the patrons slipping on the ice on a website known for displaying pranks. After a while, the pranksters became bored and left the railing to walk to the food court. As they walked away, they heard a scream and saw a mall patron fall after slipping on the remnants of the ice. The pranksters had not seen nor targeted this mall patron prior to his fall but walked over to help him up. The patron cried hysterically and was visibly shaken to the point of needing medical care for his emotional as well as physical injury.

If the pranksters are found liable for the patron's injuries, which of the following is the most plausible basis?

(A) Assault

(B) Battery

(C) Negligent infliction of emotional distress

(D) Intentional infliction of emotional distress

Two college students, dressed as robbers for Halloween, were playing tag and chasing each other in the street outside of their dormitory. One of the students hid behind a shrub and waited to surprise the other. Before the other student appeared, an elderly woman passed the shrub. The student, hearing footsteps and thinking it was the other student, jumped in front of her and shouted, "Got you!" Before the student could touch her, the elderly woman shrieked and jumped backward. She dropped a bag of groceries but was otherwise unharmed. The woman sued the student for assault.

Will the woman prevail in her suit against the student?

(A) Yes, because the woman was placed in reasonable apprehension of an imminent battery.

(B) Yes, because the student's words, coupled with the act of jumping from the shrub, constituted an overt act.

(C) No, because the woman sustained no damages for which she could collect.

(D) No, because the student did not have the necessary intent to commit a tort.

A musician's brother borrowed the musician's electric guitar. The brother told the musician that he was going to use it the next day to teach the children in his second grade class about different musical instruments. Instead, the brother went to a rowdy bar that evening and played the electric guitar with his rock band all night long. A drunk bar patron got on stage during one of the songs, grabbed the guitar from the brother, and smashed it against the ground. The brother took the electric guitar to a repair shop the next day, and was told that it would cost $750 to restore the guitar to its original condition. At the time of the incident, the guitar was worth $1,500. The musician asserts a claim against his brother for conversion.

What is the musician entitled to recover?

(A) Nothing

(B) $750

(C) $1,500

(D) $1,500 plus damages for loss of use

_____
_____
_____
_____
_____
_____
_____
_____
_____
_____
_____
_____
_____

Question 4 | 5995 | MBE TORTS | INTENTIONAL TORTS INVOLVING PERSONAL INJURY | Intentional Infliction of Emotional Distress

A defendant, intending to frighten the plaintiff, went to the plaintiff's place of work, a toy store. When the plaintiff was alone in the store, the defendant waved a knife at the plaintiff, saying, "I'm going to make sure you don't molest any more children!" It turns out the defendant had mistaken the plaintiff for someone else, who the defendant believed to have molested his nephew. The plaintiff, however, assumed the knife was just one of the toys from a shelf in the store and that the defendant was just making a tasteless joke, so he laughed it off and told the defendant to get lost. Only later did the plaintiff realize that the knife had been real, and that he had actually been in serious danger. As a result of looking back on the distressing event, the plaintiff has suffered from severe anxiety, leading to illness, which has caused him to miss work.

Which of the following tort doctrines offers the plaintiff the best chance to recover?

(A) Intentional infliction of emotional distress

(B) Assault

(C) Battery

(D) Slander

_____
_____
_____
_____
_____
_____
_____
_____
_____
_____
_____
_____
_____

The owner of a bed and breakfast catered to wealthy city residents hoping to get some rest near the beach. His bed and breakfast had doors and windows that opened out directly onto the beach. On a busy holiday weekend, a guest at the bed and breakfast threw a party during which he fell out of a second-story window onto the sand below. His injuries were minor, but he filed suit against the owner, alleging that the owner was negligent in allowing the window to fully open on an upper-level floor. During the proceedings, the guest provided evidence that within that same beach town, there were six bed and breakfasts, and all of them contained locks on their upper-level windows preventing the windows from opening more than four inches, although there was no statute requiring this precaution. The owner countered with evidence that no other guest had ever fallen out of the window, and that the windows had recently been inspected and given a positive safety rating.

Is the guest likely to recover in his negligence lawsuit against the owner?

(A)   Yes, because the owner allowed the windows to open wide enough for a guest to fall through.

(B)   Yes, because other bed and breakfasts in the area did not allow windows to open more than four inches.

(C)   No, because the windows were recently inspected and noted to be safe.

(D)   No, because there was no statute requiring window locks.

_____
_____
_____
_____
_____
_____
_____
_____
_____
_____
_____
_____
_____
_____

Question 6 | 5998 | MBE TORTS | NEGLIGENCE | The Standard of Care

A bus company operates routes between major cities. These buses are popular with students because they are inexpensive and reliable. The bus company does not have bus stations, but picks up and drops off passengers at designated, well-lit public parking areas. The plaintiff, a 20-year-old female college student, recently rode the bus. On that occasion, however, heavy traffic threatened to delay the bus, so the driver decided to let the passengers off at an unlit spot about a half-mile from the designated drop-off lot. While walking from this spot to the designated drop-off lot where her ride was waiting, the plaintiff was attacked and robbed by an unknown assailant. The plaintiff brought an action for negligence against the bus company.

Could the plaintiff recover from the bus company for her injuries?

(A) Yes, if she can demonstrate that the driver failed to meet the relevant standard of care.

(B) Yes, because common carriers are strictly liable for injuries to passengers.

(C) No, because the intervening criminal conduct of the assailant severs the chain of causation.

(D) No, because the bus company no longer owed the plaintiff a duty of care once she got off the bus.

_____
_____
_____
_____
_____
_____
_____
_____
_____
_____
_____
_____
_____
_____
_____

The plaintiff, while driving his car, had been stopped at a red light at a busy intersection for approximately 15 seconds when he was struck from behind by a speeding taxicab. The plaintiff did not see the taxicab coming towards him in his mirrors, because he had been looking down to send a text message. The jurisdiction where the accident took place, which is a contributory negligence jurisdiction, has enacted a statute prohibiting drivers from texting while driving. The statute was enacted after a study showed that most of the car accidents in the jurisdiction were caused by driving while texting. The plaintiff brings suit against the taxicab driver for damages for injuries resulting from the accident. The taxicab driver seeks to assert the defense of contributory negligence, arguing that because the plaintiff was texting in violation of the statute, he was negligent per se.

Is the contributory negligence defense likely to be successful?

(A)   No, because the taxicab driver was not in the class of people the statute was designed to protect.

(B)   No, because the plaintiff's own negligence was not the cause of the accident.

(C)   Yes, because car accidents are the type of harm that the statute is meant to prevent.

(D)   Yes, because the plaintiff's own negligence, however slight, is a complete bar to recovery.

_____
_____
_____
_____
_____
_____
_____
_____
_____
_____
_____
_____
_____
_____

Question 8 | 2950 | MBE TORTS | NEGLIGENCE | Duty

A country club hosted a celebrity golf tournament to raise money for a local hospital. The country club had a strict policy of requiring any person not currently engaged in a golf match to stay off the course while a tournament is in session. The country club made an announcement to this effect, adding that entering the course during play could result in serious injury. An adult club member, who was aware of the policy, walked onto the course during a match in order to procure the signature of a famous golf star. While on the course, the member was struck in the head with a golf ball and injured.

In a suit against the country club by the member to recover for his injuries, how will the court likely hold?

(A) Liable, because the club member was a business invitee.

(B) Liable, because the presence of famous golf stars constituted an attractive nuisance.

(C) Not liable, because the country club enjoys charitable immunity.

(D) Not liable, because the country club did not breach its duty to the club member.

_____
_____
_____
_____
_____
_____
_____
_____
_____
_____
_____
_____
_____

Question 9 | 1420 | MBE TORTS | NEGLIGENCE | Breach of Duty

A consumer bought a can of chicken soup from her neighborhood grocery store. The soup was manufactured by a large food company. Approximately two weeks later, the consumer's son ate the soup; soon thereafter, the son became violently ill. At the hospital, the attending physician diagnosed the illness as botulism poisoning, a serious disease which can arise by defects in the manufacturing process of canned foods, or can be brought on after manufacturing through temperature fluctuations in storage of the canned foods. Tests later confirmed that the can of soup was tainted with botulinium bacteria.

The consumer sued the large food company on behalf of her son. At trial, she produced no direct evidence of negligence on the part of the food company, but invoked the doctrine of res ipsa loquitur to prove liability. The applicable jurisdiction has adopted a comparative negligence standard. The company filed a motion for a directed verdict.

How should the trial judge rule on the motion?

(A) Deny the motion, because the application of res ipsa loquitur in this case is proper.

(B) Deny the motion, because the invocation of res ipsa loquitur shifted the burden of proof and production to the food company.

(C) Grant the motion, because the consumer produced no direct evidence of negligence on the part of the food company.

(D) Grant the motion, because the doctrine of res ipsa loquitur has been abolished in comparative negligence jurisdictions.

_____
_____
_____
_____
_____
_____
_____
_____
_____

A cyclist was riding his bike along a hilly road through the woods one evening wearing dark clothing and no helmet. As he coasted down a hill at a reckless speed, he hit a pothole and fell onto the shoulder of the road. A sleepy driver came over the hill behind the cyclist, weaving slightly as he struggled to stay awake. The driver could not see the cyclist because of his dark clothing, and because he was disoriented from his crash, the cyclist did not notice the approaching car. As the driver weaved, his car wandered onto the shoulder of the road and clipped the cyclist, breaking his arm. At trial, it was established that the driver was not acting as a reasonably prudent person under the circumstances when he weaved onto the shoulder of the road and that the cyclist would have been visible to a driver if he had been wearing reflective clothing.

Is the cyclist likely to recover damages from the driver?

(A) No, because the cyclist put himself in peril with his reckless speed and dark clothing.

(B) No, because the driver did not see the cyclist and therefore could not protect him from harm.

(C) Yes, because the cyclist was helpless and the driver had the last clear chance to prevent his broken arm.

(D) Yes, because the driver's negligent conduct was a substantial factor in causing the cyclist's broken arm.

A woman in great pain from a toothache made an emergency appointment with a dentist. The dentist removed her tooth. Later, she returned and the dentist implanted a new tooth. This tooth, which was made from synthetic materials by a dental laboratory, contained a defect. The dentist was unaware of the defect because he failed to exercise reasonable care in examining the tooth before implanting it. Several weeks later, when the woman bit down on an apple, the implanted tooth broke. A piece of the broken tooth caused substantial damage to her mouth. The woman brought a strict products liability action against the dentist.

Is the woman likely to prevail?

(A) Yes, because the dentist did not exercise reasonable care.

(B) Yes, because the implanted tooth was defective.

(C) No, because the dentist did not know that the implanted tooth was defective.

(D) No, because the dentist was a service provider.

_____
_____
_____
_____
_____
_____
_____
_____
_____
_____
_____
_____
_____
_____
_____

A plaintiff purchased a new car from a car dealer. A computer chip in the engine of the car had been defectively manufactured, such that the plaintiff lost control of the car, causing the plaintiff to suffer injuries. Several entities were involved in the process through which the defective chip ended up in the plaintiff's car. The defective computer chip was manufactured by a component company and then purchased by an engine builder. The engine builder then incorporated the chip into the engine and sold the engine to a car manufacturer. The car manufacturer then incorporated the engine into the car and sold the car to the car dealer. The plaintiff brought an action for strict products liability against the component company, the engine builder, the car manufacturer, and the car dealer.

From whom can the plaintiff recover for his injuries?

(A) The car dealer only, because the plaintiff was not in privity with the other parties.

(B) Any of the parties who had negligently failed to inspect the product.

(C) Any of the parties, regardless of whether the party was negligent.

(D) The component company only, because the component company is the party that manufactured the defective chip.

A chef who worked in a restaurant purchased an electric knife from a knife manufacturer that was specially designed to cut through meat. The instructions for the electric knife clearly stated that it should not be used on raw, hard vegetables, such as carrots or potatoes, because the moving blades on the electric knife would malfunction and could cause serious injury. One day, the chef's friend asked to borrow the electric knife. The chef lent the electric knife to the friend, and told him, "Don't use the electric knife to cut raw vegetables." Thinking the advice was only to avoid dulling the blade, the friend disregarded the chef's advice. When the friend used the electric knife to cut raw carrots, the moving blades on the knife malfunctioned, causing the friend to sustain a serious knife wound. The friend filed a negligence suit against the chef to recover damages for his injuries. The jurisdiction applies the common-law rules for contributory negligence and assumption of the risk.

Which of the following is the chef's best defense?

(A) The friend was contributorily negligent.

(B) The friend voluntarily assumed the risk.

(C) The chef did not owe a duty to the friend.

(D) The knife manufacturer is strictly liable for the friend's injuries.

_____
_____
_____
_____
_____
_____
_____
_____
_____
_____
_____
_____
_____
_____

Question 14 | 2981 | MBE TORTS | STRICT LIABILITY | Animals

The defendant purchased a tiger in the hopes of achieving his life's ambition of performing in a Las Vegas show. The defendant kept the tiger locked in a cage specifically designed for such animals. Unbeknownst to the defendant, however, there was a manufacturing defect in the cage that caused the lock to spring open. The tiger escaped from the cage and ran onto the defendant's yard, where the plaintiff, a painter hired by the defendant, was on a ladder painting the exterior of the defendant's home. The plaintiff panicked when he saw the tiger, causing him to fall off the ladder. The tiger ran off the property without approaching the plaintiff. The plaintiff sustained significant injuries as the result of his fall. The plaintiff has sued the defendant. At trial, the defendant provided evidence that he exercised reasonable care in containing the tiger. The jurisdiction recognizes the doctrine of contributory negligence.

Is the plaintiff likely to prevail at trial?

(A) No, because the plaintiff's own negligence on the ladder contributed to his injuries.

(B) No, because the tiger was not a direct cause of the plaintiff's injury.

(C) Yes, because the painter was an invitee, and was thus owed the highest duty of care.

(D) Yes, because the defendant is strictly liable for the plaintiff's injury.

_____
_____
_____
_____
_____
_____
_____
_____
_____
_____
_____
_____
_____
_____
_____

A water skier filed a negligence action for neck injuries he sustained while water skiing against the driver of the boat and the "spotter"—the person responsible for informing a boat driver when a water skier falls. At trial, the jury determined that all three parties were negligent. The water skier was 10% at fault for attempting a very difficult move, the driver was 30% at fault for making a sharp turn while the water skier was attempting the move, and the spotter was 60% at fault for not paying attention and failing to inform the driver when the water skier fell into the water. The jurisdiction in which the court is located recognizes pure several liability. The jury awarded the water skier $100,000 in damages.

If the water skier only tries to collect from the spotter, what is the most the water skier can recover?

(A) $90,000, and the spotter can collect $30,000 from the driver.

(B) $90,000, and the spotter can collect $45,000 from the driver.

(C) $60,000, and the spotter can collect $30,000 from the driver.

(D) $60,000, but the spotter cannot collect anything from the driver.

_____
_____
_____
_____
_____
_____
_____
_____
_____
_____
_____
_____
_____
_____
_____

The plaintiff brought his car to a mechanic for a tune-up. During the tune-up, the mechanic removed the fuse for the brake lights and inadvertently failed to replace it, causing the lights to stop working. As the plaintiff was driving his car home from the mechanic, he was involved in an accident. The plaintiff, seeing a friend walking along the road, slammed on his brakes to give the friend a ride. The defendant, who was driving the car behind the plaintiff, hit the plaintiff. The plaintiff sustained severe whiplash from the accident, and has sued the defendant and the mechanic. At trial, the jury determined that the plaintiff's damages were $10,000, and that the defendant was 50% at fault, the mechanic was 25% at fault, and the plaintiff was 25% at fault. The jurisdiction recognizes pure several liability and partial comparative negligence.

How much can the plaintiff collect from the defendant?

(A) $5,000.

(B) $7,500.

(C) $10,000.

(D) The plaintiff cannot recover from the defendant.

Question 17 | 6161 | MBE TORTS | DEFAMATION, INVASION OF PRIVACY, AND BUSINESS TORTS | Defamation

A professional football player was one of the most popular and well-known athletes on television. He regularly appeared in commercials endorsing sports equipment, cars, and performance-enhancing vitamins. After a recent drug test was administered to all professional football players, the football player's test results were leaked to the public by an unknown source. The results showed he tested positive for illegal performance-enhancing drugs. A local political activist, who campaigned against professional football players because she believed all of them used illegal drugs, stated in a televised interview that the leaked results showed that the football player was an "illicit drug user who will be suspended from playing professional football." A few days later, the drug-testing facility announced that it had mistakenly reported the football player's test results, and that he did not actually test positive for the use of illegal drugs. However, the football player had already lost a number of lucrative advertising contracts.

If the football player sues the activist for defamation, who will prevail?

(A) The football player, because the activist believed that all professional football players used illegal drugs.

(B) The football player, because he did not test positive for the use of illegal performance-enhancing drugs.

(C) The activist, because the professional football player is a public figure.

(D) The activist, because she was not the proximate cause of the damage to the football player's reputation.

- Final Tips:
  - Study where the points are (negligence, intentional torts, strict and products liability)
  - It's all about the elements
  - Don't confuse negligence and strict liability
  - Remember to double check the cause of action
  - Use the answer choices to help you

[END OF HANDOUT]

Civil Procedure

CIVIL PROCEDURE
PROFESSOR MARGARET LEMOS
DUKE UNIVERSITY SCHOOL OF LAW

CHAPTER 1:   INTRODUCTION

A. In General

- Tested on the MBE, MEE, and state essays
- Similar to state civil procedure in most states

  o State rules are often patterned on the Federal Rules of Civil Procedure

B. MBE

- Includes 25 scored questions on Federal Civil Procedure
- Important topics:

  o Pleadings
  o Discovery
  o Motions Practice

    - Motion to Dismiss
    - Motion for Summary Judgment
    - Motion for Judgment as a Matter of Law

- MOST important topic:

  o Jurisdiction

CHAPTER 2:   SUBJECT MATTER JURISDICTION: FEDERAL QUESTION AND DIVERSITY

A. Introduction to Jurisdiction

1. **Subject Matter Jurisdiction**

    Power of the court to decide *this type of the case*

2. **Personal Jurisdiction**

    Power of the court to decide the rights and liabilities of *this D*

3. **Venue**

    Among the courts that have subject matter and personal jurisdiction, which district(s) have proper venue.

B. Subject Matter Jurisdiction (SMJ)

1. In General

- Issue: Does this court have the power to decide this kind of case?
- Federal courts are courts of _____limited_____ subject matter jurisdiction.
  - State courts are generally courts of _____unlimited_____ subject matter jurisdiction.

    > **Exam Tip 1:** For the MBE, unless you are given a state statute that says otherwise, assume state courts have subject matter jurisdiction over any kind of case.

2. Pleading SMJ

- Basis for federal SMJ must be _____affirmatively_____ pleaded in every case
  - If challenged, it must be proved that there is a basis for SMJ.

3. Waiver

- _____No waiver_____ for a lack of SMJ (i.e., Parties cannot agree between themselves to litigate in a court that lacks SMJ)
- Lack of SMJ cannot be waived by failing to object or by affirmative consent

4. Objection to SMJ

- Lack of SMJ can be raised by _____any party_____ at _____any time_____, including by
  - The plaintiff, who chose to go to the wrong court.
  - The court itself
  - Anyone for the first time on _____appeal_____

C. Federal Question Jurisdiction ("Arising Under")

1. Basis

Exists for a claim that arises under _____federal_____ law.

2. Well-Pleaded Complaint

- Plaintiff's claim must be based on federal law.
- Look at the face of the _____well-pleaded_____ **complaint**.
  - Only the plaintiff's claims count for determining federal question jurisdiction; the existence of a federal defense does not matter.
  - Plaintiff does not need to anticipate or plead a response to a defense. A federal defense does not count for federal question jurisdiction even if it is important.

- ○ ***Louisville & Nashville R.R. v. Mottley***

    Example 1: *Accident on railroad, Mottleys received lifetime passes on the railroad in settlement of their claim. Congress subsequently passed a statute that prohibited lifetime passes, according to the railroad; railroad stopped honoring the passes. Mottleys brought suit, claiming (1) that the railroad failed to honor its agreement with them, (2) that the federal statute did not bar lifetime passes, and (3) if it did, then it was unconstitutional.*

    Issue: Is there federal question jurisdiction?

    Answer: ___NO___ *Mottleys' claim was for specific performance of a contract, which is a state law claim. Federal law is only raised by the defendant's argument that it is barred by the federal statute from continuing to honor its contract. These are important questions, but they are not part of the plaintiff's complaint and therefore they do not count for purposes of federal question jurisdiction; the federal question MUST appear on the plaintiff's well-pleaded complaint.*

D. Diversity Jurisdiction

1. Basis

- ○ Cases between citizens of ___diff states___, or citizens of a state and a foreign country, if the amount in controversy *exceeds* ___$75,000___, exclusive of interest and costs.

    Exam Tip 2: The amount must EXCEED $75,000, so the plaintiff must seek at least $75,000.01.

- ○ *Exceptions:* ___Probate___ and ___domestic relations___ actions cannot be brought in federal court under diversity jurisdiction even if the normal requirements are satisfied.

2. Complete Diversity

a. General rule

- ▪ The diversity statute requires ___complete___ diversity.
- ▪ Every citizenship represented on the plaintiff's side of the case must be different from every citizenship represented on the defendant's side.
- ▪ Does NOT mean every plaintiff must be diverse from every other plaintiff or that the defendant must be diverse from every other defendant

    Note 1: Diversity must only be complete as between plaintiffs and defendants.

    Example 2: *Pennsylvania Plaintiff 1 and Pennsylvania Plaintiff 2 sue a New York Defendant. Does complete diversity exist?* ___Yes___

Example 3: *Pennsylvania Plaintiff and New York Plaintiff sue a New York Defendant. Does complete diversity exist?* No

_____

_____

b. Minimal diversity (exception to complete diversity requirement)

- Exists when __any__ plaintiff is diverse from __any__ defendant, even if other plaintiffs and defendants overlap. In example above, there was minimal diversity, because there was one plaintiff from NY and one from PA.

- Minimal diversity is permitted in the following circumstances:

  - Federal Interpleader Act (statutory interpleader);
  - Class actions with claims more than $ 5 million $ (Class Action Fairness Act); and
  - Interstate mass torts if at least 75 natural persons have died in one accident and the plaintiffs and defendants are from many different states (e.g., airline crash).

  Outside these limited exceptions, the general rule is that complete diversity is required.

  Editorial Note 1: With regard to federal statutory interpleader, diversity exists if any two adverse claimants are diverse from each other (discussed later).

c. Time for determination of diversity

- Diversity must exist when the complaint is filed

  - Does NOT matter that diversity did not exist when the cause of action arose
  - Does NOT matter that diversity no longer exists when the case comes to trial

3. Citizenship of the Parties

a. Individuals

- Citizen of the state or country of domicile.

  - Must be a citizen of the United States and a domiciliary of the relevant state
  - Domicile is permanent residence = residence + an intent to remain indefinitely (or, with no intent to leave)

  Example 4: *A law student who lives in one state but does not intend to stay there to start her legal career, she resides in the state where her law school is located, but she is not domiciled there.*

- For purposes of jurisdiction, there can only be one domicile at a time

b. "Aliens" (Citizens or Subjects of a Foreign Country)

- Diversity jurisdiction exists for controversies between a citizen (or citizens) of a state and a citizen (or citizens) of a foreign country.

- A citizen of a foreign country who has been admitted to the U.S. as a permanent resident is treated as a citizen of the _State she's domiciled_.

c. **Representative parties**

- Generally, the citizenship of the _representative party_ controls.

    Example 5: *In a suit by a Trustee on behalf of a trust, the Trustee's citizenship will control, not that of the beneficiary.*

- **Exception:** For litigation involving a decedent's estate, the citizenship of the _decedent_ controls.
- **Exception:** For the legal representative (guardian) of a minor/infant or an incompetent person, the citizenship of the _infant / minor_ controls.

    Note 2: GENERAL RULE = Citizenship of the representative party controls.

d. **Class actions**

- Citizenship of the _named_ or _representative_ parties count
- Class members not named may join without regard to citizenship.

e. **Corporations**

- Can have several citizenships simultaneously
- Citizen of:

    - The state, states, or foreign countries in which it is _incorporated_; and
    - The state or country where it has its _nerve center (principal place of business)_ *(where its executive offices are located)*

    Exam Tip 3: Remember, when a corporation is a party, you still need COMPLETE diversity between plaintiffs and defendants, so you must consider EVERY state where the corporation has citizenship.

f. **Partnerships and unincorporated associations**

- Citizen of every state of which its _members_ are citizens

    Example 6: *If you sue a partnership in federal court under diversity jurisdiction, you must show _complete_ diversity between you (the plaintiff) and the citizenship of every partner in that partnership.*

- Applies to partnerships, limited partnerships, trade associations, and _____ (the rule makes it much harder to get diversity in these organizations)

4. **Devices to Create or Destroy Diversity**

    o Actions that create or destroy diversity are permitted so long as they are not "shams" or fraudulent.

- o **Moving**: permitted, even if it is done with the purpose of affecting diversity, so long as the change in domicile is genuine, not a sham
- o **Assignment of a claim**: permitted so long as the assignment is real (for value) and complete (not collusive)

  - Partial assignment of a claim for the purposes debt collection does NOT affect citizenship if the assignor retains an interest in the claim.

    Example 7: *You owe me $1,000, and you do not want to pay. I hire someone to collect that debt from you. If he is successful in collecting, he gets to keep 30% (which means that I keep 70% and the assignment is partial). Does this type of partial assignment change citizenship?* ___No___

    _____

CHAPTER 3:   SUBJECT MATTER JURISDICTION: DIVERSITY (CONT.) AND REMOVAL

A. **Diversity Jurisdiction (Cont.)**

  1. **Amount in Controversy (AIC)**

     - o Must EXCEED $___75,000___, exclusive of interest and costs
     - o ONLY relevant in diversity cases
     - o General rule: Any ___good faith___ allegation will suffice (NOT whether the plaintiff recovers $75,000)

       - Only when it appears to a legal certainty that the AIC will not be met, will the court dismiss the case for lack of AIC.

         Example 8: *In a case in which the plaintiff is seeking to recover a debt where everyone agrees the debt is $50,000, there is a legal certainty that the AIC has not been met.*

         Example 9: *If it is a tort case, a good-faith belief will suffice, even if the jury finds the damages are much less.*

  2. **Aggregation**

     - o Aggregation: Adding up smaller claims to exceed $75,000
     - o **General rule: One plaintiff vs. one defendant**: Plaintiff can aggregate all her claims, regardless of whether the claims are related.

       Example 10: *Plaintiff has four claims against the defendant, each worth $25,000. Is the AIC requirement satisfied?* ___Yes___

     - o **One plaintiff vs. two (or more) defendants**: Plaintiff may not aggregate her claims against ___multiple___ defendants

Example 11: *Plaintiff sues four different defendants, seeking $25,000 from each. Is the AIC requirement satisfied?* __No__

- Claims against *each* defendant must total more than $75,000.

- **Two (or more) plaintiffs vs. one defendant:** Plaintiffs may not aggregate their claims against the defendant

  Example 12: *Four plaintiffs (who are not bringing a class action) sue a single defendant, each seeking $25,000. Is the AIC requirement satisfied?* __NO__ *None of the plaintiffs has satisfied the AIC requirement.*

  - *EACH* plaintiff must be seeking more than $75,000 from the defendant.

- **Supplemental jurisdiction:** Smaller-value claims are sometimes permitted as a matter of supplemental jurisdiction (*discussed later*).

  Editorial Note 2: Note that if the defendants are *jointly liable*, they are treated as one defendant. Thus, if plaintiff sues two defendants on a theory of joint liability, seeking a total of $75,001, the AIC requirement is satisfied.

B. Removal Jurisdiction

Exam Tip 4: Tested with astonishing frequency, especially on essays.

1. Terminology

- **Removal** moves case from __State__ court to __federal__ court.
- **Transfer** moves case from one __federal__ court to another __federal__ court.
- No procedure for removal of a case from federal court to state court.

  - Federal court can abstain from hearing the case (in very narrow circumstances).

2. General Rule

- Removal is proper ONLY if the case could have been brought originally in __federal__ court.
- ONLY __Defendants__ may remove.

  - ALL defendants must consent to removal within __30__ days of service.

- ASK: If the plaintiff had chosen to sue in federal court in the first place, would the federal court have had __SMJ__ jurisdiction?

  Exam Tip 5: The reason this is an exam favorite is because the examiners can test federal SMJ without using the term. *"Was the motion to remove properly granted"* is a sneaky way to test SMJ.

3. Federal Question

- **Well-pleaded complaint rule:** Federal question jurisdiction on whether the federal question appears on the face of the well-pleaded complaint.

- o **Removal does not change that rule:** If the well-pleaded complaint discloses that the plaintiff's claim is based on federal law, then the defendant may remove to federal court.

  - If the plaintiff's claim is based on state law, defendant __May not__ remove to federal court, even if the defendant has raised a federal defense.

    Example 13: *Recall Louisville & Nashville R.R. v. Mottley case: Mottleys sue the railroad on a contract claim (specific performance). They tried to go to federal court because the real issues were based in federal law. However, the Supreme Court said the plaintiff's claim is a state law contract claim, so there is no federal SMJ. If there is no jurisdiction for the plaintiffs, then the defendants could not remove it to federal court.*

4. Diversity

- o Removal based on diversity jurisdiction is proper only if:

  1. There is __Complete__ diversity;
  2. The amount in controversy exceeds $ __75,000__ ; and
  3. The action is brought in a state of which no __defendant__ is a citizen.

- o **One-year limit on removal:** Must remove within one-year of the commencement of the action in state court, unless the plaintiff acted in __bad faith__ to make the case non-removable.

  Example 14: *If the plaintiffs joins a non-diverse defendant, waits a year, and then dismisses the non-diverse defendant, the other defendants can then seek removal if all of that was a ploy to defeat diversity.*

5. Removal Procedures

- o A notice of removal is filed in the __federal__ court, with a copy to the __state__ court.
- o When the removal notice is filed, the state court's jurisdiction __ends__ instantly and automatically.

6. Improper Removal

- o Plaintiff can file in federal court a petition for __remand__ , and it is on that petition that the federal court will hold a hearing.

  - If removal is proper, remand is denied, and case stays in federal court
  - If removal is improper, remand is granted, and case goes back to state court

    Note 3: KEY POINT: The decision is made by the __federal__ court. Removal is automatic, and then the decision about whether it was proper is done on a petition for remand by the __federal__ court.

CHAPTER 4: SUBJECT MATTER JURISDICTION: SUPPLEMENTAL JURISDICTION

A. Supplemental Jurisdiction

1. In General

- *Basic Rule*: Allows a federal court with subject matter jurisdiction over a case to hear additional claims over which the court would not independently have jurisdiction if ALL the claims constitute the same _Case_ or _controversy_.

- Claims constitute the "same case or controversy" if they arise out of the same common _nucleous_ of operative _fact_.

  - All the claims arise out of the same _transaction_ or occurrence.

- 28 USC § 1367: Supplemental jurisdiction allows, but does not require, the court to expand its jurisdiction.

  - Decision is within the discretion of the court and is typically made on practical grounds

2. Federal Question Cases

> *Example 15:* Plaintiff has a federal question claim and a state law claim against the same defendant. The federal question claim is the "anchor" claim, because it forms the basis for the federal court's SMJ over the case. The state law claim does not qualify on its own for federal SMJ. Nevertheless, if the two claims arise out of the same common nucleus of operative fact, the court may exercise supplemental jurisdiction over the state-law claim.

- This applies whether or not those claims involve the joinder of an additional party.

> *Example 16:* Plaintiff asserts a federal claim against Defendant 1 and a related state-law claim, arising out of the same common nucleus of operative fact, against Defendant 2. The federal court may hear both the federal claim against D1 and the state-law claim against D2.

  - Historically, this was called "_pendent_-party jurisdiction."

3. Diversity Jurisdiction Cases

- State-law claims still must be part of the "same case or controversy" (common nucleus of operative fact)

- Additionally, the statute bars supplemental jurisdiction in diversity jurisdiction cases over:

  - Claims by _P's_ against persons made party under Rules 14, 19, 20, or 24;

  - Claims by parties seeking to intervene as plaintiffs under Rule 24; or

  - Claims by parties proposed to be joined as plaintiffs under Rule 19.

  > **Editorial Note 3:** If such claims are to be part of a diversity case, they must independently satisfy the complete diversity and AIC requirements.

Note: Claims by defendants are allowed. The logic is that the plaintiff chose the federal forum, whereas the defendants have more flexibility.

> **Editorial Note 4:** Students do not need to memorize Rules 14, 19, 20, or 24. That list basically covers any mechanism for bringing additional people into the case. What you need to know for the exam is that when you have a diversity case with multiple parties, it will be very hard for a plaintiff to take advantage of supplemental jurisdiction. The only party not covered by the statute is a SINGLE defendant (*more later*).

a. **Counterclaims**

> **Example 17:** Does a counterclaim in a diversity action have to meet the jurisdictional minimum of $75,000.01? Generally, __NO__, if the counterclaim is _compulsory_.

■ A **compulsory counterclaim** is one that arises out of the same transaction or occurrence as the _opposing_ party's claim.

> **Example 18:** Plaintiff, a citizen of Maine, and Defendant, a citizen of Massachusetts, get in a car accident. Plaintiff sues Defendant seeking $100,000 in federal court under diversity jurisdiction (anchor claim). Defendant wants to countersue Plaintiff for $50,000 of his own damages. This is a _compulsory_ claim because it arises from the same event or transaction as Plaintiff's claim. Because this claim is also being brought by Defendant (and not a plaintiff), it will be permitted under supplemental jurisdiction; it need not meet the AIC requirement.

> **Note 4:** Compulsory counterclaims are usually brought by defendants, so they can usually come in without checking it against the AIC requirement. However, WATCH OUT for compulsory counterclaims brought by a PLAINTIFF, which would run into those exclusions.

■ A _permissive_ **counterclaim** is one that does NOT arise out of the same transaction or occurrence as the main claim.

● Can only be heard by a federal diversity court ONLY if it independently satisfies diversity jurisdiction (i.e., complete diversity and $75,000+)

b. **Cross-claims**

■ Claim by a _co-party_ (e.g., a plaintiff against another plaintiff)
■ **Relatedness Requirement:** Must arise out of the transaction or occurrence that is the _subject_ of the action or of a counterclaim.

> **Exam Tip 6:** Cross-claims will usually but not always qualify for supplemental jurisdiction; you still need to apply the test.

■ To qualify for supplemental jurisdiction, a cross-claim:

- Must be related to a claim over which the court has subject-matter jurisdiction (i.e., the "anchoring" claim; and
- Must not be asserted by a plaintiff against a person made party under Rules 14, 19, 20, or 24.

c. **Multiple plaintiffs, single defendant (permissive joinders and class action)**

- If the claim of one diverse plaintiff against a single defendant satisfies the jurisdictional amount, other diverse plaintiffs who have ___related___ claims against the defendant can also be heard even if their claims do NOT satisfy the jurisdictional AIC minimum.

  Example 19: Class action is brought with 5 named (representative) parties who are all diverse from the defendant. One of the representative parties has a claim for more than $75,000. Can the claims of other class members can be heard under supplemental jurisdiction, even if they do not meet the jurisdictional amount ($75,000+)? ___Yes___.

- Why? Because a **single defendant** has not been made a party by Rules 14, 19, 20, or 24.

  Note 5: *Different Basis for Jurisdiction in Class Actions*: Remember that there is also statute that allows federal subject matter jurisdiction over class actions wherein the total amount in controversy exceeds $5 million, so long as there is minimal diversity between one plaintiff and one defendant.

- Supplemental jurisdiction is available on the same logic when multiple plaintiffs do not form a class, but choose to join together in the same action. If one plaintiff has a claim worth $75K+, the others can raise claims arising from the same transaction regardless of amount.

B. **What to Remember!**

- Supplemental jurisdiction works for federal question cases across the board, as long as the additional claims are ___related___.
- In diversity cases, supplemental jurisdiction is broadly available for related claims by defendants but much more limited for claims by plaintiffs.
  o Compulsory counterclaims asserted by ___D's___;
  o Cross-claims asserted by ___D's___, so long as they arise out of the same transaction or occurrence as the anchor claim; and
  o Voluntary joinder of plaintiffs for related claims when there is single defendant.

- Supplemental jurisdiction in diversity cases does not EVER allow you to join a non-diverse defendant or non-diverse plaintiff.

CHAPTER 5: PERSONAL JURISDICTION; IN PERSONAM JURISDICTION

A. Personal Jurisdiction (PJ)

Does the court have the power to reach the involuntary party (the defendant)?

1. In General

o Personal jurisdiction is an issue in federal and state court, and rules are **generally** the same in federal and state court.

- Default federal rule—use the _long-arm_ statutes of the states in which they sit (chief means of asserting PJ over out-of-state defendants)

  > **Editorial Note 5:** As a practical matter on the exam, whether or not the fact pattern takes place in federal or state court, the court must have personal jurisdiction and the rules are generally the same.

o Must always ask two questions:

1. Has the basis for exercising PJ over an out-of-state defendant been _authorized_ by _statute_ or by rule of court?
2. Is the particular basis for exercising personal jurisdiction permitted by the _Due process_ Clause of the US Constitution?

  > **Exam Tip 7:** On a civil procedure essay involving personal jurisdiction, remember to ask and answer both of these questions.

2. Types of Personal Jurisdiction

o _In personam_ : against the person
o _In rem_ : against the thing
o _Quasi in rem_ : "sort of" against the thing

3. Constitutional Aspect

o **Remember this phrase:** Due process requires _minimum contacts_ between the defendant and the forum state such that it is consistent with traditional notions of _fair play_ and _substantial justice_ to sue the defendant here.

o In assessing minimum contacts, courts look for a _purposeful availment_ by the defendant of the protections of the forum's law.

- Contacts between the forum and the _P_ do NOT suffice.
- There must be minimum contacts between the forum and the _D_.
- Those contacts must be a result of the defendant's own _purposeful actions_.

4. Waiver

o Unlike subject matter jurisdiction, and objection to a lack of personal jurisdiction _can_ be waived. Consider two scenarios:

> ***Example 20:*** *An out-of-state defendant is sued in a state court and wants to contest personal jurisdiction. The defendant comes to the state and litigates the issue of personal jurisdiction. If the court finds that it lacks jurisdiction, then the defendant goes home. If the court finds that it does have jurisdiction, then the case goes forward on the merits, but the defendant has successfully preserved this question of personal jurisdiction for appeal.*

> ***Example 21:*** *An out-of-state defendant comes to the state, litigates on the merits to see how things are going, and then raise and objection to personal . jurisdiction when it seems that things are not going well.*

- Voluntarily litigating on the merits waives any objection to lack of PJ (a __general__ appearance)

  - A defendant waives any objection to personal jurisdiction (consents to the court's jurisdiction) by __Substatial Participation__ on the merits before raising that objection.
  - This includes almost anything other than challenging jurisdiction.

- Federal Rules: Lack of personal jurisdiction must be raised at the __first opportunity__ or it is waived.

  - If the defendant chooses to file a pre-answer motion to dismiss she must make the objection then or waive it, OR
  - If the defendant does not file a pre-answer motion, must be raised in the __answer__.

B. In Personam Jurisdiction

1. In General

- Federal courts follow the personal jurisdiction law of the states in which they sit.
- There is some variation state to state, but not much.

a. General in personam jurisdiction

The plaintiff can assert any claim whatsoever, even if it is unrelated to the defendant's contacts with the forum state.

b. Specific in personam jurisdiction

  - Plaintiff's claims against the defendant must arise out of—or directly relate to—the defendant's __Contacts__ with the forum
  - Governed by the state's __long arm__ statute

> **Exam Tip 8:** Remember: GENERAL allows suit on any claim; SPECIFIC allows claims that have a connection to the forum state.

2. **Bases for General In Personam Jurisdiction**

   a. ___Physical presence___ within the state

      - Service of process on the defendant while she is physically present in the state
      - **Exceptions:** If a person was in the state only to answer a ___Summons___
      - Persons brought to the state by brought there by ___force___ or ___fraud___.

   b. ___Domicile___

      > **Editorial Note 6:** REMEMBER: "Domicile" is where one resides with intent to remain indefinitely.

      - Domicile is independent of ___physical presence___.

      Example 22: *If you and I both live in NC, but we happen get into a car accident when we are both vacationing in California, I can sue you in NC even if you are still in California at the time I initiate my action.*

   c. **Consent**

      - Expressly ("Yes, I'd be delighted") or impliedly (by not raising the issue)
      - Can be given by ___Contract___, as long as the terms are reasonable, or by appointment of an in-state agent for receiving service of process

   d. **Corporations**

      - Corporations can consent to personal jurisdiction just like individuals, but the rules regarding physical presence are a little different.
      - Merely "doing business" in a state is insufficient to support general jurisdiction.
      - General in personam jurisdiction applies only to corporations that are essentially " ___at home___ " in the forum state.

        - The state of ___inc.___ ; and
        - The state where the corporation has its ___principal___ place of business.

      - *Exceptional cases*: It is possible in theory for a corporate defendant's operations in a state to be so continuous and systematic as to render the corporation essentially "at home" in a state that is not the corporation's place of incorporation or the state of its principal place of business, but there have been no cases as of yet.

CHAPTER 6:   SPECIFIC IN PERSONAM JURISDICTION, IN REM AND QUASI IN REM

A. **In Personam Jurisdiction (Cont.)**

   1. **Specific In Personam Jurisdiction**

      a. **Statutes**

         - Every state has a long-arm statute.

- Gives courts in personam jurisdiction over out-of-state defendants but ONLY for the particular transactions involving that state.

    - Some state statutes are very broad, e.g. "the long-arm statute extends as far as the Constitution allows"
    - Others list specific activities that give rise to jurisdiction

b. **Common Bases for Specific In Personam Jurisdiction**

- An act or omission in the state causing injury to a person or property here or elsewhere (e.g., driving car into another state)
- An act or omission _Outside_ the state causing injury to a person or property _in_ the state, provided that the defendant conducted activities here or introduced goods into the flow of commerce (probably most important)
- Any claim arising out of a contract to perform _Services_ in the state or to pay someone in the state to perform services elsewhere, or out of the _actual_ performance of such services
- Any claim arising out of a contract to _ship goods_ to or from the state, or arising out of the shipment of such goods
- Any claim regarding _local_ property
- Any action against an officer or director of a domestic corporation for acts taken in that capacity
- Any contract for insurance where the plaintiff was a resident of the state when the claim arose, or the event giving rise to the claim occurred in the state.

    Exam Tip 9: Almost everything is covered by a state's long-arm statute, so long as the claim arises out of the transaction involving that state (specific jurisdiction).

c. **Federal Exceptions**

Generally, federal courts follow the state long-arm statutes of the states in which they sit., but federal courts can assert broader personal jurisdiction in specific cases

1) **Federal Interpleader Act (i.e., "statutory interpleader")**

- Authorizes _nationwide_ service of process
- Service anywhere in the United States establishes personal jurisdiction
- For a federal court, the relevant jurisdiction is the U.S. as a whole, so _Congress_ can authorize nationwide service of process as means of asserting personal jurisdiction nationwide

    Note 6: Note that a state cannot make a similar provision authorizing nationwide service of process

2) **The Bulge Provision of the Federal Rules**

- Allows service anywhere within _____100_____ miles of the federal courthouse, even if in another state, in two situations:

  o For _impleading_ third-party defendants under Rule 14; and
  o For joining _necessary_ parties under Rule 19. *(More later on these rules.)*

3) **Unusual provision**

- Narrow authorization of nationwide service of process when the plaintiff's claim arises under federal law and the defendant is not subject to PJ in ANY state court
- Suit may be brought in federal court, so long as there are minimum contacts with the _____US_____ as a whole.
- Used rarely; most relevant with foreign defendants with no particular contact with a particular state

B. **In Rem and Quasi In Rem Jurisdiction**

1. **In Rem**

   o Suit against any kind of property, real or personal (the res), so long as the property is located in the state where you are _suing_, and it can settle everyone in the world's claim against that property (i.e., the state has physical power over the property)
   o May be piece of land (action to quiet title), goods, or intangibles (claims over bank account)

2. **Quasi-in-Rem**

   o Suit to adjudicate the claim to property of a particular defendant or defendants; the subject-matter of the suit may or may not be related to the property.

   > **Example 23:** *Plaintiff and out-of-state Defendant get into a car accident while vacationing in California. Plaintiff lives in New York and Defendant lives in Wyoming, but has a bank account in New York. Rather than suing Defendant, Plaintiff sues the bank account. Historically, quasi-in-rem jurisdiction would allow Plaintiff to sue the bank account to recover her damages.*

   o **Present rule:** The Supreme Court has held that quasi-in-rem action are subject to the same _minimum contacts_ test as applies to personam jurisdiction.

   ▪ When the property is the subject of the suit, it will constitute an important "minimum contact" between the defendant and the forum, and jurisdiction will probably be permitted as a matter of specific in personam jurisdiction.
   ▪ When the property is not the subject of the suit, the ownership of property in the state is not nearly enough to establish general jurisdiction over the defendant

CHAPTER 7: SERVICE OF PROCESS

A. Notice and Service of Process

1. In General

- Generally means service of a _Summons_ on the defendant
  - Formally gives court jurisdiction over the case
  - Gives the defendant _notice_ of the action
- Personal service—used to assert in personam jurisdiction
  - Should also be used for in rem and quasi-in-rem actions when the _identity_ of an interested party is known
  - Service by publication is only appropriate for in rem actions when that is the best that the serving party can do.
  - Constitutional test: notice must be _reasonable_ under the circumstances.
- Federal Rules authorize service in accordance with state law where the federal court sits.
  - Default rule is that service in federal court is okay as long as it follows the law of the state in which the federal court is based.

    Example 24: *State law may authorize service by mail. If it is okay for state courts, it's okay for federal courts, too.*

- Regardless, these Federal Rules for service are always allowed:
  1. In-hand _personal_ delivery;
  2. Leaving the summons at the defendant's _dwelling_ or usual place of abode with a person of suitable _age_ and discretion;
  3. Delivery of the summons to an authorized _agent_; and
  4. For persons in foreign countries, service can be made by _registered mail_, return receipt requested

  Exam Tip 10: Service by mail to the attorney of record is generally NOT accepted for service of process UNLESS state law so provides, even though other documents are served by mail.

2. Special Rules for Service of Process

a. Infant (minor)

Service on the infant AND on the _parent_ or guardian

b. Adjudicated incompetent

Service must be made on the incompetent AND her guardian

c. Partnership

Service on a _general partner_, an attorney in fact, or an authorized agent

d. Corporation

Service on an ___*officer*___, ___*director*___, managing agent, or on an agent appointed for receiving service of process (corporations doing business in the state must have an agent)

e. Non-resident motorists

- Claims arising out of in-state accidents
- Generally, service can be made on a state official who forwards a copy to the out-of-state defendant.

> **Editorial Note 7:** Note that this is a state law issue, not federal.

3. Service of Process for In Rem and Quasi-in-rem Actions

○ You must make a ___*diligent*___ effort to locate all claimants to the property (res) and serve them personally.

○ If the claimants cannot be located, then notice by ___*publication*___ is permitted.

> **Exam Tip 11:** You CANNOT rely on notice by publication if you actually know or can readily find out the ___*names*___ and addresses of the other claimants; they must be served personally.

B. Summary

- There are several bases for general in personam jurisdiction:

    ○ Consent
    ○ Domicile/"at home"
    ○ Physical presence of an individual at the time of service of process

- Specific Jurisdiction: State long-arm statutes allow very broad reach against out-of-state defendants so long as the claim arises out of the specific contact with the state.

- In every case, there must be a rule or statute authorizing PJ and the assertion of PJ must be based on minimum contacts between the defendant and the forum state such that it is fundamentally fair to sue the defendant in the state.

- PJ of federal court is usually the same as that of the state in which it sits.

    ○ Federal courts have nationwide in personam jurisdiction in statutory ___*interpleader*___ cases and expanded PJ (100 miles) under the "___*bulge*___ provision" when the defendant is trying to implead a third-party defendant (Rule 14), or trying to bring in a ___*necessary*___ party (Rule 19).

CHAPTER 8: VENUE

A. In General

- Where among the courts in this judicial system is the appropriate court to hear the case
  - Federal system: Whether this _district_ is a proper court to hear this action
- It is the _D's_ responsibility to object if venue is improper.
  - Failure to make a timely objection results in waiver.
- Federal law—claim of improper venue must be made at the first _first_ or it is waived
  - Either a pre-answer motion to dismiss if the defendant chooses to file one, or the defendant's _answer_, if no pre-answer motion is made
- State and federal venue rules are completely different.

B. Federal Rule

- Federal venue concerns which _district_ should hear a case.
- Federal venue is proper in a district:

  1) Where any defendant _resides_, as long as ALL defendants reside in the same _state_; or

  2) Where the claim arose

     - Where a "substantial part of the events or omissions" on which the claim is based occurred or where a "substantial part of the _property_" that is the subject of the action is located.

  3) If neither of the above (rare), any district where the defendant is subject to _PJ_ has venue.

- Federal venue generally does not rest on the plaintiff's _residence_.

2. Residence

  - **Individuals:** Residence means _domicile_.
  - **Business entities:** Any business entity (capacity to sue or be sued) resides in every district in which _PJ_ exists.

3. Special Provisions

For a case begun in state court and removed to federal court, venue is automatically proper in the federal district where the _State_ court sits, even if that district would not have been proper originally.

4. Transfer (one federal court to another)

> **Exam Tip 12:** Transfer is frequently tested.

- o **General rule:** transfer is only to a district with _proper venue_.
    - ▪ **Exception:** Transfer to a district without proper venue may occur when ALL parties agree.
- o A case brought in a district _with_ proper venue may be transferred for convenience to another district with proper venue.
- o A case brought in a district _without_ proper venue may be (1) dismissed or (2) transferred to a district with proper venue.

C. **Choice of Law (Which state's law applies?)**

- • If suit was brought in a district _with_ proper venue and the case is transferred to another district, the law of the transferor (<u>first</u>) forum controls.
    - o Apply the choice-of-law rules of the state in which the action began; "Take your law with you"
- • If suit was brought in a district _without_ proper venue and transferred to another district, the law of the transferee (<u>second</u>) court controls.
    - o Do NOT get to take your law with you; no advantage to filing in the wrong court

CHAPTER 9:   CHOICE OF LAW: THE ERIE DOCTRINE

A. **General Rule under Erie**

In a diversity case, a federal court applies state _Substantive_ law.

B. **State Substantive Law:**

- • The substantive rules that govern conduct, i.e. what must be proved to win a case and what defenses may be asserted;
- • State statutes of _limitations_ on state causes of action;
- • The burdens of proof on state claims or defenses; and
- • State rules on _Choice of law_

> **Example 25:** A federal court in New York with diversity jurisdiction over a state tort claim will apply state law on (i) the existence and definition of that tort, (ii) the limitations period within which that cause of action may be brought, (iii) the burden of proof for any elements of the tort claim or any defenses, and (iv) in a situation in which there is a question as to which state's law governs, the federal court will apply New York law on choice of law.

> **Note 7:** States' choice-of-law rules tend to favor applying their own law. Remember: if a case is transferred, the law of the transferor (first) state controls as long as venue is proper in the first court.

C. Federal Procedures

- *Hanna v. Plumer*: Anything covered by the Federal Rules of Civil Procedure is
  "___procedure___" for purposes of *Erie*—federal law applies, even if the substance of
  the claim is governed by state law.

D. No Federal Statute or Rule on Point

- The court must determine whether to follow state law (i.e., the matter is deemed
  "___substantive___) or to follow federal law (i.e., the matter is deemed "___procedural___").
- The twin aims of *Erie*:

  1) To avoid ___forum___ shopping; and

     - Situations in which parties have incentives to choose (or avoid) federal court based
       on perceived advantages and disadvantages of federal law versus state law)

  2) To avoid the ___inequitable___ administration of justice

     - Situations where there is a different result in state and federal courts, so winning
       and losing turns on the accident of diversity of citizenship

       Example 26: *Plaintiff is deciding between federal and state court. If the
       decision involves choosing the court based on which has the more favorable
       rules, then we run into the problems Erie was trying to avoid (forum shopping or
       inequitable administration of justice).*

- Two common applications of *Erie*:

  - If the choice of the procedure would be ___outcome___ **determinative** (change the result),
    the federal court should usually apply ___state___ law to prevent forum shopping.
  - The role of the ___jury___ in federal court is entirely controlled by federal law.

E. Federal Common Law

- Judge-made federal law that overrides (preempts) any ___inconsistent___ state or local law or rule
- Federal courts make federal common law ONLY when they encounter important federal
  interests that are not covered by a ___statute___.
- Examples where federal common law applies

  - Boundary disputes between states; and
  - ___Claim___ preclusion

- Federal courts sometimes "borrow" state law, but do so as a matter of federal common law.

F. Determining Applicable State Law

- Follow precedent from the highest ___state___ court.
- If there is no precedent, predict how the highest state court would rule.
- Give ___respectful___ attention to the decisions of lower state courts (not ___binding___).

CHAPTER 10:   PLEADINGS

A.   Commencement of Proceedings

- Federal civil action is begun by filing ___Complaint___ a with the court clerk.
- For diversity actions, ___State___ law controls when an action is begun.

B.   Types of Pleadings

1.   **The Complaint**

   o   Used to state a claim for ___relief___

   o   The plaintiff or the defendant may file a claim against a co-party, called a ___cross claim___ complaint.

   o   A defendant files a third-party complaint to implead a third-party defendant.

2.   **The Answer**

   o   Filed by the opposing party in response to the complaint

   o   It may contain responses to the allegations of the complaint, affirmative defenses, and/or ___counter-claim___.

3.   **The Reply**

   o   Used by the plaintiff to answer a ___reply___

C.   Requirements of a Complaint

- A complaint (or any pleading in which a claim is made) must include:

   o   A short and plain statement of the court's ___SMJ___ jurisdiction;

   o   A short and plain statement showing the claimant is entitled to relief; and

   o   A claim for the ___relief___ sought by the pleader.

1.   **Claim for Relief**

   o   Recovery is not limited by the claim for relief as stated in the complaint, except for ___default___ judgments.

   o   You get what you prove, not what you ask for.

2.   **Notice Pleading**

   o   Historically, pleading was difficult because each kind of claim had its own special rules of pleading, and the pleading had to match the proof.

      ▪   Litigation was often resolved on the pleadings, rather than the merits.

   o   One of the chief aims of the Federal Rules was to reform pleading.

      ▪   ___Standardize___ pleading across all civil actions

      ▪   Simplify pleading

      ▪   Shift emphasis from pleading to the ___merits___ of the case

- o The Federal Rules generally require only __notice__ **pleading**:
    - ▪ A pleading need not detail the facts of the plaintiff's case or spell out the legal theory
    - ▪ Must only give __fair notice__ of the pleader's claim
    - ▪ **Rule to remember:** All that is required is a __short__ and __plain__ statement of the claim showing that the pleader is entitled to relief.

D. Special Pleading

1. Definition

- o No particular form of words
- o Alleged with particularity/specificity/detail

2. Types of Claims Requiring Special Pleading

- o Fraud or __Mistake__ must be specially pleaded.
- o Claims for __special__ damages must be specially pleaded (i.e., damages that do not ordinarily follow from the wrong)

    > **Example 27:** *You are hit by an automobile and you claim medical expenses, pain and suffering, lost wages—all these may be alleged generally. But if you claim that you lost a major business deal because the accident prevented you from making an appointment and the opportunity slipped away, that is not the type of damages that ordinarily result from the accident, so those damages must be stated with* __particularity__

E. Recent Decisions

- • Supreme Court cut-back on notice pleading, due to concerns about excessive discovery and fishing expeditions.

    - o *Bell Atlantic v. Twombly* (2007)
    - o *Ashcroft v. Iqbal* (2009)

- • Require that the allegations in the complaint state a __plausible__ case for recovery
- • Conclusory Claims: disregard allegations not entitled to presumption of truth
- • Two-step inquiry:

    1. Identify allegations that are "conclusory" or "mere __legal__ conclusions."
    2. Look at remaining, factual, allegations, and ask whether they add up to a "plausible" case for recovery.

        - ▪ "Plausible" falls somewhere between "probable" and merely "conceivable" or "possible."

- The two cases do NOT abandon notice pleading; they curtail it by empowering district judges to dismiss, before discovery, complaints that they think are obviously _Unfounded_ (i.e., lack of factual detail, if it tells rather than shows)

> **Exam Tip 13:** The examiners cannot be demanding about how you apply these cases. You would have to go deep into the plaintiff's substantive claim, which is not what procedure questions test generally. You are most likely to see a bare pleading that raises the issue of whether a plausible cause of action has been stated. You will be expected to recognize that, even under notice pleading, unconvincing and implausible allegations with no factual support should be _____.

CHAPTER 11:   DEFENSE MOTIONS

A. Defense Motions Against the Complaint

1. Motion to Dismiss

- May be used to raise:
  - Lack of _____SMJ_____ jurisdiction
  - Lack of __PJ__ jurisdiction, (including both lack of power and defects in service of process)
  - Improper venue
  - Failure to state a claim upon which relief can be granted
  - Failure to join a _Necessary_ party
  - Forum non conveniens
- Claim of no personal jurisdiction or a claim of improper venue must be made at the ____earliest____ opportunity (either a pre-answer motion to dismiss or the answer).
- Lack of subject matter jurisdiction _Cannot_ be waived; can be raised by any party at any time, including for the first time on appeal or by the court itself.
- Most claims (including lack of PJ and venue) are waived if NOT timely raised.

  > **Example 28:** If the defendant thinks the plaintiff's claim is inadequate and files a motion to dismiss for failure to state a claim on which relief can be granted, but she also thinks the court lacks personal jurisdiction over her or is an improver venue, then the defendant must to include those objections in the motion. If the defendant does not file a motion to dismiss, then she must include the objections in the _answer_ or she will have waived them.

2. Motion for Judgment on the Pleadings

- Applies when the pleadings agree entirely on the _facts_ and only the law is in dispute
- If there is any element of factual _dispute_, you have a case for summary judgment.

3. **Motion for a More Definite Statement**

   o Asks that a pleading be made more specific

   o Judges usually disfavor this motion.

4. **Motion to Strike**

   o Can be used to delete from a pleading scandalous or prejudicial matters that are NOT _relevant_ to the case at hand

   o Also used by the plaintiff to strike a legally invalid _defense_

B. **Answer**

   1. **In General**

      o Used to respond to any form of complaint

      o May contain responses, affirmative defenses, and counterclaims

   2. **Responses**

      o The failure to respond constitutes an _admission_

      o Unless cured by amendment, the admission is binding in the action.

      o Usual practice: a "boilerplate" denial of everything not specifically admitted

   3. **Affirmative Defenses**

      o Defenses which, in fairness, require _notice_

      o Common affirmative defenses: assumption of _risk_, contributory negligence, fraud, _duress_, release, statute of frauds, and statutes of limitations (i.e., anything with a name).

   4. **Timing**

      Must ordinarily be served within _21_ days of service of the pleading to which it responds

C. **Reply**

   • Plaintiff's answer to a counterclaim

   • Rules governing _answers_ apply to a reply.

D. **Amendments to Pleadings**

   1. **As of Right**

      May be amended once at any time within _21_ days of service of the pleading or within _21_ days of the defendant's response, if there is one

   2. **By Leave of Court**

      o After the party has amended once, leave to amend must be sought from the court.

      o Amendment by leave of court should be _freely_ granted.

- Judge must have a reason for denying leave to amend
- *Example*: Amendment is too late and would be prejudicial to the other side, or the pleader has had a prior opportunity to amend but has not corrected the problem

3. Statute of Limitations and the Doctrine of Relation Back

○ In some circumstances, an amendment is deemed to _____relate_____ to the date the **original pleading** was filed.

- If the statute of limitations has NOT yet run (still open), this doctrine does not matter.
- If the statute of limitations has run out, then relation back determines whether the amended pleading is allowed (relates back) or time-barred (does not relate back).

> **Exam Tip 14:** On the exam, look for the limitations period, the date of the original pleading, and the date of the amendment. When you see that the original pleading was timely, but the amendment was not, then you know you are being asked about the doctrine of relation back.

○ **Rules to remember:**

- An amendment relates back to the date of the original filing IF it concerns the same _____conduct_____, transaction, or occurrence as the _____original_____ pleading.
- The key concept here is _____notice_____; it cannot have the effect of surprising the other party.

4. Amendment to Add or Change a Party

○ An amendment to add or change a party against whom a claim is asserted must:

- Concern the same conduct, transaction, or occurrence as the _____original_____ pleading; and
- The party _____to be added_____ (new party) must have known or had reason to know that the action should have been brought against that party but for the _____mistake_____.

Example 29: Suit is filed against a corporate subsidiary, and the complaint is later amended to name the parent company as the defendant. Meanwhile, the statute of limitations has run. Is the amended pleading timely as against the parent company? ___Yes___. The amended pleading concerned the same transaction as the original pleading and the suit filed against the subsidiary gave the parent notice of the issue.

Example 30: Suppose a plaintiff slips and falls on a sidewalk in a shopping area and sues a store. After the statute of limitations has run, it becomes clear that the plaintiff has sued the wrong store. If the plaintiff tries to amend the complaint to sue the correct store (change the defendant), the amendment is ___time___-barred because the original complaint did not give the correct store notice of the claim. Key concept: ___notice___

E. Certification of Pleadings

- **Verification:** Most pleadings are NOT verified (not sworn to), nor do they have to be.
- **Certification:** Pleadings and other documents—including motions and discovery requests—must be signed by _the attorney of record_ and provide the attorney's contact information.
  - o The signature certifies that there is an appropriate _legal & factual_ basis for filing.
  - o Attorney certifies that to the best of her knowledge after _reasonable inquiry_:
    - There is NO improper purpose (e.g., harass or needlessly increase costs);
    - The legal contentions are warranted by existing law or by a non-frivolous argument for a change in the law; and
    - The factual allegations have _evidentiary_ support or are likely to have such support after an opportunity for discovery.
- Denials must have such support or must be _reasonably_ based on lack of information or belief.
- Violation of certification requirement can be raised by court or by a party in a motion for sanctions.
  - o Move to dismiss or seek sanctions (Rule 11)
  - o The attorney can be ordered to bear the cost of _baseless_ or _improper_ filings.

CHAPTER 12: MULTI-PARTY LITIGATION

A. Capacity to Sue

- Minors (under 18) and people deemed incompetent may sue or be sued only through a _guardian_.
- Partnerships can sue or be sued as an entity if jurisdiction is based on federal question.
  - o If jurisdiction is based on _diversity of citizenship_, then every partner's citizenship counts; every partner must be listed as a party to the litigation (complete diversity applies).

B. Permissive Joinder of Parties

- Joinder by _Pls_ is governed by Rule 20.
- Any number of plaintiffs may join if:
  1) They assert claims arising out of the same _transaction_ or occurrences or series of transactions or occurrences; AND
  2) There is a common question of _law_ or _fact_.

- Any number of defendants may be joined in the same action if:

    1) The claims against them arise out of the same _transaction_ or occurrences (or series); AND

    2) There is a common question of _law_ or _fact_.

        Note 8: These rules apply assuming there is SMJ.

- **Diversity cases:** NO party can be joined whose presence would destroy _complete_ diversity, even if the joinder rules are otherwise satisfied.

    > *Example 31:* In a suit by multiple plaintiffs against a **single defendant**, if complete diversity is maintained, and if one plaintiff has a claim that exceeds $75,000, other plaintiffs with smaller claims can come in under supplemental jurisdiction.

C. Compulsory Joinder of Parties

- Joinder by _D's_ is governed by Rule 19.
- Lawyers use the terms **necessary** and **indispensable** parties.
- A **necessary party** is a person whose participation in the lawsuit is necessary for a just adjudication because:

    ○ Absent that party, complete relief cannot be accorded to the existing parties;

    ○ The necessary party has an interest in the litigation which will be _impeded_ if the litigation goes forward without that party (risk of prejudice to the absentee); or

    ○ There is a substantial risk of double or inconsistent liability.

- Necessary parties MUST be joined if feasible.

    ○ **Feasible** if (i) it will not deprive the court of SMJ (e.g., will not destroy complete diversity) and (ii) the court can assert _personal_ jurisdiction over the necessary party.

        ▪ **Bulge provision:** In addition to other grounds for serving an out-of-state party, a necessary party may be served anywhere within _100_ miles of the federal courthouse.

- If a necessary party CANNOT be joined, the court decides whether to

    ○ continue without the necessary party (typically the case) or

    ○ dismiss the suit (rare) (i.e., the party is described as being indispensable.)

D. Intervention

- Outsider who volunteers to enter a lawsuit
- Chiefly a tool for people hoping to join as _P's_

- **Intervention as of right**—May be had when the outsider claims an interest in the subject matter of the lawsuit that, as a practical matter, may be _Compromised_ by the disposition of the pending action.
- **Permissive intervention**—May be allowed whenever there is a common question of _law_ OR _fact_ between the intervenor's claim and the main claim (very relaxed standard).
  - Must ask the court's permission—matter of court's sound discretion
- Both types must be timely: "_reasonable_ promptness"
- There is no _Supplemental_ jurisdiction for either kind of intervention when jurisdiction is based on diversity.
  - Diversity case: intervenors must satisfy _complete_ diversity AND have a claim that exceeds $75,000

E. **Interpleader**

1. **In General**

   - Used to resolve the problem of competing claims to the same property
   - Designed to avoid inconsistent obligations or multiple claims
   - Property at issue is called the _Stake_
     - May be real or personal, tangible or intangible
   - Person holding the property is the _Stakeholder_
   - Persons claiming the property are _Claimant_
     - Stakeholder may also be a claimant (e.g., insurance company)
   - Stakeholder can invoke interpleader either as a plaintiff OR a defendant:
     - Stakeholder-plaintiff sues all the claimants as defendants
     - Stakeholder-defendant is one who has been sued by a claimant; all the other claimants are joined as plaintiffs

2. **Rule Interpleader**

   - Authorized by Rule 22
   - Remedy available in a lawsuit otherwise within the court's _jurisdictn_

3. **Statutory Interpleader**

   - Comes from Federal Interpleader Act and only applies in federal court
   - Has special provisions:
     - **Special jurisdictional amount:** Need only exceed $ _500_
     - Authorizes _nationwide_ service of process
     - Venue is proper in any district where any _anu_ resides.

- SMJ based on **minimal diversity** (i.e., when any two claimants are from different states)

> **Exam Tip 15:** Statutory Interpleader is meant to make access to federal court easier. All usual roadblocks are much lower: AIC need only exceed $ _500.01_ , there is nationwide service of process, venue is proper anywhere any claimant resides, and only minimal diversity is required.

CHAPTER 13: MULTI-CLAIM LITIGATION, IMPLEADER, AND CLASS ACTIONS

A. Joinder of Claims

- As between the same plaintiff and the same defendant, ALL claims may be joined (need not be related)
- **Diversity case:** Plaintiff can aggregate all claims against the same defendant to exceed the jurisdictional minimum
- **Federal question case:** If diversity is lacking for additional state-law claims, additional state-law claims can be joined only if they are covered by _Supplemental_ jurisdiction (i.e., arise from the same transaction or occurrence as the original claim).

B. Counterclaims

1. Definition

- Claim by an opposing party, usually by the defendant against the plaintiff
- Pleaded in the defendant's _Answer_

2. Compulsory Counterclaims

- A compulsory counterclaim is lost if not pleaded in the current action.

  - Permissive counterclaims can be raised now or later.

- A counterclaim is compulsory if it arises out of the same transaction or occurrence as the claim to which it responds.
- _Supplemental_ jurisdiction will generally be available for compulsory counterclaims.

  - If there is SMJ over the main claim, there is SMJ over a compulsory counterclaim.
  - **Diversity case:** Amount of compulsory counterclaim does not matter

- **Statute of Limitations:** Filing of the original complaint tolls the SOL for the original claim AND any compulsory counterclaim(s).

3. Permissive Counterclaims

- Counterclaims that _does not_ arise out of the same transaction or occurrence.
- May be pleaded now OR raised later
- **Requires an** _independent_ **jurisdictional basis:** Must be a federal claim OR there must be complete diversity of citizenship with $75,000+ in issue

- o **Statute of Limitations**: A permissive counterclaim must be timely as of the date it is filed or it's time-barred.

    > *Example 32:* *Ann, Ben, and Carol are involved in a three-car accident together. Ann sues Ben and Carol, alleging they are each at fault and seeking $100,000 from each of them. Rule 20 allows Ann to join her claims against Ben and Carol into one action because the claims arise from the same accident and will involve similar questions of law and fact. As long as the parties are diverse, there will be subject-matter jurisdiction in federal court.*
    >
    > *Suppose Ben believes the accident is Ann's fault and wants to recover $50,000 in damages from her. He should file a compulsory counterclaim against her. This claim will fall under the court's supplemental jurisdiction because it is part of the same case or controversy as Ann's claim, and is brought by a defendant.*
    >
    > *If Ann owes Ben money from an unrelated gambling debt, that would be a permissive counterclaim because it did not arise from the same event as Ann's claim. Therefore, supplemental jurisdiction would not apply, and Ben could only bring the claim if it had an independent jurisdictional basis (e.g., if the claim between these diverse parties met the AIC requirement).*

C. Cross-claims

- Claims asserted against a ___CO-party___.

    - o Plaintiff v. co-plaintiff, defendant v. co-defendant

- Must arise out of the same transaction or occurrence as the original claim or a ___counter-claim___

    > **Exam Tip 16:** Cross-claims will often fall under supplemental jurisdiction, but not always. Remember to analyze whether the cross claim satisfies federal SMJ on their own or through supplemental jurisdiction.

- Cross-claims are ___not___ compulsory.

    > *Example 33:* *In the previous example, if Ben also wanted to assert a cross-claim against his co-defendant, Carol, alleging that she is also liable for the accident, is there supplemental jurisdiction?* ___Yes___
    >
    > _____

D. Impleader (Third-Party Practice)

1. In General

Impleader is a device by which the defendant brings into the suit someone who is or may be liable to the ___D___ for all or part of the ___P's___ claim against him.

2. Vocabulary

- o **Impleaded party:** Third party defendant

- o **Original defendant:** Third party plaintiff as against the third-party defendant
- o Often applies to _Contribution_ **among joint tortfeasors**

> ***Example 34:*** *Two tortfeasors injure a plaintiff. The plaintiff sues one but not the other. That defendant has a right to seek contribution from the other tortfeasor if he is found liable to the plaintiff. The sued defendant can implead the other tortfeasor, not because the other tortfeasor may be liable to the plaintiff, but, given the right of contribution, because the other tortfeasor is or may be liable to the defendant for all or part of the defendant's liability to the plaintiff.*

- o Also often applies to **indemnification contracts**

> ***Example 35:*** *A general contractor makes contracts with subcontractors. Each contract requires the subcontractor to indemnify the general contractor for any defect in that subcontractor's work. If the building owner sues the general contractor, the general contractor (defendant) can implead the subcontractor, who may be liable to the general contractor (the defendant) for all or part of the owner/plaintiff's claim against him.*

3. **Subject Matter Jurisdiction**

- o **Diversity cases:** Impleader comes within the court's _Supplemental_ jurisdiction.
  - ▪ _Citizenship_ of the third-party defendant does NOT matter.
  - ▪ Amount of claim against third-party defendant does NOT matter.
  - ▪ Only extends to claims by the defendant against a third-party defendant

- o Supplemental jurisdiction does NOT extend to claims by the original plaintiff against the impleaded third-party defendant (because those would be claims by a plaintiff against a person made party under Rule 14).

  - ▪ Plaintiff cannot make a claim against the third-party defendant UNLESS complete diversity is met (or there is federal question jurisdiction for the claim).

> ***Example 36:*** *In previous example, Carol believes that Dave, a passenger in her car, is partially responsible for the accident. Carol is permitted to implead Dave under supplemental jurisdiction to seek contribution. Because the claim is part of the same case or controversy, Dave's citizenship and the amount in controversy do not matter. However, Ann would not be able to add a claim against Dave under supplemental jurisdiction.*

4. **Personal Jurisdiction**

Bulge provision: In addition to all other methods for asserting personal jurisdiction, impleader allows the assertion of PJ by service of process anywhere within ____100____ miles of the courthouse.

E. Class Actions

1. Prerequisites

- o Prerequisites for a class action are:
  - ▪ Numerousness (i.e., too many parties to be joined conventionally);
  - ▪ _Common_ questions of law or fact;
  - ▪ _Typicality_ of claims by the class representatives; and
  - ▪ Adequacy of _representation_
- o Burden is on proponent of class certification to establish that these prerequisites are met

2. Dismissal or Compromise (Settlement)

Requires _judicial_ approval

3. Diversity Jurisdiction

Named representatives must be completely diverse from the defendants AND at least one plaintiff has a claim worth over $75,000

4. Class Action Fairness Act of 2005

- o Allows very large class actions, involving at least ___100___ members with more than $ _5 million_ at stake
- o Only minimal diversity required (i.e., any plaintiff diverse from any defendant)

CHAPTER 14: SCOPE OF DISCOVERY

A. Mandatory Disclosures

1. In General

- o Designed to streamline discovery
- o Requires disclosure without having to wait for a discovery request

2. Three Stages

a. Initial disclosures

- ▪ _Names_ and _addresses_ (contact information) of persons with potentially discoverable information
- ▪ Copies or descriptions of relevant _documents_ or things
- ▪ Computation of the _damages_ claimed
- ▪ Applicable insurance agreement(s)

b. Disclosure of expert witnesses

- ▪ Names of expert witnesses who will be called at trial

rare on bar

- Qualifications, publications, opinions, information on which they will base their opinions, other cases in which they have testified, and __compensation__

c. **Pretrial Disclosures**

- __30__ days before trial
- List of witnesses and exhibits
- Any objections must be made within __14__ days after disclosure or they are waived unless excused by the court for __good cause__.

B. **Scope of Discovery** ≠ *just basics*

1. **In General**

- General rule is __relevance__.

   - You can discover anything that might be admissible at trial OR that might __lead to__ something that might be admissible at trial.

- **Key point:** The scope of discovery is NOT limited to __admissible__ evidence.

   Example 37: If you are at trial and you try to introduce hearsay testimony, the other side can object; it's not admissible. However, in a deposition, if you ask the deponent about hearsay, there is no viable objection. Hearsay is not __admissible__, but is __discoverable__

2. **Proportionality**

- Limited to matters that are __proportional__ to the needs of the case
- Courts consider the importance of the issues, amount at stake, parties' resources and access to information, value of discovery in the case, and, most importantly, whether the __burden__ or expense of discovery outweighs its likely __benefit__.

3. **Exceptions to Discovery**

a. **Evidentiary __Privilege__**

   Anything covered by an evidentiary __privilege__ is not discoverable.

b. **Work-product rule**

   Exam Tip 17: This is a high priority topic for the bar exam.

- **Basic idea:** Preparation for litigation by one party cannot be discovered by the other.
- The attorney work product rule protects:

   1. Documents and things (not __information__);

   Example 38: A lawyer has made notes after interviewing a witness to a car accident. The lawyer's notes are protected by the work-product rule and cannot be discovered by the other side. The other side, however, can ask for the names and addresses of the witness. The other side may then interview those *witnesses and discover the same information and introduce it at trial. Only the lawyer's notes recording the testimony of the witnesses is protected as work product.*

2. Prepared in ___anticapation of litigation___ or for trial;

   o Documents prepared before the cause of action arose (e.g., ordinary business records) are NOT protected by the work product rule.

3. By or for ___an Other party___ or her representative.

- **Result:** Creates a ___qualified___ immunity from discovery that can be overcome only if the party seeking discovery shows:

  - A ___need___ for the document or thing; and
  - That the information cannot be ___Obtained elsewhere___.

Example 39: A lawyer interviews a witness and has notes of the witness's statements. The notes are work product and are protected against discovery. But, if the witness dies after the interview, suddenly becomes senile, or refuses to talk about the matter, the other side may be able to access the lawyer's notes because it needs the information and cannot get it elsewhere.

- **Special Cases**
  Notwithstanding the above, you can:

  - ___Always___ get a copy of ___your own___ statements whether you are a party or a mere witness.
  - ___Never___ discover the ___Mental___ impressions of the lawyer.

4. Experts

o Distinguish between experts who will be called to ___testify___ and those who will not

o Other side can always discover the report of the testifying expert.

o If expert is going to testify, the other side, in fairness, has to prepare for cross-examination.

  - Can discover the amount of compensation, and the facts, data, and assumptions provided to the expert by the lawyer

    Editorial Note 8: Draft reports and communications between the lawyer and the expert are generally NOT discoverable.

o If expert is NOT going to testify, no discovery absent exceptional circumstances

5. Protective Orders

o For good cause shown, court can basically do anything, in its discretion, that justice may require.

CHAPTER 15: DISCOVERY DEVICES

[handwritten: ☆ basic mechanics of the discovery devices]

A. Six Discovery Devices

1. Oral Deposition

- Questions are asked and answered ___Orally___ and under ___oath___.
- Limited to ___10___ depositions, unless the court allows more
- Each is limited to one day of ___7___ hours, unless the court allows more.
- Any kind of notice suffices for the deposition of a ___party___; but a deposition of ___non party___ ("mere") witness requires a ___subpeona___.
- **Subpoena duces tecum**—requires the deponent to bring specified documents or things
- To depose an organization, serve notice or subpoena on organization; organization then selects person who will be deposed
- Can be taken any time after the party has made ___m and atory___ disclosures
- May be taken before any notary public who is not otherwise disqualified (usually stenographer)

2. Written Deposition

[handwritten: not used much today →]

- Questions asked in writing are delivered to an officer who asks the questions orally and the witness answers orally under oath.
- Rarely used because they are so inflexible

3. Interrogatories

- Questions asked in ___Writing___ to be answered under oath in writing
- May only be used against a ___party___
- Presumptively limited to ___25___ interrogatories, unless the court allows more
- Responses required within ___30___ days
- May respond by producing business records if the answer can be ascertained and the burden of deriving the answers is ___Substantially the same___ for the party serving the interrogatories as for the responding party

4. Discovery and Inspection of Documents and Land

- Called a request to ___documents___ and ___land___ inspection
- Applies only to documents, things, and land under the control of a ___party___
- The thing to be produced and inspected must be described with ___particularity___.
- Response is due within ___30___ days

5. Physical and Mental Examinations

- Available only against a ___party___
- Only permitted when the party's physical or mental condition is in ___controversy___
- Only for ___good cause___ shown

6. **Request for Admission**

   o Used to streamline the litigation

   o Failure to respond within 30 days is an ___admission___.

   > **Exam Tip 18:** Recall that because responses to requests for admissions (and all other documents) must be signed by the attorney of record, and the signature certifies that there is a reasonable basis and good faith for denying the request, failure to respond to a request for admission may be a violation of Rule 11.

   o Admissions are binding in litigation but have no ___preclusive___ effect (i.e., only binding in the current lawsuit; cannot be used against the party in any future proceeding)

B. **Use of Depositions at Trial**

   • Discoverability does not equal ___admissiblity___

   • Deposition of an adverse party is admissible as an ___admission___ of party opponent

   > **Editorial Note 1:** An opposing party's statement is not the same as the statement against interest exception to hearsay. *See the Themis Evidence materials for a more detailed discussion.*

   • Deposition of a mere witness can be used to ___impeach___ that witness

   • Deposition of a witness who does NOT testify can be used if the witness is dead, beyond the court's subpoena power, or otherwise unavailable

   o Can also be used if the witness is more than ___100___ miles from the place of trial.

C. **Enforcement Sanctions**

   • The court can immediately impose sanctions in three instances of complete default:

   1. Failure to attend one's own ___deposition___;
   2. Failure to respond to ___interrogatories___; and
   3. Failure to respond to a request for documents or things.

   There is no way that you can, in good faith, to fail to show up or respond.

   • In other cases, the party seeking discovery must go to court and obtain an order compelling discovery.

   > **Example 40:** *If a person shows up to her deposition but is evasive in answering questions, you may need to get an order compelling discovery. Or, if a person responds to interrogatories in a cryptic way, you need to obtain an order compelling discovery. Why? The order will clarify ambiguities, resolve disputes, and make clear what is required so that there is no possibility of good faith error.*

   o The court should first issue an order to compel based on the party's request before imposing sanctions.

   o If that order is disobeyed, the court may do what it deems is necessary.

- If the order compelling discovery is granted, the cost of compelling discovery, including attorney's fees, is often placed on the opposing party unless the court finds their refusal was substantially ___justified___ or the award of costs would be otherwise unjust.

D. Electronically Stored Information

- Normally should be preserved
- If lost through ___unreasonable___ conduct of a party, the court may order measures to cure the prejudice to the other party.
- If the material was destroyed with the ___intent___ to prejudice the other party, the court may instruct the jury to presume the information was unfavorable, or even order the end of the litigation.

CHAPTER 16:   PRE-TRIAL PROCEDURE AND MOTIONS TO TERMINATE

A. Pre-Trial Conference

- Must be attended by the attorneys who will conduct the trial
- Must file a ___pretrial   statement___ detailing claims and defenses, itemization of damages, requests for stipulations and admissions, list of all witnesses and exhibits, etc.
- Failure to comply usually means that the attorney pays the costs and the other side's ___incurred___ fees.

B. Termination Without Trial

1. Devices

- Judgment on the ___Pleadings___ ;

> **Note 9:** Rarely used; appropriate only when the pleadings agree on all of the facts

- ___Default___ judgment (defendant has not shown up);
- ___Voluntary___ dismissal (dismissal without prejudice);
- ___Involuntary___ dismissal (dismissal with prejudice); and
- ___Summary___ judgment.

2. Voluntary Dismissal

- Ordinarily ___without___ prejudice

  - **Without prejudice:** Party whose claim is dismissed can bring that claim again in a new lawsuit

- Plaintiff has a right to a voluntary dismissal once at any time prior to the defendant serving an ___answer___ or a motion for ___summary   judgment___.

  - The defendant's motion to dismiss (e.g., for lack of jurisdiction or improper venue) before filing an answer does NOT cut off the right to a voluntary dismissal.

- o After a defendant has filed an answer or motion for summary judgment, or if the plaintiff has already voluntarily dismissed once, plaintiff must seek leave of court for dismissal without prejudice.
    - Plaintiff will have to pay the costs if she ends up later filing the same action against the same defendant.

3. **Involuntary Dismissal**
   - o Typically ___With___ prejudice
   - o Involuntary dismissal for lack of jurisdiction, improper venue, or failure to join an ___indispensible___ party is ___Without___ prejudice.
   - o In all other cases, involuntary dismissal is with prejudice.
     - Dismissal with prejudice is an adjudication on the ___Merits___, which means that, under federal law, it is given full ___res judicata___ (preclusive) effect, which bars any attempt at relitigation of the same claims
   - o May be imposed for plaintiff's failure to ___prosecute___ or for failure to comply with the FRCP or any court order
   - o Standard for appellate review is **abuse of discretion**

4. **Summary Judgment (SJ)**
   - o Compare with motion to dismiss for failure to state a claim upon which relief can be granted (12(b)(6)):
     - Failure to state a claim under 12(b)(6) tests only the legal sufficiency of the plaintiff's claim.
     - Summary judgment can be used to test both the (facts) AND the law.
   - o **Partial summary judgment**: SJ can be granted for the entire case, or only for certain parties, certain claims or defenses, or certain issues.
   - o **Standard**: There is no ___genuine___ dispute as to any material fact and the moving party is entitled to judgment as a matter of ___law___.
     - "No genuine dispute" means that no reasonable ___juror___ could find for the nonmoving party.
   - o Must be supported or opposed by particular materials in the record, such as:
     - ___Deposition___
     - Answers to ___Interrogatories___
     - Affidavits
     - Stipulations
   - o Materials in the record must generally be ___sworn___ **statements** to be considered in deciding a motion for summary judgment.

SJ "know your" facts

- Pleadings are generally NOT sworn statements, but if verified, or taken under oath, they become an _affidavit_ as well as a pleading.
- Mere assertion or denial of a fact in a pleading does NOT create a genuine dispute.
  ○ Sworn statement ordinarily must be based on _personal knowledge_.

> ***Example 41:*** *Ann sues Ben for injuries in an automobile accident and then moves for summary judgment. Ann supports her motion with her affidavit, describing the accident. Ben cannot oppose summary judgment simply by relying on the denials in his answer nor by saying that he will call witnesses who will testify in a certain way. Rather, Ben must file a sworn statement based on personal knowledge that raises a genuine dispute as to a material fact. For example, Ben could file an affidavit asserting that he was out of town at the time of the accident.*

CHAPTER 17: RIGHT TO JURY AND MOTIONS TO OVERRIDE THE JURY'S VERDICT

A. Trial by Jury

1. Right to Jury Trial

- ○ 7th Amendment right to trial by jury depends on the division between law (juries) and equity (no juries) as of 1791.
- ○ Equity issues, such as a request for an _injunction_ and specific performance, do NOT require trial by jury. Neither do Admiralty issues.
- ○ Claims for damages are the classic remedy at law; triggers right to jury trial
- ○ When legal and equity issues overlap in one lawsuit, try the _legal_ issues first, no matter the order in which they arose.

> ***Example 42:*** *The plaintiff sues the defendant for an injunction (equity); the defendant counterclaims for money damages (law). The defendant wants a jury trial. What result? The court must try the counterclaim first so that it will be heard by a jury.*

2. Demand for Trial by Jury

- ○ May be made by any party either in a _pleading_ or separate motion
- ○ Must be made not later than _14_ days after service of the last pleading directed at the issue
- ○ Often made in the complaint or answer

3. Jury Selection

- ○ Minimum of _6_ jurors; maximum of _12_ jurors
- ○ All must participate in verdict unless dismissed for good cause.
- ○ Each litigant gets _3_ peremptory challenges (no need to explain or justify).

- Cannot be used for reasons of __race__ or __gender__

4. **Bench Trial**

   Judge is required to make findings of __fact__ on the __record__ and state conclusions of law

5. **Jury Instructions**
   - Parties may __request__ specific instructions.
   - Judge must inform the parties of his actions on those requests and the court's proposed instructions before final argument.
   - Court must provide an opportunity to object to proposed instructions:
     - Objections must be on the record (preserved), for stated reasons (so the appellate court can follow the argument), and made BEFORE the jury __retires__ to deliberate.
     - Only a timely objection preserves the issue for appeal.

B. **Motion for Judgment as a Matter of Law (JMOL)**
   - Formerly called Motion for Directed Verdict
   - Essentially a motion for summary judgment __after__ the trial has begun.
   - **Standard:** Viewing the evidence in the light most favorable to the __other__ party, the __evidence__ cannot support a verdict for that party, and the __moving__ party is therefore entitled to judgment as a matter of law.
     - Rule 50 provides the court must find that there is insufficient evidence for a jury reasonably to find for the nonmoving party.

   - **Credibility of a witness:** If the case turns on this issue, then there is a dispute as to an issue of material fact and the motion for JMOL will be denied; the issue is for the jury.
   - Made by defendant at the end of plaintiff's case or by either party at the close of all the evidence

C. **Renewed Motion for Judgment as a Matter of Law (formerly J.N.O.V.)**
   - A motion for JMOL made at the close of all the evidence and denied by the court may be __renewed__ after the jury returns a verdict.
   - **Standard is the same:** The evidence cannot support the jury's verdict and the moving party is therefore entitled to judgment as a matter of law.
   - **Prior motion is required:** It is a condition precedent to a post-verdict motion that the motion for JMOL had been made at the close of all evidence.

     Example 43: If the losing party appeals and the appellate court thinks the trial court was wrong to grant the JMOL, the case will need to be retried. But, if the judge instead the court lets it go to the jury and then grants the renewed motion for JMOL, the verdict is on the books if the trial court is reversed on appeal.

D. Motion for a New Trial

- Usually made with a Renewed Motion for JMOL
- Not restricted in the same way as a Renewed Motion for JMOL
- A new trial may be granted in the discretion of the court for many reasons, including:

  o Legal Errors
  o Newly discovered _evidence_
  o Prejudicial _misconduct_ by a lawyer, party, or a juror
  o Judge concludes that the verdict is against the great weight of the evidence, either in substance of the verdict or amount of _dammages_ awarded

- **Remittitur:** If the court determines that a verdict was seriously excessive, then it may offer a remittitur to reduce the verdict and grant a new trial on the condition that the remittitur is not accepted.
- The new trial order must specify the reasons for the new trial to allow for appellate review

  o If the reason is a question of law, it is reviewed _de novo_.
  o Other grounds for a new trial are reviewed for abuse of _discretion_.

CHAPTER 18: APPEALS

A. Motions to Terminate Without Trial

- Some preliminary motions are no longer relevant on appeal once there has been a full trial.
- A motion to dismiss for failure to state a claim, motion for judgment on the pleadings, motion for summary judgment, or motion for JMOL made before the jury retires are _____ if the moving party proceeds with trial once the motions are denied.
- Appellate review is based on the judgment rendered after full trial, not the earlier motion.

B. Appeals

1. Final Judgment Rule

  o Ordinarily, appeals are available only from a _final_ judgment.

    ▪ A final judgment resolves ALL the claims of ALL the parties.

  o **Partial final judgment:** The court may enter a final judgment on some claims by _expressly_ designating the order as final.
  o Judgment becomes final when entered by the _Clerk_ on the court's _docket_ (i.e., not when announced)
  o Notice of appeal must be filed in the trial court within _30_ days of entry of judgment

    ▪ A timely post-judgment motion will _toll_ the 30-day limit.

2. **Interlocutory Orders**

   a. **Interlocutory orders immediately appealable as of right:**

      - Any order granting or modifying an _injunction_
      - Any order that changes or affects _possession_ of property

   b. **Discretionary interlocutory appeal**

      - Any interlocutory order is appealable with _leave_ of _courts_.

        - BOTH the trial and appellate courts must agree to allow the appeal.

      - The trial court can issue a certificate for interlocutory appeal stating:

        - That the issue involves a _controlling_ question of law with _substantial_ ground for difference of opinion; and
        - That the immediate appeal may _materially_ advance termination of the litigation.

      - The appellate court must then agree to accept the appeal.

3. **Class Actions**

   Appellate courts have discretion to hear interlocutory appeals from orders _certifying_ or refusing to _certify_ a **class action**.

4. **Collateral-Order Doctrine**

   o Authorizes immediate appeal of "collateral orders"
   o "Collateral orders" are separable from and collateral to the main suit and too _important_ to deny immediate review.

5. **Writ of Mandamus**

   Provides for immediate appellate review of an order that is an abuse of _authority_

6. **Standards of Review**

   a. **Questions of law**

      - Appellate review is _de novo_
      - Did the trial court make an error?
      - Was the error prejudicial?

   b. **Findings of fact**

      - Jury verdicts must be affirmed if supported by _substantial evidence_.
      - Judge's findings of fact must be affirmed unless they are _clearly erroneous_

c. **Matters of discretion**

- Many issues decided by lower courts (continuances, new trials, discovery limitations)
- Standard of appellate review is abuse of _discretion_
- Any reasonable decision will be upheld.

C. Full Faith and Credit

- Courts in the U.S., both state and federal, must give full faith and credit to judgments rendered by courts of other states, provided that the rendering court had _jurisdiction_

CHAPTER 19: PRECLUSION: THE EFFECT OF PRIOR ADJUDICATION

A. Introduction

- Preclusion consists of two distinct doctrines:
  - _Claim_ preclusion (res judicata)
  - _Issue_ preclusion (collateral estoppel)

- Ask two questions IN THIS ORDER:
  1. Is the claim in the second suit precluded by the prior adjudication? If yes, the inquiry ends.
  2. If not, are there any issues in the second suit precluded by the prior adjudication?

  Exam Tip 19: Always ask these questions separately and in order.

B. Claim Preclusion (Res Judicata)

1. Rule

- A final judgment on the _Merits_ of a claim bars re-litigation of that claim by the same parties or those in _privity_ with the parties.
- Precludes re-litigation of every claim that was raised or should have been raised in the first suit.

2. Three Requirements

1. There must have been a final judgment on the _Merits_ in the first suit;
2. The second suit must be between the same _parties_ or their successors in interest; and
3. The second suit must involve the same _claim_ or cause of action.

3. Final Judgment on the Merits

- Includes a _default_ judgment, _Summary_ judgment, and dismissal _with prejudice_
- NOT necessary that there had been a trial

4. **Re-litigation Between the Same Parties**

  ○ Both parties must have been parties to the first action or successors in interest to the original parties.

  ○ A successor in interest steps into the shoes of the original party and is treated, for preclusion purposes, as the same party.

  ○ Examples of predecessors and successors in interest include:

    ▪ The assignor and assignee of a claim;

    ▪ A decedent and the executor of the estate; and

    ▪ The executor of an estate and persons who claim under the will.

  ○ **Class action**: Each member is generally bound by the judgment; they are considered to have had their opportunity in court even if not a named representative.

    > **Editorial Note 2:** However, in a class action certified under Rule 23(b)(3), a valid judgment does not bind class members who opted out of the lawsuit.

5. **Re-litigation of a Sufficiently Identical Claim or Cause of Action**

    > *Example 44:* *Father is criminally prosecuted by the government for failing to pay child support and is acquitted. Mother then brings a civil action for child support against the father. Is the second suit barred by claim preclusion?*
    >
    > *Answer:* No *The first action was a government prosecution brought by the government, and the second was a civil action brought by the mother. Different plaintiffs, different parties, different claims.*

    > *Example 45:* *A person injured by a defective vehicle sues the dealer and the dealer wins. Subsequently, the injured person sues the vehicle manufacturer for the same defect. Is the second suit barred by claim preclusion?*
    >
    > *Answer:* No *The first suit was against the dealer, and the second was against the manufacturer. No re-litigation between the same parties.*

  ○ ALL legal theories to recover for harm arising out of a single transaction or occurrence are ___one___ claim for purposes of claim preclusion.

  ○ Unless state law provides otherwise, if both contract and tort claims seek redress for the same harm, they are the ___same___ claim.

  ○ Also bars claims that could have been brought in the first case, but were not.

    > *Example 46:* Plaintiff and Defendant get in a car accident, and Plaintiff sues Defendant to recover damages for her personal injuries. Plaintiff wins. Later, Plaintiff tries to sue Defendant a second time for property damage to her car based on the same car accident. Is the claim precluded? ___Yes___ It arose from the same event and was required to be brought in the first action along with the claim for personal injury damages.

- o **Installment Sales:** Creditor must sue for all that is "due and owing" at the time of the suit.

  - All debt owed at the time of the action is one claim even if it was due in 3 or 4 separate payments.
  - Future debts or obligations are another claim.

    Example 47: *A tenant is in default on the rent for three months (January, February, and March). On April 1st, the landlord brings suit but unwisely sues only for the January rent and wins. He subsequently brings a second suit to collect the February and March rent. Can he collect?*

    Answer: __No__. *All the rent that was due when suit was brought in April is one claim, even though it involved three payments.*

    Example 48: *Suppose now that the landlord sues the tenant for all the rent due and owing as of April 1, and wins. The next month, the same dispute arises and the landlord sues again, seeking to recover unpaid rent for April. Can he collect?*

    Answer: __Yes__. *The landlord couldn't anticipate future obligations when he sued the first time, so the second suit is not precluded. The next month is a new claim.*

    Exam Tip 20: Look out for installment sales contracts that provide that if a purchaser misses a payment, the entire outstanding balance becomes due and owing (i.e., an acceleration clause). In that case, the entire balance is one claim. The seller can and must sue for everything at once or be barred.

C. Issue Preclusion (Collateral Estoppel)

1. Three Requirements

- o The same issue of __fact__ must arise in two suits;
- o That issue must have been actually and __necessarily__ decided in the first suit; and
- o The party to be __precluded__ must have been a party to the first suit.

2. Same Issue of Fact

It does not matter if the two suits involve entirely different claims, so long as they have a factual issue in common.

Example 49: *Assume that the person injured by a defective motor vehicle sues the dealer and loses. The jury found that the vehicle was not defective. Then the injured person sues the manufacturer for the same defect.*

Question: Is there claim preclusion?

Answer: __No__

_____

Question: Is there issue preclusion?

Answer: ___Yes___

3. **Actually and Necessarily Decided**

   o Only applies to issues actually litigated; not to those that ___might___ have been litigated

   o **Default judgment**: Results in full claim preclusive effect, but no issue preclusive effect because nothing was actually litigated

   o To be actually litigated, must be some sort of adversarial stance by the parties and an actual resolution of the issue by a factfinder or judge

4. **Party to Be Precluded Must Have Been a Party to the First Suit**

   o The party against whom preclusion is asserted must have been a party to the first suit or a successor in interest.

   > **Example 50:** *Assume that the person injured by a defective motor vehicle sues the dealer and loses. The jury found that the vehicle was defective. Then the injured person sues the manufacturer for the same defect. Is there issue preclusion?*
   >
   > *Answer:* ___No___ *. The manufacturer was not a party in the first case. Therefore, the first action cannot be used to prevent the manufacturer from litigating the issue of their own defense.*

   o The party invoking preclusion ___must___ have been a party to the prior action, nor in any way involved in the action.

   o NO requirement for ___mutuality___ of estoppel (at least applies to the defensive use of issue preclusion)

   > **Example 51:** *Assume that the person injured by a defective motor vehicle sues the dealer and loses. The jury found that the vehicle was not defective. Then the injured person sues the manufacturer for the same defect. Is there issue preclusion?*
   >
   > *Answer:* ___Yes___ *. Even though the manufacturer was not a party in the first case, the manufacturer can use the finding in the first case to preclude the injured party, from making the same argument she made in the first case.*

   ▪ Whether a succession of plaintiffs could invoke issue preclusion offensively is not clear.

Example 52: *Ann and Ben are involved in an auto accident with Carol and Dave. Ann sues Carol, the driver of the other car, and loses. The jury found that Carol's car was not operated negligently.*

Ann then sues Dave, the passenger in Carol's car, claiming that he caused the car to be operated negligently. Can Dave preclude re-litigation of the negligence issue in the second suit?

Answer: ___Yes___. There is no claim preclusion because the first suit was against a different defendant and thus raises a different claim. But there is issue preclusion. Ann was a party to the first suit. The issue of negligent operation of the vehicle was fully litigated and actually decided against her. Ann is precluded from re-litigating the issue of negligence.

Example 53: *Ann and Ben are involved in an auto accident with Carol and Dave. Ann sues Carol, the driver of the other car, and loses. The jury found that Carol's vehicle was not operated negligently.*

Ben, the passenger in Ann's car, then sues Carol, claiming that she operated her vehicle negligently. Can Carol, who has already litigated and won this issue, preclude Ben from re-litigating it in the second suit?

Answer: ___Yes___. No claim preclusion because a suit by a different plaintiff is a different claim. There is no issue preclusion because Ben (the party to be precluded) was not a party to the first suit. He has not had his day in court. Issue preclusion cannot be invoked against him.

D. Summary

- Remember that claim preclusion and issue preclusion are separate doctrines and must be addressed separately and in order.

    o Ask first whether claim preclusion bars the second suit. If so, that ends the matter.
    o If not, ask whether issue preclusion bars the second suit.

CONCLUSION

- Remember to concentrate your attention on the areas most often tested:

    o Jurisdiction (subject matter, personal, and venue): MOST important;
    o Pleadings, especially amendments;
    o Discovery, especially the work-product rule;
    o Motions practice, especially summary judgment and the two stages of motion for judgment as a matter of law; and
    o The effect of former adjudication, namely claim and issue preclusion

Exam Tip 21: On essay questions, subject matter jurisdiction, personal jurisdiction, and venue are often tested together. If you see one issue, be on the lookout for all three.

Exam Tip 22: Discuss claim and issue preclusion separately and in order.

Good luck!

[END OF HANDOUT]

Constitutional Law

CONSTITUTIONAL LAW
PROFESSOR JOHN C. JEFFRIES, JR.
UNIVERSITY OF VIRGINIA SCHOOL OF LAW

CHAPTER 1:   THE JUDICIAL POWER

> **Exam Tip 1:** The bar exam asks you what the law IS. Not what it should be. The examiners test only doctrine.

A. **Source, Scope, and Limitations**

- **Source:** Article III
- **Scope:** The jurisdiction of federal courts is limited to **cases or controversies**.
- **Limitations:** The Eleventh Amendment and State Sovereign Immunity

  o Article III lists the kinds of cases that come within the judicial power of the United States— the most important are **diversity** jurisdiction (i.e., disputes between citizens of different states) and **federal question** jurisdiction (i.e., cases arising under federal law).

  o A **major exception** to the judicial power is created by the _____ Amendment and by the preexisting concept of state sovereign immunity.

    ▪ Rule: You cannot sue a state for _____ damages in either state or federal court unless the state _____ or the U.S. Congress expressly says so to enforce _____ Amendment rights.

      • Note that the Eleventh Amendment protects states and state agencies, not _____ governments (i.e., no immunity for cities, counties, or towns).

      • Note also that a state's sovereign immunity applies in both _____ and _____ court, unless the state consents, or Congress expressly says so to enforce Fourteenth Amendment rights.

        o When enforcing individual rights, Congress can _____ state sovereign immunity.

        o It can force states to pay money damages for violating individual rights, but it must say so **expressly**.

        o Any lack of clarity will _____ damages.

    ▪ If you can't sue a state, then whom can you sue? Answer: A _____.

      • Injunctive relief—you can always get injunctive relief simply by enjoining the appropriate state officer (e.g., sue the state attorney general)

- Money damages—you can also get money damages, but only from the officer _____ for some kind of constitutional tort
- Damages from the state treasury are **barred** (unless the state consents or Congress expressly says so to enforce individual rights).

B. Jurisdiction of the Supreme Court

1. Original Jurisdiction

A case may be filed first in the Supreme Court (controversies between states, mostly).

2. Appellate Jurisdiction

Mostly, the jurisdiction of the Supreme Court is appellate.

a. Certiorari

- Almost all cases come to the Supreme Court by way of writ of certiorari.
- The key factor is that granting a writ of certiorari is _____ with the court.
- The Supreme Court is the _____ federal court that exercises discretionary jurisdiction.

b. Limitations on the Supreme Court's appellate jurisdiction

- Congress can make exceptions to the Court's appellate jurisdiction (i.e., Congress can effectively control the Supreme Court's docket (its appellate jurisdiction) by legislating exceptions to its appellate jurisdiction).

c. Adequate and Independent State Grounds (AISG)

- Arises *only* in the U.S. Supreme Court, and it arises only when the Supreme Court reviews a _____ judgment.

> **Exam Tip 2:** Frequently tested topic

- Rule: The Supreme Court can review a state court judgment *only* if it turned on _____ grounds. The court has no jurisdiction if the judgment below rested on an adequate and independent _____ ground.

  - **Adequate:** The state ground must control the decision no matter how a federal issue is decided. When does this happen? When the federal claimant (i.e., the party asserting a federal right) wins anyway under state law.

  Example 1:   *A criminal defendant objects to the legality of a search and seeks to suppress the evidence under both the Fourth Amendment and under the analogous search and seizure provision of the state's constitution. Suppose the state court says it is unsure about the Fourth Amendment, but under the state law, the search was illegal and the evidence must be suppressed. This kind of case cannot be reviewed by the U.S. Supreme Court—the federal claimant wins anyway under state law. Whether the evidence would also be suppressed under federal law simply does not matter.*

> **Note 1:** *Remember this key point:* The U.S. Constitution is a **floor**, not a **ceiling**, for individual rights. A state court interpreting a state constitution can always give you more protection. A state can never give you less than the federal constitution requires.

- **Independent:** The state law does not _____ on an interpretation of federal law. No AISG if state law adopts or follows federal law.
- When a state court decision is unclear as to the basis of the decision (i.e., whether it is based on the state constitution or the federal constitution), the Supreme Court _____ the federal issue.
  - If the Supreme Court **agrees** with the state court's decision of federal law, it **affirms** the decision.
  - If the Supreme Court **disagrees** with the state court's understanding of the federal issue, it **remands** the case to state court, so that the state court can reconsider state law.

Example 2: Michigan v. Long: *The defendant moved to suppress evidence under both the Fourth Amendment and the analogous search and seizure provision of the Michigan Constitution. The highest state court ruled in the defendant's favor, holding that the evidence must be suppressed, but cited state cases and federal cases indiscriminately (i.e., it did not make clear whether it was illegal as a matter of state law or federal law, or both). The Supreme Court took the case, reviewed the federal issue, found that the search was valid, that the evidence could lawfully be used under the Fourth Amendment, and remanded the case to the Michigan Supreme Court to reconsider whether the search was lawful under the state constitution.*

> **Exam Tip 3:** Again, remember that the U.S. Constitution is a _____, not a _____. State law can always provide more rights.

CHAPTER 2: THE JUDICIAL POWER (CONT'D): CONCEPTS OF JUSTICIABILITY

A. Standing to Sue

Standing requires _____, _____, and _____.

1. Injury

- Almost anything can be injury, especially if Congress says so (either past or future).
- Must be _____ (not abstract), but need not be economic

- If your freedom of movement or enjoyment of public space is impaired, that constitutes injury.
  - Mere _____ objection is **not** injury.
  - An organization has standing if its _____ have standing.

2. **Causation**

   - A defendant's conduct has caused or will cause the injury.

3. **Redressability**

   - A court can remedy or redress the injury.
   - If the injury is in the past, the remedy is _____.
   - If future injury is threatened, the remedy is an _____.
   - Past injury does not give automatic standing to seek an injunction for future injury. To get an injunction, you must show that it will happen again.

4. **Standing Examples and Commonly Tested Standing Issues**

   > ***Example 3:*** *Corporation A applies for a business license, but is turned down. Corporation B applies for the same license and gets it. Corporation A sues to enjoin the government from licensing Corporation B. Does Corporation A have standing? _____. Denying the license to Corporation B would not redress the wrong to Corporation A. The wrong to Corporation A was a wrongful denial of a license. Corporation A should sue for its own license.*

   - Federal taxpayers **always** have standing to challenge their own tax liability. However, taxpayers **do not** have standing to challenge government expenditures.

     - ***Narrow exception*** under the Establishment Clause: An establishment of religion challenge to _____ congressional appropriations can be raised by _____. (Note also that state courts often allow municipal taxpayers to challenge a municipality's expenditures.)

   - Legislative standing

     - Legislators do not have standing to challenge laws that they voted _____.

     - In some circumstances, the legislature itself as a body may have standing, if the claim concerns its institutional functions.

       - Occasional legislature standing, but no legislator standing.

   - "Third-party standing" refers to the question of whether you can raise the rights of someone else.

     - Generally, the answer is _____.

- **Exception:** Parties to an _____ or _____ can raise the rights of other parties to that exchange or transaction.

    Example 4: *Doctors who were not compensated for providing abortion services can raise the rights of women who wanted to have abortions provided. The doctor has injury because he was not paid but he wants to raise the rights of his patient to have an abortion, not his own. The doctor and the patient are involved in an exchange or transaction.*

    Example 5: *A seller of beer in a saloon can raise the rights of 18-year-old boys to buy beer at the same age as 18-year-old girls. The saloon keeper is injured because she is not making money. She wants to raise the rights of the underage boys because that is gender discrimination. She can raise the claims of those customers or would-be customers because they are parties to an exchange or transaction.*

B. Timeliness (Ripeness and Mootness)

- **Ripeness** concerns prematurity of a case. You must show _____ or an _____ threat of harm.
- **Mootness** cases are overripe and are dismissed whenever they become moot. Cases can become moot during trial or on appeal.

    - **Exception:** Controversies capable of _____, yet evading _____, are not moot, even though they look like it.

        - Such controversies always have an *internal time limit* (e.g., pregnancies and abortion).

C. Advisory Opinions

- Federal courts cannot issue advisory opinions.
- Federal courts cannot rule on the constitutionality of _____ legislation.

    > **Exam Tip 4:** Commonly tested

    Example 6: *Disputes about federal grants and aid projects were to be litigated in federal court, but the statute also provided that the court's judgment would be given effect only if the head of the relevant federal agency agreed with it. This is an unconstitutional advisory opinion. Federal courts decide cases; they do not make recommendations to executive officers.*

D. Political Questions

- A non-justiciable question when it is inappropriate for judicial resolution

    - The issue is committed to another branch of government for decision;
    - There are no manageable standards for adjudication.

- Examples of non-justiciable political questions include:
  - _____ Clause (protecting the republican form of government);
  - Foreign affairs, e.g., opening or breaking off diplomatic relations with another country;

    Example 7: *Congress enacted a law stating that American citizens born in Jerusalem could list Israel as their place of birth on their passports, which the executive branch challenged. The Court held that a dispute over the regulation of passports is somewhat related to foreign affairs but is nonetheless justiciable.*

  - _____ procedures; and
  - Political gerrymandering (drawing districts to establish a political advantage of one party over another).

    - Political gerrymandering can violate equal protection; but
    - The court has found no judicially manageable standards for determining what is and what is not acceptable in the area of drawing districts.

CHAPTER 3: THE LEGISLATIVE POWER

A. Introduction

- In theory, the federal government is a government of _____ powers. In fact, the federal government can do almost anything it likes, so long as it does not violate individual rights.

> **Exam Tip 5:** On the Multistate exam, you'll be given a federal statute, and you'll be asked to identify the strongest argument in favor of congressional power for passing that legislation. Three wrong answers:
>
> i) Promoting the _____ is not a power of Congress;
>
> ii) The federal government does not have a general _____;
>
> _____ is not a free-standing power of Congress. It works only as an add-on to some other legislative power.

- There are many powers of Congress, but the three big ones for the bar exam are: **Taxing**, **spending**, and **commerce**.

> **Exam Tip 6:** The general rule for the bar exam:
>
> i) Pick the _____ power when the law involves a tax;
>
> ii) Pick the _____ power whenever federal money is spent or disbursed;

Example 8: *There is a federal law that states that every state that receives federal highway funds has to limit its speed limit to 65 mph. What is the strongest argument Congress has to accomplish this? Answer: The _____ clause. What if the law simply caps the highway speeds at 65 mph without saying anything about federal highway funds? Answer: Regulation of _____.*

B. The Powers

1. The Commerce Power

○ Almost anything can be regulated as interstate commerce.

○ Congress can regulate:

▪ The _____ of interstate commerce (highways, seaways, airways, etc.);

▪ The _____ of interstate commerce (cars, trucks, railroads, ships, etc.); and

▪ *Intrastate* (and interstate) activity (economic or commercial) that has a _____ on *interstate* commerce.

• Substantial effect is judged in the _____. The question is whether the aggregate activity of everyone doing the same thing has a substantial effect on interstate commerce, and the answer is almost always *yes*.

• Not within the Commerce Clause: For non-economic, non-commercial activity, Congress can regulate intrastate actions only by *actually* demonstrating a substantial effect on interstate commerce (substantial effect is presumed for economic or commercial activity). Thus, Congress cannot regulate purely intrastate, non-commercial, non-economic activity for which a substantial effect on interstate commerce has not been shown.

Example 9: Wickard v. Filburn *(wheat growing case where growing crops for sale was judged in the aggregate and a substantial effect was demonstrated)*

Example 10: Gonzales v. Raich *(where the cultivation and medical use of marijuana was judged in the aggregate and a substantial effect was demonstrated)*

Example 11: United States v. Lopez *(a statute prohibited possession of a firearm within 1000 feet of a school—it could not be proved that it was an economic or commercial activity, and it could not be demonstrated that there was a substantial effect on interstate commerce)*

Example 12: United States v. Morrison *(a statute provided a federal remedy for gender-motivated violence—it could not be shown that, in the aggregate, the activity had a substantial effect on interstate commerce)*

Example 13: 2012 Affordable Health Care case *(the individual mandate required individuals to buy health insurance or to pay a penalty for not doing so—the Court said that forcing individuals who are not engaged in commercial or economic activities to buy health insurance they do not want cannot be sustained as a regulation of interstate commerce.)*

2. **The Taxing and Spending Power**

   Think of these as separate powers even though they are lumped together in one clause.

   a. **Taxing**

      ▪ The Taxing Clause is the right answer whenever Congress imposes a _____, even when the tax is actually used to prohibit the good or activity in question.

      ▪ The tax need only be _____ to raising revenue.

      Example 14: 2012 Affordable Health Care case—*the individual mandate was not sustained as a regulation of interstate commerce, but it was held to be valid under the taxing power. The individual who chooses not to buy health insurance must pay a tax, and the taxing power supports anything that is rationally related to raising revenue.*

   b. **Spending**

      ▪ The Spending Power includes spending for the _____.

      ▪ Congress can use the Spending Power to accomplish things it could not do by direct regulation under the Commerce Clause.

      Example 15: South Dakota v. Dole—*The 21st Amendment repealed Prohibition and gave states the power to control the regulation and consumption of alcohol. As a result, Congress likely cannot directly regulate the drinking age in the states. Thus, in order to pass a 21-year-old drinking age law, Congress passed a "bribe." If states wanted to receive federal highway funds, they had to raise their drinking age to a minimum of 21 years of age.*

3. **Anti-Commandeering**

   o Congress cannot force states to adopt or enforce _____ programs. It cannot commandeer state and local agencies to implement federal programs.

      Example 16: *The Brady Gun-Control Act required background checks for people wanting to purchase firearms, and it required that state and local law*

enforcement carry out those background checks. The Supreme Court said this
was unconstitutional.

- What can Congress do to enforce regulatory programs?

  - It can bribe states through use of the _____ power.
  - It can adopt its own regulatory program and enforce it with federal officers.

4. **The War and Defense Powers**

- Congress has the power to _____ and the power to maintain the Army and Navy.
- Congress has the power to provide for military discipline of U.S. military personnel.
- Congress can provide for military trial of enemy combatants and enemy civilians.
- Congress cannot provide for _____ trial of U.S. citizens who are civilians.

CHAPTER 4:   THE LEGISLATIVE POWER (CONT'D): THE POWER TO ENFORCE THE CIVIL WAR AMENDMENTS

A. **Thirteenth Amendment**

- Congress has broad power to legislate against _____ discrimination, whether _____ or _____.

- Includes purely private racial discrimination

B. **Fourteenth Amendment**

- Congress has the power to _____ violations of _____ rights by the government, but only as those rights have been defined by the courts.

  - Does not enable Congress to redefine constitutional rights by legislation
  - Only permits Congress to adopt remedies reasonably designed to enforce individual rights as they have been defined by the courts

- To be properly remedial, the legislation must have "congruence" and "proportionality." That is, there has to be a _____ between the remedial law enacted by Congress and the constitutional right as defined by the Supreme Court.

    Example 17: *The Religious Freedom Restoration Act (RFRA)*

    <u>Overview</u>: *Neutral, generally applicable regulations of conduct can validly be applied despite religious objections. Everyone can be made to obey the law whether they believe in it or not.*

Background: Religious individuals often claimed a right of accommodation of religious belief. They claimed that laws valid against everyone else could not be enforced against religious objectors unless the government showed a compelling interest. That claim was rejected by the Supreme Court, which held that neutral regulations of conduct could be enforced against anyone, including religious objectors.

Congress disagreed with the Supreme Court and passed RFRA, which declared that religious believers have the right not to obey otherwise valid laws, unless the government can show a compelling interest in enforcing the law against them.

The Supreme Court struck down RFRA, as it went beyond federal legislative power, because it was not really remedial. It was not narrowly aimed at the kinds of laws the Supreme Court had declared unconstitutional—laws aimed at religion.

Congress could have made it a crime for the government to discriminate against religious belief. Congress could have said that any government or government official who discriminated against religious belief had to pay money damages. Congress could give the Department of Justice special enforcement powers to look into religious discrimination and make sure it is rooted out. All of these actions would have been reasonable remedies against a recognized constitutional violation of discrimination against religious belief.

In RFRA, Congress said even non-discriminatory laws were invalid unless the government showed a compelling interest. That, said the Supreme Court, was not an attempt to enforce the Free Exercise right against religious discrimination as it had been defined by the court. Rather, it was an attempt to overturn the Court's decision about what the Constitution did and did not protect. Therefore, RFRA was struck down as beyond the federal legislative power.

Note: RFRA was unconstitutional only as it applied to states and localities. Requiring states and localities to accommodate religious belief was found to be beyond Congress's power under the 14th Amendment. However, Congress is free to accommodate religious belief in the exercise of its undoubted federal powers (e.g., Congress's powers over the Army and the Navy, the District of Columbia, etc.). When Congress exercised its federal powers, it may choose to accommodate religious believers, but Congress has no power to force that policy on the states.

C. Fifteenth Amendment

Congress has the power to ensure there is no racial discrimination in voting.

CHAPTER 5: THE EXECUTIVE POWER AND INTERBRANCH RELATIONS

A. The Powers of the President—Domestic

- Has the power to _____ the law, not to make it or break it

- The power to enforce is greatest when authorized by _____.
  Generally speaking, the President's powers are subject to control by statute.

- Few powers that are *exclusively executive* and, therefore, **not subject** to statutory control:

  o **Pardon Power:** The President can pardon or commute punishment for any and all _____ offenses. (Governors have a similar power for state crimes.) This power cannot be limited by Congress.

  o **Veto Power:** The President has _____ days to veto legislation. The President can veto for any reason or no reason, but cannot veto specific provisions in the legislation and accept others.

    ▪ Overriding a veto requires a _____ majority vote of each house.

  o **Appointment and Removal of Executive Officers:** Only the President (or his appointees) can _____ or _____ executive officers. Some senior officers (e.g., cabinet officers, ambassadors, federal judges) require the advice and consent of the Senate. The Senate has a power of _____. The Senate's approval power does not translate into a power of appointment.

    ▪ Who are executive officers? Anyone who _____ on behalf of the U.S.

    ▪ Just as Congress cannot hire or fire an executive officer, it cannot give executive power to any officer it can hire or fire.

B. The Powers of the President—Foreign Affairs

- Commander in Chief: The President has control over military decisions, although Congress has exclusive power to _____.

  o Congress can cut off funding to military actions.

- Treaties and Executive Agreements
    - Treaties are negotiated by the President, but require approval by a
      _____ vote of the Senate. Once a treaty is ratified
      (approved), it has the same authority as a statute.
    - Executive agreements are presidential negotiations not submitted for approval by the
      Senate. They can be authorized, precluded, or overridden by statute, but they take
      precedence over conflicting state laws. They do not have the binding status of a treaty.

C. Interbranch Relations

1. Congressional Limits on the Executive

a. Impeachment

- Applies to executive officers (e.g., President, Vice President, cabinet officers, federal
  judges)
- An accusation passed by the House of Representatives requiring a
  _____ vote.
- Once impeached, the person is tried in the Senate.
- Conviction requires a two-thirds vote of the Senate.
- Impeachment and conviction lead to _____ from office.
  No other penalty applies.

b. Impoundment

- If a statute gives the President discretion to spend or withhold funds, he may do so.
- But, if a statute unambiguously requires that certain funds be spent on certain
  purposes, then the President cannot refuse to do so. There is no power to
  _____ (withhold) funds.

c. Legislative Veto

- Unconstitutional;
- It arises when Congress passes a law reserving to itself the right to disapprove future
  executive actions by simple _____.
- If Congress wants to override executive actions, it must
  _____ the law (so that the President has an opportunity
  to veto the new legislation).
- Congress cannot evade the President's guaranteed veto opportunity by passing a law
  saying that in the future it plans to govern by resolution.

2. Delegation of Powers

- Congress can delegate its power to administrative agencies, so long as there are **intelligible
  standards** governing the exercise of that delegated power.
- Not a demanding test—almost all delegations of legislative powers are upheld.

3. **Immunities**

   a. **The President**

      ▪ Has _____ immunity from liability for official acts (broadly construed)

      ▪ Has no immunity for acts done _____ to taking office

      ▪ Has an _____ privilege not to reveal confidential communications with presidential advisers, but that privilege can be outweighed by a _____ need in a criminal prosecution (*U.S. v. Nixon*)

   b. **Judges**

      Judges have absolute immunity for all _____ acts, but may be liable for non-judicial acts (e.g., employment discrimination).

   c. **Legislators**

      ▪ United States Senators and Representatives (not state legislators) are protected by the _____ Clause.

      ▪ Senators and Congressmen and their aides *cannot* be _____ or _____ in relation to their _____ acts.

         • The official acts of a federal legislator **cannot** be introduced into evidence.

CHAPTER 6:   THE FEDERAL SYSTEM

A. Federal and State Powers

- Even though federal powers are superior, most federal powers are _____ with those of the states. (On most topics, both Congress and the states have regulatory powers. If there is a conflict, Congress wins.)

- Some powers are exclusively federal. They include the power over foreign relations and the power to coin money.

B. Intergovernmental Immunities

- The federal government is generally _____ from **direct** state regulation or taxation. However, states can tax **indirectly** (e.g., taxing the income of federal employees).

- States are not immune from direct federal regulation (e.g., pollution regulations, employment laws, etc.).

- States cannot _____ state officers from federal liability for violating federal constitutional rights.

- **Exception:** The anti-commandeering principle covered in Chapter 3. States cannot be forced to carry out federal programs. The federal government can always use the spending power to bribe states to comply.

C. **State Regulation and Taxation of Commerce**

   1. **Privileges and Immunities of State Citizenship under Article IV (Comity Clause)**

      o Technically, a subject of individual rights, but functionally belongs here because of its similarity to the next subject (Dormant Commerce Clause).

      o Forbids serious _____ against _____ individuals, absent substantial justification.

         ▪ Does not protect out-of-state _____.

         ▪ "Serious discrimination" typically involves **employment**.

      o *Rule*: There can be no legal requirement of _____ for _____ employment. States cannot require that you live or reside in the state to work in the state. However, public employment can require residency requirements.

         Example 18: *A law that requires all cab drivers to live in the city is not valid.*

         ▪ Examples of private employment requirements (can't depend on residency): Admission to the bar; other occupational licenses.

         ▪ Examples of public employment (can depend on residency): A city hiring only city residents or requiring a certain percentage of city residents on city construction projects.

      o Non-serious discrimination: States can discriminate with regard to recreational opportunities, such as hunting licenses or state park access.

   2. **Dormant Commerce Clause**

      o More important than Privileges and Immunities of Article IV because it protects out-of-state _____ as well as out-of-state individuals.

      o "Dormant" describes what the Commerce Clause means in the absence of federal regulation (when the federal commerce power is unexercised).

      o **Rule**: In the absence of federal regulation, state regulation of commerce is *valid* so long as:

         1) There is no _____ against out-of-state interests;

         2) The regulation does not _____ interstate commerce; and

         3) The regulation does not apply to wholly extraterritorial activity.

a. **No discrimination against out-of-state interests**

- Examples include: forbidding sale of only out-of-state products; taxing out-of-state products at a higher rate; requiring that manufacturing be performed in-state.

  Example 19: *A state law said that metal ore mined in the state must be processed in the state (i.e., refined) before it could be shipped out of the state. The state law is unconstitutional because it discriminates against out-of-state metal refiners.*

  Example 20: *A law limiting landfills to in-state garbage is unconstitutional because it discriminates against out-of-state garbage.*

- Hypothetically ok if there is a substantial state interest and no other non-discriminatory means is available; this is incredibly rare.

- **Exceptions** to no discrimination against out-of-state interests:

  - **State as Market Participant**—When a state is _____ or _____ goods or services, it can choose to deal with only in-state persons.

    o Examples include: Sale of cement produced by state-owned plant only to in-state purchasers; garbage stored in state-owned landfill limited to in-state garbage; law requiring 50% local workforce on state-financed construction projects.

  - **Subsidies**—A state can always choose to subsidize only its own citizens (for example, welfare benefits or in-state college tuition).

  - **Federal Approval**—Remember, the Dormant Commerce Clause applies *only* in the _____ of federal action. If Congress _____ or _____ to state regulation of commerce, nothing the state does will violate the Commerce Clause, *even if it discriminates against out-of-state interests.*

    Exam Tip 9: Commonly tested on the MBE

b. **No undue burdens on interstate commerce**

- Non-discriminatory state regulation of commerce is almost always upheld.
- Only when it is so outrageously _____ relative to the benefits of the regulation is a non-discriminatory state regulation struck down as an undue burden on interstate commerce.
- This is a balancing test, but non-discriminatory regulations are rarely struck down.

c. **No regulation of wholly extraterritorial activity**

- A state may not regulate conduct occurring wholly beyond its borders.

Example 21: *Connecticut tried to legislate that beer sold in Connecticut could not be sold at a price different from the price of beer sold in other states.*

CHAPTER 7:   STATE TAXATION OF INTERSTATE COMMERCE, PREEMPTION, AND RELATIONS AMONG STATES

A. State Taxation of Interstate Commerce

- Generally, the requirements are the same as for any other state regulation of commerce: Discriminatory taxation will be struck down unless Congress _____, and non-discriminatory taxation will be upheld unless it is unduly _____.

  o Non-discriminatory taxation is valid if the following **two requirements** are met:

    1) _____ between the taxing state and the property or activity to be taxed

      - "Substantial nexus" does not require any kind of physical presence.

    2) Must be a _____ of tax liability among states

      Example 22: *A state may tax the in-state portion of a corporation's revenue but cannot tax the entire world-wide activity of the corporation.*

- Ad Valorem Property Taxes (value-based property taxes)

  o Levied on personal property

  o Distinguish between two kinds of personal property because they are taxed differently:

    ▪ **Commodities** are the goods that move from state to state.

      - States tax all commodities within their borders on a specified date (called *tax day*), but not goods that are merely in transit—the commodities have to come to rest in the state.

      - **Rule:** Pay the full tax to every state where goods are stopped for a _____ on tax day. No taxes are due where they are merely _____.

    ▪ **Instrumentalities** are the transportation equipment that moves commodities (railroads, trucks, airplanes, etc.)

      - Fair apportionment of tax liability among states with a substantial nexus to the instrumentality.

      - Each state in which an instrumentality is used can tax the value of that instrumentality.

Example 23: *A long-haul trucker drives his rig from Maine to California. Every state through which the truck passes can tax the truck itself but each state can only tax a portion of the truck's value, roughly equal to the portion of in-state use. The state of the taxpayer's domicile taxes the full value of the truck, then turns around and gives a credit to every state that asserts taxation when the truck uses its highways. You end up with a scheme of fair apportionment of tax liability among those states with a substantial nexus to the truck. The commodities in the truck cannot be taxed if they are merely passing through; they must stop for a business purpose on tax day.*

B. Preemption

- Federal law preempts (overrides) _____ state law.
- State law is not preempted simply because it addresses the same subject matter or topic as a federal statute. There must be incompatibility or conflict.

    Example 24: *Federal law provides automobile emissions must be at least 95% pure. California adopts a more stringent requirement requiring CA emissions be 98% pure. Is this state law preempted? No. There is no conflict—you can comply with both of those standards.*

- Preempting the Field: When Congress determines that there should be no state law of any sort in a particular field, then any state law in that area is inconsistent with the federal statute and is preempted. This is **rare**.

C. Relations Among States

- *Interstate compacts* are agreements among states. States can make interstate compacts, but if the compact affects _____ rights, Congress must approve.
- Full Faith and Credit Clause: States do not have to follow other states' laws, but they do have to give full faith and credit to _____ rendered by other states' courts, so long as the rendering court had _____ to render a final judgment on the merits.

CHAPTER 8:   STATE ACTION AND PROCEDURAL DUE PROCESS

A. State Action

- The 13th Amendment (outlawing slavery and involuntary servitude) applies _____ to private parties and individuals, but it is narrow in its focus.
- Other individual rights apply to states and localities through the _____ Amendment, which requires state action.
- "State action" means _____ action, whether state or local (e.g., a county firing a sheriff is state action; a city denying a permit is state action).

- Most state action is clear, but not always. Government cannot be **significantly involved** in private discrimination.

  o Significant state involvement:

    - Government cannot _____ private discrimination.
    - Government cannot _____ private discrimination.
    - Government cannot _____ a private agreement to discriminate.
    - But, government is *not* required to _____ private discrimination.

  o Generally, the government acts constitutionally so long as its own conduct is neutral and even-handed (e.g., trespass laws, liquor licenses for private clubs).

- Anti-Discrimination Statutes

  o State action is required to show a violation of the Constitution.
  o State action is _____ if there is anti-discrimination legislation.

B. Procedural Due Process—the Right to *Notice* and a *Hearing*

   1. Consists of two questions:

   1) Is _____, _____, or _____ being taken?

   2) If life, liberty, or property is being taken, what process is due?

   2. Breakdown of loss of life, liberty, and property

   o **Life:** Death penalty requires procedural due process
   o **Liberty:** Physical confinement, probation and parole, physical injury (such as a spanking in school), any restriction on legal rights (including being punished for free speech). Injury to _____ is *not* a loss of liberty.
   o **Property**

   > **Exam Tip 10:** Out of the three, property is the most heavily tested. Most of the questions in this area concern government jobs or benefits.

   - You have a property interest in your government job or benefit whenever you have a legitimate _____ to continued enjoyment of the job or benefit.
   - A mere expectation of continued employment or benefit does not suffice.
   - Most government benefits are entitlements, and hence property.
   - How can you tell whether you have an entitlement to a government job or whether you have a mere expectation of government employment?

- Government jobs are entitlements only when the government says so—such as by providing a contractual term or discharge only "for cause."

   Example 25: *You are hired as the city planner and the boss says, "This job has a term of five years. You will not be fired during that five-year term except for cause." You have a property right in that job for five years.*

   Example 26: *Barnes was an assistant professor at a state community college. He had a three-year teaching contract and under state law, five years was required for tenure. At the end of three years, his contract was not renewed, and he sued. What is his strongest argument that he should get notice and a hearing?*

      A. He was the best teacher in the school.

      B. He was the only teacher not rehired.

      C. He was so sure of success that he moved his elderly parents to town to care for them.

      D. He had an oral promise of re-employment from the president of the college.

   Answer choice _____ is the correct answer because the president is acting as the government, and arguably Barnes had an entitlement to continued employment.

   *What is the strongest argument **against** Barnes receiving notice and a hearing? Answer: He had a three-year contract that ended.*

   o Deprivation: Notice and a hearing are not required when there is an accident. Random negligence by a state employee does not constitute a deprivation of life, liberty, or property (e.g., death by a municipal garbage truck). Deprivation requires the **intentional** taking away of life, liberty, or property.

3. **If life, liberty, or property is being taken by the government, what process is due?**

   o Procedural due process is variable, and the types of hearings can range from casual to very elaborate.

   o To decide what kind of process is due, the courts balance three factors:

      1) The _____ at stake (life, liberty, property);

      2) The _____ in protecting that interest; and

      3) The _____ in efficiency and cost.

   o **Timing** of the hearings

      ▪ Sometimes, a hearing must occur **before** the deprivation.

         • Examples include: Terminating welfare benefits; non-emergency revocations of driver's licenses.

- Sometimes, the hearing can occur **after** the action, so long as the hearing is _____ and _____.

    - Examples include: Terminating disability benefits; disciplinary suspension from a public secondary school.

  o Public employees who can be fired only "for cause" must be given some opportunity to be heard _____ to discharge, unless there is a _____ not to keep the employee on the job. If there is a significant reason not to keep a person on the job, then the discharge can come first with a subsequent hearing that is prompt and provides reinstatement with back pay (fair).

> *Example 27:* *A police officer charged with a crime can be suspended immediately because there is a significant reason not to keep him or her on the job. The hearing can come afterwards, but it must be prompt and provide reinstatement with back pay if the charges are ultimately unfounded.*

CHAPTER 9: SUBSTANTIVE DUE PROCESS

A. Standards of Review

- Both substantive due process and equal protection have the same three standards of review.

1. Strict Scrutiny

  o Is the law _____ for a _____ government interest?
  o Implicit in strict scrutiny is the requirement for the **least restrictive means**.
  o When strict scrutiny applies, the _____ bears the burden of proof. The government must show that the interest is compelling and the law is necessary to that interest.
  o Applies when there is a _____ classification or a _____ right

2. Intermediate Scrutiny

  o Is the law _____ related to an _____ government interest?
  o Applies to classifications based on _____ and _____.

> **Note 2:** While three standards of review are available in both substantive due process and equal protection claims, **intermediate scrutiny** has only ever been used to decide cases based on **equal protection** grounds.

3. **Rational Basis**

  o Is the law _____ related to a

    _____ interest?

  o The _____ bears the burden of proof.

  o Low burden of proof.

  o Applies to all other cases (residual test)

B. **Fundamental Rights**

  • Triggers the strict scrutiny test under both due process and equal protection

1. **Due Process versus Equal Protection**

  o If a law denies a fundamental right to **everyone**, it violates

    _____.

  o If a law denies a fundamental right to **only some**, it violates

    _____.

2. **Travel**

  o We have a fundamental right of _____ and settlement.

  o States can impose reasonable residency requirements for

    _____ and _____.

    ▪ Most are 30–90 days

    ▪ One year is too long for everything except _____ and

      jurisdiction to issue a _____.

  o All residents have a right to be treated equally. A state cannot have a tax scheme that
    favors long-term residents over recently arrived residents.

3. **Voting and Ballot Access**

  o Voting is a fundamental right to all _____ age 18 and over.

    ▪ _____ are unconstitutional because they burden the
      fundamental right to vote.

    ▪ Short-term (e.g., 30 days) residency requirements are permitted.

    ▪ Congress controls the residency requirements for _____
      elections. States control residency requirements for all other elections.

  o Ballot access

    ▪ States can impose requirements for candidates to be listed on a ballot, such as longer
      residency, filing fees, and nomination petitions, so long as serious candidates can
      reasonably comply.

    ▪ If the requirements become so onerous that they effectively bar access to the ballot,
      then they are unconstitutional.

4. **Privacy**

   a. **Marriage**

      There are all sorts of requirements for marriage (e.g., age or restriction on marrying close relatives), but substantial interference with the marriage—including same-sex marriage—is unconstitutional.

   b. **Contraception**

      It is a fundamental right for everyone, whether married or not, to purchase contraceptives.

   c. **Sexual intimacy**

      Perhaps not technically a fundamental right—the Supreme Court found that the government has no _____ in regulating non-commercial sexual intimacy between consenting adults, including same-sex couples.

   d. **Abortion**

      ▪ *Roe v. Wade*: A woman has a right to terminate her pregnancy until viability of the fetus. After that stage, restrictions can apply so long as there are exceptions to preserve the life and health of the mother.

      ▪ States regulate abortion in a variety of ways, but they cannot impose an _____ on the woman's right to terminate her pregnancy.

         • Informed-consent requirements are _____.
         • Twenty-four hour waiting periods are _____.
         • Parental _____ requirements (for minors) are allowed.
         • Parental _____ requirements are generally not allowed.

            ○ Narrow exception for requirement that an underage female get the consent of a parent or a judge, but requires the judge to give consent if the underage female understands the nature of the act.

         • _____ requirements are not allowed.
         • Government financing of abortion is _____.

   e. **Parental rights**

      ▪ Parents have a fundamental right to raise their children as they see fit, including the choice of religious or _____ schools.
      ▪ Can lose their rights through abandonment, _____, or neglect

f. **Family relations**

  ▪ Includes the right to live together with close relatives

g. **Obscene material**

  ▪ Fundamental right to read obscene material in the privacy of one's own home.

  ▪ However, no fundamental right to purchase, sell, import, or distribute such material.

  ▪ Does not apply to _____.

h. **Refusal of medical treatment**

  ▪ Not clear whether this is a fundamental right, but there is a liberty interest in refusing medical treatment

  ▪ No right to commit suicide

CHAPTER 10:   EQUAL PROTECTION (RACE, ETHNICITY, AND NATIONAL ORIGIN)

A. General Considerations

- Privileges or Immunities of **National** Citizenship under the 14th Amendment—means nothing today (so it is **never** the correct answer on the MBE)

  > **Note 3:** Privileges and Immunities of _____ Citizenship Clause in Article IV (Comity Clause) has a narrow but important meaning. It prohibits serious discrimination against out-of-state individuals, especially in the context of access to the _____ job market, i.e. prohibits requiring those who work in the state to live in the state.

- Two Due Process Clauses

  o Fifth Amendment applies to the federal government.

  o Fourteenth Amendment applies to _____ and

     _____.

- One Equal Protection Clause—found in the 14th Amendment

  o Applies to localities and states

  > **Note 4:** Though no Equal Protection Clause guarantee technically applies to the _____ government, equal protection concepts are applied to the federal government via the Due Process Clause of the Fifth Amendment. Therefore, states and localities have both equal protection and due process; for the federal government, equal protection and due process are called Fifth Amendment Due Process.

B. Standards of Review—Same for Due Process and Equal Protection

- Strict scrutiny, i.e., is the law **necessary** for a **compelling** interest?
- Intermediate scrutiny, i.e., is the law _____ related to an

  _____ government interest?

- Rational basis, i.e., is the law _____related to a
  _____ government interest?

  o Rational basis test is generally easily passed. However, recent Supreme Court cases have made exceptions in the field of sexual orientation.

    ▪ In the 2003 *Lawrence* case, the Supreme Court struck down laws criminalizing homosexual sodomy using language suggesting the laws did not pass the rational basis test as they reflected prejudice, not a legitimate reason for the laws.

    ▪ In the 2013 *Windsor* case, the Court used the same approach in striking down the federal Defense of Marriage Act (DOMA). The Court applied a version of the rational basis test "with teeth" suggesting that because the motivation behind the federal DOMA was animus and prejudice, the law was not a rational plan of government.

  o Laws against sexual orientation might be struck down as irrational because they are not supported by reasons other than mere prejudice.

C. **Suspect Classifications (Trigger Strict Scrutiny and Arise under Equal Protection)**

  - **Race, Ethnicity, or National Origin**—laws that disadvantage minorities will be struck down.

    o Discriminatory purpose is required: For constitutional purposes, a law is a racial classification only if the plaintiffs show it has a discriminatory _____ (not enough to show a disproportionate impact).

      > **Example 28:** *Economically restrictive zoning in Arlington Heights—a developer wanted to come in and build a large multi-family housing complex. Developer argued that the two-acre, single-family zoning ordinance has the effect of restricting the town to wealthy white people; he argued that discriminated against minorities. The Supreme Court said the zoning law was not unconstitutional as racial discrimination unless you can show it was done for the **purpose** of discriminating against minorities.*

      ▪ **Discriminatory purpose**: May be explicit on the face of the statute, or may be proved by a history of discriminatory _____, or by extrinsic evidence about the purposes of those who passed the law.

      ▪ School desegregation: De jure (by law) segregation is unconstitutional. De facto segregation is not (usually by residential housing patterns).

    o Affirmative action

      ▪ It is a racial classification; an effort to benefit a racial or ethnic minority.

      ▪ Triggers _____ and requires a _____ interest

      ▪ **Specific past discrimination**: Affirmative action is valid when it ***specifically*** corrects past discrimination *by the specific department or agency* now engaged in affirmative action.

Example 29: *New Haven Firefighters case—Nineteen firefighters sued the city of New Haven when they had all scored high enough on a standardized test to be promoted to management positions. City officials abandoned the test results because minority firefighters had not scored high enough to be considered for these positions, and then the city hired minorities anyway for these spots. The Supreme Court said the city's actions looked like a racially motivated quota and struck it down.*

- General societal discrimination does not justify affirmative action.

■ Affirmative action is allowed in the context of preferential admissions to colleges and universities.

- Preferential admissions are allowed if _____ to achieve a diverse student body and diversity is essential to the education.

  o Must be a strong showing that racial preferences are *essential* to achieving a diverse class.

  o Racial preferences must be "holistic" (can be built into an evaluation if every student is evaluated individually in a holistic way) and flexible.

  o Quotas are not allowed.

  o Separate admissions tracks or procedures for minority applicants are not allowed.

- Preferential admissions not allowed for _____ (though schools may be located and attendance zones created to maximize diversity).

CHAPTER 11:   EQUAL PROTECTION (ALIENAGE, GENDER, AND ONE PERSON-ONE VOTE)

A. Suspect Classifications Continued

- **Alienage**—Requirement of U.S. Citizenship

  o Classifications based upon U.S. citizenship are generally suspect classifications that require a compelling interest, but *two important exceptions* to strict scrutiny for alienage apply:

    ■ **Federal government**

      - Congress has plenary power over citizenship, immigration, and naturalization.

      - Federal classifications based on U.S. citizenship do *not* trigger strict scrutiny.

      - Federal classifications are valid unless _____ and _____.

- **State and local participation in government functions**
  - These are jobs that have a particular relevance to the role of government and non-U.S. citizens can be barred from these jobs.
  - States and localities may require U.S. citizenship for participation in government functions, including voting, serving on a jury, and working in any kind of government law enforcement position (including probation and parole officers), or as a public school teacher.

- **Rule**: States and localities *cannot* require U.S. citizenship for access to _____ employment or for government _____.

  > *Example 30:* *Florida required U.S. citizenship for admission to the Florida bar. Admission to the bar controls private employment as an attorney and therefore triggered strict scrutiny. It was struck down.*

  > *Example 31:* *Maryland required U.S. citizenship for Maryland's in-state tuition, a government benefit, a kind of subsidy of in-state students. Basing that subsidy on U.S. citizenship triggers strict scrutiny. The requirement was struck down. However, Maryland could and did validly require* **residency** *for in-state tuition. But Maryland was not entitled to discriminate against lawfully resident, taxpaying members of the Maryland community who were not U.S. citizens.*

  > **Note 5:** Constitutional rights of undocumented aliens—*Plyler v. Doe*: Undocumented aliens are not a suspect classification. Even so, states cannot deny undocumented children public education.

B. **Quasi-Suspect Classifications (Gender and Legitimacy)**
  - Trigger intermediate scrutiny—is the law _____ related to an _____ government interest?
  - **Gender** classifications are almost always **invalid** (e.g., Oklahoma had a law permitting women to legally drink alcohol at a younger age than men).
    - Permissible examples of gender classifications:
      - Statutory rape can be gender-specific (historically); and
      - The draft.
  - **Legitimacy** (i.e., something depends on whether parents were married at the time of one's birth) laws are almost always **invalid**, especially if punitive in nature.

C. **Non-Suspect Classifications (Age and Wealth)**
  - **Age** discrimination in employment is barred by statute, but it is not a suspect or quasi-suspect classification under the Equal Protection Clause.
    - Triggers *rational* basis

- **Wealth** is not a suspect or quasi-suspect classification, but the government has to waive filing fees for indigents when charging the fees would deny a _____ right.

  o Examples include: _____ (because marriage is a fundamental right); transcript for appeal of a criminal conviction (because appellate review is a fundamental right); transcript for appeal of the termination of parental rights.

    ▪ Bankruptcy filing fees do not have to be waived.

D. Fundamental Rights

Some fundamental rights almost always come up under equal protection.

1. Right to travel

2. Right to vote—one person, one vote

  o Requires districts of approximately equal size, i.e., approximately the same number of voters in each

  o Applies whenever you elect representatives by _____.

    ▪ Examples include: U.S. House of Representatives; both houses of a state legislature; local governments when they elect representatives by district.

      - **Exception:** Special purpose governments—A highly specialized government (e.g., for distribution of water rights) can have a franchise based on that special purpose (e.g., acreage or water entitlements).

3. Gerrymandering

Comes in two varieties—racial and political

a. Racial gerrymandering

  ▪ Vote Dilution: Drawing districts to scatter minorities so that they are not a critical mass in any one district. If done with a discriminatory _____, it's unconstitutional.

  ▪ Voting Rights Act: Requires racial gerrymandering to ensure minority success by creating majority-minority districts.

    - **Rule:** Race may be a factor in drawing district lines, but not the _____ or _____ factor.

    - Other factors include compactness and observing local, political subdivisions.

    - A bizarrely shaped district may be evidence of a predominant racial purpose.

b. Political gerrymandering (drawing districts to hurt one party)

  ▪ Can, in theory, violate equal protection. In practice, it is never struck down.

- The Supreme Court has not found any judicially manageable standards for implementing that guarantee.
- A political question (non-justiciable)

CHAPTER 12:   PRIVILEGES & IMMUNITIES, TAKINGS, AND PROHIBITED LEGISLATION

A. Privileges & Immunities Clauses Distinguished

Recall that the Privileges & Immunities Clause of *state* citizenship under Article IV prohibits serious discrimination against out-of-state _____, chiefly regarding employment.

> **Exam Tip 11:** The Privileges or Immunities of *national citizenship* under the 14th Amendment has no modern content and is *never* a strong answer that something is unconstitutional on the bar exam.

B. Takings

- Private property shall not be taken for _____ without _____.

  - **Public use**—basically anything the government wants to do with the property. It need only be _____ related to a _____ public purpose. This includes taking private property to resell to another private owner for purposes of economic development.
  - **Just compensation**—_____ at the time of the taking.

- Taking—This is where the controversy often occurs.

  - **Taking versus regulation**—If there is a taking of property, compensation is required; if there is a mere _____ on property, compensation is _____, even if the regulation reduces the value of the property.
  - **Economic impact**—The adverse economic impact of the government's action does not necessarily mean there has been a taking (e.g., a new prison built next door to a beautiful, countryside home). Many regulations can dramatically affect the value of property but that does not trigger a right to compensation.
  - **Physical occupation**—This is the key question. If the government physically occupies a private owner's property, then a taking has occurred and it owes just compensation.

    - If the government physically occupies only a tiny portion of your property, it is still a taking.

  - **No physical occupation**—Generally, no physical occupation means that no taking has occurred.

- Zoning—Not a taking and no compensation is required, so long as the zoning advances _____ interests and does not extinguish a fundamental attribute of ownership.
- Regulatory Taking—A zoning regulation can be considered a taking when it leaves **no economically viable use** for the property (rare).

> *Example 32:* *Two adjacent beachfront lots were purchased for the purpose of building a vacation home. After the lots were purchased, a new zoning law was passed, which stated that no permanent structure could ever be built on the property for environmental reasons. The Supreme Court said that no economically viable use was left for the owner, so this constitutes a taking and compensation is required.*

- Development permits—Development is often conditioned on "concessions" by the developer, such as building an access road or donating land to a park. Such exactions are valid so long as they can be seen as offsetting the _____ impact of the development.

C. Prohibited Legislation

- Bill of Attainder—A bill of attainder is a _____ punishment imposed without judicial trial and is unconstitutional.
- Ex Post Facto Laws—Unconstitutional to expand criminal liability _____, either by creating a new crime that applies retroactively to past conduct or by _____ the penalty for past conduct.
- Contract Clause—Bars states from legislative impairment of _____ contracts, unless there is an _____ need (something like an emergency).

CHAPTER 13: FREEDOM OF RELIGION

A. Establishment of Religion

1. **Three-Part Test of *Lemon v. Kurtzman*:**

   o Does the law have a _____ purpose?

   o Does the law have a _____ that neither advances nor inhibits religion?

   o Does the law avoid excessive government _____ with religion?

2. **Deficiency of *Lemon* Test**

   o Exceedingly difficult to apply

- It once was interpreted to condemn aid to religious primary and secondary schools, but **neutral aid** is now allowed (goes to everyone).
  - The government gives aid to parents and the parents are allowed to send their children to the schools of their choice.
  - The parents are making the decision as to whether a religious school gets the money.
    - The government is not picking and choosing recipients.

3. **Endorsement**
- It is a violation of the Establishment Clause for the government to endorse one religion over another and also to endorse religion over _____.
  - But, many endorsements are upheld, such as "In God We Trust" on currency.
- The Supreme Court wants to prevent _____ endorsement of religion (one that might override individual choice).
  - The Establishment Clause prohibits government endorsement of religion in a context that might prove coercive on an individual's conscience.
  - Examples:
    - Officially-sponsored school prayer is unconstitutional.
    - Officially-sponsored graduation prayer is unconstitutional.
    - Bible reading is permissible, but cannot be inspirational (e.g., as literature or poetry).
    - Display of the Ten Commandments is sometimes okay. It can be displayed for secular purposes (e.g., historical or promoting morals), but not to inspire religious belief.
      - Can teach the Ten Commandments in school as an example of an early legal code.
      - Cannot post the Ten Commandments in a classroom and leave it there every day of the school year—designed to inspire religious belief.
      - Cannot post the Ten Commandments in a _____ if the context makes plain that the purpose is to endorse religious belief.
    - Laws prohibiting teaching evolution have been struck down.
    - Legislative prayer is okay for historical practices.
    - Nativity scenes are okay on public property if there is something else there to dilute the religious message (e.g., Hanukkah symbols, Rudolph the red-nosed reindeer).

B. **Free Exercise of Religion**

1. **Religious Belief**

   Protected _____ (entitled to hold any belief or none at all)

2. Religious Conduct

- Protected qualifiedly

  - Laws regulating religious conduct because of its religious significance are unconstitutional (i.e., laws aimed at religion).
  - Neutral regulation of conduct: Neutral, generally applicable laws must be obeyed despite religious objections.

    - No right to accommodation.
    - No constitutional right to exemption from neutral, generally applicable regulations of conduct (e.g., *Peyote* case).

    Example 33: *Religious Freedom Restoration Act (RFRA) overruled the Peyote decision: Even neutral, generally applicable laws could not be enforced against religious objectors unless the government had a compelling interest. Insofar as RFRA applied to state and local governments, the Supreme Court struck it down as beyond federal legislative authority (Congress cannot force states to accommodate religious beliefs). RFRA would not be beyond federal legislative authority insofar as it applied to the federal government's own actions. Can states and localities require a religious accommodation for themselves? Yes.*

    - **Exception:** "Ministerial exception"—in 2012, the Supreme Court held that the First Amendment requires a ministerial exception to employment laws.

      - Non-discrimination employment laws cannot be applied to _____.
      - Plaintiff was a commissioned minister working as a teacher in a religious school. The school fired her in a plain violation of the Americans with Disabilities Act. She sought reinstatement as provided by the statute.
      - The Supreme Court held that the First Amendment precludes claims concerning the employment relationship between a religious _____ and its ministers.
      - The federal government cannot regulate employment relations between a religious institution and its ministers.
      - The term "minister" was construed **broadly**.

  - Campus Access: A state university that allows student groups to meet on campus must allow student religious groups equal access.

CHAPTER 14:   FREEDOM OF EXPRESSION (TIME, PLACE, AND MANNER)

A. Regulation of the Content of Expression

Content-based regulations of speech trigger _____ and are usually

_____.

1. Expressive Conduct (a.k.a. Symbolic Speech)

o Laws regulating expressive conduct are upheld if:

■ They further an _____ interest;

■ That interest is _____ to the suppression of expression; and

■ The burden on expression is no greater than necessary.

Example 34: *Laws against flag desecration are*

_____ *because they suppress an expressive type*

of speech to show disapproval.

Example 35: *Laws against public nudity are*

_____ *because public order must be kept, which*

is unrelated to speech.

o The key: If the government is trying to suppress a particular message, then the law will be struck down; if the government is trying to pursue an interest unrelated to the suppression of expression, then the law will be _____.

2. Vagueness and Overbreadth

o **Vagueness**: Vague laws are ones that give no clear notice of what is prohibited and thus violate due process.

o **Overbreadth**: Overbroad laws are ones that go too far in regulating speech. These laws burden _____ more speech than is necessary to protect a _____ interest and thus violate the First Amendment.

Example 36: *Laws that prohibit all nudity in drive-in movies are overbroad.*

> **Exam Tip 12:** Vagueness and overbreadth are almost always seen together on the bar exam.

3. Prior Restraints

o Are especially disfavored and will be struck down even when other forms of regulation might be upheld.

o Injunctions against speech are almost impossible to get.

B. Regulation of the Time, Place, or Manner of Expression (Content-neutral)

• Apply principally in a _____ forum.

- A public forum is a place traditionally reserved for speech activities. These places include
_____, _____, and
_____ around public buildings (but not airports).
- Only time, place, and manner may be regulated in a public forum. There are **three requirements**:

    1) Content neutral: Must be content neutral on its face and as
    _____. Also, must not allow executive
    _____.

        Example 37: *A local D.C. ordinance prohibited picketing within 500 feet of a foreign embassy if the picketing sign brought the foreign government into odium or disrepute. This is plainly content-based and is thus, unconstitutional.*

        Example 38: *Parade permit laws giving permits to first come, first served are constitutional. Parade permit laws giving the chief of police discretion are unconstitutional because the law may not be applied in a content-neutral way.*

    2) Alternative channels of communication must be left open: Time, place, or manner law must be a guideline for speech, not a flat prohibition of speech.

        Example 39: *Laws against amplified sound trucks during the night-time hours are fine. Laws against amplified sound during all times and all places would be struck down.*

    3) Must _____ serve a _____
    state interest: Under this test, most content-neutral time, place, or manner regulations are upheld.

        - Does not require a compelling interest

- Nonpublic forum

    o This includes all kinds of government property that is not a public forum (e.g., government offices, jails, power plants, military bases, etc.). Here, the government has great power. Basically, any _____ regulation of speech will be upheld.

        ▪ Viewpoint discrimination is invalid: One clearly unreasonable kind of regulation would be to discriminate based on viewpoint (e.g., between members of different political parties).
        ▪ Disruption of the functions of government: One should go outside to the public sidewalk surrounding the building since that is a public forum.

- Limited public forum

    o Describes a place that is not a traditional public forum, but that the government chooses to open to all comers (e.g., a municipal theater that anyone can rent).

- o In such areas, only time, place, or manner regulations are allowed, but this is a narrow category.

> *Example 40:* *A school auditorium is not a public forum, limited or otherwise. Just because a school auditorium is open to some speech does not mean it has to be open to all.*

CHAPTER 15:   FREEDOM OF EXPRESSION (CONTENT-BASED RESTRICTIONS ON SPEECH)

A. Regulation of Unprotected and Less Protected Expression

There are some categories of speech that can be regulated because of content.

1. Obscenity: Defined by the rule of "S"

- o **Sexy**: Must be erotic; appeal to the prurient interest. (Gore and violence are not legally obscene.)
- o **Society sick**: Must be _____ to the _____ person in the society. The society may be the nation as a whole, or a particular state, or a major metropolitan area.
- o **Standards**: Must be defined by the proper standards for determining what is obscene, not vague and/or overbroad.

> *Example 41:* *Tax on films displaying frontal nudity. Not a valid law because frontal nudity is not a good enough standard.*

- o **Serious value**: The material must lack serious value. If material has serious value (artistic, scientific, educational, or political), it cannot be held legally obscene. This determination is made by the _____, not the jury, and it must be based on a _____ standard, not a local one.
- o Footnotes on obscenity:
  - ▪ Minors: A lesser legal standard can be applied to minors, but the government cannot ban adult speech simply because it would be inappropriate for minors.
  - ▪ Child pornography: Can be prohibited whether or not it is legally obscene, and possession can be punished even if it is in the privacy of your own home.
  - ▪ Land use restrictions: Narrowly drawn ordinances can regulate the zoning of adult _____, but cannot ban them entirely.

> **Note 6:** Courts have recently begun to distinguish legally obscene speech from pornography. Merely establishing that speech constitutes pornography is generally insufficient to establish that the speech is obscene.

2. Incitement

Speech is not protected if it is an incitement to _____ violence.

3. **Fighting words**

   o Words likely to provoke an immediate _____.

      ▪ General vulgarity is not enough.
      ▪ Must be aimed/targeted at someone, and that person might hit back.
      ▪ In theory, fighting words are _____ protected speech.
      ▪ In fact, all fighting words statutes on the bar exam are unconstitutionally
        _____ and/or _____ (e.g.,
        laws against "hate speech").

4. **Defamation**

   o False statements of fact (not opinion) damaging to a person's reputation can be prohibited.
   o Public officials and public figures can recover for defamation only on proof of
     _____ or _____ falsity.
   o Private plaintiffs can recover on proof of _____ falsity.

      Example 42: United States v. Alvarez: *The Supreme Court struck down the*
      Stolen Valor Act. The Stolen Valor Act made it a crime to falsely claim receipt of
      military declaration or medals. The Act was struck down by the Supreme Court
      as applied to a local politician who lied about receiving the Congressional Medal
      of Honor. The Justices held that the fact that the statement was a blatant self-
      serving lie did not exempt it from First Amendment protection. The prohibition
      was content-based and was not supported by one of the five recognized
      categories of unprotected speech. The statute was unconstitutional.

5. **Commercial Speech**

   o Most regulations of commercial speech are _____. So long as
     the advertising is _____ and
     _____, it must be allowed.
   o **Test:** Regulation of commercial speech must directly advance a
     _____ government interest and be
     _____ tailored to that interest.
   o Misleading speech: Misleading commercial speech (unlike political speech) may be
     prohibited.

B. **Government Speech**

   • The First Amendment restrictions basically do not apply to the government as a speaker.
   • Government as a speaker is free to express a point of view (e.g., advertising the military).
   • The government does not have to accept all monuments donated by a private person simply
     because it accepts one—when the government is controlling the message, it is entitled to say
     what it wants.

- But specialty license plates bearing messages requested by purchasers are still government speech, so the government can refuse to issue plates that would be offensive to other citizens.

C. Corporations

Corporations have the same First Amendment right to speak as individuals.

CHAPTER 16: REGULATION OF THE MEDIA, REGULATION OF ASSOCIATION, SPEECH BY GOVERNMENT EMPLOYEES, AND CAMPAIGN FINANCE

A. Regulation of the Media

1. No Special Privileges

The press and media have no special privileges. They have the _____ rights as everyone else.

> **Exam Tip 13:** When asked about a law on the media, ask whether that law could be applied to you.

Example 43: *Confidential sources for the media. Does a reporter have a constitutional right to refuse to answer grand jury questions about a confidential source? Think of it in terms of yourself: You will not answer questions because you promised that you would not reveal a confidential source. Can the government force you to talk? Yes, you can be put in jail (held in contempt). The same is true of the media and press.*

Example 44: *Open trials—The press has the right of access to open trials.*

2. Broadcasters

- The only special case is broadcasters.
- Traditionally, because of early limits on the broadcast spectrum, the government had greater regulatory authority over broadcasters than over print media or the Internet.

B. Regulation of Association

- Freedom of association: Cannot be punished or disadvantaged because of political associations.
- Loyalty oaths: Public employees can be required to take a loyalty oath to the Constitution, but most loyalty oaths are struck down as _____ and/or _____.
- Bar membership: States can investigate good character, but they cannot deny admission based on political affiliations.
- Political parties: States cannot require _____ primaries (i.e., one in which you do not have to be registered as a member of the particular party to participate in the primary).

C. **Speech by Government Employees**

- General rule: Government employees generally cannot be hired or fired based on political _____, political _____, or any act of _____.

  o Can be fired for disrupting the workplace or not doing their jobs.

- **Exception:** This general rule does not apply to confidential advisors or policy-making employees (e.g., the President's cabinet officers).

D. **Campaign Finance**

- The use of money to support a political campaign is _____ and the regulation of that money raises First Amendment issues.

- Contributions versus expenditures:

  o Contributions _____ be regulated, provided that the limits are not _____ low.

  o Direct expenditures in support of a candidate, a campaign, or a political issue _____ be regulated.

    ▪ The rationale is to prevent corruption: a candidate could theoretically act in a certain way in exchange for a larger, direct contribution.

- Independent expenditures versus coordinated expenditures:

  o Independent expenditures *cannot* be regulated.

  o A coordinated expenditure is a disguised contribution (the campaign is in control) and _____ be regulated as contributions can be regulated.

- The constitutional protection of direct independent expenditures applies not only to individuals, but also to corporations, including nonprofits, and unions.

- The Supreme Court has consistently rejected _____ of campaign resources as a valid rationale for restricting campaign expenditures.

  > *Example 45:* *Congress passed the Millionaires' Amendment, which basically said that if your opponent spends a lot of his or her own money, then your contribution limit is automatically raised. The Supreme Court struck it down.*

[END OF HANDOUT]

Contracts & Sales

CONTRACTS AND SALES
PROFESSOR GEORGE S. GEIS
UNIVERSITY OF VIRGINIA SCHOOL OF LAW

CHAPTER 1:   INTRODUCTION

A. Introduction

- The MBE emphasizes certain topics over others and covers some ground that is rarely studied in first-year Contracts.

  a. Has an enforceable contract been formed?

  b. Has the contract been performed (or, has the performance been excused)?

  c. What are the remedies for breach?

- Always come back to these three questions if you get lost or confused.

1. What is a Contract?

- A contract is just a _____ .

- Look for an agreement plus a special legal basis for enforcing the promise (e.g., bargained-for consideration).

  > **Example 1:**   *I promise to give you $1,000 next week. You say "OK, I accept." Is this a contract? _____ .*

- The law of contracts and sales spans two parallel universes. **What universe are you in?**

  - **Universe One**—_____

    - We are in this universe whenever a contract deals with real estate or _____ .

      > **Example 2:**   *You hire me to mow your lawn. Is this contract governed by the common law? _____ .*

  - **Universe Two**—_____ of the UCC

    - We are in this universe whenever a contract deals with _____ .

      Note 1: The UCC governs all parties who enter into a goods contract, not just merchants.

      > **Example 3:**   *You agree to buy five dozen pencils from Staples. Is this contract governed by common law? _____ .*

      Note 2: The law of contracts is often the same in both universes, with some key differences arising on the MBE.

- o **Mixed contracts**—What universe are you in if the contract has elements of both services and goods?

  > *Example 4:* *You agree to purchase a hot-water heater from Boilermaker Inc. for $1,000. As part of the deal, Boilermaker promises to install the hot water heater in your home. Is this contract governed by the UCC?* _____.

  - ▪ **Rule #1**: The _____ rule. You cannot be in two universes at the same time, so mixed contracts must fall into one universe or the other.

    - • **Exception**: _____ contracts—the agreement is divided into two mini-contracts

      > *Example 5:* *You agree to purchase a hot-water heater from Boilermaker Inc. for $950. As part of the deal, Boilermaker promises to install the hot-water heater in your home for an additional $50. Is this latter installation part of the deal governed by the UCC?* _____.

  - ▪ **Rule #2**: The _____ rule. Does a good or a service play a bigger role?

    > *Example 6:* *You commission the famous artist Andy Warhol to paint your portrait for $1 million. Does the UCC apply?* _____.

    > *Example 7:* *You commission my mother-in-law, Mickey, to paint your portrait for $10. Does the UCC apply?* _____.

CHAPTER 2:   FORMATION—MAKING AN OFFER

A. In General

- • Has an enforceable contract been formed?
- • Four big topics within this question:

  1. **A**greement (offer and acceptance)
  2. **C**onsideration (and related theories for when you have to keep your promises)
  3. **D**efenses to formation (incapacity, duress, etc.)
  4. **S**tatute of Frauds (enforceability)

     > **Note 3:** If it helps, remember "**A**ll **C**ontracts **D**on't **S**tink."

B. Agreement

- • A contract is typically created by agreement. This can be broken down into the offer and the acceptance:

  - o Offer: "Will you go to the football game with me?"
  - o Acceptance: "Sure"

      o Counteroffer: "How about we go skating instead?"

C. Offer

- An offer is a manifestation of a willingness to enter into an agreement (by the offeror) that creates a _____ (in the offeree).

> **Note 4:** Think of the offer as a caterpillar: Cute and fuzzy, but fragile.

1. Creating a Legal Offer

- o Offer and acceptance are governed by the _____.

  - ▪ The outward appearance of words and actions matters—not secret intentions.

- o Key question—whether an offeror displays an objectively serious _____ to be bound

  > *Example 8:* *I offer to "sell you my Jeep Wrangler for $5,000." But I have my fingers crossed behind my back, and in my mind I'm thinking: "Of course I don't mean it; there is no way I'll sell the Jeep to you." If you say "OK," do we have a contractual agreement?* _____.

  > **Note 5:** Watch out for situations involving humor or anger—the offeror may not be displaying a serious intent to be bound under the objective test.

  > *Example 9:* *You see me on the side of the road with the hood of my Jeep Wrangler open and wires pulled out everywhere. I kick the side of my Jeep and yell "I'd sell this stupid junker for $5!" You yell back, "I ACCEPT." Do we have a contractual agreement?* _____.

  - ▪ Expressions of opinion?

    > *Example 10:* *We are talking casually in the law school parking lot when I lean against my Jeep Wrangler and ask you, "How much do you think this old thing is worth?" You reply (generously), "I don't know, maybe about $10,000." I say "OK, I accept." Do we have a contract?* _____.

- o An offer must usually be directed to a specific offeree. In other words, you cannot accept an offer unless it is directed at you.

  > *Example 11:* *You hear that there are a lot of good deals to be had on Wall Street. So you walk down through the trading pit, saying "I accept. I accept. I accept." Do you have any contracts with the stock traders?* _____.

  - ▪ Limited exception—contest offers or reward offers that promise something to anyone who accomplishes a certain task

    > *Example 12:* *I've lost my pet cat, Monster, and I take out a newspaper advertisement promising $100 to anyone who finds my cat by this Friday. You*

see the ad, find Monster, and come by my house on Thursday to collect the
reward. Do we have a contractual agreement? _____.

- How specific must your offer be? Two slightly different rules for the two different universes:

  - **Common law**—All _____ terms must be covered in the agreement.

    - This typically means the parties, subject, price, and quantity.

  - **UCC**—The law is more willing to fill the _____ and find a contract, even if the agreement leaves out some key terms.

    - Under the UCC, the only **essential** term is the _____.
    - The _____ does not need to be stated.

    Example 13:   Beth offers to pay Seth $50 every week to wash her car each Saturday for the next year. Is this deal covered by the common law? _____. Is it a valid offer? _____; it names the parties, the subject, the price, and the duration (quantity of washes).

    Example 14:   Beth offers to pay Seth a "fair price" every week to wash her car for the next year. Is this a valid offer? _____.

    Example 15:   Bob offers to buy 500 windshield wiper blades next week from Sue for $5 each. Is this deal covered by the common law? _____. Is it a valid offer? _____.

    Example 16:   Bob offers to buy 500 windshield wiper blades next week from Sue for a "fair price." Is this a valid offer? _____.

    Example 17:   Bob offers to buy windshield wiper blades next week from Sue for a "fair price." Is this a valid offer? _____ because there is no _____ term.

    Example 18:   Bob offers to buy "all the windshield wiper blades that I need for the next 10 years" from Sue for a "fair price." Is this a valid offer? _____, as a requirements contract.

- **Requirements contract:** "I don't know how many I need over the next year, but I promise to buy all of them from you."

  - The buyer is offering to buy 100% of whatever amount is needed from this individual seller.

- **Output contract:** "I don't know how many I will make over the next year, but I promise to sell all of them to you."

- The seller is offering to sell 100% of whatever amount is produced to this individual buyer.
  - o Both output and requirements contracts are specific enough under the UCC, even though they don't state an exact quantity term—they provide a formula for calculation.

- A valid offer must convey the power of acceptance to the other side (i.e., the offeree can simply say "I accept" and know that he has concluded the deal).

> **Exam Tip 1:** Here are two common fact patterns testing this concept:
>
> _____ —a preliminary communication that reserves a final right of approval with the speaker. It does not convey a power of acceptance to the other side.
>
> _____—usually understood as an invitation to deal (e.g., "Make me an offer for the advertised item; I'll probably accept it."). There are some exceptions:
>
> - Reward advertisements (*see* Example 12, above)
>
> - Advertisements that are very specific and leave nothing open to negotiation, including how acceptance can occur

Example 19: I tell you that "you'd better decide fast if you want to buy my house, as I expect to have a ton of offers next week." You say, "I accept." Is this a contract? _____.

Example 20: I place an advertisement in the paper promising "to sell my 1994 Jeep Wrangler for $5,000, first come, first served." You show up at my house waving a check and say, "I accept." Is this a contract? _____.

CHAPTER 3:   TERMINATING THE OFFER AND IRREVOCABLE OFFERS

A. Terminating the Offer (Squashing the Caterpillar)

- Look for one of six recurring fact patterns on the MBE (but also beware of irrevocable offers):

1. **The offeror_____ the offer by express communication to the offeree.**

   Example 21: I offer to sell you my house for $100. A split second later I yell "I revoke." Is there a squashed caterpillar? _____.

   Example 22: I offer to sell you my house for $1 million. A day later, I decide that I don't want to move and mutter to myself in my office "Forget it. I revoke that offer." Is there a squashed caterpillar? _____, the revocation must be _____ to the offeree.

2. **The offeree learns that the offeror has taken an action that is absolutely inconsistent with a continuing ability to contract. This is called a _____ revocation.**

Example 23: I offer to sell you my house for $1 million. A day later, you are talking with Mickey and learn that she bought my house that morning for $1.1 million. You run to my house waving a check and say, "I accept." Is this a contract? _____.

Example 24: I offer to sell you my house for $1 million. A day later, you are talking with Mickey and learn that I offered to sell her my house that morning for $1.1 million. You run to my house waving a check and say, "I accept." Is this a contract? _____.

Example 25: I offer to sell you a signed contracts textbook for $100. A day later, you are talking with Mickey and learn that she bought a signed contracts textbook from me for $100. You run to my house waving a check and say, "I accept." Is this a contract? _____, because there are lots of books available to sell.

3. The offeree _____ the offer.

>   *Example 26:* I offer to sell you my Jeep for $5,000. A split second later, you yell, "NO... I mean YES!" Is there a squashed caterpillar? _____.

4. The offeree makes a _____.

- ○ Operates as a rejection plus a new offer

>   *Example 27:* I offer to sell you my Jeep for $5,000. A split second later, you say "I offer to buy it for $4,500." I remain silent. Ten seconds later, you say "OK, OK, I'll buy it for $5,000." Is there a contract? _____, the counteroffer squashes the caterpillar.

>   **Note 6:** Be careful to distinguish a counteroffer from a mere counter-inquiry or indecision.

>   *Example 28:* I offer to sell you my Jeep for $5,000. A split second later, you say "Maybe not; I better check my bank balance." I remain silent. Ten seconds later, you say "OK, OK, I'll buy it for $5,000." Is there a contract? _____.

5. The offeror _____.

>   **Note 7:** Death of one party after the contract has been formed does not usually terminate the contract; we're talking here about **offers**.

6. A reasonable amount of time passes.

>   *Example 29:* I offer to sell you 1,000 barrels of oil for $100 each. You remain silent, and I never revoke. Five years later, when the price of oil has jumped to $500, you call me up and accept. Is there a contract? _____.

>   **Note 8:** Remember that even if an offer is squashed, the offeror can always throw out a new offer with the exact same terms as before ("revival").

B. Irrevocable Offers (Caterpillar's "Power Shield")

- The offeror is normally free to revoke at any time prior to acceptance.

> ***Example 30:*** *I offer to sell you my house for $1 million, and I promise not to revoke this offer for one week. Five minutes later, I say "Never mind. I revoke the offer." Can you still accept? _____.*

- An "irrevocable offer" can arise in four ways.

1. Option

> ***Example 31:*** *I offer to sell you my house for $1 million. You also pay me $100 in exchange for a promise that I will not revoke this offer for one week. Five minutes later, I say "Never mind. I revoke the offer." Can you still accept? _____.*
>
> *What if the $100 will go toward the $1 million purchase price if you exercise the option? _____.*

2. Firm Offer

- A merchant in the UCC universe can make a firm offer to buy or sell goods (i.e., a binding, free option).

  - **Merchant**—someone who regularly deals in the type of good at issue

    - I.e., a _____ _____, or a person holding himself out as having knowledge or skills particular to the goods

  - For purposes of this rule, a merchant is any business person, when the transaction is commercial in nature.

- A firm offer must be written, signed by the _____, and contain an explicit promise not to revoke.
- Time period—either: (i) as long as stated in the offer, or (ii) for a reasonable time period not to exceed 90 days

> **Editor's Note 1:** According to UCC 2-205, the "reasonable time" is not to exceed three months.

> ***Example 32:*** *I offer to sell you a contracts textbook for $100 and I promise via a signed writing not to revoke this offer for one week. Five minutes later, I say "Never mind. I revoke the offer." Can you still accept? _____, because Professor Geis is not a merchant.*

> ***Example 33:*** *Your law school bookstore offers to sell you a contracts textbook for $100 and it promises via a signed writing not to revoke this offer for one week. Five minutes later, the bookstore says, "Never mind. I revoke the offer." Can you still accept? _____.*

Example 34: *Your law school bookstore offers to sell you a contracts textbook for $100. Five minutes later, it says, "Never mind. I revoke the offer." Can you still accept? _____.*

Example 35: *Your law school bookstore offers to sell you a contracts textbook for $100 and it promises via a signed writing not to revoke this offer for one week. Ten days later, you stop by the bookstore to accept the offer. Can you still accept? _____, as long as a reasonable amount of time has not squashed the caterpillar (the offer).*

The firm offer has expired, and the bookstore may now revoke the offer. However, there is no indication that the bookstore has revoked the offer. The default question is whether a reasonable amount of time has passed (see Example 29).

3. **Unilateral Contract—Offeree has Started Performance**

   o A unilateral offer to contract cannot be revoked by the offeror if the offeree has started to perform.

      ▪ Unilateral contract—arises from a promise that requests acceptance by an _____ of the promisee

         • Compare this with a request for a return promise, which is a "bilateral contract."

         Example 36: *"I promise to pay you $1,000 if you promise to paint my house." Unilateral or bilateral? _____.*

         Example 37: *"I promise to pay you $1,000 if you take the action of painting my house." Unilateral or bilateral? _____.*

   o Because a unilateral contract can be accepted only by performance, the law gives the promisee the right to finish.

         Example 38: *I promise $10,000 to the winner of a swim race to Alcatraz Island. The swimmers dive off the dock and are going strong toward the island. When they're about halfway, I stand up on Fisherman's Wharf with my bullhorn and yell "I REVOKE!" Can the winner of the race insist on the prize? _____, this is a unilateral offer with part performance.*

         Note 9: The offeree is not required to complete performance and can stop at any time.

         Example 39: *You are swimming in the Alcatraz race, but you get tired and swim to a boat. Can I sue you for breach of contract? No; there's no agreement.*

4. **Detrimental Reliance**

- Arises when an offeree _____ and detrimentally relies on the offer in some foreseeable manner

    - Look especially for a general contractor/subcontractor context.
    - This is a special variant of the reliance theory of contractual liability (sometimes called "promissory estoppel").

        Example 40: *A builder who is bidding on a law school building project receives an offer from a subcontractor to supply all of the carpet for $20,000. Armed with this knowledge, the builder offers to renovate the building for $100,000. Before the law school accepts the bid, the subcontractor calls to revoke its carpet offer. Can the general contractor builder still accept the carpet offer from the subcontractor? _____ .*

CHAPTER 4:   ACCEPTANCE

A. Acceptance

- Acceptance—a manifestation of a willingness to enter into the agreement by the offeree

1. **Acceptance is governed by the _____ test.**

    - Starting place: "The offeror is master of the offer."
    - The offeree must accept the offer according to the rules of the offer.

        Example 41: *I offer to sell you my Jeep for $50 and state that in order to accept this offer, you must spring into a handstand, walk across the room to me on your hands, and sign this piece of paper. You look at me funny, just stand there, and say "I accept." Is there a contract? _____ .*

    - **Unilateral versus bilateral offers**—The offeror decides which type of offer to make, and the offeree must play by those rules.

        Example 42: *"I promise to pay you $1,000 if, and only when, you paint my house." You say, "I accept." Is there a contract? _____ , you haven't done what I said you must do to accept.*

        Example 43: *Bob sends a letter to Sue, reading "please ship me 500 windshield wiper blades next week for $5 each." Sue mails back a letter saying, "I accept." Unilateral or bilateral offer? Unclear without more information. Is there a contract? _____ , under the modern approach.*

        Note 10: Under the modern approach, if there is an ambiguity about whether the offer is unilateral or bilateral, acceptance can be by either performance or a return promise.

Example 44: *Bob sends a letter to Sue, reading "please ship me 500 windshield wiper blades by next week for $5 each." Sue ships 500 wiper blades the next day. Is there a contract? _____ .*

> **Note 11:** **TRICK** What if the seller tries to accept by shipping the wrong goods? The UCC treats this as acceptance plus breach.

Example 45: *Bob sends a letter to Sue, reading "please ship me 500 Bosch windshield wiper blades by next week for $5 each." Sue ships 500 Sloshed wiper blades the next day. Is there a contract? _____ , but also a breach.*

B. Other Acceptance Rules

1. The offer must be _____ to the person trying to accept it.

2. Even with an open-to-all offer, you must _____ about that offer in order to accept it.

   Example 46: *I've lost my pet cat, Monster, and I take out a newspaper advertisement promising $100 to anyone who finds my cat by this Friday. You never see the ad, but you find Monster roaming near my house and return the cat to me. Later, you learn about the reward offer and come by to collect. Do we have a contractual agreement? _____ .*

3. You must _____ your acceptance to the other party in order for it to become effective.

   Example 47: *You offer to buy my contracts textbook for $50. I say "I'll think about it." That night, while I'm alone brushing my teeth, I say to myself "that's a good offer… I should really accept that offer… in fact, I do accept that offer right now… I accept!" The next morning, you call me up and revoke the offer. Is there a contract? _____ .*

   o The requirement of communicating an acceptance can raise some timing issues. This is the subject of the _____ rule.

4. **Mailbox Rule**

   o General rationale—to determine when an acceptance has been legally communicated when there is some delay between sending and receiving
   o **The Rule**—An acceptance sent by mail is effective when the letter is _____ .
   o Does not apply:

   1) If the offeree sends something else _____ (e.g., rejection, counteroffer);

   2) To other types of communications (e.g., revocations, rejections);

   3) To _____ contracts; or

   4) It is unclear whether this applies to other media (e.g., fax, e-mail).

Example 48: *I send you an offer. You mail back your acceptance. I call you before I receive your letter and revoke. Is there a contract? _____.*

Example 49: *I send you an offer. You mail back your acceptance. The letter gets lost and never shows up. Is there a contract? _____.*

Example 50: *I send you an offer. You mail back your acceptance. You change your mind and call me up before I receive your letter to reject the offer. Is there a contract? _____, unless I detrimentally relied on the rejection.*

Example 51: *I send you an offer. You mail back a rejection. You change your mind and mail back an acceptance a few hours later. Both letters arrive at my house on the same day. Is there a contract? _____. It depends on _____.*

5. Acceptance Without Communication (By Silence)

o There are some exceptions to the requirement that you must communicate an acceptance to the offeror.

o Look for one of the following:

- Unilateral _____ offers or contests (e.g., my lost cat Monster)
- Unilateral offer in which the parties are geographically close (such that the offeror will see that performance has occurred)
- A _____ of silence serving as acceptance (such that the offeree should reasonably notify the offeror if she does not accept)
- The offer says that acceptance must come by silence, and the offeree _____ to accept the offer by silence.

Example 52: *I've lost my pet cat, Monster, and I take out a newspaper advertisement promising $100 to anyone who finds my cat by this Friday. You see the ad, find Monster, and come by my house on Thursday to collect the reward. Can you get the money even though you never communicated your acceptance to me? _____.*

Example 53: *Mickey buys her weekly keg of beer by calling up Pabst on Monday and leaving a message requesting delivery on Friday. One Monday, she leaves her message as usual, but Pabst does not deliver the keg that Friday. Distraught, Mickey asks if she has a contract for this keg. Does she? _____.*

Example 54: *I offer to sell you my Jeep for $500,000, saying "you may accept this offer by remaining silent for five seconds." You stare at me but don't say a word. After five seconds pass, do we have a contract? _____, unless you intend to accept.*

6. Implied-In-Fact Contracts

- ○ You can communicate an acceptance without writing or speaking.
- ○ This communication by gestures or actions is called an "implied-in-fact" contract.

> *Example 55:* *I walk into Cheapcuts, a popular haircut franchise where the service offerings and prices are posted above the cash register. The energetic receptionist offers to put my name in, and I sit down to wait. A short time later, someone comes forward and calls my name. I follow, and she cuts my hair. When I walk toward the exit, the receptionist tells me that I owe them $15. Must I pay—even though I never said a single word?*

_____

CHAPTER 5: COUNTEROFFERS AND UCC § 2-207

A. Common Law

- • The **common law** universe uses the _____ rule.

  - ○ The terms in the acceptance must match the terms of the offer exactly—or it is not an acceptance, but a counteroffer.

- • A conditional acceptance is another form of counteroffer.

  - ○ Look for: "if," "only if," "on the condition that," "but," etc.

    > *Example 56:* *I offer to mow your lawn on Saturday for $50. You say, "OK, if you come over on Sunday." Do we have a contract? _____.*

B. UCC § 2-207

- • The UCC universe is more forgiving for acceptances that do not match the terms of the offer exactly.

  - ○ The UCC replaces the mirror-image rule with § 2-207.

- • In some cases, a purported acceptance that does not match the terms of the offer exactly can still count as a legal acceptance.

  - ○ But, do not assume that all terms in the purported acceptance will govern the contract.

    > **Note 12:** It does not matter whether the parties are merchants for this part of § 2-207.

    > *Example 57:* *I run a business on the side: Geis's Chainsaws. You send me a purchase order requesting a chainsaw for $400. On the back of this form is an indemnification provision saying "**seller** agrees to indemnify **buyer** in the event of a lawsuit related to the chainsaw."*

*I send back a confirming memo that is exactly the same as the purchase order, except for a provision on the back saying "**buyer** agrees to indemnify **seller** in the event of a lawsuit."*

Editor's Note 2: Prof. Geis misspoke with regard to the seller's confirming memo. The seller's memo has the opposite indemnity provision of the buyer's provision.

The most likely outcome—we do not ever notice the difference, because nobody ever gets hurt. But it is possible that a dispute arises and one of us tries to back out of the deal. Is there a contract and, if so, which indemnity term, if any, controls?

1. Acceptance

Text of **§ 2-207(1):** "A definite and seasonable expression of acceptance [or a written confirmation] which is sent within a reasonable time operates as an acceptance even though it states terms additional to or different from those offered or agreed upon, unless acceptance is expressly made conditional upon assent to the additional or different terms."

> **Example 58:** *You send a purchase order requesting acceptance by this Friday. I send back my confirming memo two weeks later. Is there a contract? _____, because the purported acceptance is not timely.*

> **Example 59:** *You send a purchase order. I send back a timely confirming memo saying "Thanks, but I no longer sell chainsaws; however, I have a hand saw which you can have on the same terms." Is there a contract? _____, because this is not a definite acceptance of the original offer.*

> **Example 60:** *You send a purchase order. I send back a timely confirming memo saying "OK, on the condition that you agree to indemnify me against a lawsuit for harm arising from the chainsaw." Do we have a contract? _____.*

> **Example 61:** *Same facts as Example 60, but my acceptance letter has a bunch of terms on the back, all of which match yours, except for a clause that says "Buyer agrees to indemnify seller against a lawsuit for harm arising from the chainsaw." Do we have a contract? _____, under § 2-207(1).*

2. The Additional Term

o The new term in the acceptance may control under **§ 2-207(2)**, but only if all of the following are true:

1) Both parties are _____;

2) The new term does not materially alter the deal;

3) The initial offer did not expressly limit acceptance to its terms; and

4) The offeror does not _____ within a reasonable time to the new term.

- o It is very difficult for the new terms in the acceptance to govern the contract.

> ***Example 62:*** *Same facts as Example 61. Is my indemnity term part of the contract? _____.*

> ***Example 63:*** *Does the answer change if the buyer is Lowe's? _____, if the indemnification is _____.*

3. The Knock-Out Rule (Different Terms)

- o Arises when the acceptance has a *different* term from the initial offer (as opposed to just an *additional* term)
- o **Minority**—When the different term does not govern under § 2-207(2), the initial offer controls the terms.
- o **Majority**—"Knock out" both of the different terms; neither term will govern and the general gap-filling provisions of the UCC will apply.

4. Acceptance Based on Conduct

- o Parties might fail to make a contract but still act as though there is an agreement (e.g., exchange goods for money).
- o Under UCC § 2-207(3), only the terms that _____ agree on become part of the contract, with all other terms supplied by the UCC default rules.

C. UCC § 2-207—Confirming Memo

- • Arises when the parties have a contract (usually by verbal agreement) and one party sends a confirming memo with additional terms
- • Section 2-207(1): [A definite and seasonable expression of acceptance or] **a written confirmation which is sent within a reasonable time operates as an acceptance** [even though it states terms additional to or different from those offered or agreed upon, unless acceptance is expressly made conditional upon assent to the additional or different terms.]

> **Exam Tip 2:** If you see this fact pattern (early agreement + written confirmation with new terms), work through the same steps as above for § 2-207(2). But recognize that the new terms will very rarely come in.

CHAPTER 6:   CONSIDERATION, INCLUDING MODIFICATION AND PREEXISTING DUTY RULE

A. Consideration (and Related Theories)—The "C" in "All Contracts Don't Stink."

1. Bargained-For Consideration

- o Consideration—a deal in which the parties exchange promises involving a legal _____ or _____

> *Example 64:* I promise to pay you $1,000 if you do not watch the next season of The Bachelor. You do not watch the show, but I refuse to pay you the money. Who is the promisor? Professor Geis. Who is the promisee? You.
>
> Did I benefit from the exchange of promises? Not in a legal sense. Did you incur a legal detriment, even though not watching the show is good for you? _____. Is there bargained-for consideration? _____.

- Not doing something that you are legally entitled to do is a legal detriment.

o Gift promises and conditional gifts do **not** count as bargained-for consideration.

> *Example 65:* Every year for Christmas, Mickey gives me a tacky tie, and I give her an ugly sweater. Can she sue me this year if I refuse to give her a present? _____, we are exchanging gifts, not bargaining.

> *Example 66:* I promise to give you my Jeep if you come to my house to pick it up. Is there bargained-for consideration? _____. I am not bargaining for you to come. This is a conditional gift.

2. Tricks Regarding Consideration

a. Adequacy of consideration (nominal consideration)

- A pretense of consideration is insufficient.

> *Example 67:* I promise to sell you my Jeep for $1. Is there bargained-for consideration? _____, $1 is inadequate.

- A difference in economic value between the items exchanged is not grounds for finding inadequate consideration.
- As long as there is enough value, even subjective value to the person receiving it, consideration will be adequate.

b. Illusory promise

> *Example 68:* You promise to buy my Jeep for $5,000 on December 1, "if you feel like it." Is there bargained-for consideration? _____.

- A promisor must clearly commit to the deal or there is no consideration (i.e., there must be a way for the promisor to _____).
- Look for situations where one side is not really committing to the deal under the objective test. Examples:
  - "I would like to buy your car when I have more money."
  - "When the economy gets better, I will pay $5,000 for your car."
- Satisfaction contracts _____ illusory; they are real contracts with consideration.

  Example 69: *I promise to pay Mickey $500 if she paints a portrait of my family that meets my satisfaction. She says OK. Is there bargained-for consideration? _____.*

- Output and requirements contracts _____ illusory promises.
  - There is a way for a party to breach:
    - By requiring the product and purchasing from others; or
    - By making the product and selling to others.

c. **Past consideration is not consideration.**

  Example 70: *You are trying to win a race to Alcatraz, when the sharks start to circle. I swing my boat over to pick you up. Grateful, you promise to pay me $500 for the rescue. Is there bargained-for consideration? _____.*

d. **Promising not to sue**

- Settling a legal claim can be sufficient consideration, but only if:
  a) The plaintiff has a _____ belief in the validity of the claim; or
  b) There is reason to doubt the validity of the claim due to uncertain law.

B. Contract Modification

- Contract modification might require new consideration to be valid (the pre-existing duty rule)

1. Common Law

- Follows the **preexisting duty rule**—a promise to do something that you are already legally obligated to do is not consideration.

  Example 71: *You rent an apartment from Slumlord for one year; the rent is $2,000 per month. Later that year, you start running short on cash, and you both agree to modify the rent to $1,500 per month. Can Slumlord sue you at the end of that month for the extra $500? _____, at common law. (There is no bargained-for consideration for the modification of the contract.)*

- o **Exceptions:**

    1) A change in _____ ;

    2) A third party promising to pay; or

    3) Unforeseen difficulties that would excuse performance.

        Example 72: Same facts as Example 71, except you agree to re-rent the apartment for another year when the rent is lowered to $1,500 per month. Can Slumlord sue you at the end of that month for the extra $500? _____.

        Example 73: Same facts as Example 71, except Slumlord's sister (Slumlady) agrees to cover $500 of your monthly rent if you stay in the apartment. Is there bargained-for consideration? _____.

- o Promising partial payment for release from a debt obligation—ask whether the debt is currently due and undisputed. If so, the modification _____ binding.

        Example 74: Mickey owes me $50,000, due today. I promise to release her from this debt if she can pay me at least $1,000. If she does, can I sue her for the other $49,000? _____, because the modification is not valid.

        Example 75: Same facts as Example 74, except that the debt is not due until next year. If Mickey accepts the deal and pays me the $1,000 today, can I sue her next year for the other $49,000? _____, because the debt is not currently due.

2. UCC Modification

- o The UCC universe does not follow the preexisting duty rule.
- o Ask whether the modification is made in _____. If so, it is binding even _____ new consideration.

        Example 76: Mickey contracts with Pabst to buy her weekly keg of beer for $75. Later in the week, Pabst calls back to say that there is a worker shortage that week, and it can't get her the beer unless she pays $100 (so Pabst can outsource delivery to FedEx). Mickey says, "OK, charge what you must; I need my beer." Is the price modification binding? _____.

        Example 77: Same facts as Example 76, but Pabst knows that Mickey will do anything for her beer. On Friday morning, Pabst calls to say, "you better pay us $1,000 or we won't deliver your keg this afternoon." Mickey says, "OK, charge what you must." Is the price modification binding? _____.

CHAPTER 7: CONSIDERATION SUBSTITUTES (PROMISSORY LIABILITY)

A. Promissory Estoppel (or Reliance)

- Can arise when one party makes a _____, and the other party _____ on that promise to take some action
- Three key elements for a claim under reliance:

    1) A promise is made that would be _____ to induce reliance;

    2) The promisee does indeed take detrimental action in reliance on the promise; and

    3) _____ can only be avoided by enforcement of the promise.

    Example 78: *Grandpa Moneybags promises to pay his granddaughter Katie $100,000 next month so that she doesn't have to work anymore. Katie quits her job. Is this bargained-for consideration? _____. Does Grandpa nevertheless have to keep his promise? _____, under a reliance theory.*

    Note 13: Charities do not need to prove detrimental reliance (the second element) when pursuing a reliance theory to collect on a charitable-gift promise.

    Note 14: Remember that reliance was discussed earlier with respect to irrevocable offers (a type of caterpillar "power shield").

B. Quasi-Contract

- Sometimes called a "contract implied-in-law."
- Arises when you would have made a contract if you could have, but you could not, or when one party conferred a benefit on another party, and it would be fair to pay for that benefit
- Quasi-contract elements:

    1) The plaintiff confers a _____ on the defendant;

    2) The plaintiff reasonably expected to get paid; and

    3) It would be _____ to let the defendant keep the benefit without paying.

    - Look for an opportunity to decline or a good reason why there was no opportunity to decline.

    Example 79: *I am teaching away for this bar review course, when I suddenly grab my chest and keel over with a heart attack. A student rushes out to hire a doctor, who saves my life. Later, that student asks me to pay her back for the doctor's fee. Must I? _____.*

Example 80: *I learn about this cool thing called quasi-contract and rush over to paint your house while you are taking the bar exam. When you come home, I stick out my hand and demand a reasonable payment for the paint job. Will I recover? _____.*

- Quasi-contract damages are often limited, as justice requires, to the fair value of the benefit conferred.

> **Note 15:** When you see a situation that does not satisfy the normal requirements for a contract but still strikes you as unfair, ask whether quasi-contract might apply.

C. Moral Obligation Plus Subsequent Promise (the "Half Theory")

- A few jurisdictions have some case law suggesting that a moral obligation plus a subsequent promise to pay can be binding.
- Normally, this would be past consideration and thus not binding.

Example 81: *Recall the facts of Example 70. You are trying to win a race to Alcatraz, when the sharks start to circle. I swing my boat over to pick you up. Grateful, you promise to pay me $500 for the rescue. Is there bargained-for consideration? _____. Might I argue moral obligation plus subsequent promise? _____.*

D. The Seal

- Does a seal on a document act as a consideration substitute in most jurisdictions? _____.

CHAPTER 8: DEFENSES PART 1: MISUNDERSTANDING, INCAPACITY, AND MISTAKE

A. Defenses to Contract Formation—The "D" in "All Contracts Don't Stink."

- Seven Defenses:

    1) Misunderstanding

    2) Incapacity

    3) Mistake

    4) Fraud/Misrepresentation/Nondisclosure

    5) Duress

    6) Illegality

    7) Unconscionability

1. Misunderstanding

    o Arises when each party attaches a different meaning to the same words

- For this defense, you must show that:

1) The parties use a _____ that is open to two or more reasonable interpretations (the objective test cannot apply);

2) Each side attaches a different meaning to the term; and

3) Neither party knows, or should know, of the confusion.

   Example 82: *I verbally contract to sell you a bike for "twelve fifty." You think I'm trying to unload the bike by selling it for $12.50. I think you recognize that this is a rare edition bike and you are willing to pay $1,250. Do we have a contract? _____.*

   Example 83: *Same facts as Example 82, except I know that you would never pay $1,250 for the bike and must think the price is $12.50. Is there a contract? _____. For how much? _____.*

2. Incapacity

- Who lacks the capacity to make a contract?

1) _____ (under the age of 18)

2) People who are mentally ill—two standards:

   - The person cannot understand the nature and consequences of his actions; or
   - The person cannot act in a _____ in relation to the transaction (if the other side knows or has reason to know this).

3) Very intoxicated persons (if the other side knows or has reason to know this)

- What happens if you make a contract with a person who lacks capacity?

   - The contract is _____—the incapacitated party can disaffirm.

   - **Contract for necessities**—the party without capacity must still pay _____ (not necessarily the contract price)

      - **Necessity**— something you really need to live (e.g., food, clothing, or shelter)

   - A party without capacity can ratify the deal by keeping the benefits of the contract after capacity is obtained.

   Example 84: *Amelia is 16 years of age but looks much older. She buys a used airplane for $5,000. The wings fall off as she pulls away from the dealer's lot. Can Amelia get her money back? _____.*

   Example 85: *Same facts as Example 84, except the plane flies OK. Amelia turns 18 and continues to use the plane. Can she get her money back now? _____.*

Example 86: Same facts as Example 84, except Amelia is now 32 years of age and takes LSD prior to buying the plane. She has no idea what she is doing, but witnesses say she seemed perfectly lucid while negotiating and buying the plane. Can Amelia get her money back? _____.

3. **Mistake**

   o A mistake is a belief that is not in accord with a _____ fact.

      Example 87: Mickey contracts with her stockbroker to buy a share of Google stock for $500. When the price drops to $400 the following month, can she get out of the deal by saying, "I made a mistake; I thought the price was going to go up?" _____.

   a. **Mutual mistake (affecting both parties)**

      ▪ Allows the adversely affected party to rescind if:

         a) There is a mistake of _____, existing at the time that the deal is made;

         b) The mistake relates to a _____ assumption of the contract and has a material impact on the deal; and

         c) The impacted party did not _____ of mistake.

      Example 88: We are walking along a trail, when I lean down to pick up a shiny rock. "Wow," I say, "look at that diamond. I'll sell it to you for $10,000." You agree and pay me the money but are sad to learn later that the rock is plain quartz. Can you get out of the contract? _____, for mutual mistake.

      Example 89: Same facts as Example 88, except I say "Wow, look at that shiny rock; I wonder what it is," and then you say, "I don't know what it is, but it is pretty amazing." I say, "whatever it is, I'll sell it to you for $10,000." You agree. Can you get out of the contract? No, this is a "compromise of conscious ignorance."

      Editor's Note 3: Professor Geis misstated the party names while reciting Example 89. The correct party names and facts appear above.

   b. _____ **mistake (one party)**

      ▪ Allows the adversely affected party to rescind if:

         a) She can prove all of the elements of mutual mistake; **and**

         b) Either:

            i) The mistake would make the contract unconscionable; or

            ii) The other side knew of, had reason to know of, or caused the mistake.

Example 90:   *Mickey decides to move to an annual purchasing model for her beer kegs and solicits 25 brewers for offers. Twenty-four of the brewers quote her prices in the $100,000 to $120,000 range. But one brewer makes a mistake about the quantity of kegs she lists and quotes a price of $10,000 for the year's supply. Can Mickey snap up the last deal? _____.*

Note 16: Only the adversely affected party can claim the defense.

CHAPTER 9:   DEFENSES PART 2: FRAUD, DURESS, ILLEGALITY, AND UNCONSCIONABILITY

A. **Defenses to Contract Formation (Continued)**

  4. **Fraud, Misrepresentation, and Nondisclosure**

  o **Misrepresentation**—a statement at the time of contracting that is _____.

    ▪ Can be intentional (fraudulent) or accidental

  o To assert this defense, the party must show:

    1) A misrepresentation of a _____ (not opinion);

    2) That is _____ OR fraudulent (intentional); and

    3) That is made under circumstances in which it is justifiable to _____ on the misrepresentation.

    Example 91:   *Before buying my Jeep Wrangler for $3,000, you ask me how the car runs. I say, "it's a great car." In actuality, it only runs on four out of six cylinders, and the radiator leaks. Can you get out of the contract? _____, if this is an opinion.*

    Example 92:   *Same facts as Example 91, except you ask me if the car runs OK, and I say "yes," knowing that it has all the mentioned problems. Can you get out of the contract? _____, due to intentional fraud.*

    Example 93:   *Same facts as Example 92, except I don't know about these problems. Can you get out of the contract? _____, due to material misrepresentation.*

    Example 94:   *Same facts as Example 93, except the only thing wrong with the car is that the cigarette lighter doesn't work. Can you get out of the contract? _____.*

  o **Fraud in the Execution**—you trick someone into signing something that they do not even know is a contract

    Example 95:   *You're walking down the street when you run into Dave Matthews. You ask for his autograph and then laugh when he hands back the paper. If you show that he just signed a contract promising to play music at*

your birthday party for just a $100 fee, is Dave bound? _____, this is
fraud in the execution.

- ○ **Nondisclosure**—the other party does not learn the truth about something, but now you just remain quiet

    - ▪ Normally, you do not need to tell the other side about all material facts related to the deal.

        > **Editor's Note 4:** Professor Geis erroneously states that this common law principle of "buyer beware" continues to apply to the sale of a residence. It does not. See MBE Real Property outline III.B.4.

    - ▪ **Except:** A special (fiduciary) relationship or active _____

        > *Example 96: I'm selling my house, but I have a bad termite problem. I hide the ripples in the floor with carpets and put plants on the damaged stairways. You buy the house but soon learn of the termite infestation. Can you get out of the contract for nondisclosure? _____.*

5. Duress

- ○ An improper threat that deprives a party from making a meaningful choice to contract
- ○ _____ duress—arises when one party makes threats to induce another party to contract (or modify a contract)

    > *Example 97: Pabst threatens to breach a contract with Mickey to sell her beer unless Mickey agrees to extend the contract for another year at double the price. Mickey has exhausted her credit with every other brewer and feels that she has no choice but to accede to this threat. Is Mickey bound for the next year? _____.*

- ○ Undue influence—arises when a party puts very intense sales pressure on another party, who often seems weak-minded or susceptible to high-pressure sales tactics.

6. Illegality

> **Editor's Note 5:** Because they do not impact the requirement that contracting parties have a "meeting of the minds," the defenses of illegality, contracts against public policy, and unconscionability are enforcement defenses, not formation defenses. This means that they do not prevent the formation of a contract, but will impact its enforceability.

- ○ Illegal contracts are unenforceable.
- ○ But, a contract entered in _____ of an illegal act (that is not itself illegal) will still be enforced.

    > *Example 98: Mobster Tony Soprano agrees to pay Paulie $10,000 to knock off Artie. Is this legally binding as a contract? _____, because it is for an illegal action. Tony cannot sue Paulie for breach if he refuses to perform the contract.*

> *Example 99:* *Same facts as Example 98. Paulie hires a taxi to drive him over to Artie's restaurant. Can Paulie claim an illegality defense to avoid paying the cab driver? _____.*

- Typically, the law will just leave the parties where they stand. There is a modern trend toward allowing less-guilty parties to recover restitution (i.e., get their money back).

  > *Example 100: Same facts as Example 99, except Tony pays Paulie the $10,000 up front. If Paulie refuses to perform, can Tony get the money back? _____. The losses will lie where they may.*

- **Contracts against public policy**—are not enforced

  - These are contracting situations that are not formally illegal but present some other policy concern (e.g., a broad exculpatory agreement).

7. Unconscionability

- This is the ultimate contract defense. Everything seems fine, but a court simply looks at the deal and says, "No, this shocks my conscience. It's unconscionable."
- Two varieties of unconscionability:

  1) _____ unconscionability—a defect in the bargaining process itself, usually:

     - A hidden term (surprise); or
     - An absence of meaningful choice (no other contracting option).

  2) _____ unconscionability—a rip-off in some term of the contract

- Some jurisdictions require both varieties to be present before a deal is stuck down; others may act if only one variety is present.

  > *Example: When you started law school, you signed a license to use Westlaw products. Buried on page 110 of a 235-page contract is a clause in which you agree to pay 25% of your salary for the first five years after you graduate law school.*

CHAPTER 10:   STATUTE OF FRAUDS (PART 1)

A. Statute of Frauds—The "S" in "All Contracts Don't Stink."

- The Statute of Frauds (SOF) is a barrier that some contracts must meet in order to become legally binding.
- **Goal**—to prevent false assertions about a contract that was never really created

  > *Example 101: I walk up to you one day and say, "I'm so glad that you agreed to sell me your mansion for just $50,000." You stare at me puzzled and reply,*

"Who are you? We've never met." I laugh and say, "See you in court." Will I win the lawsuit? _____; the Statute of Frauds will bar my claim.

- You should always ask two questions here:

    1) Does the Statute of Frauds apply to this transaction? Are we in SOF world?

    2) If so, has the Statute of Frauds been satisfied?

- Contracts in SOF world require a higher and special form of proof—typically a writing signed by the defendant or some performance on the purported deal.

B. Is the Contract in the Statute of Frauds World?

- Recall that the Statute of Frauds applies to only a few types of contracts:

    1) **M**arriage—a contract made in consideration of marriage (like a prenup)

    2) **S**uretyship—a contract promising to guarantee the debt of another

    3) **O**ne year—a contract that by its terms _____ be performed within one year from its making

    4) **U**CC—applies to goods contracts for a price of _____ or more

    5) **R**eal property—a contract for the sale of an interest in real property

    Note 17: Remember Mr. SOUR (or M. SOUR) the mascot of Lemonhead candy.

    Example 102: *Mickey buys beer on credit from Pabst, promising to pay $499 at the end of the month for her five kegs. Pabst sues her at the end of the month for failure to pay. Are we in Statute of Frauds world? _____.*

    Example 103: *Same facts as Example 102, except Pabst now sues me, claiming that I had offered to pay Mickey's bill if she could not. Are we in Statute of Frauds world? _____, suretyship.*

- **The main-purpose exception**—if the main purpose in agreeing to pay the debt of another is for the surety's own economic advantage, then we _____ in SOF world.

    Example 104: *Same facts as Example 103, except Pabst sells beer to Mickey that she brings over to my house for weekly parties. Pabst sues me, claiming that I had offered to pay Mickey's bill if she could not. Are we in Statute of Frauds world? _____, because of the main purpose exception.*

- The one-year rule is interpreted very narrowly; the question is whether there is _____ for the contract to be performed within one year.

    Example 105: *I verbally contract with the mayor of Charlottesville to build an exact replica of the Egyptian pyramids at the edge of town for $50 billion. Are* *we in Statute of Frauds world? _____. It may be difficult, but it is not impossible to complete the contract within one year.*

Example 106: I verbally contract with the mayor of Charlottesville to manage all city elections through 2028 for $50 per election. Are we in Statute of Frauds world? _____.

Example 107: I contract on April 1 to hire a 1L student as my RA for three months during the summer after her 2L year of law school. Are we in Statute of Frauds world? Yes. The length of the employment is only three months, but it won't even start until after one year from now.

> **Editor's Note 6:** The Statute of Frauds applies to a contract that cannot be performed within one year from its making.

Example 108: Luke Skywalker hires me to teach him contract law for the rest of his life. Are we in Statute of Frauds world? _____. It is possible that Skywalker could die within one year.

- All contracts involving real property are not automatically in SOF world; only those transferring an interest in the property.
- Leases of less than one year are usually not in SOF world.

Example 109: Skywalker hires Chewbacca to build a house on an acre that Skywalker owns on Endor. Is this contract in Statute of Frauds world? _____. It involves land but does not transfer an interest in land.

Example 110: Skywalker agrees to sell his Endor acre to Chewbacca for $5 million. Is this contract in Statute of Frauds world? _____.

Example 111: Mickey verbally contracts with Pabst to buy exactly $500 in beer. Are we in Statute of Frauds world? _____, under the UCC part of the SOF.

CHAPTER 11: STATUTE OF FRAUDS (PART 2)

A. Has the Statute of Frauds been Satisfied?

- Two main ways to satisfy the SOF—by _____ or by _____. The exact requirements differ between our parallel universes.

1. Service Contracts that Cannot be Performed within One Year

- o Full performance of a services contract **by either side** satisfies the Statute of Frauds.

Example 112: Skywalker verbally agrees to hire Chewbacca to build a house on his Endor property. In exchange, Skywalker will provide "charm lessons" to Chewie for the next three years. Is this contract in Statute of Frauds world? _____.

Chewie builds the house, but Skywalker refuses to provide the lessons, asserting a Statute of Frauds defense. Is Skywalker right? _____.

- o Part performance of a services contract does not satisfy the Statute of Frauds.

2. A Writing Signed by the Party Against Whom the Contract is Asserted

- o Do you need both signatures on the writing? _____.
- o Does the writing have to be a formal contract? _____.
- o It must cover the fundamental facts:

    1) Show that a contract has been made;

    2) Identify the _____; and

    3) Contain the _____ elements of the deal.

3. Real Estate

- o A signed writing will satisfy the Statute of Frauds.
- o Part performance of a real estate contract can satisfy the Statute of Frauds if **any two** of the following three elements are met:

    1) Possession;

    2) Payment;

    3) Improvements _____.

    Example 113: *Chewbacca claims that Skywalker agreed to sell his Endor acre for $5 million. There is no signed writing, but Chewie now possesses the land and has erected a nice house by the lake. Is this contract in Statute of Frauds world? _____. Is the Statute of Frauds satisfied? _____.*

4. Goods (UCC)

a. Signed writing

- ▪ A signed writing will satisfy the SOF, but the requirements differ a little:

    - • There is no need to mention the _____;
    - • The writing must mention the _____ of goods sold.

- ▪ The contract is only enforceable under the SOF for the quantity mentioned in the writing.

    Example 114: *Mickey verbally contracts with Pabst to buy 100 kegs of beer for $75 each. Later, Pabst sends her a signed confirmation order stating that the parties agree to contract for 50 kegs of beer (no price is listed). Even later, Pabst* *asserts a Statute of Frauds defense and refuses to sell Mickey any beer. Can Mickey satisfy the Statute of Frauds? _____, but only for 50 kegs.*

b. Part performance

- **Part performance** satisfies the SOF, but only for the quantity delivered and accepted.

   Example 115: Same facts as Example 114, except there is no confirming memo. Mickey changes her mind and decides to order some kegs of Fat Tire beer. Later, Pabst delivers 25 kegs to Mickey, and she eagerly stores the kegs in her basement. Can Pabst satisfy the Statute of Frauds? Yes, but only for the 25 kegs delivered and accepted. Is Mickey contractually obligated to buy the other 75 kegs from Pabst? _____, the Statute of Frauds will bar that claim.

c. Custom-made (or specially manufactured) goods

- These are *exempted* from the Statute of Frauds.
- The maker can satisfy the SOF as soon as it makes a _____ _____ toward the manufacturing of the goods.

   Example 116: I contract verbally with Brooks Brothers to buy 100 white dress shirts with "GSG" monogrammed on the sleeve for $10,000. Brooks Brothers sends me the shirts, but I change my mind and send the shirts back. Can I assert a Statute of Frauds defense if Brooks Brothers sues for the $10,000? _____, the custom-goods exception applies.

d. A judicial admission

- Includes a statement in a pleading or during testimony, etc.
- This satisfies the Statute of Frauds under the UCC.

e. Confirming memo

- The **failure to object** to a confirming memo within 10 days will satisfy the Statute of Frauds—but only if both parties are _____.

   Example 117: Mickey verbally contracts with Pabst to buy 100 kegs of beer for $7,500. Later, Pabst sends her a signed confirmation memo with all of the material terms. Mickey has changed her mind, crumples up the memo, and throws it in the corner. Ten days later, does Pabst satisfy the Statute of Frauds? _____. Mickey is not a merchant.

   Example 118: Same facts as Example 117, except the buyer is now Whole Foods. Ten days after the memo arrives at Whole Foods, does Pabst satisfy the Statute of Frauds? _____, even though there is no signed writing by Whole Foods.

5. Miscellaneous Statute of Frauds Problems

○ **Agency law**

- Do you need a signed writing to authorize an agent to form a contract that is in Statute of Frauds world? _____.
- This is known as the "_____ rule."

- ○ **Modification**
  - Suppose you have a deal that is in SOF world, and the requirements are met. Now the parties want to modify that deal. Must the modification also satisfy the Statute of Frauds requirements? _____.
  - Ask whether the deal, with the alleged modification, would be in Statute of Frauds world.
    - If so, the Statute of Frauds requirements must be met for the modification;
    - If not, there is no Statute of Frauds requirement, even though the initial deal was in Statute of Frauds world.

    Example 119: Mickey contracts with Pabst to buy five kegs of beer for $500. Later, Pabst sends her a signed confirmation memo with all material terms. Mickey alleges that they later modified the deal to three kegs only for $300. Does she need to supply written proof of this alleged modification? _____. Because the contract (as modified) is not within the SOF world, the modification is not required to satisfy the SOF.

    If Mickey argues that the deal was modified to 10 kegs for $1,000, then the modification must satisfy the SOF because the modified contract is in SOF world.

CHAPTER 12: PERFORMANCE AND THE PAROL-EVIDENCE RULE

A. Second Main Question: Has the contract been performed?

- Four big topics within this question:
  1) **P**arol-evidence rule
  2) **W**arranties
  3) **C**onditions
  4) **E**xcuse of performance obligations (impracticability, frustration of purpose, etc.)

  Note 18: Remember "Pizza With Crawling Escargot"

B. The Parol Evidence Rule (PER)—The "P" in "Pizza With Crawling Escargot."

- First, determine what the agreement entails.
  - ○ If the parties have reduced their contract to a comprehensive writing, then earlier statements or writings related to this agreement are not part of the deal under the PER.

- o Does the PER apply to later written or verbal statements about the deal? _____, that's a modification.
- o Does the PER apply to earlier written documents? _____.

- Gateway Question: Have the parties created an integrated writing?

    - o _____ integration—the contract expresses all terms of the agreement.
    - o _____ integration—there is a final writing, but some terms are not included.

- How do you distinguish an agreement that is not integrated from one that is completely or partially integrated?

    - o Look for a _____ clause (evidence of complete integration).

        > *Example 120:* Disney signs a contract with Hugh Grant to make a movie for $2 million. It contains the following language right above the signature line: "This is the entire agreement between the parties. No representations or promises have been made save for those set out in this memorandum." Hugh argues that Disney had verbally promised to provide a free house in Beverly Hills while he was filming, and failed to do so. Can he introduce this evidence? _____.

        > *Example 121:* Same facts as Example 120, except Hugh argues that during the meeting, but after the written contract was signed, they verbally agreed that $2 million was not enough and that he would get $3 million. After the meeting, Disney sent Hugh a check for $2 million. Can Hugh introduce evidence that Disney promised to pay Hugh $3 million? _____.

    - o Courts may also ask whether, under the circumstances, an extrinsic term of the agreement would "naturally be omitted" from the writing.

        - ▪ If so, it may not violate the parol-evidence rule and can be introduced as evidence if it does not contradict the writing.

            > *Example 122:* Same facts as Example 120, except Hugh argues that Disney verbally offered him, prior to signing, a sequel part for $5 million. Can he introduce this evidence? Tough call.

    - o The UCC universe is more forgiving.

        - ▪ Presumes that a writing is, at most, only a partial integration—**unless** the parties would have _____ included a disputed term in the writing

- Situations in which the PER does not apply to bar earlier evidence:

    1) Will not bar evidence relevant to a defense against contract formation (duress, mistake, fraud, etc.)

2) Even if a writing is completely integrated, a party can introduce evidence of a
_____ deal.

> *Example 123: Same facts as Example 120, except Hugh now argues that Disney verbally offered, prior to signing, to sell him a season pass to Disneyland for $1,000. Can he introduce this evidence? _____.*

3) Even if a writing is completely integrated, a party might be able to introduce evidence of a prior communication that is designed to interpret an
_____ in the final agreement.

> *Example 124: Same facts as Example 120, except the parties disagree over what "movie" means in the contract. Disney believes that Hugh will make "Mrs. Doubtfire 2." Hugh claims that they had verbally agreed that he would make "Driving Miss Daisy 2." Can Hugh introduce this evidence? _____, as long as the term "movie" is sufficiently ambiguous.*

- Some people confuse the parol-evidence rule with the Statute of Frauds.

  o If the question does not have a signed writing, think
  _____.

  o If the question does have a signed writing, along with an earlier discussion of the deal, think
  _____.

CHAPTER 13: WARRANTIES AND EXPRESS CONDITIONS

A. Warranties—The "W" in "Pizza With Crawling Escargot"

- A warranty is a promise about a term of the contract that explicitly shifts _____ to the party making the promise.

  > *Example 125: I agree to sell you my Jeep for $5,000, but we don't discuss any other term. If the wheel falls off as you drive away, can you get out of the deal? It's uncertain. The buyer would need to argue mistake, duty to disclose, etc.*
  >
  > *What if I include a warranty that the Jeep will run fine for the next 1,000 miles? _____, you can get out of the deal.*

- You can also _____ all warranties.

  > *Example: I might sell the Jeep on an "as is" basis.*

  > **Exam Tip 4:** Three types of warranties might arise on the exam. These apply in the UCC universe.

1. Express Warranty

  o A promise that affirms or describes the goods and is part of the basis of the bargain is an express warranty unless it is merely the seller's opinion.

- The use of a sample or model creates an express warranty that the goods sold will be like the sample.

> *Example 126:* *You walk into an AutoZone store to buy some hubcaps. The clerk shows you some floor samples that are bright gold and says these are our best model. You buy that model of hubcaps but find that they are an ugly yellow color when you pull them out of the box. AutoZone has breached an _____ warranty.*

2. **Implied Warranty of Merchantability**

- This warranty is triggered only when the seller is a _____ dealing in the goods at issue.
- Warrants that the goods are fit for

_____.

> *Example 127:* *You walk into an AutoZone store to buy some polish for your hubcaps. The clerk waves you over to aisle 12 where you pick up a can of hubcap polish. When you spray it on your hubcaps, they turn an ugly yellow color. AutoZone has breached an implied warranty of*
>
> *_____.*

> *Example 128:* *You walk into an AutoZone store and the clerk tells you that their delivery van is for sale. You buy it, but it breaks down the next day. Has AutoZone breached the implied warranty of merchantability? _____, this is a one-off good; AutoZone is not a merchant in vans.*

- Can a merchant disclaim this warranty? _____, if it is very clearly done.

  - Look for VERY CONSPICUOUS language; and
  - Look for the term "merchantability."

> **Editor's Note 7:** Unless the circumstances indicate otherwise, the warranty can be disclaimed by use of "as is," "with all faults," or similar language that makes plain that there is no implied warranty. The disclaimer may be oral, but it must use the term "merchantability" and must be conspicuous if in writing.

3. **Implied Warranty of Fitness for a Particular Purpose**

- Triggered when a buyer relies on a seller's expertise to select a special type of good that will be used for a special purpose
- Warrants that the goods will satisfy this special purpose

> *Example 129:* *Same facts as Example 127, except you can't decide between three different types of hubcap polish. You ask the clerk which one is right for your aluminum-alloy hubcaps, and he picks up a can and says, "THIS is the brand you want." When you spray it on your hubcaps, they turn an ugly yellow*

color. AutoZone has breached an implied warranty of

_____.

- ○ Can a nonmerchant extend this warranty by implication? _____, as long as the buyer relies on any seller's expertise.
- ○ Can this warranty be disclaimed? _____.
    - Must use CONSPICUOUS language, such as "as is"
    - Disclaimer must be in _____.

B. Conditions—The "C" in "Pizza With Crawling Escargot"

- • Another way to shift risk by stating that one party's contractual obligation will only kick in if some future event takes place

    > *Example 130: Your rich and eccentric Aunt promises you $5,000 if you pass the bar exam—on the express condition that you study with Bar Breeze. You take Themis and easily pass the exam. Must your aunt pay you the $5,000? _____.*

- • Conditions can be express or implied.
- • The most important implied condition is the "constructive condition of exchange."

1. Express Conditions

- ○ Express conditions are created by language in the contract.
    - Look for magic words like "only if," "provided that," "on the condition that," "only in the event that," etc.
- ○ Express conditions must be _____, unless the condition is somehow excused.

    > *Example 131: Mark contracts to work for The Egg House for 10 weeks building a new henhouse for the chickens. The parties agree that Mark will get $10,000 for building the house, along with a bonus of $5,000 awarded on the condition that he shows up every day for work. Mark finishes the henhouse, but he doesn't come to work for the last two days in week 10 because he is really sick. Can Mark collect the $5,000 bonus? _____.*

a. Satisfaction conditions

- How are these conditions met? It depends on the nature of the performance.

    Preferred approach—use an _____ standard of satisfaction.

    - ○ If most reasonable people would be satisfied, then the condition is met.
- • Contracts involving aesthetic taste—such as art or tutoring services—use a _____ standard.
    - ○ The party can still breach if they claim dissatisfaction in bad faith.

Example 132: I promise to pay Mickey $500 if she paints a portrait of my family, and the painting meets with my satisfaction. She says OK. After she is finished, the portrait is revealed, and all of the art critics rave over the masterpiece. But I hate it. Must I pay Mickey the $500? _____.

b. Waiver

▪ The party receiving the protection of the condition may waive the condition by _____ or _____.

Example 133: You agree to buy my Jeep for $5,000 on the express condition that you can get a car loan for this amount at an interest rate of 10% or less. You can only get a loan for 12%, but you still want to buy the Jeep. If you waive the financing condition, must I sell you the Jeep? _____. Can I waive the financing condition? _____.

▪ A condition will also be waived if the other party

_____

with or hinders the occurrence of the condition.

● This will be judged by a good-faith standard.

Example 134: Same facts as Example 133, but you decide that you don't want the Jeep after all. You refuse to provide any documentation to the bank considering your loan and tell the loan officer that you're a lazy deadbeat. Will the financing condition excuse your performance? _____.

CHAPTER 14: IMPLIED CONDITIONS

A. The Constructive Condition of Exchange (CCE)

One party's performance is conditioned on the other side's performance.

Example 135: You agree to buy my Jeep for $5,000 next Friday. The day we meet I refuse to sign over the pink slip. Do you have to pay me the $5,000? _____.

B. Common-Law Universe

● The doctrine of substantial performance states that a party will satisfy the CCE if there is not a

_____.

Example 136: Shaquille O'Neal hires me to build him a house. I build the doorways all at standard height (6'6") instead of the 8' listed in the contract. Shaquille is mad because he must duck to get from room to room. Has there been substantial performance? _____, this is a material breach, a "big deal."

● Substantial performance only works to satisfy the CCE if the failure is not _____.

Example 137: I hire you to build the Geis Tower, a 150-story building in Charlottesville, Virginia, for $100 billion. When you finish, I conduct the final walkthrough and notice that the lobby walls are made of baby blue marble from North Carolina, not dark blue marble from Virginia, as called for in the contract specs. Can I avoid paying you the $100 billion? _____. Assuming the breach was innocent, the CCE has been satisfied.

Example 138: Same facts as Example 137, but our contract includes the following express condition: "Geis's payment obligation under this contract is expressly conditioned on the use of dark blue Virginia marble in the lobby." Must I pay the $100 billion? _____. This is an express condition, not a constructive condition.

- If payment must be made (because there is only a minor problem) can the nonbreaching party recover **damages** for the deficiency? _____.

  - o Typically measured as the cost to complete the performance
  - o Sometimes limited to the diminution in market value

- Can a breaching party who fails to satisfy the CCE due to a **material** breach get paid anything?

  - o _____—maybe quasi-contract

- Can a breaching party who fails to satisfy an **express** condition get paid in quasi-contract?

  - o Usually not, express conditions must be strictly satisfied.

- **Divisibility**—If a contract is clearly divisible, then it will be broken into mini-contracts for the purposes of determining if there has been substantial performance.

    Example 139: Mickey contracts with Best Buy to install a kegerator in each of the 20 rooms in her house for $2,000. If Best Buy only installs five kegerators before it abandons the job, is this substantial performance? _____, the contract is not divisible; Mickey is paying for the full job.

    Example 140: Same facts as Example 139, except Mickey agrees to pay Best Buy $100 for **each** of the 20 kegerators. If Best Buy installs only five kegerators before it abandons the job, can it collect anything on the contract? _____, if the contract is divisible: Best Buy can collect 5 × $100 = $500.

C. UCC Universe: Performance

- The UCC requires _____.

    > **Exam Tip 5:** Do not discuss substantial performance or material breach if the contract involves goods.

  - o Exceptions—contract explicitly changes the default rule; installment contracts

- Perfect tender has two main obligations:

1) Perfect _____

2) Perfect _____

> *Example 141: Mickey contracts for 500 pints of Fireball whiskey for $5,000. Fireball sends Mickey only 495 pints. Is this perfect tender? _____, Mickey can reject all of the whiskey.*

> Note 19:Rejection of the goods is not the same as rejection of an offer.

1. Revocation of Acceptance

- The buyer may **revoke an acceptance** of the goods if the goods seem OK when delivered but a defect is discovered within a reasonable time.

> *Example: Under the facts in Example 141, Fireball delivers all 500 pints of the whiskey, and Mickey stores the bottles in her cellar. A month later, she opens a bottle to find that it is cola (not whiskey). She can revoke her acceptance and send the bottles back.*

2. Seller's Right to Cure

- If the seller **fails to tender perfect goods** and time is left on the contract **or** the seller had reasonable grounds to believe that the buyer would accept a replacement, then the buyer must give the seller a chance to _____.

3. Delivery

- The default method of delivery under the UCC is **one** delivery of the goods.
- The UCC allows for _____ contracts (agreement for delivery in separate lots).

  - The buyer can reject a specific delivery that is not perfect only when there is

    _____

    in the installment that cannot be cured.

> *Example 142: Same facts as Example 141, except Mickey contracts for one pint of Fireball whiskey to be delivered each day at 5:00 p.m. for 500 days. Delivery #345 comes at 5:15 p.m. Can Mickey reject that delivery? _____. Even though it was not perfect tender, the UCC allows Fireball some leeway because this is an installment contract.*

4. Method of Tender/Delivery

a. Tender at Seller's place of business

  - If the goods are to be tendered at the seller's place of business, then the seller just needs to give the goods to the buyer.

b. _____ contract [F.O.B. Seller's place of business]

- If the contract is a shipment contract, then the seller must take three actions to satisfy perfect delivery:

  a) Get the goods to a _____;

  b) Make arrangements for _____; and

  c) _____ the buyer.

c. _____ contract [F.O.B. Buyer's place of business]

- If the contract is a destination contract, then the seller must get the goods to the **buyer's** business and notify the buyer.

  Example 143: I contract with Brooks Brothers (located in New York) to buy "100 white dress shirts for $10,000 F.O.B. my house in Charlottesville." Has Brooks Brothers satisfied its delivery obligation when it gives the shirts to FedEx and sends me an e-mail saying that they are coming? _____, because "F.O.B. my house in Charlottesville" makes this a destination contract.

5. Risk of Loss Problem

- Arises when there is a **goods** contract followed by **damage** or destruction of the goods **before** the buyer receives them. Who will bear the loss, the seller or the buyer?

  1) Check whether the parties have already dealt with the risk problem in the contract. If so, their agreement will control.

  2) If not, ask whether either party has **breached** (typically another part of the contract).

     - If so, the breaching party bears the risk of loss.
     - Is this true even if the breach is totally unrelated to the delivery damage? _____.

  3) If there is no breach, and the goods are being shipped, then ask what type of delivery contract it was:

     - If it was a **shipment** contract, then the risk of loss during delivery rests with the _____.

     - If it was a **destination** contract, then the risk of loss during delivery rests with the _____.

  4) In all other cases, ask whether the seller is a **merchant.**

     - If so, the risk of loss stays with the seller until the buyer _____ the goods.
     - If not, the risk of loss moves to the buyer when the seller _____ the goods.

Example 144: I contract with Brooks Brothers to buy "100 white dress shirts for $10,000." Brooks calls to tell me that the shirts are ready, and I can pick them up at the store when I like. That night, the store burns down, and my shirts are destroyed. Do I have to pay for them? _____. (In this risk of loss problem, you continue to the last step in analysis. Seller is a merchant. Therefore, the risk of loss stays with the seller.)

Example 145: Professor Geis contracts with the law school bookstore to sell 10 used copies of his book for $10 each. He tells the bookstore manager that he has left the books outside his office, so she can get them whenever. That night, a pack of law-review editors steals and burns all of the books. Does the bookstore have to pay for them? _____. (Again, you go through all the steps. Because Professor Geis is not a merchant, the risk of loss moves to the buyer and the bookstore has to pay for the books.)

CHAPTER 15:   EXCUSES

A.   Excuses—The "E" in "Pizza With Crawling Escargot"

- There is a contract, but something has happened to prevent one side from having to perform.

1.   Impossibility and Impracticability

- ○ Look for these common fact patterns:

  - ▪ Performance becomes _____ after the contract is formed;
  - ▪ The subject matter of the contract is _____; or
  - ▪ In a services contract with a "special person," the performing party _____ or is incapacitated.

- ○ BUT, something that just makes performance more expensive than expected will not normally excuse performance.
- ○ Look for something that hinders the *ability* to perform, not just the *cost* to perform.

  Example 146: Mickey contracts with a local tavern, The Whisky Jar, to bartend for one year in exchange for free drinks. If "Prohibition II" is passed, outlawing alcohol consumption in Virginia, must Mickey perform this contract? _____.

  Example 147: You contract to reroof my house for $10,000, but before you can perform, my house burns down. I insist that our contract requires you to rebuild my house and then reroof it. Am I right? _____.

  Example 148: You contract to dig a wine cellar for me for $10,000. After you start performing, you hit some big rocks and realize that it will cost you twice as much to finish the job, resulting in a loss on the contract. Are you excused from performing? _____.

o Look for an unforeseen event in which the non-occurrence of the event was a basic assumption of the contract, and the party seeking discharge was not at fault.

2. **Death after a Contract**

   o Dying does not normally excuse liability on a contract that has been made.

      ▪ The estate will normally be on the hook for any contractual obligations.

         Example 149: Old Man Jones finds out that he only has a few more months to live. So, he goes out and borrows $1 million from a bank and invests the money in jewelry. When he dies, is his debt contract with the bank excused? _____.

   o Ask whether there is something special about the person performing on the contract, such that it makes no sense to continue if they die.

         Example 150: You hire the Rolling Stones to play your birthday party next month for $1 million. If, sadly, Mick Jagger dies before the big date, can the rest of the band show up and play for the $1 million? _____, your contractual obligation is excused. Likewise, the band's obligation is excused as well.

3. **Frustration of Purpose**

   o Performance can still occur, but something has happened to undermine the entire reason for the creation of the contract.

   o This is very rare—the event must be extreme and not previously allocated to one of the parties.

         Example 151: You are excited for the season opener of your favorite football team, especially after paying $2,000 for season tickets. You sit down 20 rows up on the 50-yard line, when right before kickoff, a tall man in an Abe Lincoln hat sits down in front of you. He refuses to remove the hat, and you can't see the game. Can you get out of your contract for the football tickets? _____.

         Example 152: You rent an apartment in Chicago at $5,000 for one day because it has a prime view of Wrigley Field, and the Cubs are scheduled to play in the World Series that afternoon. The game is unexpectedly canceled one day before because of an earthquake. Is performance excused due to impossibility? _____. What about being excused for frustration of purpose? _____.

4. **Performance is Excused Because the Initial Contract has been Modified or Canceled**

   o Can both parties agree to just walk away from a contract? _____, as long as there is some performance remaining from each side.

      ▪ Otherwise, there is no consideration for this modification.

Example 153: I contract to sell you my Jeep for $5,000. We meet to swap the money for the pink slip, but both of us want to back out. Can we just say forget it? _____.

Example 154: I contract to paint your house for $5,000. After I finish the job, we agree to rescind the deal. Is this valid? _____.

B. Accord and Satisfaction

- The parties to an earlier contract agree that performance will be satisfied instead by the completion of a different performance.

  - The new performance is called the _____.
  - The excusal of the initial performance obligation is called the _____.

    Example 155: Pabst owed Mickey $500. Later, the parties agree that if Pabst delivers 100 cases of beer, then it does not need to pay Mickey the $500. If Pabst delivers the cases of beer, can Mickey still sue for the money? _____.

- If the accord is not performed, the other side can sue on **either** the original obligation **or** the new promise.

    Example 156: Same facts as Example 155. If Pabst delivers nothing, then Mickey can sue for the $500 or the 100 cases of beer.

- **Distinguishing accord and satisfaction from modification:**

  - If the party to perform has **an option** to satisfy a contract obligation by doing something else, then it is an accord and satisfaction.
  - In a modification, it is clearer that the parties have **changed** the performance obligation.

C. Novation

- Arises when BOTH parties agree that a substitute person will take over the contractual obligations.

  - Can one side decide to create a novation by asking someone else to do the work? _____, this is called a "delegation," (discussed later).

- If there is a valid novation, then the original promisor will be excused from performance.

    Example 157: Mickey contracts with Pabst to buy five kegs of beer for $500. Later, both parties agree that Blatz will take over the deal. If Blatz fails to deliver any beer, can Mickey sue Pabst? _____, the novation has excused Pabst.

CHAPTER 16:   ANTICIPATORY REPUDIATION; EXPECTATION DAMAGES (PART 1)

A.   Third Main Question in Contract Law: What are the remedies for breach?

1.   Constructive condition of exchange (CCE)

- **Common law**—failure to substantially perform means the other side may withhold their own performance

  ▪ Cannot withhold payment if the other side has substantially performed, but may be entitled to recover for the breach

- **UCC**—perfect tender: Seller must strictly perform all obligations or be in breach.

  ▪ The doctrine of material breach applies to installment sales.

B.   Anticipatory Repudiation

- Closely related to the CCE, but it deals with a slightly different question:

  - What are your remedies when the other side says they are not going to perform on the contract (repudiation) before performance is due?

    Example 158: I hire you to build the Geis Tower, a 150-story building in Charlottesville, Virginia, for $100 billion by December 31. On July 31, when you're about halfway finished with the project, I let it slip that I'm broke and never going to pay you the money. Do you have to keep working on the tower? _____, as long as my repudiation is clear and unequivocal.

- If a party clearly and unequivocally repudiates, the nonbreaching party has two options:

  1) Treat the repudiation as a _____ and sue immediately for damages

     • BUT, if you have completed the entire performance and are only waiting for payment, **you cannot sue early.**

  2) Ignore the repudiation, demand performance, and see what happens

     Example 159: Same facts as Example 158. If you decide to sue me for money damages, must you wait until December 31, or can you sue on July 31? You can sue on _____.

     Example 160: Same facts as Example 159, except you completed the Geis Tower ahead of schedule on June 30. If you decide to sue me for money damages, must you wait until December 31, or can you sue on July 31? You _____.

- Can a party **retract** its repudiation? Yes, as long as the other side has not:

  - Commenced a _____; or
  - Acted in _____ on the repudiation (by materially changing its position).

- **UCC**—Reasonable grounds for insecurity about the other side's performance allows you to demand an _____ of performance.
  - If the party fails to respond within a reasonable time, you can treat this as repudiation.

    Example 161: I agree on January 1 to buy 100 white shirts from Crooks Brothers for $1,000. Half of the money is due on February 1; the balance and the shirts are due on March 1. In the middle of January, I see a news exposé about financial trouble at Crooks Brothers, and it fails to return my phone calls. I send a letter demanding adequate assurance of performance on January 15. If they say, "don't worry, we're almost done with the shirts," must I make the $500 February 1 payment? _____. What if they don't respond? _____.

C. Money Damages

Note 21: Money damages are the typical remedy in contract law.

1. Expectation Damages

- This is the normal way to calculate damages in contracts.
- Goal—to put a party in the same _____ it would be in if the contract had been performed as promised.
- Measured by comparing the **value of the performance** without the breach to the value of the performance with the breach.

    Example 162: I hire you to build the Geis Towers, a 150-story building in Charlottesville, Virginia, for $100 billion. You never start the project and tell me that you are breaching the contract. What are my expectation damages if I hire a replacement builder for $110 billion? _____

    _____

    Example 163: Same facts as Example 162, but the replacement builder costs only $80 billion. What are my expectation damages? _____; I've benefitted from your breach. Do I have to pay you? _____.

- **UCC**—work through this basic formula to determine any expectation damages question.

    Example 164: Buyer breach. Mickey contracts with Pabst to buy a keg of beer for $100. Mickey repudiates the contract, and Pabst sells the keg to a liquor store for $80. What are Pabst's expectation damages? _____

    _____.

    Example 165: Buyer refusal to pay. Mickey contracts with Pabst to buy a keg of beer for $100. Mickey gets the keg but breaches the contract by refusing to pay. The current price for a keg of Pabst has risen to $110. What are Pabst's expectation damages? _____.

Example 166: Seller breach. Mickey contracts with Pabst to buy a keg of beer for $100. Pabst fails to deliver the keg, and Mickey has to buy her keg from Blatz for $120. What are Mickey's expectation damages? _____

_____.

When Pabst refuses to deliver, can Mickey buy a keg of Utopias for $25,000 and sue Pabst for $24,900? _____, cover must be similar.

Example 167: Seller breach. Mickey contracts with Pabst to buy a keg of beer for $100 (paid up front). When Pabst delivers the keg, it is only half full, but Mickey is desperate to get her keg and keeps the keg. It can be shown that a half keg of Pabst costs $60 at the corner liquor store. What are Mickey's expectation damages? _____

_____.

Example 168: Same facts as Example 167. Can Mickey send the keg back instead? _____, under the perfect-tender rule.

CHAPTER 17:   EXPECTATION DAMAGES (PART 2)

A. Limits on Expectation Damages

- There are three major limits on the calculation of expectation damages.

1. Expectation Damages

- o Must be proven with _____.

  Example 169: Will Ferrell decides to run for president and agrees to pay CNN $5 million for ten 30-second advertising slots. CNN forgets to run the ads. Ferrell argues that but for this breach, he would have been elected president, and he sues for the four-year salary of the president. Can he get this as expectation damages? _____, there is too much uncertainty.

- o Also arises with an unproven business venture—trouble proving lost profits from a consistent sales track record

2. Unforeseeable Consequential Damages

- o Not recoverable unless the breaching party had some reason to know about the possibility of these special damages at the time of contracting (the *Hadley* rule)
- o Two categories of damages:

  1) **General damages**—the type of loss that almost anyone would incur from a breach

     - Includes incidental damages—the cost of storing rejected goods, or finding a new buyer, or finding a replacement vendor

  2) **Consequential damages**—losses that are unique or special to this plaintiff

Example 170: I hire FedEx to deliver Super Bowl tickets to a buyer on eBay for $20. FedEx refuses to honor the contract, and I have to pay UPS $50 for rapid delivery to get the tickets there in time. I also use up $5 in gas driving to UPS. What are my expectation damages against FedEx? _____

_____.

Example 171: Same facts as Example 170, except I cannot get another carrier to deliver the tickets in time, and as a result, the buyer doesn't pay me the $2,000 ticket price. Because I bought the tickets for $200, can I sue FedEx for my lost profits of $1,800? _____, this is an unforeseeable consequential damage.

Example 172: Same facts as Example 170, except I also provide FedEx with the exact details of my transaction. Can I now recover my lost profits? _____, assuming that there are no other disclaimers in the contract.

3. Mitigation

o A breached-against party must take reasonable steps to reduce damages from breach.

Example 173: I agree to pay you $10,000 to fix my roof, which has major holes (I tell you this). You breach the contract. Can I sit in my bed and ring up the cash register every time it rains? _____, I have to hire someone else to do the job.

o If a party refuses to mitigate, the law will calculate damages as if the party did mitigate.

o The defendant bears the burden of proving a mitigation failure.

Example 174: Same facts as Example 173, but I don't hire a new roofer for several months. My oriental carpets (worth $25,000) are ruined from rain and snow. Eventually, I hire another roofer to do the job for $12,000. I sue you for $25,000 + $2,000 = $27,000. Should I receive this amount? _____

What is my recovery if you can show that there was another roofer able to do the job for $9,000 at the time that you told me of the breach? _____

o Mitigation efforts must be reasonably similar to the original contract.

Example 175: Shirley MacLaine contracts with MGM to make a movie entitled "Bloomer Girl" for $10 million. MGM decides not to make the movie, but it offers her a replacement part for $10 million in a country-western movie. If MacLaine refuses to take the part, can MGM argue that she has failed to mitigate, such that expectation damages are zero? _____, this is not reasonably similar mitigation.

B. Special Problems with Expectation Damages

1. Lost Volume Profits (LVP)

o If the paying party breaches, then normally the selling party needs to mitigate by reselling the goods or services to another person.

o But if the seller is a retailer who sells this type of product all the time, the seller might try to argue for LVP.

> *Example 176: Outrigger contracts to sell Mickey a speedboat for $15,000 (which cost Outrigger $10,000 to buy from the manufacturer). The following week, Mickey repudiates the sale. The very next day, Will Ferrell walks in to buy the same boat for $15,000. Mickey argues that Outrigger's damages are zero because it fully mitigated her breach with the sale to Ferrell. Is she right? _____, if Outrigger can show that it had plenty of boats to sell and few buyers. If Outrigger does get LVP, how should these be calculated? _____*
>
> _____

2. Incomplete Performance

o If the paying party breaches in a partially completed building contract, can the builder continue to work on the job? _____, this runs counter to mitigation—it would be "running up the damages."

o Adjust the recovery to take account of the fact that the builder did not need to finish the job

o Use this formula:

▪ *Expectation Damages = Contract Price – Amount already Paid – Amount that Would Be Needed to Finish the Job*

> *Example 177: I hire you to build the Geis Towers, a 150-story building in Charlottesville, Virginia, for $100 billion, with $10 billion due every month. You start the project, and I pay you for the first three months. After that, I tell you that I'm repudiating the contract and won't pay another dime. You had expected to build the tower for $85 billion (netting a $15 billion profit), but you have spent only $45 billion thus far. Can you recover the $70 billion balance on the contract price? _____, you didn't do all of the work. What should you get?*
>
> *Expectation damages = _____*
>
> _____
>
> _____

3. Economic Waste and Diminution in Market Value Damages

o The normal measure of expectation damages is the cost to complete the job.

> *Example 178: I hire you to build the Geis Towers, a 150-story building in Charlottesville, Virginia, for $100 billion, with $10 billion due each month. You*

start the project, and I pay you for the first three months, and then you repudiate the contract. I have to pay someone else $80 billion to finish the job. How much can I recover from you under expectation damages? The cost to complete the job: _____

_____

- o Sometimes cost-to-complete damages will dramatically overcompensate the plaintiff.

    Example 179: I hire you to build the Geis Towers, a 150-story building in Charlottesville, Virginia, for $100 billion. When you finish, I'm conducting the final walk-through and notice that the lobby walls are made of marble from North Carolina, not marble from Virginia (as called for in the contract specs). I sue you for breach and demand $20 billion (to tear it down) plus $100 billion (to rebuild it with the right marble). Should I get the $120 billion in cost-to-complete damages? _____.

- o **Diminution in market value ("DMV")**—How much lower is the market value of what you got versus what you wanted?

    - ▪ The breaching party normally must have acted in an innocent and unintentional manner for DMV damages.

    Example 180: Same facts as Example 179. If you can show that your use of North Carolina marble was unintentional, what damages must you pay for the breach? DMV, probably zero, or maybe a slight amount if I can show that Virginia marble would increase the market value of the Geis Towers.

CHAPTER 18:   OTHER MONEY DAMAGES AND SPECIFIC PERFORMANCE

A. Reliance Damages

- • Goal—to put a party in the same economic position that it would be in if the contract had never been _____ in the first place

    Note 22: RELIANCE DAMAGES = GROUNDHOG DAY DAMAGES

- • Ask what loss has the plaintiff incurred that would never have taken place but for the breached contract?

    Example 181: Recall the facts of Example 169, in which Will Ferrell decides to run for president and agrees to pay CNN $5 million for ten 30-second advertising slots. CNN forgets to run the ads. Ferrell cannot recover the four-year salary of the president. Can he get anything under reliance damages? _____, the cost of making all the ads.

- • A party _____ recover both expectation and reliance damages; typically, the plaintiff must elect one or the other.

B. Restitution Damages

- Goal—to give the plaintiff an amount equal to the economic benefit that the plaintiff conferred on the defendant
- This can sometimes equal reliance damages, but it need not.

> *Example 182: Owen Wilson pays $50,000 to Dr. Plastic, a famous surgeon who promises to "make Wilson's nose perfect." Wilson also incurs $20,000 in hospital costs related to this procedure. Dr. Plastic botches the job, and Wilson sues for restitution damages. What does Dr. Plastic owe Wilson? _____, the benefit that Owen Wilson conferred upon Dr. Plastic.*

> *Example 183: Same facts as Example 182, but Wilson sues for reliance damages. What does Dr. Plastic owe Wilson? _____* _____

> *Example 184: Same facts as Example 182, but Wilson sues for expectation damages. How would these be calculated? _____* _____

C. Liquidated Damages

- Stated in the contract as an explicitly negotiated amount due upon breach
- Courts are wary about awarding punitive liquidated damages and will do so only if:

  1) The amount of liquidated damages was _____ at the time of contracting; and

  2) Actual damages from breach would be uncertain in amount and difficult to prove.

> *Example 185: Same facts as Example 182, but Wilson and Dr. Plastic agreed that the doctor would pay Wilson $500,000 if the operation was a failure. Will these liquidated damages be enforced? _____. What if the liquidated damages were $500 million? _____. This is likely to be viewed as a penalty that will not be enforced.*

D. Punitive Damages

- Punitive damages are almost never allowed in contract law.
- Don't worry about these unless you see a breach that also seems like a tort (e.g., fraud or some other very extreme situation).

E. Specific Performance/Injunction

- Equitable relief is the exception, not the norm in contract law.
- Awarded only when monetary damages are considered inadequate for some reason.
- Specific performance is presumptively available for _____ transactions.

Example 186: Hugh Grant contracts to buy a Napa Valley winery for $25 million. If the seller breaches, can Grant get specific performance? _____. What if the seller has already transferred the land to another bona fide purchaser? _____.

- Specific performance is presumptively not available for contracts of _____ service.

  o Rarely, a court might grant an injunction prohibiting a breaching party from performing similar services for a competitor for a reasonable period of time/place (the *Lumley* doctrine).

    Example 187: Hugh Grant contracts to make a movie with Disney for $3 million. If Grant breaches, can Disney get specific performance, forcing Grant to act in the movie? _____.

    Example 188: Same facts as Example 187. Can Disney get an injunction prohibiting Grant from acting in another Hollywood movie for the next three months? _____, under the Lumley *doctrine.*

- **UCC**—Specific performance is available only for **unique goods** like art or custom-made items.

    Example 189: You purchased the original Saturday Night Fever dance floor in an auction, but the seller refuses to perform on the contract. Can you get specific performance? _____.

- **Right of reclamation**—arises when an unpaid seller tries to reclaim goods that were sold on credit when the buyer is insolvent

  o To assert this remedy, the following facts must be present:

    1) The buyer is _____ at the time of receipt of the goods;

    2) The seller must demand the return of goods within 10 days of receipt (or within a reasonable time if the buyer misrepresented his solvency to the seller in writing within three months before delivery); and

    3) The buyer still has the goods.

    Example 190: Mickey is broke, but she contracts for 500 pints of Fireball whiskey for $5,000 on credit. Fireball sends all 500 pints but learns of Mickey's financial situation and asks for the whiskey back five days later. Must Mickey return the whiskey? _____.

CHAPTER 19:   THIRD-PARTY BENEFICIARIES

- Three main concepts:

    1) Third-party beneficiary contracts

    2) Assignment

    3) Delegation

A. Third-Party Beneficiary Contracts

- Whether a third party can sue to enforce a contract made by two other people

1. Identify the Parties

- **Promisor**—the person making the promise that the outsider is trying to enforce
- **Promisee**—a contractual counterparty to that promise; this person could presumably enforce the contract, but is not doing so.
- **Third-party beneficiary**—the outsider suing the promisor for the breach

    Example 191: Abe agrees to pay Beth $50 if Beth mows Cam's lawn. Beth never shows up, and Cam files a lawsuit against Beth. Who is the promisor? _____. Who is the promisee? _____. Who is the third-party beneficiary? _____.

2. Types of Third Parties

- The critical issue is whether the third party is an intended or an incidental beneficiary.

    - _____ beneficiaries have the right to sue.
    - _____ beneficiaries do not.

- To determine whether a given third party is an intended or an incidental beneficiary, ask whether the initial counterparties (promisor and promisee) intended to convey enforcement rights to the third party in the event of a breach.

    Example 192: Same facts as Example 191. Is Cam an intended beneficiary? _____. Can the promisee, Abe, sue Beth? _____.

    Example 193: Same facts as Example 191. Don lives across the street from Cam, and he has to buy $15 in weed killer when weeds blow over from Cam's yard into Don's yard because Beth didn't mow the lawn. Can Don sue Beth for breach? _____, Don is an incidental beneficiary.

    Example 194: Same facts as Example 191. Earl runs a gas station that Beth uses to gas up her lawn mower. Earl would have earned $5 in profits if Beth had performed on her contract with Abe. Can Earl sue Beth for breach? _____, Earl is an incidental beneficiary.

- A _____ beneficiary arises when the promisee strikes a deal with the promisor in order to repay some earlier debt to the third party.

> **Example 195:** *Cam loaned Abe $500 last month. In satisfaction of this debt, Abe agrees to pay Beth $500 if Beth mows Cam's lawn 10 times. Beth never shows up, and Cam files a lawsuit against Beth. Cam can sue Beth because he is a creditor beneficiary.*

- A donee beneficiary arises when there is no preexisting obligation, but the promisee clearly intends to confer a gift of enforcement on a third party.

> **Example 196:** *Abe buys a policy from Bottomless Life Insurance. Under this contract, Abe will pay $500 per year to Bottomless, and Bottomless will pay $500,000 to Cam when Abe dies. Can Cam sue Bottomless if it fails to pay the claim? _____, because he is a donee beneficiary.*

3. **Revoking Third-Party Rights**

- The initial counterparties might try to revoke or modify the third-party's right to enforce the contract.
- Ask whether the third party knows about the promise and has changed position in reasonable reliance on the promise.
  - If so, the third party may be able to make out a claim under promissory estoppel (see Example 78)
- A third party will not lose enforcement rights if any of the following facts is true, as these facts cause the right to vest:
  - The beneficiary _____ on the rights (similar to promissory estoppel);
  - The beneficiary _____ to the contract; or
  - The beneficiary _____ to enforce the contract.
- The promisor can assert any contract defense against the third party that he would be entitled to assert against the promisee.

> **Example 197:** *Abe points a gun at Beth's head and promises to "sell" Beth a contract law casebook if Beth pays $225,000 to Cam. Beth says "OK" but doesn't pay the money to Cam. Would Beth have a contract defense against Abe? _____, duress. Can she assert this defense to avoid having to pay Cam? _____*

CHAPTER 20: ASSIGNMENT AND DELEGATION

A. Assignment

- Assignment—the transfer of **rights** under a contract
- Delegation—the transfer of **duties** under a contract
- You can distinguish assignment from a third-party beneficiary contract because you will typically see two steps in an assignment:

    1) The formation of a contract; and

    2) The transfer of the benefits of the contract from an original counterparty to some third party.

- Almost all contract benefits can be _____, in whole or in part, unless the contract explicitly prohibits or invalidates assignments.

    > ***Example 198:*** *I offer to pay you $1,000 to paint my house. Can you assign the offer to Mickey? _____, an offer must be directed at a specific person by the offeror.*

    > ***Example 199:*** *I offer to pay you $1,000 to paint my house. You accept. Can you assign the $1,000 payment to Mickey such that she can sue me for failure to pay? _____.*

    > **Note 23:** Terminology for Example 199: Professor Geis is the guarantor; you are the assignor; Mickey is the assignee.

    > ***Example 200:*** *Same facts as Example 199. Can Mickey sue me for the money if you don't paint the house? _____. All defenses transfer to (i.e., can be asserted against) the assignee.*

    > ***Example 201:*** *I agree to pay Mickey $1,000 if you paint my house. Mickey is an intended third-party beneficiary.*

- If the contract states that rights are not assignable, you must determine whether the contract _____ assignments or _____ assignments.

    o The contract **prohibits assignments**—the assigning party has breached when he makes the assignment, but the third party can still recover from the guarantor.

       ▪ The power to assign persists, even if the right to assign does not.

          > ***Example 202:*** *I agree to pay you $1,000 to paint my house, but the contract states that the rights under this contract are not assignable. You nevertheless assign the $1,000 payment to Mickey. Have you breached? _____. Can Mickey sue me if I don't pay her the money? _____.*

    o The contract **invalidates assignments**—the third party cannot recover because there is no power or right to assign.

Example 203: I agree to pay you $1,000 to paint my house, but the contract states that all purported assignments of rights under this contract are void. You nevertheless assign the $1,000 payment to Mickey. Can Mickey sue me if I don't pay her the money? _____ .

- What happens if someone assigns the same rights twice? It depends on whether the assignee has paid consideration for the rights:

    o If the rights are **assigned without consideration**, the assignment is generally revocable and the last assignment controls.

        > **Editor's Note 8:** Assignments without consideration (i.e. gratuitous assignments) are generally revocable. However, a gratuitous assignment cannot be revoked if (i) the obligor has already performed, (ii) promissory estoppel applies, or (iii) a document evidencing the assigned right or a written assignment signed by the assignor was delivered to the assignee.

    o If the rights are **assigned for consideration**, then the first assignment for consideration is typically irrevocable and will hold.

        ▪ **Limited exception:** A later assignment will take priority if the second assignee does not know of the initial assignment and is first to obtain payment or a judgment (i.e., a bona fide purchaser for value without notice).

        Example 204: I agree to pay you $1,000 to paint my house. You assign the payment rights to Mickey. You then wise up and assign the payment rights to your best friend. Can Mickey sue me if I don't pay her the money? _____ . Can your best friend sue? _____ .

        Example 205: Same facts as Example 204, except Mickey trades you 100 bottles of Fireball whiskey for the assignment of payment rights. You then assign the rights to your best friend. Can Mickey sue me if I don't pay her the money? _____ . Can your best friend sue? _____ .

B. Delegation

- A delegation occurs when a party to a contract "outsources" her duties under the contract.
- This is generally acceptable, as long as the contract does not prohibit delegation and as long as the other party does not have some special interest in having a specific individual perform.

    Example 206: I agree to pay you $1,000 to paint my house. You delegate your painting obligation to your best friend, who is also a painter. Is that OK? _____ .

    > **Note 24:** Terminology for Example 206: You are the delegating party; your friend is the delegatee; Professor Geis is the obligee.

Example 207: If your friend does a lousy job, are you still on the hook for breach? _____. Contrast this outcome with novation, described above in Example 157.

Example 208: Same facts as Example 206. Your friend does a great job, and I refuse to pay. Can your friend recover from me? _____, all you have done is transfer the duties, not the benefits. What if you delegated the duties and assigned the rights to your friend? _____, the friend can recover from me.

- A delegatee is generally not liable for breach unless she receives _____ from the delegating party.

Example 209: I agree to pay you $1,000 to paint my house. You delegate your painting obligation to your best friend and promise to pay her $800 to do the job. She does a lousy job. We know already that I can sue you. Can I sue your friend? _____, the friend has been paid consideration to do the job. Contrast this with Example 207, in which I cannot sue your friend.

Example 210: I commission the famous artist Andy Warhol to paint my family portrait for $1 million. He delegates this duty to Mickey for $50. Is this OK? _____, under the special-person exception.

> **Exam Tip 6:** The bar examiners will often use "assignment" when they are referring to both an assignment and a delegation. Just take the context of the question into account.

CHAPTER 21: FINAL REVIEW

A. Which Universe—Common Law or UCC Article 2?

B. The Three Big Questions in Contract Law:

1. **Has an enforceable contract been formed? ("All Contracts Don't Stink")**

   - A—_____
   - C—_____
   - D—_____
   - S—_____

2. **Has the contract been performed? ("Pizza With Crawling Escargot")**

   - P—Parol Evidence Rule
   - W—_____
   - C—Conditions
   - E—_____

3. **What are the remedies for breach?**

   - Anticipatory repudiation

- o _____ damages (expectation, reliance, restitution)
- o Specific performance
- **Third-party after-party**
    - o Third-party beneficiaries
    - o Assignment and delegation

C. **Hot Topics from Past Exams:**

1. **Rejecting an offer**

2. **Revoking an offer (and irrevocable offers)**

3. **Statute of Frauds**

4. **Parol evidence rule**

5. **Warranties**

6. **Rejecting goods**

7. **Money damages**

8. **Third-party beneficiary**

9. **Assignment**

10. **Delegation versus novation**

Exam Tip 7: Remember your DNA twitches.

GOOD LUCK!

[END OF HANDOUT]

Criminal Law

CRIMINAL LAW
PROFESSOR PAMELA S. KARLAN
STANFORD LAW SCHOOL

CHAPTER 1:   JURISDICTION AND ACTUS REUS

A. **Jurisdiction**

- The United States has the power to criminalize and to prosecute crimes that:

  - Occur _____;
  - Occur on _____ and _____; or
  - Are committed by U.S. nationals abroad

- States can only punish crimes having some _____ to the state. For example:

  - A crime that occurs _____ or _____ inside the state
  - Conduct outside the state that involved an _____ to commit a crime inside the state
  - A _____ to commit a crime if an overt act occurred within the state

    Example 1: *Doug lives in Delaware and is visiting South Carolina for vacation. In South Carolina, he meets Ken from Kansas in a bar. Doug hires Ken to kill Doug's wife, Vicki. Ken goes to Delaware, kidnaps Vicki, and her body is later found in Pennsylvania (where she was killed).*

    Can Ken be convicted of murder in Delaware? _____ _____.

    Suppose Ken leaves the bar in South Carolina and rents a car to drive to Delaware. Can Ken be prosecuted for conspiracy to commit murder in South Carolina even if no crime occurred there? _____ _____.

    Can Ken be prosecuted in Kansas? _____ _____.

B. **Actus Reus**

- No such thing as a "_____" crime. Wanting or hoping to commit a crime is not itself a crime.

1. **There must be some _____ in the world**

    Example 2: *A thief shoves a gun into the side of a victim and says, "Your money or your life." The shoving of the gun is the actus reus.*

  - Act can be _____

Example 3: A thief walks up to a victim and says, "Give me $100,000 or I will break your mother's legs next week." The act of speaking is the actus reus.

2. **Act must be _____ (i.e., willed by the defendant)**

    o   Involuntary act does not satisfy the actus reus requirement

        Example 4: Steve can't get to sleep because he's worried about the bar exam. His doctor recommends that he take Ambien, a popular sleep medication. One of Ambien's side effects is that users sometimes sleepwalk or eat while not fully awake. One night after taking his Ambien, Steve arises from his bed, sleepwalks into the common area of the dormitory, reaches into the refrigerator, and eats Cecelia's jar of caviar.

        Can Steve be charged with larceny? _____
        _____.

        Example 5: A husband is in bed one night with his wife. In the middle of a dream, the husband rolls over on top of the wife and suffocates her to death.

        Is the husband guilty of homicide? _____
        _____.

    o   "Voluntary" does not necessarily mean the person wanted to do it. It means that he had motor control over the act.

        Example 6: Tom goes into a store in an attempt to rob the store. He points a pistol at Jerry and says, "Tie up your coworkers or else I'll blow your head off." Jerry, in tying up his coworkers, has committed the actus reus necessary for battery, but he almost certainly will have a defense of duress.

3. **The failure to act can be sufficient actus reus**

    o   Failure to comply with a _____ duty;

        ▪   E.g., the failure to file a tax return, failure to register for selective service, etc.

    o   _____ between defendant and victim;

        ▪   E.g., parents' failure to take care of their children

    o   Voluntarily assuming a duty of care that is cast aside

        Example 7: Anna and her friends are on the beach when they see you drowning. Anna shouts, "I'll save you!" She starts swimming out to you when she looks at her watch and realizes that it's time for her favorite TV show. She turns around and swims back to shore. If you drown, can Anna be held criminally liable? _____
        _____.

○ The defendant causes a _____ and fails to mitigate harm to the victim caused by the peril

> *Example 8:* *On the way into the bar exam, you see a student spill his drink all over himself. You notice that he is about to touch a live wire. If you do nothing and let the student get electrocuted, you cannot be held criminally liable. However, if it were your wire and you should have grounded it, you could be held criminally liable.*

> *Example 9:* *Nancy is a home healthcare worker who cares for an elderly woman named Mona. One evening, while Nancy's friend Dave is visiting Nancy at Mona's house, Mona begins to choke on her dinner. Dave hears Mona choking. Nancy is in the kitchen listening to her iPod. Dave says, "Hey, that old lady is turning blue and gasping." Nancy decides to wait until the end of a track to check on Mona. Mona chokes to death.*

> *Can Dave be charged with any crime related to Mona's death?* _____
> _____.

> *Can Nancy?* _____
> _____.

CHAPTER 2: MENS REA, TRANSFERRED INTENT, AND MERGER

Exam Tip 1: Mens rea is one of the most important criminal law topics tested on the MBE.

A. Mens Rea—The Common Law States of Mind

1. Specific Intent

○ Defendant committed the actus reus and did it for the very purpose of causing the _____ that the law criminalizes

> *Example 10:* *Burglary is defined as the entering of a dwelling with the intent to commit a felony once inside. You have a suspicion that your neighbor might be a hoarder. One day, you climb into your neighbor's house through a window to look around. Once inside, you happen to see a newspaper from the day that you were born. You take the newspaper and leave the house.*

> *Have you committed burglary?* _____
> _____.

○ Memorize the four categories of crimes that are specific intent crimes under the common law.

Note 1: Remember **FIAT!**

1) F_____: not most murders; on the MBE, the question will expressly state if a defendant is charged with first-degree murder

2) I_____: "CATS"—conspiracy, _____, and solicitation

3) A_____ with attempt to commit a _____

4) T_____: e.g., larceny, embezzlement, forgery, burglary, and robbery

> **Exam Tip 2:** The main reason to memorize the FIAT crimes is that there are some defenses—most notably voluntary intoxication and unreasonable mistake of fact—that are available only for specific-intent crimes.

2. Malice

- I "**AM**" certain that there are only two malice crimes: _____ and _____
- Malice exists when the defendant acts in reckless disregard of a high degree of harm. The defendant realizes the risk and acts anyway.

> *Example 11:* Arson is the malicious burning of the dwelling of another. Lynn is at Paul's house for a Fourth of July cookout. Some of the fireworks seem to be duds, so Lynn tosses them onto the grill. Some explode and catch Paul's house on fire. Lynn is charged with arson. At trial, she argues that she didn't want to cause Paul's house to burn down.
>
> *Can Lynn be convicted of arson?* _____
> _____.

3. General Intent

- Catch-all category
- The intent to perform an act, and the act is unlawful
- The defendant does not need to know that the act is unlawful; it is sufficient to intend to perform the act that the law condemns
- Generally, acts done knowingly, recklessly, or negligently under the Model Penal Code (MPC) are general-intent crimes.
  - Examples include: battery, kidnapping, rape, and false imprisonment.

> **Exam Tip 3:** General intent crimes most likely to be tested on the MBE include manslaughter and battery.

4. Strict Liability

- There is no state of mind requirement; the defendant must merely have committed the act

1) Statutory/Regulatory offenses

    Example 12: *A statute requires that food items be labeled with the expiration date. If a company sells those food items without an expiration date, they've committed a crime under this statute. Even if the company did not intend to sell the food without an expiration date or even if it was an honest mistake, the company is liable under strict liability.*

2) Morals offenses

    Example 13: *Humbert is attracted to younger women. He knows the age of consent in his state is 16. He meets Lolita in a bar, where patrons must show ID to enter. Lolita tells Humbert that she is 18 and she suggests they go back to her apartment to have sex. Humbert agrees and they have sex. Later, Humbert is charged with statutory rape, because Lolita is under the age of consent. At trial, Humbert states that he saw her ID and really thought that Lolita was 18. Suppose the judge believes Humbert, can he still be convicted of statutory rape?*

    _____.

Exam Tip 4: If an MBE question contains a statute, read it carefully for mens rea language.

"With intent to…" = _____ crime

"Knowingly or recklessly…." = _____ crime

No mens rea language = Consider _____

B. Mens Rea—The Model Penal Code States of Mind

- The MPC expresses mens rea as: purpose, knowledge, recklessness, and negligence. The MPC also recognizes some strict liability crimes.
- Hierarchy of mental states:

    1) Purpose—highest level of culpability

    2) Knowledge

    3) Recklessness

    4) Negligence—lowest level of culpability

- Look for the mens rea requirement in the statute through words like "knowingly" or "intent to"
- If there is no mens rea language, assume the prosecutor must prove

    _____

1. Purposely

The defendant's conscious objective is to engage in the conduct or to cause a certain result

> *Example 14:* *Patricia raises her gun, points it at Vic, screams "die, you two-timing no-good piece of garbage," and fires, killing him. She has acted purposely.*

2. Knowingly or willfully

Requires that the defendant be _____ that his conduct is of the nature required to commit the crime and that the _____ is practically certain to occur based on his conduct

> *Example 15:* *Patricia is angry at Vic but can't stand the sight of blood. So she decides to kill Vic by putting arsenic in his coffee Thermos. She knows Vic shares his coffee with his co-worker, Virgil, but she does not care what happens to Virgil. Both men drink the coffee and die. With respect to Vic, Patricia has acted purposely, but with respect to Virgil, she has acted knowingly, since she didn't have the intent that Virgil die, although she knew that the result was practically certain to occur.*

3. Recklessly

Requires the defendant to act with a conscious disregard of a substantial and unjustifiable _____ that constitutes a gross deviation from the standard of conduct of a law-abiding person

> *Example 16:* *Patricia is a Golden State Warriors fan who lives in downtown Oakland. When the Warriors win their 77th regular season game, she's so excited that she takes her semi-automatic gun out of the house and fires several dozen rounds into the air. Several of the rounds hit Vic. She didn't want to hit him, and she actually didn't know he was standing nearby, but she acted recklessly.*

4. Negligently

The defendant _____ aware of a substantial and unjustifiable risk and acts in a way that grossly deviates from the standard of care of a reasonable person in the same situation

C. Transferred Intent Doctrine

- When a defendant has the requisite mens rea for committing a crime against Victim A, but actually commits the crime against Victim B, the law _____ the intent from Victim A over to Victim B.

> *Example 17:* *Ralph is a professional jewel thief. He is hired to steal a valuable diamond pin from Mrs. Rich at a charity ball. In preparation, Ralph studies her picture from old newspapers. However, Mrs. Rich has had a lot of work done on her face since the picture. So at the ball, Ralph approaches Miss Humble, who*

resembles the picture he studied, believing her to be Mrs. Rich, and steals jewelry from her instead.

Can Ralph be charged with larceny—a specific-intent crime—against Miss Humble? _____.

Can he be charged with attempted larceny against Mrs. Rich? _____

_____.

Note 2: Transferred intent does not apply to attempted crimes, only to completed crimes.

D. Vicarious Liability

- Holds a person or entity liable for an actus reus committed by someone else
- A corporation can be liable for the actions of its high-level employees or the Board of Directors.

E. Merger

- A defendant can be convicted of more than one crime arising out of the same act.
- A defendant cannot be convicted of two crimes when the two crimes merge into one.
- Two categories of merger:

    1) _____ offenses; and

    2) The merger of an _____ and a completed offense

1. Lesser-included Offenses

- o Lesser-included offense—an offense in which each of its elements appears in another offense, but the other offense has something additional

    Exam Tip 5: Think of each element as a different geometric figure.

    If the elements of Offense # 1 are a circle and a square,

    And the elements of Offense # 2 are circle, square, and triangle, then

    Offense #1 is the lesser-included offense of Offense #2; Offense #2 is the greater-included offense of Offense #1.

    Remember: A defendant cannot be convicted of both Offense #1 and Offense #2.

    Example 18: *Ralph tries to steal Miss Humble's pin by gently prying it free from her jacket. But she notices Ralph and resists. Ralph then pushes her over and runs off with the jacket. His conduct would satisfy the elements for both larceny and robbery, but since:*

    Robbery = _____ + _____ of force

    Larceny is a lesser-included offense of robbery. Robbery is a greater-included offense of larceny. Ralph can be convicted of robbery but not of larceny, because larceny _____ into the robbery.

2. **Inchoate and Completed Offenses**

   ○ **Attempt**—A defendant who actually _____ a crime cannot also be convicted of _____ that crime.

> **Example 19:** If you attempt to rob someone and you succeed in robbing them, you can only be convicted of robbery, not also attempted robbery.

> **Example 20:** If you try to rob Person A, but actually rob Person B, you can be convicted of attempted robbery of Person A and actual robbery of Person B.

   ○ **Solicitation**—Merges into the completed offense

> **Example 21:** If the defendant solicits another person to commit a murder, and the other person commits the murder, the defendant is liable for the murder, but not for solicitation because it merges into the murder.

   ○ **Conspiracy** and a completed substantive offense do not merge!

      ▪ A defendant can be convicted of both _____ to commit a crime and committing the crime itself.

CHAPTER 3: PRINCIPALS, ACCOMPLICES, AIDERS, AND ABETTORS

A. Children

- At common law, children under the age of _____ were never capable of committing a crime.
- Children ages _____ to _____ were rebuttably presumed to be incapable of committing crimes.
- Children at least _____ years old could be charged as adults.

> **Exam Tip 6:** On the MBE, children are more likely to be the victims of crime than the perpetrators.

B. Principals

- Defendants whose _____ or _____ form the actus reus of the crime
- Can be more than one principal to a particular crime
- Ask: Who committed the actus reus that gives rise to the offense?

C. Accomplices

- Theory for holding people other than the principal responsible for the crime committed by the principal; same degree of responsibility as the principal
- People who _____ the principal either before or during the commission of a crime
- Must act with the _____ of assisting the principal to commit the crime; bystanders, even approving ones, are not accomplices

Example 22: *You go to a bar after the exam and a bar fight breaks out. If you applaud during the fight, you are not liable for assault as an accomplice.*

- Liable as an accomplice for both the _____ crime and any other _____ crimes that occur in the course of the criminal act

  Example 23: *Irving decides to rob a bank. He asks Oscar to drive a getaway car. Irving then goes to Paul's house and asks to borrow Paul's gun, telling him he wants to go target shooting. Paul lends him the gun. During the bank robbery, Irving shoots a teller. Oscar takes his share of money from the robbery and buys a pound of heroin. Irving, Oscar, and Paul are all charged with robbery, attempted murder, and possession of heroin with intent to distribute.*

  For which crimes can they be convicted?

  Irving: _____

  Oscar: _____

  Paul: _____

  Note 4: Irving and Oscar might also be held liable for conspiracy (discussed below).

- An accomplice can be _____ even if he or she cannot be a principal or even if the principal cannot be convicted.

  Example 24: *A statute makes it a crime for a public official to take bribes. Mayor Benedict wants to take a bribe, but wants to do it where no one will see. His friend, Claudio, owns a cabin in the woods. Mayor Benedict asks Claudio if he could use his cabin as the location to exchange bribery money. Claudio agrees and offers to chain off the road. Claudio could be guilty of aiding and abetting the bribery as an accomplice. But, he could not be guilty as a principal because he is not a public official.*

  Example 25: *You assist a six-year-old child to commit murder. Your little nephew tells you that he really wants to kill his classmate Bobby. You give your nephew a gun and he shoots Bobby. Your nephew cannot be convicted of murder because he is under the age of seven, but you can be convicted of aiding and abetting as an accomplice.*

  Example 26: *If you help a diplomat commit a crime, the diplomat has diplomatic immunity, so the diplomat might not be held liable as a principal, but you can still be held liable as an accomplice.*

- **Exception:** A person protected by a _____ cannot be an accomplice in violating the statute

> ***Example 27:*** *If a statute prohibits sex with an underage person, the underage person is not an accomplice to that crime.*

D. Accessories After the Fact

- People who assist the defendant _____ the crime has been committed (e.g., obstruction of justice or harboring a fugitive)

> ***Example 28:*** *After the bank robbery, Irving asks his accountant for help with laundering the money from the robbery. If the accountant helps Irving, he is not guilty of aiding and abetting the bank robbery, but instead would be guilty of a **separate crime** as an accessory after the fact (e.g., a financial crime).*

E. Aiders/Abettors and Conspiracy

- In addition to accomplice liability for the substantive crime, individuals who aid or abet a defendant to commit a crime may also be guilty of the separate crime of _____ if there was an agreement to commit the crime and an overt act was taken in furtherance of that agreement.

> ***Example 29:*** *Oscar and Irving might also be guilty of conspiracy to commit robbery in addition to the substantive crime of robbery.*

F. The Mental States of Accomplices

- **Majority and MPC Approaches**—the accomplice must act with the _____ of promoting or facilitating the commission of the offense; the accomplice must _____ that her acts will assist or encourage the criminal conduct.
- **Minority Approach**—the accomplice is liable if he intentionally or knowingly aids or causes another person to commit an offense.
- **Criminal Facilitation**—under the majority rule, a person who is not guilty of the substantive crime (because he did not act with intent) may nevertheless be guilty of the lesser offense of criminal facilitation for simply assisting

CHAPTER 4: NEGATING MENS REA

A. Mistake

- Often, a defendant will claim that some mistake—regarding either facts in the world or the state of the law—negates his _____ and thus he cannot be convicted of a crime for which there are both actus reus and mens rea elements.

1. Mistakes of Law

- Mistakes about what the law _____ and what it _____
- _____ of the law is no excuse.

> ***Example 30:*** *You thought the speed limit was 80 mph because last time you drove on that highway there was a sign that said 80 mph. In reality the speed limit was 65 mph. The fact that you didn't realize the speed limit was 65 mph is not a defense.*

- ○ Three potential exceptions:

  - 1) Reliance on high-level government _____

    > ***Example 31:*** *If a regulation states that something is permitted and you are later prosecuted for that conduct because the regulation was wrong, the regulation might negate the mens rea element.*

    > **Note 5:** Relying on your own lawyer's advice does not generally fall into this exception.

  - 2) Lack of notice

  - 3) Mistake of law that goes to an element of _____ intent (applies only to the "FIAT" crimes or specific-intent crimes)

    > ***Example 32:*** *Quentin, a solo practitioner, practices law out of his rented apartment. He drills holes in the wall of his apartment for bookshelves. The landlord tells Quentin to stop drilling and grabs Quentin's drill. Quentin pushes the landlord, causing him to fall and injure his shoulder. Quentin is charged with battery and with the statutory crime of "knowingly damaging the property of another person, [with the intent to deprive that person of the property]." Quentin argues that he thought a tenant was allowed to alter the walls of his apartment. He argues that he was defending his own property when he pushed the landlord.*

    > *Quentin had the mistaken belief that he was protecting his own property. Is that a defense to a charge of battery? _____ _____.*

    > *Can Quentin's mistake about the property be a defense to violating the statute? _____ _____.*

2. Mistakes of Fact

- ○ **Key starting point:** Determine whether the crime is a specific intent crime (FIAT), a _____ crime, or a strict liability crime.

- **a.** **Strict Liability:** Mistake of fact is _____ a defense to strict liability crimes

  - ▪ Must be a voluntary act, but the defendant's state of mind is irrelevant

Example 33: *You live in a jurisdiction where selling alcohol to a minor is a strict liability crime. If you work in a wine shop, checking IDs is not sufficient to avoid liability for selling alcohol to a minor.*

b. General Intent: Mistake of fact is a defense only if the mistake is
_____ and goes to the criminal intent.

c. Specific intent: Mistakes of fact are a defense whether the mistake is
_____ or _____. The only question is whether the defendant held the mistaken belief.

Example 34: *Roger is out of town on a business trip and he is very jetlagged. He picks up a rental car at the airport but he's not paying attention to what color it is. He goes to a restaurant and gives his keys to the valet. After his meeting, Roger gives his ticket to the valet and the valet goes to get his car. The valet returns, not with Roger's cheap rental car, but with a Porsche. Roger gets into the Porsche and drives off.*

Roger is charged with larceny (which requires taking away the property of another person with the intent to permanently deprive the other person of the property; a specific-intent crime) and with joyriding (which requires taking the automobile of another person without permission for a short period of time).

Can Roger be convicted of larceny if the jury concludes that no reasonable person would confuse an economy car with a Porsche? _____ _____.*

Can Roger be convicted of joyriding, even if the jury believes that he thought the car was his? _____.

B. Insanity

- Four Different Tests:

    1) **M'Naghten:** Defendant either did not know the _____ of the act or did not know that the act was _____ because of a mental disease or defect

        Example 35: *A defendant did not realize that he was shooting at a human being; he thought he was shooting at a pumpkin because he was delusional.*

    2) **Irresistible Impulse:** Defendant has a mental disease or defect that prevents the defendant from _____ himself

    3) **Durham Rule:** Defendant would not have committed the crime _____ his having a mental disease or defect (rarely used because so defendant-friendly)

4) **Model Penal Code**: Due to a mental disease or defect, the defendant did not have
_____ to appreciate
the wrongfulness of his actions or to _____ his conduct to the law

> **Note 6:** All four tests require that the defendant have a mental disease or
> defect. Being a sociopath is not enough to constitute insanity.

- Majority—the _____ has the burden of proving insanity either by
  a preponderance of the evidence or clear and convincing evidence.

  o Some jurisdictions require the defendant to introduce evidence of insanity, and then the
  burden of persuasion shifts to the prosecution to prove sanity beyond a reasonable doubt.

C. Intoxication

- Covers alcohol, drugs, and medications
- Can be _____ or _____

1. Involuntary intoxication

o Occurs when a person:

  - Doesn't realize that she received an intoxicating substance (e.g., "date rape" drugs);
  - Is _____ into ingesting a substance; or
  - Has an _____ or unanticipated reaction to prescription
    medication.

o Can be a valid defense to _____-intent, _____-intent, and
  _____ crimes when it negates the mens rea necessary for the crime

2. Voluntary intoxication

o Occurs when a person intentionally ingests the substance, knowing it is an intoxicant

o Voluntary intoxication is a defense only to _____-intent crimes (FIAT crimes),
  and only if it prevented the defendant from forming the mens rea

  - Not a valid defense if the defendant got drunk in order to commit the crime

    *Example 36: Terry is a member of a gang. As an initiation rite, she must break
    into her boyfriend's house and steal one of his mother's shoes. Terry is timid
    and nervous, so she drinks six shots of bourbon to get her courage up. She's
    now quite drunk. She then climbs through an open window and begins
    rummaging around in the mother's closet. She gets one of the mother's shoes
    and leaves the house. While weaving down the driveway, the mother comes
    home and confronts Terry. Terry tries to hit the mother over the head with the
    shoe. But Terry's hand-eye coordination is not so good, so she misses. Terry
    then jumps into her car and drives off. Unfortunately, she runs over Ursula and
    kills her. Suppose Terry is charged with burglary, assault, and vehicular
    homicide.*

Starting point: She got drunk in order to commit the crime. If she'd simply gotten drunk with friends and then burglarized a house, she could not be convicted of burglary because it is a specific-intent offense. But because she drank in order to commit the burglary, she _____ be convicted, even of the specific-intent crime of burglary.

Assault (with attempt to commit battery) is a specific-intent crime, but it's not the crime she got drunk in order to commit, so if she didn't have the _____, she can't be convicted of assault.

Vehicular homicide is not a specific-intent crime, so she's guilty even though she had no desire to run over Ursula.

- o Under the MPC, voluntary intoxication is only a defense to crimes for which a material element requires purpose or knowledge and the intoxication prevents the formation of that mental state.

CHAPTER 5:   INCHOATE CRIMES

> **Note 7:** Remember CATS: Conspiracy, Attempt, Solicitation

A.   Conspiracy

1.   Definitions and Elements

a.   Common law conspiracy requires:

- An _____;
- Between two or more people;
- To commit an _____ act.

b.   Modern conspiracy statutes

Add a fourth element: The performance of an _____ in furtherance of the conspiracy

c.   Model Penal Code (MPC)

Only the defendant must actually agree to commit the unlawful act. The other people with whom the defendant agrees can be undercover agents, for example.

- o **Agreement** can be _____ or _____
  - Simply _____ a crime is going to occur and doing nothing about it does not turn a bystander into a co-conspirator; there must be an agreement.

    Example 37: *Anna lives in a common law jurisdiction. She agrees with Bob to rob a bank, but she doesn't know that Bob is an undercover police officer. Anna also wants to steal an emerald from a jewelry store in a nearby state, which is* *an MPC jurisdiction. She asks Ranier for help with stealing the gem. She doesn't know that Ranier is also an undercover officer.*

Is Anna guilty of conspiracy to commit bank robbery? _____
_____.

Is Anna guilty of conspiracy to commit larceny? _____
_____.

- ○ **Purpose of the conspiracy:** Unlawful act

  - ▪ If what the conspirators agree to do is not a crime, there is no conspiracy even if they think what they're doing is wrong.

    Example 38: Harry and Sally hear that gray-bellied sapsuckers are exotic birds and that someone will pay $10,000 for one of these birds. They know that stealing eggs from endangered species' nests is a crime. Harry and Sally agree to go to the nest of the gray-bellied sapsucker and steal the eggs to sell them. But it turns out that gray-bellied sapsuckers aren't endangered, so it's not actually a crime to catch one. So they are NOT guilty of conspiracy, because what they conspired to do was not a crime—even though they thought it was.

- ○ **Overt act:** Can be lawful or unlawful, as long as it _____ the conspiracy

    Example 39: Zacarias Moussaoui and other 9/11 hijackers joined a health club together in Georgia. They did it to build strength so they could overpower the pilots and crew during the hijackings. This is an overt act because it furthered the conspiracy.

2. **Scope of a Conspiracy**

   - ○ At common law, each co-conspirator can be convicted both of:

     1) _____; and

     2) All substantive crimes committed by any other conspirator acting in _____ of the conspiracy.

     Example 40: Goldie, Frank, and Myrtle all agree to steal goods from a sporting goods store in the mall. Goldie will enter the store to steal the goods, Frank is the lookout, and Myrtle is driving the getaway car. Goldie tells Frank to blow a whistle if a security guard comes by. After Goldie enters the store, Frank panics when he sees a guard and shoves the guard, who falls and breaks his arm. Goldie comes out of the store with the goods, including some starter pistols. Myrtle later uses the starter pistol to rob a convenience store. Who is liable for what?

     Conspiracy to rob the store: _____

Battery of the guard: _____

_____

Robbery of the convenience store: _____

- ○ Relationships of co-conspirators

  - ▪ **Chain Conspiracy**: Co-conspirators are engaged in an enterprise consisting of many steps; each participant is liable for the substantive crimes of his co-conspirators

    Example 41: *A conspiracy to distribute drugs involves many people in a causal chain (manufacturer—distributer—dealer). The conspirators need not know each other, but they have all agreed to participate in the same conspiracy and each can be held liable (1) for the conspiracy and (2) for the substantive offenses committed along the way.*

  - ▪ **Spoke-Hub Conspiracy:** Involves many people dealing with a central hub; participants are not liable for the substantive crimes of their co-conspirators because each spoke is treated as a separate agreement rather than one larger general agreement

    Example 42: *A bank employee agrees to process fraudulent loan applications. This employee would serve as the "hub." Each individual seeking a fraudulent loan is a "spoke." But the spokes are not generally responsible for the actions of the other spokes.*

    Example 43: *A pawn shop operates as a "fence" to sell stolen goods. Each robber is responsible for conspiracy to sell stolen property, but not for the goods from other robbers.*

3. **Withdrawal from a Conspiracy**

   - ○ **Common law**—it's _____ to withdraw from a conspiracy, because the crime is completed the moment the agreement is made.

     Example 44: *You and Professor Kramer agree to commit a crime. The next day, she calls and says she no longer wants to participate in the crime. Professor Kramer can still be convicted of conspiracy because you both agreed to commit the crime. But if you go ahead and commit the crime without Professor Kramer, she will not be convicted of the actual crime because she has withdrawn.*

   - ○ **Federal and MPC**—a conspirator can withdraw prior to the commission of any _____ by communicating her intention to withdraw to all other conspirators or by informing _____.

     - ▪ After an overt act—a conspirator can withdraw only by helping to _____ the success of a conspiracy.

Example 45: In an MPC jurisdiction, if Professor Kramer withdraws from the conspiracy after an overt act—either by notifying you or law enforcement—she may not be held liable for conspiracy if the notification was timely enough to thwart the success of the conspiracy.

o   Even if a defendant cannot withdraw from the conspiracy (e.g., because a conspiracy had already been formed), the defendant can limit his liability for substantive crimes by informing the other conspirators of withdrawal or timely advising legal authorities.

B. Attempt

* Attempt is a _____ crime

1. Requirements

1) Specific intent to commit a particular criminal act; and

2) _____ step towards perpetrating the crime

Example 46: You work at a bank and plan to embezzle funds. Waking up and getting dressed does not constitute a substantial step.

Example 47: Bringing special equipment to the scene of the crime or lying in wait will typically constitute substantial steps.

o   Attempt is a specific-intent crime even when the completed offense is only a _____ crime.

Example 48: Attempted murder is specific-intent crime, but murder is a ~~general-intent~~ malice crime.

> **Editorial Note 1:** Common-law murder is a malice crime, not a general-intent crime.

2. Defenses

o   Defenses for specific-intent crimes can be used as a defense to attempt

Example 49: Aaron is standing on an overpass. For a joke, he throws bowling balls onto the highway below. If a bowling ball hits and kills someone, Aaron will be guilty of murder (because he acted with a maligned and depraved heart). But if the ball doesn't hit anyone, Aaron cannot be charged with attempted murder because he lacked the specific intent required to commit murder (i.e., he didn't intend to kill).

o   Certain defenses like voluntary intoxication and unreasonable mistake of _____ are available even if they wouldn't be available had the crime been completed.

3. Merger

o   Attempt merges into a _____ offense.

- o You _____ be convicted of both attempted murder and murder of the same person in the same episode.
- o You can be convicted of both _____ to commit murder and murder.

C. Solicitation

- Occurs when an individual _____ invites, requests, or commands another person to commit a crime
- If the person agrees, the crime is _____ instead.
- If the person commits the offense, the solicitation charge will _____ into the completed offense.

> ***Example 50:*** *Amy offers to pay Doug $1,000 to commit a murder. This is a solicitation. If Doug says yes, this is a conspiracy to commit murder. If Doug actually commits the murder Amy will be guilty of the murder and conspiracy, but not solicitation.*

> ***Example 51:*** *Wallace goes into a bar and offers a guy $10,000 to kill her boss. That is solicitation. If the guy agrees, that is conspiracy to commit murder. If the guy actually kills the boss, Wallace is guilty of both conspiracy and murder.*

CHAPTER 6:   HOMICIDE

A. In General

1. Definition

- o Homicide: The _____ of a living human being by another human being
  - ▪ Animals cannot commit a homicide and killing an animal is not a homicide;
  - ▪ Victim cannot already be dead;
  - ▪ Suicide is not homicide; but _____ someone to commit suicide can be a homicide.

2. Causation

- o There must be a _____ relationship between the defendant's actions and what happened to the victim
- o **Actual Causation:** Victim would not have died "_____" what the defendant did
- o **Proximate Causation**: Defendant's act is a _____ cause of the victim's death (death is the natural and probable result of the conduct)

> ***Example 52:*** *A defendant shoots the victim, and the victim dies in the hospital because the doctor was negligent. That death is a foreseeable consequence of shooting someone. So, the defendant's act was both the actual and proximate cause of the victim's death.*

- Independent actions by a third person are generally not a foreseeable cause

  Example 53: Bernie, the defendant, commits securities fraud. One of his victims—who was defrauded of money—commits suicide. Bernie is not the proximate cause of the victim's death, even though he may be viewed as the actual cause.

  Exam Tip 7: Consent is not a defense to any type of homicide.

Assisted suicide is a homicide by the assister, except in jurisdictions that permit assisted suicide.

B. First-Degree Murder

- Specific-intent crime

  Exam Tip 8: The question will generally tell you if the case involves first-degree murder. Otherwise, assume the question involves common law murder.

- Typically defined as a _____ and _____ murder, or a killing that results during the commission of an inherently dangerous felony (i.e., felony murder is frequently classified as first-degree murder)

C. Common-Law Murder

1. Definition

- o _____ killing of another human being committed with _____ aforethought
- o Lawful killing of another is not murder (e.g., state execution or a police officer's justifiable use of deadly force)

2. Four Kinds of Malice

- **a.** _____: The defendant acted with the desire that the victim end up dead.

  - Intent need not be premeditated; it can be formed in the moment before the killing.

- **b. Intent to inflict** _____: The defendant intended to hurt the victim badly, and the victim died.

- **c.** _____ **or** _____: The defendant acted with a cavalier disregard for human life and a death resulted.

  - Defendant must realize that his conduct is really risky but need not have any intent regarding the outcome of his actions.

    Example 54: Recall the example about dropping bowling balls off an overpass.

  - Majority and MPC—defendant must actually realize that there is a danger

- Minority—a reasonable person would have recognized the danger

d. _____: The death occurred during the commission or attempted commission of a _____ felony

- The "BARRK" felonies—burglary, _____, robbery, rape, and

_____

> **Note 8:** The dangerous felony must be independent of the killing itself. E.g., aggravated assault that resulted in a death is not felony murder; it is a different type of common law murder.

- Deaths caused by other felonies get the label of misdemeanor manslaughter.
- Felony murder can involve:

a) Someone who _____ the felony

Example 55: *The defendant attempts to rob the victim and the victim resists. The defendant punches the victim and the victim dies.*

b) When a _____ is killed during a felony

Example 56: *The defendant tries to rob a bank and the guard gives chase. The defendant turns around and tries to shoot the guard. Instead, the defendant hits a pedestrian on the street.*

c) Third person killed by the resister or police officers (minority)

Example 57: *You rob a bank. After robbing the bank, you get into a shootout with the police. If a police officer misses you and shoots a bystander, you are liable in a minority of jurisdictions.*

- **Majority—agency theory**: A defendant is only responsible for the crimes of the defendant's "agents." Because the victim, police, or third party are not the defendant's agents, the defendant is not responsible for their conduct.

d) If a co-felon is killed by a resister or a police officer, then the defendant is not guilty of felony murder

Example 58: *If the defendant is riding with the getaway driver and the police shoots and kills the getaway driver, the defendant is not liable for felony murder.*

D. Manslaughter

1. Definitions

- All _____ killings of another human being that are not first-degree murder or common law murder
- Two types: _____ and _____

2. Voluntary Manslaughter

o   Occurs when a defendant intends to kill the victim, but his state of mind is less blameworthy than murder

o   Acted in the "_____" or "under extreme emotional disturbance"

o   Test: Is the situation one in which most people would act without _____ and without time to _____?

> ***Example 59:*** *Rufus comes home and finds his wife, Amy, in bed with Luke. Rufus shoots Luke and Amy. This is acting in the heat of passion or heat of the moment. People are not expected to stop, think rationally, and calm down in this situation.*

> **Note 9:** Hearing about your spouse's affair is not sufficient.

> ***Example 60:*** *Frank was sexually abused as a young teenager. Five years later, he testifies at the highly-publicized trial of his abuser and was forced to describe the abuse he had suffered. Several days later, a group of young teenagers surrounded Frank and began taunting him, suggesting that he had "asked for it." Frank lashes out at the group and strangles one of them.*
>
> *Would Frank be entitled to a manslaughter instruction? Probably not under the heat of passion defense, but maybe under the emotional disturbance. Need more facts to determine whether it was reasonable to strangle somebody for a taunt.*

3. Involuntary Manslaughter

o   A criminally _____ killing or killing of someone while committing a crime other than those covered by felony murder (i.e., misdemeanor manslaughter)

o   A defendant who engages in criminally negligent conduct and causes a death is guilty of involuntary manslaughter (e.g., traffic deaths).

> ***Example 61:*** *Lisa goes jogging with her dog. A city law makes it a misdemeanor to let a dog off its leash on public property. Lisa ignores the law. While unleashed, Lisa's dog attacks and kills a small child. In this situation, Lisa may be guilty of misdemeanor manslaughter, because letting her dog off its leash was the "but-for" cause of the child's death.*

CHAPTER 7:   PROPERTY CRIMES

A. Larceny

1. Definition

- ○ Larceny requires:
  - ▪ Taking;
  - ▪ Another person's property;
  - ▪ Without his consent (trespassory); and
  - ▪ With the _____ to deprive him of it permanently.

2. Elements

a. Property—tangible personal property (e.g., wristwatch, goods from a store)

- ▪ Not intangible property (e.g., copyright), real property, or services

  Note 10: There are modern "theft of services" statutes that criminalize obtaining a service, e.g., a massage, and then not paying for it. That conduct does not fall under common law larceny.

b. Taking—involves any _____ of property, however slight

Example 62: *Hank goes into an electronics store to shoplift an MP3 player. He lifts the player off of the counter and heads for the door. Even before he leaves the store, he has satisfied the "taking" element of larceny.*

c. Trespassory taking (without consent)

- ▪ Consent must be real, not obtained by trick (discussed below)
- ▪ The defendant bears the burden of proving that there was consent

d. Intent—an intent to deprive the person of the property permanently

- ▪ "Borrowing" property, even without the owner's consent, is not larceny, as long as you intend to _____
- ▪ If the property is destroyed in your care, you have not committed larceny.

Example 63: *A teenager sees a fancy car with the keys in it. The teen jumps in, thinking he will just drive the car around the block a few times and then return it. But he crashes the car. Is he guilty of larceny? _____ _____.*

(Note: he may be guilty of other crimes, like joyriding.)

Example 64: *One day before class, you realize that you forgot your textbook. In the law school library, you see someone else's textbook lying on a desk. You borrow the book with the intention of returning it after class. During your class, there is a fire alarm and you leave the book behind. The sprinklers malfunction and start spraying water inside the classroom, ruining the borrowed textbook.*

Are you guilty of larceny? _____

_____.

- o Larceny is a _____ crime.

  - As long as the defendant thinks it's his property—however unreasonably—he is not guilty of larceny.

    Example 65: You take the wrong black umbrella from an umbrella stand in a restaurant. Even if you intend to keep that umbrella forever, you are not guilty of larceny because you were mistaken (this is true even if the mistake was unreasonable).

3. Embezzlement: A Variation of Larceny

- o A defendant starts out having the victim's consent to have the property but commits embezzlement by _____ the property to his own use.

  Example 66: Jake is a teller at King Savings Bank. One day Lou, a depositor at the bank, comes to the window and hands Jake a check, made out to Zach and endorsed over to Lou, for deposit to Lou's account. Jake knows that Lou is an enforcer for an organized crime family, and strongly suspects that Lou obtained Zach's check through force. Believing the check to be ill-gotten gains, Jake instead deposits the check to the account of the Make-a-Wish Foundation, a local charity.

  Is Jake guilty of larceny because he stole Lou's check? _____

  _____.

  Is Jake guilty of embezzlement? _____

  Even though the money was not rightfully Lou's in the first place? _____.

  Even though he didn't keep the money for himself? _____.

4. False Pretenses: Another Variation of Larceny

The defendant obtains title to someone else's property through an act of

_____.

  Example 67: Paying for goods with counterfeit money or a bad check

5. Model Penal Code and other Modern Changes

Under the MPC and in many jurisdictions, crimes such as larceny, false pretenses, and embezzlement are treated as a single statutory crime of theft (which includes both tangible and intangible property).

B. Robbery

1. Definition and Elements

- Common law robbery is a simple equation:

  - Robbery = _____ + _____

- **Robbery requires**:

1) Taking;

2) Another person's property;

3) Without his consent;

4) With intent to deprive him of it permanently; and

5) The taking occurs from the victim's _____ or in his _____

6) Either by violence or putting the victim in fear of _____ physical harm

2. Extortion: A Variation of Robbery

Involves threats of _____ harm (including non-physical harm)

> *Example 68:* *Xenia approaches Chris at a party and admires her necklace. Xenia tells Chris, "Give me that necklace or else I'll tell your husband that I saw you coming out of a hotel room last weekend with Ben." Chris turns to walk away and Xenia grabs the necklace, pulling it off Chris's neck. Of which crimes is Xenia guilty?*
>
> *Robbery: _____*
>
> *Attempted extortion: _____*
>
> *Extortion: _____*

C. Burglary

1. **Definitions**

   o **Common law burglary requires:**

   - Breaking and
   - Entering
   - The _____
   - Of another
   - At night
   - With the specific intent to commit a _____ once inside

   o The common law elements have been relaxed, so that **modern law burglary requires:**

   - Breaking and
   - Entering
   - The property
   - Of another
   - With the specific intent to commit a felony inside

2. **Elements**

   o **Breaking** can involve pushing open or smashing a door or window, or obtaining entry by

   _____

   > **Note 11:** Someone who comes inside with the owner's consent and then steals something is guilty of larceny (and possibly robbery if he uses violence or threat of violence) but not burglary because there was no "breaking."

   o **Entering** involves breaking the _____ of the dwelling.

   > *Example 69:* *Sticking your hand through a window constitutes "entering."*

   o A "**dwelling**" at common law is a structure regularly lived in

   - Modern statutes can also include a commercial building

   o **Of another:** Cannot burglarize yourself

   o With the _____ to **commit a felony** once inside

   - The usual felony is larceny, but it could be another felony, such as battery.

   > *Example 70:* *Breaking into another's house because of curiosity is not burglary because there is no intent to commit a felony once inside.*

   > *Example 71:* *Nick has several friends staying at his beach house. One afternoon, he notices that Mary has an expensive diamond watch. That evening, while everyone is down at the beach for the sunset, he sneaks back to the house, pries open the kitchen window, enters Mary's bedroom, forces open her jewelry box, and steals the watch.*

Meanwhile, Quinn, Nick's neighbor, notices the half-open window. He's always wanted to see the inside of Nick's house, but Nick has been very standoffish about inviting him in. So Quinn raises the window slightly higher to squeeze into the house. While roaming about the house, he notices Wayne's wallet on the nightstand and takes $250 from the wallet. Nick and Quinn are each charged with burglary. Are either of them guilty of burglary?

Nick: _____

Quinn: _____

CHAPTER 8:   OTHER CRIMES

A. Battery

1. Definition

- ○ Unlawful
- ○ Application of force
- ○ To another person
- ○ That causes:

    - ▪ Bodily _____ OR
    - ▪ An _____ touching

2. Elements

- ○ **Unlawful**: Consent is a complete defense to battery (e.g., boxing match).
- ○ **Application of force**: Need not be a great deal of force; the slightest touch can constitute force in some cases
- ○ Battery is a _____-intent crime, so voluntary intoxication and _____ mistake of fact are not available defenses.
- ○ Does not require actual physical contact between the defendant and the victim (e.g., throwing a rock that hits someone)

B. Assault (Two Forms)

1. _____

- ○ If a defendant has taken a substantial step toward completing a battery but fails, he will be guilty of assault
- ○ It is a _____-intent crime because it is an attempt; specific-intent defenses are available.

2. Fear of Harm

- ○ Intentionally placing another in _____ of imminent bodily harm
- ○ This form of assault is a _____-intent crime.

Example 72: *Thomas has a crush on Ursula. After getting drunk one night, Thomas concludes that Ursula truly loves him. He goes to her room and knocks, but she won't open the door, so Thomas breaks it down. Once inside, he tries to kiss Ursula. But she's fast and he's drunk, so she gets away. Thomas falls over and grabs Isaac—who is also in the room—injuring Isaac's arm.*

Is Thomas guilty of battery against Ursula for trying to kiss her? _____
_____.

Is Thomas guilty of attempted battery (assault)? _____
_____
_____.

Did Thomas commit a battery against Isaac? _____

He also committed assault by breaking down the door because he put them in fear of imminent bodily harm and his voluntary intoxication is not a defense.

C. Rape

1. Common-law rape requires:

- o Unlawful
- o Sexual intercourse
- o With a female
- o Against her will by _____ or _____ of force

    > **Exam Tip 10:** The MBE will not likely test on common-law rape because the elements have been relaxed or eliminated in most modern statutes.

2. Most modern rape statutes

- o Gender-neutral
- o Require _____ rather than the force requirement

3. Intent

- o Rape is a _____-intent crime; voluntary intoxication _____ be used as a defense

4. Statutory Rape

- o Regulatory morals offense that involves _____ sexual intercourse with a person under the age of _____
- o Statutory rape is a _____ offense

    - So long as the defendant knows that he is having sex, he cannot claim ignorance or mistake about the victim's age.

5. **Other Sex Crimes at Common Law**

> **Exam Tip 11:** These are extremely unlikely to be tested on the bar exam.

- ○ Adultery: Having sex with someone who is not your spouse
- ○ Fornication: Sex between unmarried people
- ○ Crimes against nature: Bestiality
- ○ Incest: Sex between people who are too closely related to one another
- ○ Bigamy: Marrying someone while you are still legally married to someone else
- ○ Seduction: A man tells a woman that he will marry her if she has sex with him

D. **Kidnapping**

- • **Requires:**
  - ○ Unlawful
  - ○ _____ of another person
  - ○ Against that person's will
  - ○ Either by _____ or _____ the victim

  > *Example 73:* *Olivia and Paul decide to rob a grocery store. Alex, the clerk, manages to trip the alarm and Olivia grabs Scott and puts him into the meat locker. A hostage situation ensues, and police eventually get Olivia to release Scott. Now Olivia and Paul are charged with kidnapping Alex and Scott.*
  >
  > *Are they guilty of kidnapping Scott? _____*
  > *_____.*
  >
  > *Are they guilty of kidnapping Alex? _____*
  > *_____.*

E. **Arson**

1. **Definition**

   - ○ **Common law arson requires:**
     - ▪ _____
     - ▪ Burning
     - ▪ Of another person's
     - ▪ _____

2. **Elements**

   - ○ **Malice:** Intent to act in a way that will cause burning, or is substantially likely to do so
   - ○ **Burning:**
     - ▪ Common law—there had to be burning (fire) as opposed to an explosion or smoke damage. It also required damage to the _____, not just the contents inside.

- Modern statutes—it is arson even if there is no damage to the structure of the building or if the fire was caused by an explosion.

- ○ **Another Person**:
  - Common law—you could not torch your own house.
  - Modern statutes—burning your own home is arson.

- ○ **Dwelling**:
  - Common law—had to be a _____, not another structure
  - Modern statutes—burning down a _____ building is arson.

F. Perjury

- Willful act of _____ promising to tell the truth, either verbally or in writing, about material matters
- The person must know what they are saying is false, must _____ to say something that is false, and the falsity must go to a _____ matter.

> **Example 74:** *Pauline is a called as a witness in a burglary case. She says that she was walking down the street and she saw the defendant break into the victim's house and then come out. It would not be a material falsehood for her to say that just before she saw the defendant, she had been at a friend's house not doing much of anything—when in reality, she was at the friend's house sleeping with her friend's husband. This is not a material falsehood, at least not vis-à-vis the burglary case.*

- **Subornation of Perjury**: A person persuades someone else to commit perjury, such as paying someone to testify falsely

G. Bribery

- **Common law**: Corrupt payment of something of value for purposes of influencing an _____ in the discharge of his official _____
- **Modern law**: Allows a bribery charge even if the person being bribed is not a public official
- Offering a bribe and receiving a bribe are both felonies.
- Recall that a person can be convicted of bribery even if the person could not "be bribed."

> **Example 75:** *If the defendant aids and abets the bribing of a public official by helping the official accept the bribe, the defendant can be guilty of bribery even though he could not receive the bribe and did not offer the bribe.*

CHAPTER 9: DEFENSES

A. Intoxication

- **Ask two questions:**

  1) Was the intoxication _____ or
     _____?

  2) Is the charged crime a _____-intent crime or a
     _____-intent crime?

  o **Specific-intent crimes (FIAT or MPC statute with "purposely"):** Can use either voluntary or involuntary intoxication as a defense, if the defendant could not maintain the state of mind necessary for the offense

  o **General-intent crimes:** Can use only _____ intoxication as a defense

B. Insanity

- Involves a defendant who, because of a _____ disease or defect, is unable to conform his conduct to the law.

C. Mistake of Fact

- Is this a specific-intent crime or a general-intent crime?

  o General-intent crimes: Only _____ mistakes of fact may be used as a defense.

  o Specific-intent crimes: _____ mistakes of fact are potential defenses, even unreasonable mistakes.

D. Self-Defense

- Two Kinds of force:

  o _____ force: Intended or likely to cause death or serious injury (e.g., shooting someone)

  o _____ force: (e.g., locking a door; pushing someone)

1. Non-deadly force

  o A victim is entitled to use non-deadly force any time he _____ fears _____ unlawful harm.

  > *Example 76:* *If someone is trying to kiss you and you don't want them to, you can swat their hand away, slap their face, or use another type of non-deadly force.*

2. Deadly force

o A victim is entitled to use deadly force only if he _____ believes that deadly force will be used against him, or under the MPC, reasonably believes that the crime will result in serious bodily injury.

o **Retreat**

- **Majority Rule:** Retreat is _____ even when entitled to use deadly force

- **Minority Rule**: _____ retreat rather than using deadly force if safe to do so

    Example 77: Jan sees you coming toward her house with a weapon in your hand. In a minority jurisdiction, if she can get inside, lock the door, and call the police, she cannot go upstairs to get her rifle and blow your head off from a window.

- Even in minority jurisdictions, retreat is never required when the person employing deadly force is in his own home.

    Exam Tip 12: On the MBE, the question will tell you if you are to assume a duty to retreat. Otherwise, assume that you can use deadly force to resist deadly force or another serious crime.

E. Defense of Others

- An individual has the same right to defend other individuals against a criminal that she has to defend herself.

    Example 78: You and a friend are walking down the street. Someone approaches your friend and says, "Give me your money or I'm going to blow your head off." You are entitled to use deadly force to protect your friend, as if you were protecting yourself.

F. Defense of Property

- Right to use only _____ force to protect property

    Example 79: If you see someone trying to steal your car, you cannot use deadly force to prevent the theft of property.

    Exam Tip 13: The bar examiners often use a scenario involving deadly force designed to protect property during the owner's absence; e.g., the use of booby traps or spring guns. This is not an appropriate use of force.

G. Duress

- Defendant claims he committed a crime only because he was threatened by a third party and _____ believed that the only way to avoid death or injury to himself or others was to commit the crime.

- In order to be a defense, there must be a threat of death or serious bodily harm. Mere injury, particularly injury to property, is not sufficient.
- Defense for all crimes other than _____

> *Example 80:* Don decides to rob a grocery store. On the way out of the store, he leaps into a passing car driven by Fred, puts a gun to Fred's head, and orders Fred to drive him out of town. "Faster, faster," Don yells. Fred knows that the speed limit is 65, but he cranks the engine up to 90 miles an hour. As a result, he is unable to stop before running over Glenda. Fred is charged with felony murder with respect to Glenda's death.
>
> Is Fred guilty? _____
>
> _____.

H. Necessity

- Available in response to _____ forces; i.e., it is the lesser of two evils

> *Example 81:* After Hurricane Katrina flooded New Orleans, many people were trapped in the city. One such person is Harold, who is trapped in his house without potable water. He breaks into a neighbor's house looking for drinkable water. Harold could assert a necessity defense, because he could claim that without getting water from his neighbor's house (which was a burglary), he might have died. Thus, breaking into the house was the lesser of two evils.

GOOD LUCK ON THE EXAM!

[END OF HANDOUT]

Themis
Bar Review

Criminal Procedure

CRIMINAL PROCEDURE
PROFESSOR PAMELA S. KARLAN
STANFORD LAW SCHOOL

CHAPTER 1:   BASIC CONCEPTS, ARRESTS, AND SEIZURES

A. Basic Principles

- Constitutional protections apply only to _____ actions

    Example 1:   *If parents severely beat a child, they do not violate the Cruel and Unusual Punishments Clause.*

    Example 2:   *A snoopy neighbor enters your house and steals several things—including your marijuana plants. He brings the plants back to his home and calls the government to notify them of what he found. This is not a search.*

- Two important exceptions:

    o Private persons acting as government _____

    Example 3:   *The government calls your neighbor and asks her to break into your house to look for marijuana plants. This is a search under the Fourth Amendment.*

    Example 4:   *The government asks one inmate to speak with another inmate in order to get the second inmate to answer some questions. This is an interrogation within the meaning of the Fifth and Sixth Amendments.*

    o Defense counsel (both public and private) are treated as government actors for purposes of the Sixth Amendment with respect to effective assistance of counsel.

B. Arrests and Seizures of Persons

1. In General

o Police can approach anyone in a public place, and unless the encounter escalates to a _____, there is no real constraint on what the police can do and no protection against what they discover (e.g., "tailing" a suspect, canvassing a neighborhood and asking questions).

o **Seizure**—Occurs when an officer, by means of _____ or show of _____ intentionally terminates or restrains the person's freedom of movement

- Physical force—grabbing suspect by the arm, blocking ability to move, shooting a suspect
- Show of authority—showing a badge and saying, "Stop!"
- Test: Whether a reasonable person would feel free to _____ the officer

- Seizure—Ramming a suspect's car in an attempt to stop the car
- Not a seizure—Running over a third party while chasing a suspect (because the officer did not intend to stop the third party)

2. **Types of Seizures**

   a. **Stop and Frisk/Terry Stops**

   - An officer stops an individual when the officer has a _____ suspicion, based on _____ facts, to believe the suspect is or is about to be engaged in criminal behavior.
   - Burden Hierarchy:
     - Beyond a reasonable doubt → conviction
     - Probable cause ("more likely than not") → arrest
     - Reasonable suspicion → stop
   - An officer's reasonable _____ of law can give rise to reasonable suspicion
   - During a Terry Stop, an officer can pat-down a detainee for _____ but cannot frisk for _____.
     - If the pat down reveals objects whose shape makes their identity obvious, the officer can seize those objects (i.e., it's obvious that the objects are contraband).
     - If probable cause develops during a Terry Stop, the officer can then make an arrest.
   - Consequences of a stop that is not based on adequate suspicion:
     - If the initial stop is unlawful, but the officer develops the basis for a lawful arrest during the stop, evidence seized during the arrest _____ be used at trial
     - If the arrest is unlawful, evidence seized during the arrest _____ be used at trial

   Example 5: *In* Utah v. Strieff, *police were outside of a house where they thought there might be drug activity. Strieff came out of the house and the officers stopped him based merely on a hunch (which is insufficient to support a stop). During the stop, the police ran a warrant check, which revealed a warrant for Strieff's arrest. During a search incident to arrest, the officer discovered drugs.*

   b. **Traffic stops**

   - Officers must have _____ to stop a car
   - Once there is lawful stop, officers may pat down an occupant for _____ if they have reasonable suspicion that the person has a weapon.
   - **Checkpoints**—Officers _____ need reasonable suspicion to stop drivers if they pull over everyone.

c. Arrests

- There must be _____ to believe that the arrested individual has committed a crime.
- Can be with or without an arrest _____
- **Pretext arrest**: As long as the police have probable cause to believe an individual committed a crime, it is irrelevant whether the officer stopped that person for the crime for which there is probable cause or some other crime.

  Example 6: *Undercover officers are walking the streets of D.C. looking for illegal drug activity. They see a man driving a car—he appears nervous and somewhat suspicious. He then makes a turn without using his turn signal. Police can pull over this driver because he failed to use his turn signal—even though they were really concerned about drug activity. They did not have probable cause to stop him for the drugs, but he could be pulled over because they had probable cause to believe that he committed some crime.*

  Note 1: Pretext arrests are fine under the Fourth Amendment. However, there may be an Equal Protection issue if the officers choose who to stop based on race or other discriminatory criteria.

d. Warrants

- Authorizes an officer to arrest a particular person
- An arrest warrant is issued by a _____ and detached magistrate based on a finding of _____ to believe that the individual has committed a particular crime.
- Warrant must name the person and identify the _____
- Allows officers to enter an individual's home to arrest that individual

  - Does not authorize officers to enter a third party's home or business
  - Officers must also have a search warrant to search the premises for the individual (or meet an exception to the warrant requirement)

- Absent an arrest warrant, officers can only arrest someone inside a dwelling if:

  a) There are _____ circumstances (e.g., felony hot pursuit or danger to others); or

  b) There is _____ to enter.

e. Warrantless arrests

- An officer can arrest an individual without a warrant in a _____ place, either for a crime committed in the officer's _____ or based on probable cause to believe the individual committed a _____.
- If the crime was not committed in the officer's presence, the officer can make an arrest only for a _____.

> *Example 7:* You just robbed a bank (a felony) and fled the scene. An officer arrives and a witness describes you to the officer. The officer walks around the area and notices you because you perfectly match the suspect's description. The officer can arrest you because he has probable cause.

- An arrest that is illegal does not prevent prosecution for the crime. But, it may result in the exclusion of _____ discovered during the arrest.

C. Searches Incident to Arrest

- A lawful arrest permits the arresting officers to make a contemporaneous search of the person arrested and the immediate _____ to:

  o Protect officers from weapons or other dangers; and
  o To prevent the _____ or concealment of evidence

- Any evidence discovered during a search incident to a lawful arrest can be used against the person arrested.

- **Arrest on the street:** Can search the suspect and his _____

- **Arrest at home:** Can search the suspect and his immediate arrest area

- **Arrest in a car**: May search _____ compartment of a vehicle as long as the person/suspect still has _____ to the vehicle at the time

  o Officers cannot arrest a suspect, put him in the back of the squad car, and then go back and conduct a search of the car

  > **Editor's Note 1:** Note that if it were reasonable to believe that the vehicle contains evidence of the offense of the arrest, such a search would be proper, even though the suspect would no longer pose a threat to the officers.

- Inventory search—When the police arrest a driver and impound his car, it may be searched for inventory purposes.

- Special rule for cellphones—officers may seize a cellphone during an arrest and check the phone for dangers, but police need a _____ to search the phone's digital information

CHAPTER 2: SEARCHES

> **Exam Tip 1:** "Searches" is a topic that is often tested.

A. What is a "Search"?

- Occurs when _____ conduct violates a reasonable _____ of privacy

1. Government Conduct

> *Example 8:* It is not a search if your mother or private employer goes through your things.

- ○ Can occur with _____ intrusion upon private property

    Example 9: *The police bring a drug-sniffing dog onto your porch, or place a GPS device on your car*

- ○ A search can occur without a _____ intrusion

    Example 10: *The defendant was growing marijuana in his basement and used grow lamps. A government agent set up a thermal imaging device on the public street and found that the basement was unusually warm. The agent used this information to obtain a search warrant. The use of the thermal imaging device was a search in violation of the defendant's reasonable expectation of privacy.*

    - ▪ Using some types of **technology** constitutes a search.

2. Reasonable Expectation of Privacy

- ○ Places where we do have an expectation of privacy against the government:

    - ▪ Homes
    - ▪ _____
    - ▪ Offices
    - ▪ _____
    - ▪ Backyard of your home (curtilage)

- ○ Places where we do not have an expectation of privacy against the government:

    - ▪ Public streets
    - ▪ _____ (even if they're private property)
    - ▪ Garbage cans left out in the street
    - ▪ _____ property

    > **Exam Tip 2:** Be aware of who holds the reasonable expectation of privacy and who is claiming the search. The government's actions are valid unless it is the defendant who has the reasonable expectation of privacy.

- ○ You have a reasonable expectation of privacy in your car, though it is more limited.

    Example 11: *Quentin goes into the dressing room of a men's store and hides a valuable leather belt in his underwear. Wendy, a store security guard monitoring a hidden camera in the dressing room, sees Quentin. As Quentin is leaving the store, Wendy grabs him, thrusts her hands into his pants, and grabs the belt. Wendy calls the police and Quentin is subsequently charged with larceny. He argues that the belt should be excluded from evidence because the search violated his constitutional rights. What result?* _____

    _____

    _____

B. The Warrant Requirement

- Generally, the government needs a _____ to conduct a search if there is a reasonable expectation of privacy.

- Three requirements:

    1) A search warrant must be issued by a _____ magistrate

    2) Must be based on probable cause to believe that the items sought are _____, instrumentalities, or _____ of crime

        Example 12: *There has been a bank robbery. The loot that was stolen from the bank is the fruit of the crime; the gun used to commit the robbery is an instrumentality of the crime; the bloody shirt the robber wore is evidence of the crime.*

    3) Must describe the _____ and _____ to be searched with particularity

- If a warrant does not meet the above requirements, the warrant is _____, and the items seized pursuant to the warrant will be _____ from the prosecution's case-in-chief.

- Wiretapping constitutes a search.

    o Must have probable cause and a warrant
    o Must specifically identify whose conversations are to be intercepted
    o Must include an end date for the warrant
    o Must perform minimization

C. Exceptions to the Warrant Requirement

- There are seven major exceptions; think of them as seven _____ from the warrant requirement:

    o Exigent circumstances
    o Search incident to arrest
    o Consent
    o Automobiles
    o Plain view
    o Evidence obtained from administrative searches
    o Stop and frisk

1. Exigent Circumstances

    o Officers are entitled to secure premises (i.e., prevent people from moving things) while they obtain a warrant, but sometimes this is not sufficient.
    o If officers are in "hot pursuit" or there is an _____, they may conduct a search without getting a warrant first.

Example 13: *A woman runs out of a building and tells an officer that there is a man inside with a bomb who is threatening to blow everyone up. The officer may enter the building and search without first obtaining a warrant.*

Example 14: *If officers believe that a suspect dropped a weapon in a place where a small child might pick it up, officers may look for the weapon without first obtaining a warrant.*

- o This exception does not apply when police create the exigency.
- o Absent exigent circumstances, police need a warrant for a DUI blood draw.

2. Search Incident to Lawful Arrest

- o If the arrest was lawful, a search warrant is unnecessary.
- o **Scope**—limited to the immediate area around the individual
- o **Automobile**—arrestee must be within reach of the passenger compartment to search it
- o **DNA**—samples may be collected as part of search incident to arrest
- o **Cellphones**—_____ search digital contents

3. Consent

- o A defendant can consent to a search.
- o Consent does **not** require the officer to _____ the subject of his right to refuse. (e.g., "Mind if I look in that ....?")
- o Consent can involve outright deception.
- o **Third Parties:**

    Example 15: *You give your bags to a friend and say, "Please hold my knapsack while I run into the library for a second." A police officer approaches your friend and asks to look in the knapsack. If your friend agrees, the officer need not obtain your consent to search the knapsack because the friend had apparent control over the property.*

    - ▪ Officers cannot search over the objection of a present occupant.
    - ▪ Officers can search if the suspect is not present and the other occupant consents.

4. Automobiles

- o Recall that police are allowed to conduct a warrantless search of an automobile incident to arrest if the arrestee is within reach of the passenger compartment (and to conduct an inventory search of an impounded vehicle).
- o If police have **probable cause** to believe an automobile contains _____, they can search those parts of the vehicle that might contain contraband, even without an arrest.

Example 16: *If police have probable cause to believe that there are drugs in a car, they may search the parts of the car (and containers in the car) that might contain the drugs. (Might be the whole car)*

Example 17: *If police have probable cause to believe that there are submachine guns in a car, they may search the trunk and passenger compartment. They cannot search inside a wallet or lipstick container or in other areas where they could not reasonably expect to find the contraband.*

5. Plain View

o   If police are _____ present, they can seize any item in "plain view" (or "plain smell"), even if that item was not named in the warrant.

Example 18: *If police are legally present in a house to search a computer for evidence of child pornography and they see marijuana on the table, they can seize the marijuana.*

6. Evidence Obtained From Administrative Searches

o   Police do not need search warrants to conduct administrative searches.

o   Two kinds:

4)   Administrative warrants (e.g., fire or health inspections of a building)

5)   Warrantless administrative searches—used to ensure compliance with various administrative regulations; examples:

- Airplane boarding areas
- International borders
- Highly regulated industries (liquor stores, gun shops, etc.)
- Searches of students in public schools
- Special needs searches; e.g., drug testing of railroad employees after an accident
- Roadblocks for drunk driving or seeking information

7. Stop and Frisk

o   Terry stops merely require reasonable suspicion; can conduct a limited search for weapons (i.e., a frisk)

CHAPTER 3:   INTERROGATIONS

A. The Fifth Amendment

- Provides, among other things, that no person shall be _____ in any criminal case to be a witness against himself.

1. **Scope of the Privilege**

   ○ Applies to _____, not corporations or unions

   > ***Example 19:*** *A corporation's records custodian cannot claim the privilege on behalf of the corporation.*

   ○ Applies to _____ evidence, not physical evidence

   > ***Example 20:*** *Fifth Amendment protection does not apply to blood tests or handwriting exemplars*

   ○ Applies to testimony that would be a link in the chain leading to prosecution or conviction

   ▪ As long as there is reason to believe the testimony might lead to future criminal prosecution, an individual is entitled to invoke the Fifth Amendment.

   > ***Example 21:*** *Laura is a witness in a bank robbery case. When asked if she saw the suspect rob the bank, Laura can refuse to answer the question if by answering, she would somehow incriminate herself. Suppose Laura was a law enforcement officer and was supposed to be watching another suspect at the time of the robbery. By admitting that she was at the bank, she might incriminate herself with regard to theft of government services.*

   ○ If someone is given _____ from prosecution for their statements, they cannot continue to refuse to answer.

2. **Statements Made by an Individual**

   ○ Must be made by the individual to the _____

   > ***Example 22:*** *Jana comes home and tells her parents that she just robbed a bank. The government can force her parents to testify about what Jana said to them. She would have no Fifth Amendment protection.*

   > ***Example 23:*** *Remember that other privileges or protections may apply via evidence law. Suppose that after robbing the bank, Jana had an appointment with her doctor and told him about the bank robbery because she was feeling anxious and wanted some tranquilizers. Those statements are protected by the doctor-patient privilege.*

   ○ Key starting point for the privilege against self-incrimination: *Miranda v. Arizona*

   ▪ Statements made as a result of _____ are inadmissible unless they are accompanied by procedural safeguards (i.e., the *Miranda* warnings)

   ▪ "Custodial": The person being questioned has been arrested or is not otherwise _____ (e.g., in the back of a police cruiser).

   • If not in custody, no warning is required. Any statement (or silence) can be used.

- Someone who is already imprisoned is not necessarily treated as "in custody" for purposes of custodial interrogation. The prisoner is not "in custody" if he is free to be taken back to his cell.

- "Interrogation": Involves either the official asking questions or engaging in other words or _____ that police know or should know will elicit a response

  - Does not include _____ statements
  - Does not include _____ booking questions

3. Miranda Warnings

- Before conducting custodial interrogations, the police must inform the suspect:

  - You have the right to remain _____;
  - Any statement you make may be used against you in court;
  - You have the right to consult an attorney and to have the attorney _____ during questioning; and
  - You have the right to have an attorney appointed if you cannot afford one.

- Interrogators must ask whether the defendant _____ the rights

  - I.e., Defendant understands English, can hear, and actually heard what was said

- No magic words: As long as the substance of the Miranda warnings is communicated, it will be sufficient

- The police must cease questioning if either of the following occurs:

1) Invoking the right to remain silent

- If a defendant says she does not want to talk, the interrogation must _____.
- The right must be affirmatively invoked; it is not enough to just remain silent.
- After a _____ period of time, police can go back to the suspect, give warnings again, and seek to talk to the person again.

2) Invoking the right to counsel

- Right must be affirmatively invoked: "I want a lawyer."
- If the right to counsel is invoked, all questioning must stop until either:

  i) The lawyer is present; or

  ii) The defendant affirmatively _____ contact with police. Police cannot generally go back to the defendant.

- It is not enough to say, "I think I should talk to somebody," or "I want to talk to my... (Parents, doctor, etc.)"
- Police do not have to tell the defendant that a lawyer is trying to reach them.

4. The Public Safety Exception

- ○ When public safety is at risk, the police do not have to give Miranda warnings before questioning.

    Example 24: *If there is a ticking time bomb in a grocery store, the police need not give Miranda warnings before questioning people. Or if police are called to a school and told that a man planted a bomb inside, they can arrest the man because they have probable cause and can question him about the bomb's whereabouts before giving Miranda warnings.*

5. Interrogation Tactics

- ○ The confession must be _____
- ○ Statements obtained by _____, even after Miranda warnings, are inadmissible.

    Example 25: *"We will prosecute you," is not a threat. "We will beat you up," and "We will go and arrest your children," are threats.*

- ○ Confessions can be the product of _____

    Example 26: *It is permissible to tell a suspect (who was caught on video wearing a mask) that police have the capability to peel off the stocking mask through photo-technology.*

    Example 27: *Police can also use the colander and copy machine "lie detector."*

B. Consequences of Fifth Amendment Violations

- Two categories:

  - ○ Statements obtained involuntarily
  - ○ Statements obtained in violation of Miranda

1. Involuntarily Obtained Statements

- ○ An involuntarily obtained statement is _____ admissible against a defendant.

    Example 28: *Police may never put a gun to a suspect's head and say, "Confess or die." Any incriminating statement made by the suspect is inadmissible.*

- ○ Whether to overturn a conviction depends on the harmless error standard.
- ○ Evidence obtained as the result of an involuntary statement (e.g., "Tell us where the body is buried" while a suspect is at gunpoint) is fruit of the poisonous tree and is _____ inadmissible.

2. Statements in Violation of Miranda

- ○ Inadmissible in the prosecution's case in chief, but can be admitted in order to _____ the defendant to challenge his credibility.

o Evidence obtained as a result of a voluntary statement taken in violation of Miranda is

_____

CHAPTER 4:   THE SIXTH AMENDMENT RIGHT TO COUNSEL; IDENTIFICATION PROCEDURES

A. The Sixth Amendment

In addition to the Fifth Amendment right to counsel for custodial interrogations, the Sixth Amendment explicitly provides a criminal defendant with "the _____ of counsel for his defense."

1. **Sixth Amendment Right to Counsel vs. Fifth Amendment Miranda Right**

   o **How is it invoked?**

   ▪ Sixth Amendment right automatically attaches once there has been an indictment, information, or other formal charges

   • Exists unless a defendant knowingly and intelligently _____ the right

   ▪ Fifth Amendment right (protected by *Miranda*) must be _____ invoked by the defendant

   Example 29: You are arrested and brought to the police station. Unless you ask for a lawyer after getting Mirandized, you will not get one. But if you are charged in court, you get an attorney unless you affirmatively waive the right to counsel.

   o **To what charges does the right apply?**

   ▪ Sixth Amendment right to counsel is offense-specific; a defendant has a Sixth Amendment right to counsel only with regard to the offenses for which he has actually been _____ (and any lesser-included offenses)

   ▪ With respect to unrelated charges, the defendant can be questioned, either expressly or through undercover government agents.

   Example 30: You are charged with burglary, so you have a Sixth Amendment right to counsel regarding that burglary and a lesser-included offense, such as larceny. But police can still question you about an unrelated robbery for which you have not been charged.

   o Sixth Amendment applies whether you are in _____ or not

   ▪ Fifth Amendment *Miranda* right applies to custodial interrogation for any charge, but not to non-custodial interrogation

2. **When Does the Sixth Amendment Right to Counsel Apply?**

   o Applies to all _____ prosecutions and to any misdemeanor prosecutions in which jail time or suspended jail sentence is imposed.

      Example 31: *If you are charged with a misdemeanor and are not sentenced to any jail time, you do not have a Sixth Amendment right to counsel.*

   o Applies to all _____ stages of the prosecution

      ▪ Examples of critical stages:

         • Evidentiary hearings
         • Post-indictment lineups
         • Post-indictment interrogations
         • All parts of the trial process, including guilty pleas, and sentencing

      Note 2: There is also a right to counsel in appeals as of right, but this right is provided by the Equal Protection Clause, not the Sixth Amendment.

      ▪ Examples of non-critical stages are:

         • Investigative lineups (pre-indictment)
         • Witnesses looking at photo arrays
         • Discretionary appeals and post-conviction (habeas) proceedings

B. **Identification Procedures**

   1. **Types of Procedures**

      o There are two kinds of identification procedures: _____ and
         _____

         ▪ **Photo arrays**: Neither the defendant nor his lawyer has the right to be _____,
            but police must turn over the array to the defendant.
         ▪ **Pre-indictment lineups:** Defendant has no right to counsel.
         ▪ **Post-indictment lineups:** Defendant has a right to have _____ present.

            • If violated, evidence that the witness identified the defendant at the lineup must be excluded.

   2. **Admissibility**

      o **Lineup evidence at trial**

         ▪ If the defendant moves to suppress evidence that a witness picked the defendant out of a lineup, the court will consider whether the lineup was _____
            _____
         ▪ If it was, the court can exclude the testimony.

- o **In-court identification**
  - The prosecution must establish by _____ evidence that the witness would have identified the defendant even without the suggestive lineup.

    Example 32: *Ingrid is charged with art theft. The prosecution alleges that she stole a small but valuable sculpture from an art gallery by putting it into a large shopping bag. The police ask Oscar, who works at the gallery, to view a photo array of five potential perpetrators. Ingrid is the only blonde-haired woman in the array and she appears quite a bit younger than the others. Oscar identifies Ingrid. The police then place Ingrid in a lineup. Preeta, another gallery employee, views the lineup. The Assistant D.A. asks Preeta, "Do you see the person who walked out of the gallery with a large shopping bag?" Preeta says no, but adds that she "saw the third person from the left" – Ingrid – "reach into a lady's pocket and steal her wallet." The A.D.A. knows that another patron at the gallery, Sarah, had filed a complaint with the police that her pocket had been picked on the day of the alleged sculpture heist. So the A.D.A. obtains a search warrant for Ingrid's house, and the police find Sarah's wallet. Ingrid is now charged with larceny against Sarah as well as art theft. Which of the following statements about the use of evidence are true?*

    A) Is the wallet admissible at Ingrid's trial for larceny even though Ingrid's lawyer was not present at the lineup? _____

    _____

    B) Is Oscar's identification inadmissible at Ingrid's trial because Ingrid's lawyer was not present? _____

    _____

CHAPTER 5: THE EXCLUSIONARY RULE AND ITS EXCEPTIONS

Exam Tip 3: This is one of the most important Criminal Procedure topics on the MBE.

- **Rule**: Illegally obtained evidence, either _____ evidence obtained by an illegal search or a statement obtained through an illegal _____, is inadmissible at the criminal trial of the person whose rights were violated.
- The Exclusionary Rule applies at _____, not to pretrial proceedings (e.g., grand jury proceedings).

A. Standing

- The violation must have been of the _____ rights, and not someone else's rights.

Example 33: *Police enter Ellen's house without a warrant and while there, they find a photograph of Robert holding a sawed-off shotgun. Robert would have no standing to object to introduction of the photograph at his trial for possessing an illegal weapon, because it was Ellen's Fourth Amendment rights that were violated.*

Example 34: *Lucy is arrested but police do not give her Miranda warnings. If she makes a statement that she robbed a bank with you, you cannot suppress her statements at your trial (because it was a violation of Lucy's rights, not your rights).*

- One slight qualification: If the driver of a car is arrested without probable cause, passengers are deemed to have been seized as well, so they _____ challenge the constitutionality of the stop.

B. The Exclusionary Rule

1. Definition

- Evidence obtained in violation of the _____, _____, or _____ Amendments cannot be introduced at trial to prove a defendant's guilt.
- _____ of the Poisonous Tree: The exclusionary rule also applies to evidence obtained as a result of the initial violation.

  Example 35: *Police illegally search your house and find a safe deposit box key. They take the key to the bank, look inside the deposit box, and find some incriminating items. Those items are considered fruit of the poisonous tree, because but for the first illegal search, they would not have found the items in the safe deposit box.*

2. 5½ Exceptions

- **Knock and announce:** Officers executing an arrest warrant at a residence are required to knock and announce they are police.

  - If they fail to do so, and discover evidence, that evidence does not have to be

    _____.

- **Inevitable discovery:** If the evidence would have been discovered anyway through _____ means, it will be admissible.

  Example 36: *Officer Thomas was searching Ulysses' house without a warrant. Officer Young, who had probable cause, was in the process of acquiring a search warrant.*

- **Independent source:** Relevant evidence discovered on the basis of an independent source will be admissible.

- **Attenuation in the causal chain:** Intervening events and the passage of time can remove the taint of the unconstitutional conduct.

Example 37: *An officer unlawfully discovered some betting slips in a flower shop. He told a second officer what he had seen. This second officer then spoke with a former employee of the flower shop who admitted that a bookmaking operation was run out of the shop. Here, there were enough steps in the chain of causation that the evidence gained from talking to that former employee need not be suppressed.*

Example 38: *In* Utah v. Strieff, *police were watching a house with a suspected drug operation. They decided to stop and question the next person who left the house. The police stopped and questioned Mr. Strieff without adequate suspicion to do so. During the course of questioning, the officers discovered an outstanding arrest warrant for an unrelated event. The officer arrested Mr. Strieff and conducted a search incident to the arrest. During the search, the officer found drugs. The Court held that there was attenuation between the initial illegal stop and the discovery of the drugs. The arrest was lawful and that was sufficient to remove the taint and admit the evidence.*

- o **Good faith**
  - ▪ Biggest of the exceptions to the exclusionary rule
  - ▪ It applies to officers who rely on either:
    - a) An _____ that was later declared unconstitutional; or
    - b) A warrant that, while facially valid, is later found to be defective.
  - ▪ If officers are acting in good faith reliance, they are entitled to use the evidence that was obtained.
  - ▪ Officers can rely on a warrant unless:
    - • The warrant was obtained by _____
    - • The warrant was obtained in reliance on an unacceptably bare-bones affidavit (defective on its face)
    - • The magistrate wholly abandoned his _____
- o **(Half) Exception**—Isolated _____ by law enforcement personnel does not necessarily trigger the exclusionary rule.
  - ▪ To trigger the exclusionary rule, police conduct must be sufficiently deliberate so that exclusion could meaningfully _____ it.

Example 39: *In* Herring v. United States, *Herring went to a police station to pick up his truck, which had been impounded. At the station, an officer who was familiar with Herring asked the clerk to see if there was an arrest warrant for him. There was not. The officer then asked her to call the next county and ask whether there was a warrant there for Herring. The clerk said there was. The officers pulled Herring over after he left the police station without probable cause, arrested him, and conducted a search incident to arrest. They found some incriminating evidence. In the meantime, the clerk discovered that there was no longer a valid warrant for Herring's arrest.*

Mr. Herring moved to suppress the evidence on the grounds that he was arrested without probable cause and without a warrant. The Supreme Court held that the good faith exception should apply—even though the police may have been negligent.

3. **Key Points**

   o Remember that suppression is an issue only after you conclude that there has been an underlying _____ in the first place.

      ▪ Fourth Amendment: Was there a search? Was there a seizure? If yes, was there probable cause?
      ▪ Fifth Amendment: Was there a Fifth Amendment interrogation violation? Was the defendant in custody? Was there an interrogation? Was the defendant given warnings? Did he invoke his rights?
      ▪ Sixth Amendment: Did the Sixth Amendment right to counsel attach? Was this a critical stage?

   o If there was a violation, ask whether the exclusionary rule applies to that kind of violation.
   o Then ask whether one of the _____ to the exclusionary rule makes the evidence admissible anyway.
   o If the question involves whether a conviction should be overturned (rather than whether the evidence should be suppressed), apply the harmless error rule:

      ▪ Ask, if this piece of evidence had not been admitted, would it make a difference to the outcome?

CHAPTER 6:   PRETRIAL PROCEDURES

A. The Initiation of Charges

   • Under the Fifth Amendment's Presentment Clause, all federal felony charges must be initiated by _____ by a grand jury unless the defendant waives indictment.

      o An indictment requires _____ to believe the defendant committed the crimes charged.

   • The Fifth Amendment Presentment Clause has not been incorporated to the states, so states can choose whether to proceed by grand jury indictment or by _____

      o If proceeding by information, there must be a preliminary hearing before a neutral judge to determine whether there is _____.

B. Proceedings before the Grand Jury

- Grand juries can consider evidence that has been obtained _____ and _____ evidence in deciding whether there is probable cause to indict.
- **Defendants** do not have the right to testify before the grand jury or to call witnesses.
- **Witnesses** do not have the right to _____ within the grand jury room, although they can leave the grand jury room to consult with their lawyers.
- Grand jury proceedings are held in _____
- The grand jury does not have to be _____

C. Competence to Stand Trial

- Test: Whether the defendant comprehends the _____ of the proceedings against him and can _____ his lawyer in defending the case
- If a defendant is competent to stand trial, he is also competent to plead _____ and _____ the right to trial.

D. Guilty Pleas

- The majority of defendants do not go to trial; the charges are either dismissed or the defendant pleads guilty
- When a defendant pleads guilty, he _____ various trial rights, such as the right to put the prosecution to its proof, to confront and produce witnesses, to trial by jury, to challenge the introduction of evidence, to appeal if there is a conviction.
- For a guilty plea to be valid, the defendant must _____ and _____ waive these rights. This is accomplished through plea allocution, where the judge:

  - Informs the defendant of his rights and ensures the defendant understands those rights;
  - Informs the defendant of the possible sentences;
  - Informs the defendant of immigration consequences (the judge is not required to inform the defendant of all collateral consequences, such as difficulty getting student loans);
  - Makes sure there is a factual basis for the plea;
  - Determines that the plea did not result from _____, coercion, threats, or promises

- If a defendant challenges his plea agreement and succeeds in reopening the case, the prosecution can reinstate charges that it had dropped.
- The defendant is entitled to _____ assistance from counsel in the plea bargaining process.

E. Bail

- The Eighth Amendment forbids the setting of _____ bail, but does not state outright that bail must be offered pending trial.

- **General rule:** Bail is available unless the defendant poses either a flight risk or a
  _____ to the community.
- There is a presumption _____ bail.
- Courts can impose pretrial release conditions on defendants, such as house arrest, avoidance of particular people, or reporting requirements.

CHAPTER 7:   THE TRIAL PROCESS

A. The Jury

1. Sixth Amendment Right to a Jury Trial

A defendant has a right to jury trial for all _____ offenses, for which the authorized punishment is more than _____ months.

> **Note 1:** The Sixth Amendment right to *counsel* attaches in misdemeanor cases only if a sentence of incarceration is actually imposed.

2. Jury Size

- **Federal:** A jury in a federal criminal case must have _____ members and must decide the case _____
- **States:** Can use juries of _____ or more in criminal cases; juries do not have to be unanimous (though a six-person jury must be unanimous)

3. Jury Selection

- Begins with a venire or jury pool
  - Must represent a fair _____ of the community from which no distinctive group is excluded
- The petit or petty jury is selected through the process of voir dire.
  - Two ways to remove potential jurors: challenges _____ and peremptory challenges.
    - The actual jury that is seated must be impartial, but it does not have to reflect a fair cross-section of the community.
  - **For-cause challenges**—Used to ensure an _____ jury
    - Jurors can be removed for cause when they reveal something that will prevent them from being impartial and deliberating _____
      - E.g., if a juror knows one of the parties or the victim; if a juror was a friend of one of the witnesses; or worked for the defendant's company
    - There is _____ to the number of challenges for cause.

- **Peremptory challenges**—Can generally be made for any reason, including hunches
  - Exception: Neither side can challenge jurors on the basis of _____ or _____ (Batson doctrine)
  - Each side is statutorily limited in the number of peremptory challenges.

B. Speedy and Public Trial Rights

1. Speedy Trial Rights

- Defendants can be injured by the passage of time between an alleged crime and their trial
- Statutes of limitations give defendants repose.
  - Statutes of limitations normally begin to run when the crime _____.
  - For continuing offenses, the statute of limitations does not begin to run until the end of the offense (e.g., a conspiracy starts on the day of agreement but continues until the conspiracy's purpose has been achieved or abandoned).

    Example 40: *In January 2003, Prof. Karlan entered into a conspiracy to distribute drugs. The conspiracy continued until 2007. The statute of limitations begins to run from 2007, not 2003.*

- Two constitutional provisions that protect against delay:
  - The _____ protects against pre-accusation delay. It's relatively toothless, as long as the limitations period has not run.
  - The _____ Clause of the Sixth Amendment protects defendants against delay that occurs between the time of arrest or indictment (whichever comes first) and the time of trial.

- A court faced with a Speedy Trial Clause claim looks at **four factors:**
  1) Length of the delay;
  2) _____ for the delay;
  3) Whether the defendant _____ to a speedy trial; and
  4) _____ to the defendant

2. Public Trial Rights

- The Sixth Amendment and First Amendment, taken together, protect the rights of the defendant (Sixth) and the public (First) to attend public trials.
- Courts have some discretion to close particular proceedings if there is a substantial likelihood of _____.

3. The Confrontation Clause

o The Sixth Amendment guarantees a defendant the right to _____ the witnesses against him, as well as the right to compulsory process to produce his own witnesses.

a. Crawford Doctrine

- If a statement is _____ (i.e., made under circumstances which would lead a reasonable person to believe that the statement would be used at a later trial), then the Sixth Amendment bars admission of the statement if:

  - The declarant is _____; and
  - The defendant had no prior _____ to cross-examine the witness.

  Example 41: In Melendez-Diaz v. Massachusetts, *the prosecution tried to admit a forensic report into evidence without calling the forensic analyst who prepared the report as a witness. The Court determined that the defendant was entitled to cross-examine the analyst and so the report was inadmissible without that opportunity.*

- For non-testimonial statements, look to the rules of evidence.

b. Bruton Doctrine

- A defendant's own statements are always _____ against him. This is true even if the defendant does not testify at trial.
- If there are co-defendants, a non-testifying co-defendant's statements are _____ against the other defendant.

  Example 42: Pam and her brother Peter are on trial for robbing a bank. During the investigation, Pam said, "It's true, I drove the getaway car. But Peter talked me into the whole thing and Peter is the one who held the gun to the teller's head." Pam's statement is admissible against her, but the statement also incriminates Peter. They go to trial together. If Pam takes the stand, Peter may of course cross-examine her about the statement, and there's no Confrontation Clause problem. But if Pam doesn't testify, the statement could still be used against Pam; the statement becomes inadmissible against Peter because he cannot cross-examine Pam. (Courts have been required to redact or alter the confession so that it no longer refers to the non-testifying co-defendant.)

c. Defendant's right to present witnesses

- The defendant has the right to testify on his own behalf. He also has the right to compulsory process to obtain witnesses in his defense.

4. **Burden of Proof**

   o The prosecution must prove every element of the crime _____

   _____

   o Distinguish elements of the crime from affirmative defenses

      ▪ The government can place the burden of proof with regard to affirmative defenses on

      _____

   o Affirmative defenses can include insanity, self-defense, entrapment, or mistake.

CHAPTER 8:   RESPONSIBILITIES OF JUDGES, PROSECUTORS, AND DEFENSE COUNSEL

A. Judges

   • The Due Process Clause requires that judges possess neither actual nor
     _____ bias.

   • Actual bias consists of interests that would impair the judge's _____

      Example 43: A judge was paid for issuing search warrants, but not when he
      failed to issue a search warrant. The Supreme Court held that this was actual
      bias toward issuing warrants.

      Example 44: A judge had been a district attorney in the jurisdiction when the
      death penalty was imposed and had approved the death sentence. Later when
      the case was being appealed, the judge had become a justice on the court
      deciding the appeal. It violated Due Process for the justice to sit on the case
      because it might hinder his impartiality.

B. Prosecutors

   1. **Four Prosecutorial Duties**

      a. **Brady doctrine—Prosecutors must turn over all material**
         _____ **evidence to the defense; includes two types of
         evidence:**

         1) Evidence that tends to show that the defendant is _____ of
            the crimes charged

            Example 45: Two witnesses to a bank robbery described the suspect as a
            white, middle-aged, Jewish woman wearing a double strand of pearls, a red
            shirt, and a black suit. However, several other witnesses described the robber
            as a six-foot-five Samoan male wearing flip-flops and a sarong. The prosecutor
            is obligated to turn over all of this information to the defense, as it suggests
            that the suspect described by the first two witnesses may not have committed
            the crime.

2) Evidence that would enable the defense to _____ the credibility of prosecution witnesses

> ***Example 46:*** *The prosecutor must disclose if one of the government's witnesses is testifying because the prosecutor promised to drop charges against the witness.*

> ***Example 47:*** *If one of the witnesses in the bank robbery example above first described the robber as a tall Samoan male but later said it was a short white woman, this must be disclosed to the defense. This allows defense counsel to impeach that witness by questioning his credibility.*

- _____ evidence—disclosure could change the outcome of the case
- *Brady* material includes inconclusive lab reports, witness descriptions that do not match the defendant, cooperation agreements with witnesses, etc.

  - Includes evidence within the control of the government (including the police)

- If the defendant pleads guilty after negotiations, the prosecution is not required to share the Brady information

  - Many states and some D.A.s offices have an open file policy allowing the defense to see the information.

b. A prosecutor may not knowingly present _____ testimony.

c. A prosecutor may not contact (or direct others to contact) a defendant outside the presence of his _____ (i.e., cannot violate the defendant's Sixth Amendment right to counsel).

d. A prosecutor may not comment on a defendant's _____ to testify at trial or make unfair remarks about the defendant to the jury (i.e., cannot violate the defendant's Fifth Amendment right to remain silent).

- A prosecutor _____ comment on a defendant's silence before his *Miranda* rights attached.

2. Prosecutorial Misconduct

- Prosecutorial misconduct that has a reasonable possibility of affecting the verdict may require a _____ or reversal of a conviction.

C. Defense Counsel

- The Supreme Court has held that the Sixth Amendment not only guarantees defendants the right to the assistance of counsel, it also guarantees them _____ assistance of counsel at all critical stages of prosecution.

1. **Conflicts of Interest**

   o Joint representation can lead to a conflict of interest.

      Example 48: *Co-defendants represented at the same trial by the same lawyer can create a conflict of interest. For instance, one defendant may want to plead guilty while the other wants to proceed to trial.*

   o If there is an actual conflict, the judge must _____ the defendants that joint representation is a risk and give them the opportunity to get separate counsel.

      ▪ If they choose not to get separate counsel, the judge must get an affirmative waiver in which the defendants acknowledge that there is a conflict and that they would prefer to go forward with joint representation.

   o If a conflict of interest actually affects counsel's behavior, there is a _____ of prejudice. The defendant is not required to show actual innocence in order to obtain a new trial.

      Example 49: *Harry and Sally are represented by the same lawyer at trial. Because he represents them both, the lawyer decides not to cross-examine a particular witness because the testimony could be damaging to Sally. Harry need not show that the cross-examination by itself would have changed the outcome. He only needs to show an actual effect on the lawyer's behavior.*

2. **Effective Assistance**

   o The Strickland test—assesses whether a defendant was denied effective assistance:

      ▪ **Performance:** Did defense counsel's performance fall below the wide range of _____ conduct that lawyers might engage in?

      Example 50: *The defendant shot the victim in the buttocks and was charged with assault with intent to kill and attempted murder. The defendant's lawyer told him that he would be acquitted if he went to trial because the elements of the crime of attempted murder means you have to intend the victim's death; by shooting someone in the buttocks you can't be intending to kill them. Here, the lawyer got the law totally wrong. Shooting at someone is enough to show intent to kill.*

      Example 51: *Sleeping Lawyer: The decision of a junior lawyer not to wake a senior lawyer was found to be a tactical decision designed to get sympathy for the defendant.*

      ▪ **Prejudice:** There is a _____ probability that, had counsel performed effectively, the result would have been different.

      Example 52: *In this jurisdiction, suppression motions must be brought no later than thirty days before trial. The defendant's lawyer fails to bring the motion in time, filing it three days before trial. The judge denies the motion. There is clearly a failure of performance. But if the evidence had been seized legally, the lawyer's failure to file a timely motion would not have resulted in a different outcome. This would not be ineffective assistance because the defendant was not prejudiced.*

- Cases that go to trial: Defendant must show that there was a reasonable probability that he would not have been _____ if the lawyer had done a proper job
- Guilty pleas: Defendant must show that he would not have pleaded guilty if his lawyer had not given him bad advice or performed ineffectively

o If a defendant is denied effective assistance of counsel, his conviction must be reversed because the defendant has already shown that he was prejudiced

3. **Choice of Counsel**

o Defendants who can afford retained counsel are entitled to the counsel of their choice as long as the lawyer is:

- Properly _____ in the jurisdiction (including pro hac vice rules);
- Available for _____; and
- No conflict or other reason to disqualify the lawyer.

o A defendant who is denied the retained counsel of his choice is entitled to have his conviction _____.

o Indigent defendants: _____ to appointment of the lawyer of their choice.

- As long as they receive _____ assistance, they have received all the Constitution guarantees them.

4. **Proceeding Pro Se**

o Defendants are entitled to _____ the right to counsel and to represent themselves as long as they do it knowingly and voluntarily.

o The competence standard for waiving counsel: are they competent enough to understand what they are doing.

o A defendant who proceeds pro se does not have a constitutional right to a "back-up" lawyer.

CHAPTER 9: SENTENCING AND POST-TRIAL PROCEDURES

- There are three primary constitutional provisions that regulate sentencing:

    o The Cruel and Unusual Punishments Clause of the Eighth Amendment

    o The Double Jeopardy Clause of the Fifth Amendment

    o The Apprendi line of cases under the Sixth Amendment

A. The Cruel and Unusual Punishment Clause

1. Length of Prison Sentences

   o The Supreme Court has given the government free rein to authorize virtually any length sentence for virtually _____

   > ***Example 53:*** *"Three-strike" laws—Life sentences without parole for recidivists are constitutional, even if the offense that results in the life sentence is a minor crime.*

   o Exception: LWOP for crimes committed while a juvenile are _____.

   > **Editorial Note 1:** A sentence of LWOP for ***non-homicide*** crimes committed while a defendant was a juvenile is unconstitutional. However, a sentence of LWOP for a ***homicide*** committed while a defendant was a juvenile may be constitutional, provided that the sentence is not mandatory.
   >
   > **Exam Tip 4:** This is very unlikely to be tested because the details involved are too case-specific.

2. Capital Punishment

   o The death penalty can be imposed in cases only when the victim _____.

   - It is constitutionally disproportionate to apply the death penalty in non-homicide cases.

   o The death penalty cannot be imposed on:

   - Defendants who were under the age of _____ when they committed the crime
   - Defendants who suffer from mental retardation
   - Defendants who are _____ at the time of execution

   o The state must provide a variety of special safeguards before executing a defendant, including a bifurcated trial process, the opportunity to present mitigating evidence, and a process that sufficiently narrows the class of death-sentence eligible offenses.

   > **Exam Tip 5:** The states' death penalty procedures are sufficiently distinct from one another that it seems unlikely that the MBE will test on those procedures themselves.

3. Other Types of Sentences or Punishments

   o The Eighth Amendment also prohibits the imposition of cruel or unusual/degrading punishments.

- Courts have extended this protection to conditions of confinement (e.g., overcrowding).
- You must have been convicted of a _____ for the Eighth Amendment to apply.

> **Example 54:** *Torturing a suspect to get the suspect to confess violates the Fourth and Fifth Amendments, but it does not violate the Cruel and Unusual Punishment Clause.*

B. The Double Jeopardy Clause

- Provides three separate protections:
  - Protection against prosecution for the same offense after _____
  - Protection against prosecution for the same offense after _____
  - Protection against _____ prosecutions or punishments for the same offense

1. Defining the "Same Offense"

> **Example 55:** *You are prosecuted for and acquitted of a homicide. If the government finds more or new evidence, you cannot be prosecuted again.*

> **Example 56:** *You are prosecuted and convicted of larceny and sentenced to three years in jail. The prosecutor cannot prosecute you again in an attempt to get a longer sentence.*

- **The Blockburger test:** Ask whether each statutory provision requires proof of an element that the other does not.

> **Example 57:** *Offense #1 = A + B and Offense #2 = A + C (These are separate offenses and you can be prosecuted and punished for both.)*
>
> *Larceny = (taking the property of another) + (intent to permanently deprive)*
>
> *Conspiracy to commit larceny = (agreement to take property)*

> **Example 58:** *Offense #1 = A + B and Offense #2 = A + B + C*
>
> *These are not separate offenses; Offense #1 is a _____ offense.*
>
> *Larceny = (taking the property of another) + (intent to permanently deprive)*
>
> *Robbery = (taking the property of another) + (intent to permanently deprive) + (use or threat of force)*
>
> *If you are prosecuted for and convicted of larceny, you cannot be indicted and prosecuted for robbery in the same episode.*

- **Two warnings about the same offense test:**
  - Offenses with different _____ are separate offenses for double jeopardy purposes.

> *Example 59:* *Killing two victims with one shot can be prosecuted as two separate crimes.*

- **Separate Sovereigns Rule:** If two different sovereigns have jurisdiction over the crime committed (e.g., a state and the U.S. or two different states), they can each try the defendant separately. The Double Jeopardy Clause does not bar a defendant from being tried, convicted, and punished in both jurisdictions.
- **Charged v. punished:** A defendant can be charged and tried for an offense and a lesser-included offense at the same trial, but the defendant can only be _____ for one offense.

2. **The Attachment and End of Jeopardy**

   o Jeopardy attaches when the _____ is sworn in or, in a bench trial, when the _____ is sworn in.

     - Before the trial begins, the prosecutor can add, drop, or change the charges against a defendant without Double Jeopardy problems.

   o **Acquittal:** If the defendant is acquitted, it is the _____ of the case and the defendant cannot be _____ by the same jurisdiction for the same offense.

     - The prosecution cannot _____ from an acquittal.

   o **Conviction:** If the defendant is convicted and he either does not appeal or his conviction is affirmed, that is the end of jeopardy and he cannot be retried by the same jurisdiction for the same offense.

     - If the jury convicts the defendant, and he appeals and gets the conviction reversed, he can be retried unless the reversal was based on a finding of _____ evidence.

   o **Mistrial**—Two kinds of mistrials:

     - Manifest necessity: Defendant _____ be retried

       > *Example 60:* *The jury is deadlocked or defense counsel engages in misconduct*

     - No manifest necessity: Defendant _____ be retried by that jurisdiction

C. **The Apprendi Doctrine (Sixth Amendment)**

   - The Sixth Amendment right to a jury trial prohibits judges from _____ criminal sentences beyond the statutory maximums based on facts other than those decided by the jury beyond a reasonable doubt.

     > *Example 61:* *Normally the sentence for a particular crime was five years, but a judge was entitled to raise the sentence to more than that if the judge determined that it was a hate crime. The Supreme Court has held that it violates the Sixth Amendment because all of the facts that are necessary to*

authorize a particular sentence must be found by a jury, and the jury must find those beyond a reasonable doubt.

- Many statutes give the judge wide discretion to sentence the defendant.

    Example 62: *A statute states that a defendant convicted of robbery can be sentenced between 5 and 10 years' imprisonment. The judge has discretion within this range.*

    Example 63: *A statute states that the maximum sentence for robbery is 8 years, but if the victim was unusually vulnerable, the sentence can be doubled. A jury would have to find beyond a reasonable doubt that the victim was unusually vulnerable in order to enhance the sentence.*

- Exception: Sentence enhancement based on prior _____ convictions need not be found by a jury.

BEST OF LUCK!

[END OF HANDOUT]

Evidence

EVIDENCE
PROFESSOR SHERMAN J. CLARK
UNIVERSITY OF MICHIGAN LAW SCHOOL

CHAPTER 1:   PRESENTATION OF EVIDENCE (PART 1)—INTRODUCTION OF EVIDENCE

A. Role of Judge and Jury

1. In General

- The jury decides questions of _____; the judge decides questions of _____.

- The question of whether a piece of evidence gets in is a question of _____.

    - The _____ decides whether evidence is admissible.
    - Includes whether there is a privilege or whether witnesses are qualified

2. Preliminary Questions

- Many evidentiary issues are decided prior to trial through motions in limine or preliminary hearings.
- Sometimes preliminary questions of law hinge on factual questions.
- The _____ decides fact questions that go to the admissibility of evidence.
- For preliminary factual decisions, the court is _____ by the Federal Rules of Evidence (FRE).

3. Preliminary Hearings

- Conducted _____ the presence of the jury in three circumstances:

    1) When the issue is the admissibility of a _____ in a criminal trial;

    2) When the defendant in a criminal case is a _____ and makes that request; and

    3) When the interests of _____ otherwise require (unfair prejudice to a party)

4. Weight and Credibility

The _____ decides the weight and credibility of the evidence.

B. Challenge to Evidence Ruling

1. Challenging on Appeal

- Evidentiary ruling can be reversed on appeal only if:

    1) A substantial _____ of a party has been affected (i.e., not harmless error); and

2) The judge was _____ of the mistake at trial and given a chance to correct it

- Notify court by _____ or by offer of proof

2. Plain Error Rule

- Plain error—error that was obvious on its face
- Appellate court will sometimes reverse the case to prevent a miscarriage of justice, even if no objection or offer of proof was made at trial

> **Note 1:** You should not rely on the plain error rule. You should actively preserve the record for appeal.

3. Notifying the Court to Preserve it for Appeal

a. Objection

If the court has *admitted* evidence that should have been excluded, must object and explain why the evidence should have been excluded

b. Offer of proof

- If the court *refuses to admit* evidence that should have been admitted, must make an offer of proof on the record
- Offer of proof—explain to the court what the evidence would have been and why it should have been admitted
- Not necessary if the substance and logic of the evidence is straightforward and clear on the surface

C. Limited Admissibility (Rule 105)

- Evidence may be admissible for _____ purpose, but _____ purpose.
- Upon request of the objecting party, the court will give the jury a _____ instruction
  - I.e., the evidence can only be used for one purpose, but not another illegitimate purpose

> **Exam Tip 1:** Pay attention not just to the type of evidence but the purpose for which the evidence is being used.

D. Rule of Completeness (Rule 106)

- If a party introduces part of a _____ statement, the opposing party may introduce other portions of that statement that are necessary to put the admitted portion into perspective.
- Can be introduced immediately; no need to wait for the party's turn to present its case
- Other portions may be introduced even if they might otherwise be _____.
- Sometimes called a "curative admission"

E. Judicial Notice

- The court's acceptance of a fact as true without requiring formal proof
- It is about so-called _____ facts—facts that the jury would otherwise have to decide
- If not subject to reasonable _____, the court will instruct the jury to accept that fact as proven
- Facts that are not subject to reasonable dispute:
  - Generally known within the territorial jurisdiction of the court; or
  - Accurately and readily determined by sources whose _____ cannot reasonably be questioned

    Example 1: *A question of whether a particular city is north or south of another city, or whether July 5th in a certain year was a Friday*

- **Civil case**—court will instruct the jury that it ***must*** accept the fact as proven
- **Criminal case**—court will instruct the jury that it _____ (but need not) find that fact

CHAPTER 2: PRESENTATION OF EVIDENCE (PART 2)—MODE OF PRESENTATION; BURDENS AND PRESUMPTIONS

A. Mode and Presentation of Evidence

1. Trial Process

- Begins with the _____ (civil case) or _____ (criminal case) introducing its case first, then the defendant will present its case
- Order of presentation of evidence and witnesses is within the court's _____ to control
- Court may call and question witnesses.
  - All parties can cross-examine those witnesses.
  - Every party should have an opportunity to _____ outside the hearing of the jury.

2. Form of Questions—Leading Questions

- Suggests the _____ within the question

    Example 2: *"Isn't it true that you were walking down the street on that Friday?" or "Isn't it true that you were not wearing your glasses that day?"*

- Generally, not permitted on _____ examination
- **Exceptions:**
  1) To elicit preliminary background information not in dispute;

2) The witness has trouble communicating due to age or infirmity; or

3) When you call a _____ witness or adverse party

3. Refreshing a Witness's Recollection

- Arises when a witness is having trouble remembering
- Allowed to help the witness remember by showing them a document (or something else), typically a person's notes
- The witness looks at the notes, remembers, puts the notes aside, and proceeds to testify from present memory—called _____ refreshed

> *Example 3:*   *A witness cannot recall what occurred on the night in question. The attorney asks, "Would it help you remember what happened that night if I sang to you part of the Aria from La Boheme, which was playing at the time the event happened?" The witness says, "Yes it might." The attorney sings the song and the witness suddenly remembers everything that happened.*

- The document _____ become evidence and the witness _____ _____ read from it
- The opposing party is permitted to see and inspect the document, and even show it to the jury.

> **Note 2:** Contrast with **Past Recollection Recorded** (discussed later):
>
> - Arises when the witness still cannot remember after trying to refresh their memory
>
> - Permits the witness to read the notes into evidence under a hearsay exception
>
> - Requires that the witness cannot remember, the record was made when it was fresh in their memory, and the record accurately reflects their memory

4. Cross-examination

- Courts limit the _____ of cross-examination to the _____ of direct examination.
- Courts are permitted to allow broader inquiry.
- Allowed to use _____ questions

5. Other Improper Questions

a. Compound questions

A question that asks for several answers

> *Example 4:*   *"Isn't it true that you went to the bank and then you took out the money and then you went home and never did anything else?"*

b. **Facts not in evidence**

   A question that assume facts not in evidence

   > *Example 5:* *"Do you still hate your mother?"*

c. **Argumentative questions**

   Not really a question; just intended to bother or harass the witness

   > *Example 6:* *"What the heck makes you think you can get away with that?"*

d. **Questions calling for inappropriate conclusions**

   Call for a conclusion that the witness is not _____ to make

   > *Example 7:* *"How did the executives in the company feel when they received your letter?"*

e. **Repetitive questions**

   - Have already been "asked and answered"
   - A lawyer can continue to ask the question if the witness has not actually answered it.

6. **Exclusion of Witnesses**

   o Witnesses must be excluded from the courtroom upon the request of _____ party to prevent the witness from hearing the testimony of others.

   > **Editorial Note 1:** If a party requests exclusion or the court deems it necessary, the witness **must** be excluded, subject to the exceptions below.

   o Some witnesses **may not** be excluded:

   - A witness who is essential to the presentation of the case;
   - A person, such as a crime victim, who is permitted by state rule to remain in the courtroom; or
   - A party in the case

B. **Burdens and Presumptions**

1. **Burden of Proof**

   a. **Burden of** _____

      A party must produce enough evidence to get the issue to the jury.

   b. **Burden of** _____

      A party must convince the jury to decide the case in its favor.

   c. **Civil cases**

      Usually, the standard is a _____ of the evidence.

d. Criminal cases

_____ standard

2. Presumptions

a. Rebuttable presumption

- Shifts the burden of _____ on a particular issue, but not the burden of _____
- Useful for things that are difficult to prove directly

    Example 8: *The issue of whether someone received a letter. If you can show that you correctly mailed the letter, there is a presumption that the recipient received the letter. This shifts the burden of production to the other side to prove that they did not receive it.*

- If counterproof is introduced, the presumption is eliminated (the bubble bursts) and there is sufficient evidence for the jury to decide the issue.

b. Destruction of evidence

If a party destroys evidence, there is a presumption that it would have been adverse to that party.

c. Conclusive (or irrebuttable) presumption

Rules of _____ that happen to use the language of presumption

CHAPTER 3: RELEVANCE (PART 1)—GENERAL CONSIDERATIONS AND CHARACTER EVIDENCE

A. General Considerations

1. FRE 401 and 402

- ○ Evidence must be _____.
- ○ If evidence is irrelevant, it is _____.
- ○ All relevant evidence is admissible, unless excluded by a specific rule.

    Editorial Note 2: The Professor misspoke when restating the above rules. Irrelevant evidence is ***inadmissible*** and relevant evidence is generally ***admissible***, unless it is excluded by a specific rule.

- ○ **Relevance**—makes the fact in issue _____ than it would be without the evidence

    Example 9: *Evidence that the defendant was seen in a particular city on a given weekend is not sufficient to convict the defendant of a crime. However, it could be relevant to the issue of whether the defendant committed the crime.*

- ○ Evidence is relevant if it is both _____ (related to some issue in the case) and _____ (having a tendency to prove or disprove some fact).

2. Direct vs. Circumstantial Evidence

- ○ **Direct evidence—** _____ to what it is offered to prove (e.g., eyewitness testimony)

- ○ **Circumstantial evidence—**Evidence from which a fact can be inferred

Exam Tip 2: Keep in mind, the issue with relevance is *how* a particular piece of evidence makes a certain *fact more likely*.

3. Exclusion of Relevant Evidence (FRE 403)

- ○ Even if the evidence is relevant and there is no particular rule excluding it, the court has discretion to exclude relevant evidence if certain risks _____ outweigh its probative value.
- ○ Risks—confusion of the issues, unfair _____, misleading the jury, or waste of time

Exam Tip 3: This rule is weighed in favor of admissibility. The probative value must be substantially outweighed by the risks.

4. Relevance Conditioned on Fact (FRE 104(b))

- ○ Sometimes, the relevance of evidence hinges on some fact that is best for the jury.

    Example 10: *A letter is offered into evidence. There are no issues with its admissibility. But, there is a question as to whether the person received the letter. The relevance of the letter depends on a question of fact—whether it was received. If it was received, it demonstrates that the party was on notice. If it was not received, then it is irrelevant.*

- ○ Courts will simply admit the evidence on the condition that the jury will decide that preliminary fact later.

B. Character Evidence

1. In General

- ○ Rule about the _____ argument or inference
- ○ Prohibits the argument that a person acted in conformity with a particular character trait
- ○ Prevents a party from proving a character trait in order to show action in conformity

    Example 11: *The defendant started this fight because he's a violent person. A violent person is much more likely to start a fight, so it's likely he started this one. This is evidence of a character trait used to show action in conformity and is generally prohibited.*

- o Rationale—too prejudicial, not that probative of the current conduct, and it distracts the jury's attention

2. **Methods of Proving Character**

    - o When admissible, can only be proved through _____ or _____ testimony
    - o Cannot be proved by specific bad acts

3. **Other Relevant Use for Character Evidence**

    - o Character evidence cannot be used to prove propensity.
    - o Can be used for some other relevant purpose (i.e., when character is at issue)
    - o If character is an _____ in the case, then it can be proved

        Example 12: Character evidence may be permitted in a child custody case when there is a question about whether a parent is violent.

        Example 13: Character evidence may be permitted in a negligent entrustment case to prove carelessness.

        Note 4: Character is generally only at issue in civil cases.

CHAPTER 4:   RELEVANCE (PART 2)—CHARACTER EVIDENCE (CONT'D) AND HABIT EVIDENCE

A. **Character Evidence (cont'd)**

    1. **Impeachment** (covered fully in later lecture chapters)

        Propensity argument can be made to impeach (e.g., the witness is a liar)

    2. **Civil Cases**

        - o Propensity argument can almost never be made.
        - o Except: in a civil case involving child molestation or sexual assault, the plaintiff _____ introduce evidence of the defendant's _____ of that sort.

            Note 5: Recall that in civil cases, if character is at issue, evidence of that trait is admissible to prove an essential element of the case (i.e., for a non-propensity purpose).

    3. **Criminal Cases**

        a. **Basic rule**

            The prosecution _____ allowed to introduce the bad character of the defendant.

b. **Defendant's good character**

- A defendant is permitted to introduce a _____ trait of character.

    Example 14: *If a defendant was accused of assault, the defendant is permitted to introduce evidence that he is a peaceful person.*

    Example 15: *If a defendant was accused of embezzlement, the defendant could introduce evidence that he is an honest person.*

- **Opens the door**—prosecutor is free to _____ the defendant's claims by attacking the defendant's character

    - Prosecutor can cross-examine the defendant's character witnesses with questions about _____ from the past.

- Defendant is limited to witnesses who will testify about _____ or _____

    - Defendant _____ permitted to bring _____
    - On cross-examination, prosecutor _____ inquire about _____

    Example 16: *The defendant has his neighbor take the stand and say, "In my opinion, the defendant is not violent," or "The defendant has a reputation for nonviolence." The prosecution gets to cross-examine the neighbor and can ask the neighbor the following questions, if the prosecution has a reasonable basis for doing so: "Have you heard that the defendant started a fight last week?" "Did you know that the defendant beat up four kids on his block within the last two years?"*

- The prosecution cannot prove the incident; must accept the witness's answer

    Example 17: *The neighbor in the above example says, "No, I've never heard that." The prosecution cannot introduce evidence about the earlier incident.*

c. **Victim's character**

- A defendant may bring evidence about the _____ character.

    - May introduce evidence of a _____ trait of the victim

    Note 6: As a practical matter, only happens in a homicide or assault case (violent cases) when the defendant is arguing that the victim started the altercation (self-defense).

    Example 18: *The defendant is on trial for assault. He claims that it was self-defense because the victim attacked him. The defendant can introduce evidence that the victim is a violent person.*

- **Opens the door**—the prosecution can introduce evidence that the victim is not violent using reputation or opinion, but not specific acts.

  - The prosecution can then introduce evidence that the _____ has the _____ that he or she accused the victim of having.

  Example 19: In the above example, after the defendant introduces evidence that the victim is violent, the prosecution can introduce evidence that the victim is nonviolent AND evidence that the defendant is violent.

4. Prior Acts

- In some circumstances, evidence of a defendant's past crimes or bad acts can be introduced
- "_____" evidence—not used for_____; used for some other purpose:

  - _____

    Example 20: If the prosecution wants to argue that the motive for a murder was to cover up a prior embezzlement scheme, the prosecution can introduce proof of that embezzlement.

  - _____

    Example 21: The defendant is caught in possession of drugs, and there is a question as to whether the defendant had intent to sell those drugs. The prosecution can introduce prior convictions of selling drugs.

  - Absence of mistake

    Example 22: A young man marries a wealthy older woman who drowns in the bathtub. It happens with three different women. The prosecution may introduce the prior deaths to prove absence of mistake.

  - _____

    Example 23: The prosecution wants to prove that the defendant has a certain modus operandi. The prosecution may be able to introduce evidence of that modus operandi in prior crimes.

  - Common plan or scheme

    Example 24: The prosecution may introduce the prior bad acts if understanding a series of crimes is the only way to provide context to the crime at issue.

B. Habit Evidence

- Allowed to prove action in conformity with the habit

    Example 25: *Evidence that every morning the defendant drove a certain way to work and stopped at the same coffee shop and got the same drink.*

- Something that is routine, regular, or automatic
- Can also be the habit of an _____

CHAPTER 5: REVIEW OF CHAPTERS 1–4: PRESENTATION OF EVIDENCE AND RELEVANCE

A. Presentation of Evidence

- _____ decide questions of admissibility.

    o Includes preliminary _____ questions that go to admissibility

    Example 26: *A statement might be admissible if the person who made the statement was an agent of a party. Admissibility under hearsay depends on a factual determination of whether the declarant was an agent.*

    o The court is not bound by the FRE in deciding preliminary questions of fact.

- Party can preserve an error for appeal by:

    o _____ to evidence the party thinks should not have been admitted; or

    o Making an _____ with regard to evidence the party thinks should have been admitted

- Evidence is often admissible for one purpose, but not another; the court will give a limiting instruction upon a party's request (FRE 105).

- Judicial notice—if question is not subject to _____ _____, the court will not require evidence

    o Court will instruct the jury to find that fact; or

    o In a criminal case, instruct the jury that it may find that fact

- Leading questions are generally prohibited on _____ examination, except:

    o Preliminary information;

    o Witnesses that need help testifying; and

    o _____ witnesses

- Cross-examination is supposed to be within the scope of _____ examination; can and should use _____ questions

- Other improper questions—assume facts not in evidence, call for an inappropriate or unsupported conclusion, compound, harassing or repetitive, argumentative

- Burden of proof—plaintiff in a civil case and prosecution in a criminal case
  - Burden of _____ and burden of

  _____
  - Civil case—generally _____ of the evidence
  - Criminal case—beyond a reasonable doubt
- Presumption—shifts the burden of _____ on a particular fact

B. Relevance

- Evidence that makes a _____ fact _____
  than it would be without the evidence
  - FRE 403 allows a court to exclude relevant evidence if certain risks—prejudice, confusion, misleading the jury, waste of time— _____ outweigh the probative value.
- Character evidence—the propensity argument is generally prohibited
  - Permitted in criminal cases if introduced by the defendant
    - Opens the door—prosecutor can rebut the defendant's evidence
  - Defendant can also offer a pertinent character trait of the _____ (violence)
    - Opens the door—prosecutor can rebut with evidence that the _____ is not violent and also introduce evidence that the _____ is violent
- Introducing evidence for some purpose other than propensity
  - Civil case—character is an _____ in the case
  - MIMIC evidence using prior bad acts

CHAPTER 6: WITNESSES (PART 1)—COMPETENCE AND IMPEACHMENT

A. Competence

- Anyone who has _____ of the
  matter about which they are going to testify and is willing to make an _____ to tell
  the truth is competent to testify.

1. State Rules on Competency

- Some states have particular competency requirements.

  Example 27: *Minimum age for a child to testify*

  - FRE—whether the child has personal knowledge and is mature enough to understand the obligation to tell the truth and is willing to promise to do so

- o Dead Man's statute (not included in FRE)—limits the ability of witnesses to testify about _____ with people who are deceased

    > *Example 28:* *The decedent passed away and the next day, the neighbor says that the decedent promised to sell his car for $11. Courts may limit the neighbor's ability to testify against the decedent's estate.*

- o Under the *Erie* doctrine, a federal court sitting in diversity jurisdiction, using state law to decide the case, will defer to state competency rules.

2. Judge as Witness

A judge is _____ from being a witness in a trial over which she is sitting.

3. Juror as Witness

- o A juror may not testify as a witness in a trial in front of the jury in which he sits.
- o After the verdict or an indictment (grand jury), the parties might be tempted to ask the jurors to testify about what happened in the jury room in the context of a motion for a new trial or on appeal.
- o **FRE 606(b):** a juror _____ testify as a witness in an inquiry into the validity of a verdict or indictment as to:

    - Any statement made during _____ ;
    - Any incident that occurred during deliberations; or
    - The effect of anything upon any juror's mind

- o Exceptions—a juror may testify after trial about whether:

    - Extraneous, _____ information was improperly brought to the jury's attention;

        - E.g., provided with inadmissible evidence

    - An _____ was improperly brought to bear on a juror;

        - E.g., a juror was bribed or threatened

    - A clerical or technical error was made in entering the verdict onto the verdict form; or
    - A juror made a clear statement that he relied on _____ stereotypes or animus in convicting a defendant

B. Impeachment—calling into question the witness's credibility

1. Three Basic Ways to Impeach a Witness

- o Show that the witness is dishonest; bad character for _____
- o _____
- o _____ competence

2. Bias

- ○ Showing that the witness has some reason to lie or shade the facts
- ○ E.g., relationship with a party, the witness is being _____ to testify, the witness has agreed to testify in return for a reduced sentence, the witness has an _____ in the outcome of the case, etc.

3. Sensory Competence

- ○ The witness is _____ in some way.
- ○ The witness did not see or hear things as well as she thinks.

> **Example 29:** *How far away were you? How much did you have to drink? How dark was it that night? Were you wearing your glasses?*

CHAPTER 7:   WITNESSES (PART 2)—IMPEACHMENT (CONT'D)

A. Character for Truthfulness or Untruthfulness

1. Character Witness Testimony (FRE 608(a))

- ○ Can introduce character witnesses who will testify that the target witness is dishonest
- ○ May be attacked through _____ or _____, not prior specific incidents

2. Specific Acts (FRE 608(b))

- ○ May _____ the witness about specific acts of dishonesty

> **Example 30:** *Isn't it true that you lied on a job application a year ago? Isn't it true that you falsely claimed on your resume to have an advanced degree that you don't have? Isn't it true that you stole money from your partners when you had a business years ago?*

- ○ Must be probative of untruthfulness
- ○ Only permitted to ask; must take the witness's answer
- ○ Must have a _____ basis for asking the question

3. Criminal Convictions (FRE 609)

a. Crimes involving _____ or _____ _____

> **Example 31:** *perjury, fraud, embezzlement*

b. Convicted of _____

- ▪ Crimes punishable by _____ or more than _____ in prison
- ▪ Court will allow impeachment with the prior felony conviction **unless** the risk of prejudice _____ the probative value

- **Criminal defendant**—evidence of a prior felony conviction is admissible only if its probative value _____ the prejudicial effect ("reverse 403")

c. **Old convictions**

- If more than _____ have elapsed since the conviction (or release from confinement, whichever is later), then evidence of the conviction is admissible only if:

  - The probative value of the conviction, supported by specific facts, _____ its prejudicial effect; and
  - The proponent gives an adverse party reasonable advanced notice

d. **Pardon**

A conviction _____ be used for impeachment if the witness has been pardoned or received a certificate of rehabilitation if the action was based on a finding of innocence or the witness has not been convicted of another felony.

B. **Prior _____ Statements**

> **Example 32:** *A witness takes the stand and says, "The car was blue." You can cross-examine the witness and say, "Didn't you tell your mother-in-law three weeks ago that the car was red?"*

- Can be done with any kind of statement
- Can be proved by _____ evidence, but only if the witness is given the opportunity to explain or deny the evidence

C. **Impeachment of a Hearsay Declarant**

- When an out-of-court statement comes in under a hearsay exception, the declarant (the person who made the statement) is acting like a _____ and can, therefore, be impeached.
- Impeachment may be made by any evidence that would be admissible if the declarant had testified as a witness.

D. **Rehabilitation of a Witness**

- Rehabilitation may be accomplished in one of three ways:

  1) Give the witness a chance to _____;

  2) Prior _____ statement—if the witness has been accused of changing his or her story, or being bribed or pressured or having an improper motive, can be rehabilitated with a statement that the witness made before the alleged motive arose; or

  3) If the witness has been _____ as having a bad character for truthfulness, then evidence can be introduced bolstering the witness's character for truthfulness (either reputation or opinion evidence).

CHAPTER 8: WITNESSES (PART 3)—TESTIMONY

A. Lay Witnesses

- In general, we want _____ and not _____ from witnesses.
- Old rule—prohibited lay witnesses (non-experts) from offering opinions or conclusions
- Opinions from lay witnesses are _____ with respect to _____ impressions, such as appearance, intoxication, speed, etc.
- To be admissible, a lay witness's opinion must be:

  o Based on the _____ of the witness; and
  o Helpful to a _____ of the witness's testimony or the determination of a fact in the case.

- Implicit requirement—cannot be based on any _____, technical, or specialized knowledge

B. Expert Witnesses

1. Subject Matter of Testimony

o An expert witness may offer opinions or conclusions if:

- The subject matter is scientific, technical, or other _____ information; and
- It will help the trier of fact understand the evidence or determine a fact in issue.

o Courts have generally rejected expert testimony about witness _____.

2. *Daubert* Test

o Courts require that the expert:

1) Be qualified by knowledge, _____, experience, _____, or education;

2) Base his testimony on sufficient _____ or _____;

3) Base his testimony on reliable principles and methods; and

4) Apply the principles and methods _____ to the facts of the case.

> **Editorial Note 3:** The *Daubert* test is a four-part test. The Professor mistakenly skipped the third requirement listed above.

3. Ultimate Issue

o Experts _____ express an opinion on the ultimate issue in most types of cases.

> ***Example 33:*** *An expert in a design-defect case may testify that the vehicle was defective in its design.*

o Courts do not allow experts to testify about whether a criminal defendant had the requisite _____ of any element of a crime or defense.

4. **Basis of Expert Opinions**

   o An expert may base his or her opinion on:

   ▪ Personal _____;
   ▪ Evidence presented _____; or
   ▪ Information reasonably relied upon by experts in that particular _____.

      • May base opinion on facts that would otherwise be inadmissible at trial
      • The basis for the expert opinion may not necessarily be admissible unless the probative value of the information in evaluating the expert's testimony ***substantially outweighs*** any prejudice.

5. **Court-Appointed Expert**

   o The court _____ appoint an expert witness
   o Must let each party know what the witness found
   o Each party can depose the expert and call or cross-examine the expert.

CHAPTER 9:   REVIEW OF CHAPTERS 6–8: WITNESSES

A. **Competence**

- Anyone can testify if they:

   o Have _____ knowledge;
   o Can appreciate the obligation to tell the truth; and
   o _____ to tell the truth (i.e., take an oath).

- _____ and jurors may not be witnesses on cases in which they are sitting.
- Jurors cannot testify after trial as to what was said in the jury room, what happened in the jury room, or what impacted their deliberations.

   o May testify about extraneous _____ information or improper outside influence
   o May testify if a juror has made a clear statement that a conviction was based on _____ stereotype or animus

B. **Impeachment**

- Adversary may _____ (attempt to call into question) the witness's testimony
- Ways to impeach:

   o _____
   o _____ competence

- o Bad character for _____
  - ▪ Introduce reputation and opinion testimony
  - ▪ Inquire on cross-examination about prior acts
  - ▪ Conviction of crimes
    - • Crimes involving _____ or _____ statement; and
    - • Felonies
- o Prior _____ statement
  - ▪ Extrinsic evidence permitted as long as witness is provided a chance to explain
- • After impeachment, can attempt to rehabilitate the witness
  - o Allow the witness to _____ or clarify
  - o Introduce a prior _____ statement
  - o Introduce evidence of the witness's good character for truthfulness if that character was attacked

C. Testimony

- • A lay (non-expert) witness is permitted to testify as to her opinion when it is:
  - o Rationally based on the _____ of the witness; and
  - o Helpful to a clear understanding of the testimony or the determination of a fact in issue.
- • Lay witnesses cannot offer opinions based on specialized, scientific, or technical knowledge.
- • Expert testimony is scientific, technical, or specialized knowledge that will help the trier of fact
  - o Must be qualified
  - o Must be based on sufficient facts and data and the methods must be applied reliably to the case
  - o Expert opinion can be based on:
    - ▪ _____ knowledge;
    - ▪ Witnesses or evidence made known at trial; or
    - ▪ Other things, even if not admissible at trial, if they are the sorts of things that are reasonably relied upon by experts in that field

CHAPTER 10: TANGIBLE EVIDENCE (PART 1)—AUTHENTICATION

A. In General

- • Includes documents and other physical items
- • First step—must be _____
- • Must show evidence sufficient to support a finding that the thing is what the party claims it is
  - o Does not mean that the court must find that the document or thing is authentic

- o The jury will decide this fact question

B. Real Evidence—Ways to Authenticate

- _____—testimony of a witness that recognizes and identifies the item
- Distinctive features or _____
- Chain of _____—technique accounting for the whereabouts of an item along an unbroken chain

C. Documentary Evidence—Ways to Authenticate

- By _____ of the parties
- Eyewitness testimony combined with distinctive features
- Ancient Documents

  - o At least _____ old;
  - o In a condition unlikely to create _____; and
  - o Was found in a place where such documents would be if they were authentic

- Reply letter doctrine—authenticated by evidence that it was written in response to another letter
- Handwriting verification

  - o _____ or _____ comparing it to a known sample; or
  - o Lay witness with personal knowledge of the handwriting (from before the current litigation)

- Self-authenticating documents (FRE 902)—include:

  - o Public documents bearing a government seal
  - o Certified copies of public records
  - o Official publications issued by public authority
  - o Trade inscriptions
  - o Notarized documents
  - o Commercial paper

D. Oral Statements

- Voices and recordings may need to be authenticated as to the identity of the speaker.

1. Voice identification

Can be authenticated by any person who has heard the voice at any time

2. Telephone conversations

  - o Caller recognized the speaker's voice
  - o The speaker knew _____ that only a particular person would know

- o The caller dialed the number believed to be the speaker's and the speaker
  _____ upon answering the phone
- o The caller dialed a business and spoke with a person who answered questions about business regularly conducted over the phone

CHAPTER 11: TANGIBLE EVIDENCE (PART 2)—THE BEST EVIDENCE RULE AND PAROL EVIDENCE RULE

A. The Best Evidence Rule (Original Document Rule)

- **Rule**—No describing the documents instead of showing them, unless you really need to
- Limits the ability to present other evidence of the _____ of a document when the contents are _____
- No witness testimony about the contents when you could just produce the actual document

1. Duplicates

- o Duplicates are fine, unless:
  - There is a genuine question about the _____ of the original; or
  - In _____, the original should be required.

2. Contents "at issue"

- o The document is used as _____ of an event

   Example 34: A witness testifies about who robbed the bank but the only reason she knows the robber's identity is because she saw a picture of the person robbing the bank. The best evidence rule requires that the picture be produced.

- o The document has actual _____, such as a contract or will
- o The witness is testifying based on facts only learned from the document

   Example 35: The witness did not actually see the bank robbery but saw a video of the robbery. The witness is called to testify about the robbery. The witness's knowledge of the robbery is based on facts learned from the video, so the video should be produced under the best evidence rule.

  - Contrast with situation where a witness actually saw what happened but there also happens to be a recording—the witness is permitted to describe his or her personal knowledge; does not mean there is a best evidence problem

3. Exceptions to the Best Evidence Rule

a. Unavailable

  - May introduce other evidence of the contents if:

- The original has been _____ or _____
  (unless done by the proponent in bad faith);
- The original cannot be obtained by any judicial process; or
- The party against whom the document is introduced had _____
  of the original and knew that it was going to be at issue at trial.

b. Public records

Can use a _____ copy instead of the original

c. Voluminous writings

- May be presented in the form of a _____ or _____
- Originals or duplicates must be made available for inspection by the other party

d. Admission by a party

The testimony, either in court or deposition, or a written statement of the party against whom the evidence is introduced

Example 36: A party wrote a letter in which she said, "As you know, your lease permits you to have small dogs." At trial, an issue is the size of the dog that the tenant had. The letter can be introduced against that party as proof of what the lease said.

B. The Parol Evidence Rule

1. General Rule

- Excludes evidence that, if introduced, would _____ the terms of a written contract
- Many contracts are explicitly described as _____ integrations—they contain all of the terms of the agreement.
- No _____ evidence that would change the terms may be admitted.

Example 37: There is a contract that says you will paint the Professor's house and he will pay you $400. The contract explicitly states that it is completely integrated. The parol evidence rule prevents the introduction of evidence that (before signing the contract) the Professor agreed to pay extra.

2. Partial Integration

- Excludes extrinsic evidence that would _____ the terms of the agreement
- Allows evidence that might _____ the terms

3. Exceptions to the Parol Evidence Rule

- Extrinsic evidence about a contract can be admitted to:

- Clarify an ambiguity;
- Prove a _____ of trade or course of dealing;
- Show _____, duress, mistake, or illegal purpose; or
- Show whether consideration has or has not been paid.

CHAPTER 12: REVIEW OF CHAPTERS 10–11: TANGIBLE EVIDENCE

A. Authentication

- Does not mean that the court must find that the document or thing is authentic.
- Court simply must find that there is evidence *sufficient to support a finding* that it is what the party claims.
- Ways to authenticate:

  - _____
  - Testimony of a witness—often coupled with distinctive features
  - Reply letter doctrine
  - Chain of custody
  - Ancient documents
  - _____ verification
  - Self-authenticating documents

B. Best Evidence Rule

- Relates to proving the _____ of documents
- If the contents are at issue, we want to see the actual document, not witness testimony about it
- Duplicates are fine, unless there is a reason to require the original.
- _____ are appropriate if the originals are too voluminous.
- If the document is lost or missing through no fault of the proponent, then a witness can testify as to the contents of the document.
- Courts will allow other evidence of the contents of a document on a _____ matter.

  > *Example 38:* A witness says, "I was reading the newspaper about how the Yankees beat the Red Sox, and all of a sudden I looked up and there was a giant car accident." The witness has described the contents of a document—the newspaper—but that is collateral. The case is about a car accident.

CHAPTER 13: PRIVILEGES (PART 1)

A. General Principles

- FRE—no specific, codified privilege provisions
- Federal courts are instructed to:

- o Defer to general principles of federal common law when it comes to most privileges; and
- o When deciding state law issues when sitting in diversity jurisdiction, apply _____ law regarding privileges.

B. Attorney-Client Privilege

1. Rule

- o Protects a _____ communication between a client and a lawyer if the communication was for purposes of securing _____
- o Neither the lawyer nor the client can be forced to testify about the communication.

2. Confidential

- o Client must have made reasonable efforts to keep the communication confidential
- o Communications made in the presence of *unnecessary* _____ will not be privileged.
- o Presence of persons *necessary* to the communication (e.g., a translator or the lawyer's assistant or agent) will not undercut the privilege
- o An unknown secret eavesdropper _____ destroy the privilege.

3. Communication

- o Only the communication is privileged; not underlying _____ or evidence that the client has or knows

  > **Example 39:** If the client was involved in some kind of civil fraud and tells a lawyer, "I was involved in this business transaction that may have been fraudulent and here is what we did. Am I in legal trouble?" This communication is privileged. If the client was later subpoenaed to testify about his conduct, he could not claim the privilege saying that he spoke to his lawyer about what happened. He could still be asked about what happened; not asking him to testify about the conversation with the lawyer, which would be privileged. The underlying facts are not protected.

- o Does not protect pre-existing _____
- o Must have been made for purposes of securing _____

4. Who Holds the Privilege?

- o The _____ holds the privilege and has the right to decide whether to disclose the communication (i.e., waive the privilege).
- o The attorney must _____ the privilege by refusing to talk about such confidential communications.

5. Waiver

- o Failure to _____ the privilege in a timely manner
- o _____ disclosure of the information

- o Express waiver, even by contract
- o Failure to take precautions (i.e., careless conduct) on the part of the lawyer

6. Corporate Client

- o Issue: who is the client?
- o Some courts—the "control group"
    - People with sufficient power to control the conduct of the corporation
    - E.g., CEO, board of directors
- o Federal courts—the focus should be on the nature of the communication
    - A communication made by an employee about matters within the _____ of employment for purposes of seeking legal advice is _____, even if the employee is not a member of the "control group."

7. Exceptions to the Privilege

- o Future _____ or _____
    - If a client communicates to a lawyer for purposes of getting help with what the client _____ or _____ is a crime or fraud, the communication is not privileged.
- o _____ between the lawyer and the client

8. Work-Product Doctrine

- o Documents prepared by a lawyer in _____ _____
- o Such documents may not be privileged, but will be protected
- o Can obtain some types of work product from the opposing party if:
    - The party can demonstrate a _____ for the information; and
    - Show that it cannot otherwise be obtained without _____ _____

    Example 40: *The opposing party already interviewed a witness. By the time you take the case, that witness has died.*

- o Work product that cannot be obtained—_____ impression work product (core work product)
    - Reveals the attorney's trial tactics, conclusions, theories of the case, etc.

CHAPTER 14: PRIVILEGES (PART 2)

A. Physician-Patient Privilege

- Not recognized under federal law, but recognized by many states
- Statements made by a patient to a doctor for the purpose of obtaining _____

  _____
- **Exceptions**—privilege does not apply if:

  - The information was for reasons other than treatment;
  - The communication was made for some _____ purpose;
  - A _____ exists between the doctor and patient; or
  - The patient agreed to waive the privilege

B. Psychotherapist-Patient Privilege

- Recognized in federal courts and most jurisdictions
- Applies to confidential communications between a patient and a psychiatrist, psychologist, or licensed social worker for the purpose of treatment
- **Exceptions**—does not apply if the communication was:

  - The result of a court-ordered _____; or
  - Taken as part of a _____ proceeding

C. Fifth Amendment Protection against Self-incrimination

- Prevents a witness from being required to give incriminating testimony against himself
- Applies only to people (not _____)
- Applies only to current statements (not prior statements)
- Does not apply to blood samples, voice samples, breathalyzer, etc.
- If no risk of criminal trouble, there is no privilege

  - State can ensure no risk through immunity.

D. Spousal Privileges

1. Confidential Marital Communications

- Protects communications made between spouses in confidence in reliance on the sanctity of marriage
- Held by _____ spouses

  - Spouse can refuse to reveal confidential communications
  - Spouse can also prevent the other from revealing the communications
- Survives _____ marriage

2. **Spousal Immunity**

   o Gives a spouse the right to refuse to testify in a _____ case against the other spouse

   o Applies to currently married spouses

   o Covers testimony about anything, whether before or during marriage, but only applies while married to the person

   > **Exam Tip 4:** Remember that under the federal system, the witness spouse holds the privilege; the defendant cannot prevent the spouse from waiving their privilege if they choose to testify against their spouse.

3. **Exceptions**

   o Neither of the spousal privileges apply when:

      ▪ One spouse is _____ the other; or

      ▪ When one spouse is charged with a _____ against the other spouse or the children of either of them.

CHAPTER 15:   PUBLIC POLICY EXCLUSIONS

A. Liability Insurance

- Evidence that a person was or was not insured against liability is not admissible to prove _____ or wrongdoing.

- **Except**—when evidence of insurance coverage is relevant for some other purpose

   o E.g., might be relevant to show _____

B. Subsequent Remedial Measures

- Evidence of repairs or changes made _____ an accident is not admissible to prove _____, culpable conduct, defective product or design, or an inadequate warning.

   > *Example 41:* Someone slips on ice on your front walk. The next day, you go out and apply a non-slip substance to the walk. Later, the person sues you for slipping. The person cannot present evidence that you took remedial measures after the accident.

- **Except**—when evidence of subsequent remedial measures is relevant for some other purpose

   o E.g., ownership, control, feasibility

C. Settlement Offers or Negotiations

- A settlement offer made by any party is not admissible to prove the validity or the amount of a _____ claim.

- Cannot be used as a prior inconsistent statement to impeach
- **Except**—may be admissible if it serves another purpose, such as proving bias
- Cannot be unilaterally waived by either party

D. Offers to Pay Medical Expenses

- Not admissible to prove liability for _____
- Statements made or conduct accompanying the offer may be admissible.

E. Plea Negotiations

- Not admissible in a civil or criminal case
- Includes: withdrawn guilty pleas, nolo contendere pleas, offers to plead guilty, and statements made while negotiating a plea

F. Past Sexual Conduct

1. Victim's conduct (Rape Shield Laws)

In general, evidence of a victim's past sexual behavior or sexual predisposition _____ admissible in a criminal proceeding involving _____.

a. Exceptions in a criminal case

- Evidence of a victim's past sexual conduct is admissible to:

  - Show that the defendant was or was not the source of _____ evidence, such as semen or bruises; or
  - Show the victim's past sexual conduct with the defendant to show _____

- May be admissible in certain circumstances when exclusion would be too unfair to the defendant (exclusion would be unconstitutional)

b. Exceptions in civil cases

- Evidence of the victim's past sexual conduct or predisposition is admissible only if its probative value _____ the danger of harm to the victim and unfair prejudice to any party.
- Evidence of reputation is admissible only if the _____ brings it up.

2. Defendant's Conduct (FRE 413–415)

In a criminal or civil case in which a defendant is accused of committing an act of sexual assault (and the like) or child molestation, evidence that the defendant committed any other sexual assault or child molestation is admissible to prove any relevant matter.

CHAPTER 16:   REVIEW OF CHAPTERS 13–15: PRIVILEGES AND PUBLIC POLICY EXCLUSIONS

A. **Privileges**

- **Attorney-client privilege**—protects a confidential communication between a client and a lawyer for purposes of securing legal advice

    o _____ holds the privilege

    o Corporate client—federal courts: the focus should be on the context of the communication

    o **Exceptions:**

        ▪ Future _____ or _____

        ▪ Disputes between an attorney and client

    o **Work-product doctrine**—protects material prepared by an attorney in anticipation of litigation

        ▪ May obtain if a substantial need and cannot obtain it without undue hardship

        ▪ _____ impression work product cannot be obtained.

- **Physician-patient privilege**—recognized in some states, but not the federal courts

    o Protects communications made by a patient to a doctor for purposes of _____ _____

- **Psychotherapist-patient privilege**—recognized in federal courts

    o Protects confidential communications made with a psychotherapist, psychologist, or licensed social worker for the purposes of seeking mental health support

- **Fifth Amendment privilege against self-incrimination**—prevents a person from having to testify against himself in a criminal case

- **Spousal privileges**

    o Confidential communications made in reliance on the sanctity of marriage

        ▪ Held by both spouses (can refuse and can prevent other spouse)

        ▪ Survives the marriage

    o Spousal immunity—spouse cannot be forced to testify against other spouse in a _____ case

        ▪ Held by the _____ spouse

    o Neither privilege applies if one spouse is suing the other or one spouse is charged with a crime against the other spouse or either of their children

B. **Public Policy Exclusions**

- **Liability insurance**—cannot be admitted to prove that a person was negligent or liable for wrongdoing

- **Subsequent remedial measures**—cannot be admitted to prove negligence or that a product was defective
- **Settlement offers and statements made during settlement negotiations**—cannot be admitted to show the _____ or amount of a disputed claim
- **Offers to pay medical expenses or the payment of medical expenses**—cannot be admitted if offered to prove liability for an injury
- **Statements made in an effort to reach a plea bargain**—inadmissible
- **Rape Shield Laws**—generally prohibit defendants from introducing the victim's past sexual conduct or alleged predisposition
  - *Criminal case*—victim's past sexual conduct may only be admitted when:
    - Necessary to explain particular _____ evidence;
    - Offered to show consent—evidence of past sexual conduct with the defendant; or
    - It would be so _____ to prevent the defendant from introducing such evidence that it would be unconstitutional.
  - *Civil case*—evidence of the victim's past sexual conduct or predisposition is only admissible if the court finds the probative value _____ _____ the risk to the victim or others.
- Defendant's past sexual conduct (FRE 413-415)—admissible for any relevant purpose, including propensity

CHAPTER 17:   WHAT IS HEARSAY

A. Definition

- An _____ statement offered to prove the _____ of the matter asserted

1. Out-of-Court Statement

  - Spoken or _____
  - The person who made the out-of-court statement is the _____.
  - Statement can also be assertive nonverbal conduct (e.g., pointing).

    Example 42: A witness is asked at trial, "Who committed the crime?" The witness responds, "I don't know exactly, but when I asked my brother who committed the crime, he pointed at Smith, the defendant." The witness is describing an out-of-court, nonverbal statement, that is intended as an assertion of who committed the crime.

2. Offered to Prove the Truth of the Matter Asserted

  - When the declarant is acting like a _____, the hearsay rule is implicated.

- The declarant and the witness might be the same person; the out-of-court statement could still be hearsay
- If the statement is used for some other purpose (other than the truth of the matter asserted), it is not hearsay.

> *Example 43:* *Someone was trapped in a burning car following a car accident. One question was whether the person was killed on impact or whether he survived and burned to death. There was evidence that the trapped person was yelling, and yelled, "Tell my Mom I love her." This is not hearsay because it is not being offered to prove the truth of the matter asserted. It is being offered to show he was still alive.*

> *Example 44:* *But consider if the trapped person yelled, "I'm alive. I survived the impact!" This is also not hearsay; it coincidentally proves what it asserts (he was still alive).*

B. Common Non-Hearsay Uses

1. Verbal Acts or Legally Operative Facts

The statement is offered to prove that the statement was made (verbal conduct)

> *Example 45:* *A defendant is on trial for extortion. There is evidence that the defendant, over the phone, said, "You better do what I say or I'm going to hurt you." The statement is conduct.*

2. Effect on the _____

A statement offered to show the effect on the person who heard it

> *Example 46:* *There is a question about whether an insurance company received notice that a ship sank. Evidence of a letter sent to the insurance company that stated the ship sank would be nonhearsay. It is not being offered to prove the ship sank; rather, it is being offered to prove the insurance company had notice.*

3. State of Mind

- A statement offered as circumstantial evidence of the declarant's _____ state

> *Example 47:* *A person says, "I am King Henry the VIII." The statement may be introduced to show the person is not of sound mind.*

- Circumstantial evidence can be used to show knowledge.

> *Example 48:* *There is a question about whether someone spoke French. Evidence of that person making a speech in French would be admissible to prove that the person spoke French. It doesn't matter what the speech was about; the speech is not being offered for its truth.*

C. Multiple Hearsay

- Be aware of hearsay within hearsay (double or multiple hearsay)
- If there are multiple levels of hearsay, you will need an exception or exclusion for each level of hearsay for the statement to be admissible.

> *Example 49:* A witness is going to read a letter from the witness's brother in court. The letter says, "Dear brother, yesterday I was talking to our beloved mother and she told me that the red car was speeding." The letter is hearsay and the mother's statement is hearsay. There would have to be a hearsay exception for both.

CHAPTER 18: WHAT IS NOT HEARSAY

A. In General

- Many statements that meet the definition of hearsay will be admissible under an exception.
- The first two categories (discussed in this chapter) are actually exclusions from the definition of hearsay—they meet the definition of hearsay but have been excluded from the rule.

B. Certain Prior Statements of Testifying Witnesses

- The declarant must testify as a witness and be subject to cross-examination for these exclusions to apply to their earlier statements.

1. Prior _____ Statements

- Must have been made under _____ at a trial, hearing, or deposition

- Only prior inconsistent statements made under oath at a trial, hearing, or deposition are admissible as substantive evidence.

> *Example 50:* The witness on the stand at trial says, "The light was red." In the past, the witness told his mother that the light was green. That statement can be used to cast doubt on the witness's credibility (i.e., impeach), but it cannot be used to prove the light was green.

> *Example 51:* If, however, the witness on the stand says, "The light was red," and under oath at a deposition or prior proceeding said the light was green, then the statement can be used to cast doubt on the witness's credibility AND as actual proof that the light was green.

2. **Prior** _____ **Statements**

- Can be used to rehabilitate a witness when accused of recent fabrication or improper motive
- Can also be used as proof of the truth of the matter asserted (substantive evidence)

3. **Prior Statements of** _____

- A previous out-of-court identification of a person (after perceiving that person) is admissible.
- Classic example: _____ at a police station
- Remember: requires that the declarant _____ as a witness and be subject to cross-examination

    - Does not apply if the witness died (or is otherwise unavailable at trial)

C. **Admissions of a Party Opponent**

1. **General Rule**

- If a statement that is being introduced against a party is the party's own prior statement, then it is _____.
- Applies to anything a party said

    > **Editorial Note 5:** This type of statement must be offered by the ***opposing*** party. A party cannot introduce its own hearsay statements using this exclusion.

2. **Adoptive Admissions**

- A statement made by someone else, which is then expressly or impliedly adopted

    > ***Example 52:*** *Someone asks you, "Did you rob that bank?" You reply, "Yes, indeed I did." This entire exchange is admissible because the person's statement (technically hearsay) is adopted or incorporated into your statement. You expressed agreement with the person's question ("Yes, I did rob that bank"), though you never directly said, "I robbed a bank."*

- Can sometimes adopt a statement by _____—Requirements:

    - The party heard the statement and _____ it;
    - The party had the ability to _____; and
    - A reasonable person similarly situated would have denied the statement.

3. **Vicarious Admissions**

- Statements made by persons authorized to speak on a party's behalf—speaking agents (e.g., PR reps, lawyers)
- Statements made by agents or employees if made within the _____ of employment

4. Co-conspirators

Statements made by co-conspirators during and _____
of a conspiracy are admissible against other co-conspirators.

5. Preliminary Questions

o In deciding whether there was a conspiracy or an agency relationship, the court cannot base its finding solely on the contents of the statement itself.

o Pure "boot-strapping" is not permitted; there must be some other evidence to support the finding.

CHAPTER 19: HEARSAY EXCEPTIONS (PART 1)—DECLARANT UNAVAILABLE

Threshold requirement—must show the declarant is _____ to testify as a witness

A. Unavailable Declarant

- "Unavailable" if the declarant:
  - o Is exempted from testifying on grounds of _____;
  - o _____ to testify;
  - o Lacks _____ of the subject matter;
  - o Is dead or too ill; or
  - o Is absent and cannot be subpoenaed or otherwise made available

- Not considered unavailable if a party wrongfully renders the declarant unavailable for the purpose of preventing testimony
- Unavailability alone does not make a declarant's out-of-court statement admissible.

B. Exceptions

1. Former Testimony

- o Given by an unavailable witness _____ at a prior hearing or deposition
- o Admissible in a subsequent trial if the party against whom the testimony is being offered had an _____ and similar _____ to develop the testimony by direct or cross-examination at the prior trial, deposition, or hearing

> **Example 53:** *A witness testifies at a trial and is cross-examined by the party. Later, that trial is overturned, and the court orders a new trial. The witness has died since the first trial. The opposing party can introduce the witness's former testimony because it was under oath at a trial and the party already had an opportunity and similar motive to develop the testimony.*

2. **Dying Declarations**

   o Requirements:

   - Individual believes she is dying;
   - Individual believes death is _____; and
   - Statement relates to the _____ or circumstances of death.

   o Admissible in a _____ case or a _____ case
   o The declarant does not actually have to die
   o Remember, the declarant must be unavailable in some way

3. **Statements Against Interest**

   o At the time it was made, the statement was against the declarant's pecuniary, proprietary, civil, or penal interest, such that a _____ person would not have made the statement unless it were _____

   o Exonerating statements:

   > *Example 54: A defendant is on trial for a crime. The defendant brings in a witness who testifies that his friend Danny (the declarant) told the witness that he committed the crime, which proves that the defendant did not.*

   - Statements that would subject a declarant to _____ liability are not admissible unless corroborating circumstances clearly indicate the trustworthiness of the statement.

   > **Note 10:** Do not confuse with party admissions. There is no "against interest" requirement in the party admissions doctrine and the statement against interest exception is not limited to parties.

4. **Statements of Personal or Family History**

   Statements concerning the unavailable declarant's own birth, adoption, marriage, familial relationship, etc. are admissible under this exception.

5. **Forfeiture by Misconduct (Declarant Unavailable Due to Party's Wrongdoing)**

   o If a party engages in wrongdoing for the purpose of making the declarant unavailable to testify, and renders the declarant unavailable, then:

   - The party cannot claim the declarant is unavailable; and
   - The door is open to use anything the declarant said against the party.

CHAPTER 20: HEARSAY EXCEPTIONS (PART 2)—DECLARANT'S AVAILABILITY IMMATERIAL

These exceptions do NOT require that the declarant be unavailable.

> **Exam Tip 6:** Steps for a hearsay problem:

1. Determine whether the statement is hearsay by definition.

- Look for an _____ statement.

- Determine whether it is being used for the _____ _____.

2. See whether it falls within the definition of non-hearsay.

3. Determine whether the declarant is _____ in order to use that set of hearsay exceptions.

4. See whether the remaining exceptions might allow admission of the hearsay statement.

A. Present Sense Impression

- Statement made _____ the declarant was _____ the event (or immediately thereafter)
- Describes or explains the event

> *Example 55:* A witness is asked, "What happened in the car accident? Did you see it?" The witness says, "I did not, but my brother was watching the accident unfold while I spoke to him on my cellphone. While he watched the accident, he said, 'Oh my goodness, bro! This car was going really fast, ran a red light, and just smashed into the bank."

B. Excited Utterance

- Statement relating to a _____ event or condition while the declarant is still under the _____ of excitement caused by the event or condition

> *Example 56:* A person comes running out of a bank that was just robbed and says, "Oh my goodness! I can't believe it. He came in with a gun and I thought he was going to shoot me! He was wearing a green shirt."

C. State of Mind (mental, emotional, or physical condition)

- Statement of a declarant's _____ physical, mental, or emotional condition is admissible to prove the existence of that condition.
- A statement of _____ can be used to prove action in _____ with that intent.

> *Example 57:* On Tuesday, a person said, "I intend to go to Cleveland tomorrow." The statement can be used not only to prove the person's intent to go to Cleveland, but also that the person actually went to Cleveland on Wednesday.

D. Statements Made for Purposes of Medical Diagnosis or Treatment

- Describe a declarant's medical history or past or present symptoms, or even the _____ of an injury, if pertinent to _____ or diagnosis

- Need not be made directly to the doctor

Editorial Note 6: The statement need not necessarily be made by the patient.

E. Past Recollection Recorded

Note 11: Recall that when a witness cannot remember something while testifying, you can refresh the witness's recollection. This can be done by showing them a document or item (or by many other methods).

Example 58: *You call the grocery store manager who was working the night of a slip and fall. You ask how recently the floor had been waxed. The manager cannot remember because it occurred a year and a half ago. You show the manager his wax log to refresh his memory, but he still cannot recall exactly when the floor had been waxed. That information is important to your case, but the wax log itself is hearsay.*

- When a witness has inadequate memory to testify about a matter for which a record exists, the witness may *read* the record to the jury if:

  - The record concerns a matter about which the witness once had knowledge;
  - The record was prepared or adopted by the witness when the matter was _____;
  - The record accurately reflects the witness's knowledge; and
  - The witness testifies he has _____ memory of the event to testify fully and accurately (even after consulting the writing while on the stand).

- The witness may *read* it to the jury, but it is not provided to the jury (not introduced into evidence).
- The _____ may introduce it to the jury.

CHAPTER 21: HEARSAY EXCEPTIONS (PART 3)—DECLARANT'S AVAILABILITY IMMATERIAL (CONT'D)

A. Business Records

- Any record or writing of an act or event made in the course of a _____ conducted business activity
- Admissible if the record was made:

  - At or near the _____ of the event it records;
  - By a person with _____ of the event and under a duty to report it (or transmitted by such a person); and
  - As part of the _____ practice of the business to make that kind of record

- Medical records are often included as business records (only to the extent that entries relate to diagnosis or treatment).

- Records prepared in anticipation of _____ are not admissible as business records.
- Courts have discretion to exclude business records if the source of information or the method or circumstances indicate a lack of _____.

B. Public Records

- Certain records of public _____ and administrators (e.g., fire department, health department, public utilities, etc.)
- May be excluded if the circumstances indicate a lack of _____
- There are three sorts of things which may be admissible if set forth in a public record:

  - _____;
  - _____; and
  - _____

- Law enforcement—police reports being used against criminal defendants

  - Can only introduce the activities; not what was observed or concluded
  - Rationale—the officer should actually testify and be subject to cross-examination
  - Police report may still come in under the recorded recollection exception (officer cannot remember).

C. Learned Treatises (scientific, historical, or medical)

- May be used to _____ expert witnesses and as substantive evidence
- May be used as substantive evidence once it is established as a reliable authority, an expert relied on it, or it was used to cross-examine an expert

D. Judgment of Previous Conviction

- Admissible to prove any fact that was _____ to the judgment

E. Other Exceptions

- Records of vital statistics
- Records of religious organizations
- Marriage and baptismal certificates, and other family records
- Statements in ancient documents
- Market reports and commercial publications

F. Reputation

- There is a hearsay exception for the reputation or character of a person.
- Available in the narrow circumstances when reputation/character evidence is admissible

CHAPTER 22:   REVIEW OF CHAPTERS 17–21: HEARSAY

A. **What is Hearsay**

- **Definition—**_____ statement being used to prove the _____ of the matter asserted

  o   Declarant is being treated like a witness (source of information)

- **Other uses that are not hearsay:**

  o   _____ (e.g., agreeing to a contract)
  o   Effect on the recipient (e.g., to prove notice or duress)
  o   Declarant's mental state

B. **What is Not Hearsay**

- Prior _____statements—if made under _____ at a trial, hearing, or deposition
- Prior_____ statements
- Prior statements of _____
- Admissions of a party _____

  o   Need not be a formal admission or be against interest
  o   Adoptive admissions
  o   Vicarious admissions
  o   Co-conspirators—during and in furtherance of the conspiracy

C. **Exceptions When Declarant is Unavailable**

- **Unavailable witness:**

  o   Exempt on grounds of privilege
  o   _____ to testify
  o   Lack memory
  o   Death or illness
  o   Absent and cannot be subpoenaed

- **Exceptions that require a showing of unavailability:**

  o   _____ testimony

    ▪   Given at an earlier trial, hearing, or deposition
    ▪   Person against whom the testimony is offered had an opportunity and similar motive to develop testimony by cross-examination

  o   _____ declaration
  o   Statements against _____
  o   Statement of personal or family history
  o   Statements introduced against a party that wrongfully caused the declarant's unavailability

D. Exceptions When Declarant's Availability Is Immaterial

- Present _____
- Excited utterance
- State of mind
  - Includes intent—can be used to prove action in conformity
- Statements for the purposes of medical diagnosis or treatment
  - Statements about the cause of an injury may be admitted if reasonably pertinent to diagnosis or treatment.
- Past _____ recorded
  - May be *read* to the jury; may be introduced into evidence by the opposing party
- Business records—in the course of a regularly conducted business activity
- _____ records
  - Activities, observations, and conclusions of public agencies and officials
  - Police reports—when used against criminal defendants, can only use activities
- Learned treatise
- Conviction
  - To prove someone was convicted of a crime (impeachment)
  - To prove the person actually committed the crime (requires a hearsay exception)

CHAPTER 23: CONSTITUTIONAL LIMITATIONS TO THE HEARSAY RULE

A. The Confrontation Clause (Sixth Amendment)

1. Face-to-Face Confrontation

- Criminal defendants have the right to be _____ with the witnesses against them.
- Witnesses must testify in front of the accused; strong preference for face-to-face confrontation
- Sometimes particular accommodations are necessary to protect the interest of a vulnerable witness, such as a child.

2. Out-of-Court Statements

- Basic principle of *Crawford*: out-of-court statements that are _____ give rise to Confrontation Clause problems.
- **Testimonial**—made with the primary purpose of ascertaining past criminal conduct
- Testimonial statements can only be admitted against a criminal defendant if:
  - The declarant is now _____; and

- The defendant had a prior opportunity to _____
    that declarant.
  - Statements made for the purpose of getting help (emergency doctrine) should not be considered testimonial.

> **Exam Tip 7:**   Think of the Confrontation Clause as an entirely separate hurdle for prosecutors.

B. The Due Process Clause (Fourteenth Amendment)

- If evidence rules restrict a criminal defendant's ability to mount a defense, the rules might violate the Due Process Clause.

GOOD LUCK!

[END OF HANDOUT]

Real Property

REAL PROPERTY
PROFESSOR ZACHARY A. KRAMER
ARIZONA STATE UNIVERSITY – SANDRA DAY O'CONNOR COLLEGE OF LAW

> **Editorial Note 1:** The Professor refers to specific Example numbers throughout this lecture. The content does not always match these references due to formatting changes.

CHAPTER 1:   OWNERSHIP

A. Basics

Different ways property can be transferred (i.e., alienated):

1. _____:

   Example 1:   *Oliver sells his home to Anna for $325,000.*

2. **Gift:**

   Example 2:   *Oliver gives his lucky pen to Anna, "in the hope that it will bring her as much luck as it has brought him."*

3. _____:

   Example 3:   *Oliver dies in a tragic fishing accident. In his will, he gives his stamp collection to his wife Anna. When is this gift effective? At Oliver's* _____.

   > **Note 1:** Gifts in a will are effective when the decedent dies.

4. _____ **succession:**

   Example 4:   *Oliver dies without a will. He is survived solely by his wife, Anna, who is his* _____ *at law (i.e., a person who survives the decedent and takes by intestate succession).*

B. Estates in Land

Ownership interests: Divided in time between _____ interests and future interests

- Key distinction is timing of _____.

  Example 5:   *Oliver transfers Blackacre "to Anna for life, then to Ben."*

  Who has the right to possession presently?

  _____.

  Who has the right to possession in the future?

  _____.

Example 6:   *Oliver transfers Blackacre "to Anna once she passes the bar exam."*

Who has the right to possession presently?

_____.

Who has the right to possession in the future?

_____.

- Someone must be in possession of the property at all times.

C. Fee Simple

- Fee simple is the _____ possessory estate.
- Why is it the largest? It is capable of _____.

  o Inheritable: Upon the owner's death, the owner can pass it by will or by intestate succession; can also be transferred by gift or sale during owner's life.

  > *Example 7:*   *O transfers land to A. A has a fee simple absolute. A dies without a will. B is A's only heir. B then has a fee simple absolute. B dies without a will, leaving C as an heir. C has a fee simple absolute.*

- To create a fee simple:

  o Look for magic words: "and his/her _____ "

     ▪ But these words are *not* required: "O to A" and "O to A and her heirs" are the same thing.

  o Watch out for ambiguous grants. If ambiguous, it creates a

     _____.

     > *Example 8:*   *Oliver conveys Blackacre "to Anna forever." What does Anna have? A _____.*

- Fee simple absolute is the default estate; there is a presumption that the grantor conveys the most that she has.
- Don't be fooled by words of _____ or

  _____.

  > *Example 9:*   *Oliver conveys Blackacre "to Anna, my hope and wish being that on her death, Anna will give the property to her son, Ben."*

  What interest does Anna have? _____.

  What interest does Ben have? _____.

  Note 2: Precatory words such as "my hope and wish" are not enough to show actual intent.

- No future interest associated with a fee simple.
  - Capable of lasting _____.

CHAPTER 2:   DEFEASIBLE FEES

A. Defeasible Fees

- May be _____ by the occurrence of an event;
- Capable of lasting forever but also of being terminated early;
- Condition will _____ the fee simple.

B. Fee Simple Determinable

- Limited by specific _____ language

> *Example 10:* *Oliver conveys Blackacre "to Anna _____ the land is used as a farm."*

- Examples of durational language include:
  - "_____ the land is used as a farm;"
  - "_____ its use as a farm;"
  - "Until it is no longer used as a farm."

> **Note 3:** The fee simple lasts while the period is in play (e.g., while used as a farm), but as soon as the period ends (e.g., when the land is no longer used as a farm), the fee simple ends.

C. Fee Simple Subject to Condition Subsequent

- Limited by specific _____ language

> *Example 11:* *Oliver conveys Blackacre "to Anna, _____ the land is not farmed, Oliver may re-enter and re-take the property."*

- Examples of conditional language include:
  - "Provided that the land is not farmed;"
  - "On the condition that the land is not farmed."

- Focus on the language to the grantor: Suggests that the grantor must exercise a right in order to take possession.

> *Example 12:* *Oliver conveys Blackacre "to Anna, but if the land is not farmed, Oliver may re-enter and re-take the property." When, if ever, is Oliver entitled to possession? When the condition is met and Oliver reclaims it.*

D. Future Interests Associated with Defeasible Fees

1. Possibility of Reverter

- Future interest held by a _____ following a

  _____.

- Interest vests _____ after the durational period ends.

  > **Example 13:** Oliver conveys Blackacre "to Anna and her heirs, so long as the
  > land is used as a public park." What future interest does Oliver have? Oliver
  > has a _____. If the land isn't used as a park, the
  > interest vests in Oliver as a fee simple because it reverts back to the grantor.

2. Right of Entry

- Future interest held by the _____ following a

  _____.

- Does not vest automatically; it must be _____.

  > **Example 14:** Oliver conveys Blackacre "to Anna and her heirs, but if the land is
  > not used as a public park, Oliver can re-enter and re-take." Oliver has a
  > _____. In order for Oliver's interest to become
  > possessory, Oliver must exercise the right of entry and reclaim the interest.

  Note 4: The right of entry is also known as the power of termination.

E. Fee Simple Subject to Executory Interest

- Will end upon the happening of an event and the future interest will vest in a
  _____ (i.e., someone other than the grantor)

- Held by another _____ and not the grantor.

  > **Example 15:** Oliver conveys Blackacre "to Anna and her heirs, but if liquor is
  > served on the premises, then to Ben and his heirs."
  >
  > Anna has a fee simple subject to executory interest.
  >
  > Ben has an _____. If liquor is ever served, Ben
  > will divest Anna of her interest and hold a fee simple.

  Note 5: Look to who holds the future interest to distinguish a fee simple
  subject to executory interest (third party holds) from a fee simple subject to a
  condition subsequent (grantor holds).

F. Executory Interest

- Future interest that will _____, or terminate, an earlier interest.
- The word for terminating a prior interest is to "_____."

  > **Example 16:** Oliver conveys Blackacre "to Anna and her heirs, but if liquor is
  > served on the premises, then to Ben and his heirs."

Ben has an executory interest. Why? Because Ben will

_____ *Anna's interest if liquor is ever served.*

Whose interest is being divested? _____.

Problem 1: *Oliver conveys Blackacre "to Anna."*

Anna has a _____.

Oliver has _____.

Note 6: Always presume a party conveys the most that it has to convey.

Problem 2: *Oliver conveys Blackacre "to Anna while the land is used for school purposes."*

Anna has a _____.

Oliver has a _____.

Problem 3: *Oliver conveys Blackacre "to Anna while the land is used for school purposes, then to Ben."*

Anna has a _____.

Ben has an _____.

Oliver has _____.

Problem 4: *Oliver conveys Blackacre "to Anna, but if Anna gets a pet, Oliver may re-enter and re-take."*

Anna has a _____.

Oliver has a _____.

CHAPTER 3:   THE LIFE ESTATE

A. Definition

- Present estate that is _____ by a

  _____.

- Whose life?

  Example 17: *Oliver conveys Blackacre "to Anna for life." This life estate is measured against* _____ *life.*

  Example 18: *Oliver conveys Blackacre "to Anna for Ben's life." Anna's life estate is measured against* _____ *life. This is known as a life estate "pur autre vie" (meaning measured against the life of someone else).*

B. **Creation**

- Magic words to create a life estate are "_____."
- If ambiguous, look for the grantor's intent to create an estate that will end upon the _____ of the measuring life.

> *Example 19:* "To A to live in your house." Some argue that this language creates a fee simple for A. Others argue that this language creates a life estate. Both arguments have merit. Resolve based on whether it should be inheritable or limited just for the person while they are alive.

C. **Termination**

- Ends naturally when the measuring life _____.
  - Transferable

    > *Example 20:* Oliver conveys Blackacre "to Anna for life." Anna later transfers her interest to Ben. When will Ben's interest terminate? _____.

- Can a life tenant (of a life estate measured by the life tenant's life) pass the property by will?
  - _____, the life estate ends at the life tenant's death.

- Can a life tenant (of a life estate measured by the life tenant's life) pass the property by intestate succession?
  - _____, the life estate ends at the life tenant's death.

    > *Example 21:* Oliver conveys Blackacre "to Anna for life." Anna dies, leaving her son Ben as her sole heir. Does Ben inherit Anna's life estate? _____, Anna's interest ended on her death.

D. **Future Interests Following a Life Estate**

- If possession of the land goes back to the grantor after the life estate ends, then the grantor retains a _____.

    > *Example 22:* Oliver conveys Blackacre "to Anna for life."
    >
    > Oliver retains a _____. Upon Anna's death, Oliver takes the property in _____.

- If possession of the land goes to a *third party* (transferee) after the life estate ends, then the third party takes a _____.

    > *Example 23:* Oliver conveys Blackacre "to Anna for life, then to Ben."
    >
    > During Anna's life, Ben has a _____. What happens when Anna dies? Ben takes possession in _____. Oliver has

_____ _because Anna has the present interest (life_
estate) and Ben has the future interest.

E. Waste

- Comes into play when more than one party has an interest in the same piece of real property

    Example 24: _Oliver conveys Blackacre "to Anna for life." Anna has been_
    dumping hazardous materials onto the property, which have caused serious
    damage to Blackacre. The doctrine of waste gives Oliver a claim to stop Anna
    from injuring the land. Why? Because Oliver has a

    _____.

- Three kinds of waste:

    o _____ waste: Waste caused by
      _____ conduct, which causes a
      _____ in value.

    Example 25: _Dumping hazardous materials on the property_

    o _____ waste: Waste caused by
      _____ toward the property, which causes a decrease in value.

    Example 26: _Harm caused to property through tenant's failure to take action_
    after a storm

    o _____ waste: Special situation where a life tenant or other
      person in possession changes the use of the property and actually
      _____ the value of the property.

    Example 27: _Renovation of a house, construction of a dam, fixing a fence_

- Not unique to estates and future interests
- Situations where the doctrine of waste applies include:

    o Landlord v. tenant;
    o Co-tenant out of possession v. tenant in possession (concurrent estates);
    o Mortgagee (bank/lender) v. mortgagor (borrower).

    > **Exam Tip 1: How to Spot a Waste Problem:**
    >
    > 1. Do multiple parties have simultaneous interests, (e.g., life tenant, remainder, future interests, landlord v. tenant)?
    >
    > 2. Is there a change in the value of the property due to the actions/inactions of the party in possession?
    >
    > 3. Will the waste substantially change the interest taken by the party out of possession?

CHAPTER 4: FUTURE INTERESTS

A. Remainders

- A remainder is a future interest that follows what present possessory estate? _____.

    o A remainder _____ follow a vested fee simple. Why? A future interest following a vested fee simple would have to divest the prior interest (the fee simple) but a remainder does not function that way because it instead waits for the prior interest to end.

- Can be _____ or _____.
- RAP generally applies only to _____ remainders.

    o Vested Remainder—an interest that is:

    1) Given to an _____ grantee (i.e., someone who can be identified); and

    2) Not subject to a _____ (i.e., there is no condition that must be satisfied in order for the interest to vest).

    ▪ If the remainder fails either 1 or 2, it is a contingent remainder.

    Example 28: Oliver conveys Blackacre "to Anna for life, then to Ben."

    What does Anna have? A _____.

    Is Ben an ascertainable grantee? _____.

    Is there a condition precedent? _____.

    Ben has a _____ remainder.

    Note 7: If the holder of a vested remainder dies, the interest passes to the holder's heirs.

    Example 29: Oliver conveys Blackacre "to A for life, then to A's firstborn grandchild." At the time of the conveyance, A does not have any grandchildren.

    What interest does the firstborn grandchild have? A _____.

    Is the firstborn grandchild an ascertainable grantee? _____.

    The firstborn grandchild has a _____ remainder.

    Note 8: If a contingent remainder does not vest before it becomes possessory (e.g., A does not have any grandchildren before A dies), the grantor has a reversion.

Example 30: *Oliver conveys Blackacre "to Anna for life, then to Ben if Ben survives Anna." What kind of remainder does Ben have?*

Is Ben an ascertainable grantee? _____.

Is there a condition precedent? Yes, Ben must survive Anna.

Ben has a _____ remainder.

Oliver has a _____.

B. Class Gifts—Vested Subject to Open

1. Vested Subject to Open

o Vested remainder in a _____; and

o Full class membership is _____.

- At least one person in the class must be vested for it to be vested subject to open; if no one in the class has vested, the remainder is contingent.

- When all members of a class are identified, the class is _____.

    Example 31: *Oliver conveys Blackacre "to Anna for life, then to Anna's children who reach 21." Anna has three kids—Ben is 25, Carmen is 18, and David is 15.*

    What is Ben's interest? _____.

    Why is it subject to open? Because _____ might make it to 21.

    When will we know when the class closes and who the class members are? _____.

    If more of Anna's children reach 21, what happens? They will _____ divest Ben.

    Note 9: In property law, it is presumed a party can have a child at any time before the party's death, regardless of age.

- **Watch out!** At least one member of the class must be vested. If no one in the class is vested, then the remainder is _____. In the above example, if Ben were 20 instead of 25, his remainder would be contingent.

2. RAP Applies to a Vested Remainder Subject to Open.

o Rule of Convenience: A class-closing mechanism to avoid application of _____ to a class gift.

o If the grant does not have an express closing date, the Rule of Convenience closes the class when any member of the class becomes entitled to _____.

Example 32: *Oliver conveys "to Anna for life, then to Ben's children." Ben has one child. When will this class close under the Rule of Convenience? On _____death.*

C. Special Cases

1. Doctrine of Worthier Title

- ○ Prevents against remainders in a _____ heirs
- ○ Creates a presumption of a reversion to the grantor

Example 33: *Oliver conveys "to Anna for life, then to my heirs." What future interest does Oliver retain under the Doctrine of Worthier Title?*

_____.

2. Rule in Shelley's Case

- ○ Prevents against remainders in a _____ heirs
- ○ Uses the doctrine of merger to create a fee simple

Example 34: *Oliver conveys "to Anna for life, then to Anna's heirs." What estate does Anna have under the Rule in Shelley's case?*

_____.

D. Executory Interests

- • Subject to the Rule Against Perpetuities ("RAP")
- • Definition: Future interest that _____ (i.e., divests) a prior _____ interest

- ○ Two kinds of executory interests:

  - ▪ **Springing** executory interest: Divests the _____;
  - ▪ **Shifting** executory interest: Divests a prior _____.

Example 35: *Oliver conveys Blackacre "to Anna for life, then to Ben one year after Anna's death."*

What interest does Anna have? A _____.

What happens immediately after Anna's death?

_____.

Whose interest does Ben divest? _____.

What interest does Ben have? A _____ executory interest.

Example 36: *Oliver conveys Blackacre "to Anna, but if the land is used for commercial purposes, to Ben."*

What interest does Anna have? A _____.

Under what condition will Ben take the property? If the land

_____.

Whose interest does Ben divest? _____, who is a

prior grantee.

What interest does Ben have? A shifting executory interest.

Example 37: *Oliver conveys Blackacre "to Anna after she is admitted to the*
bar."

What interest does Anna have? A _____

executory interest.

Whose interest does Anna divest? _____, the

grantor.

What interest does Oliver have? A _____.

Exam Tip 2: Count the parties:

If there are **two parties** (Grantor + Grantee), it is most likely a **springing** executory interest because the grantee will divest the grantor.

If there are **three parties** (Grantor + Grantee + Grantee), it is most likely a **shifting** executory interest because a grantee will divest another grantee (the executory interest will shift from one grantee to another).

CHAPTER 5:   THE RULE AGAINST PERPETUITIES (RAP)

A. What is going on here?

Three questions to set the RAP context:

1. **Why do we have such a silly rule?**

   o Practical tension: Parents want to keep property in the family but do not trust their children **v.** courts' unease about uncertainty

   o Thus: RAP prevents _____ vesting.

2. **What's the goal of the rule?**

   o Testing for _____;

   o Operates like a statute of limitations for contingent future interests.

3. **Why 21 years?**

   o Approximately two generations—a life plus 21 years;

   o Beyond that, we can't say what will happen.

B. Method—When, What, Who?

   1. When: Identifying when the interests are created

   - Inter vivos transfers: Interests created at time of the grant
   - Devise (will): Interests created at testator's _____, not when the will is drafted

   2. What: Determine if interests created are subject to RAP

   - RAP applies to:

     - _____ remainders;
     - _____;
     - _____ gifts (subject to open), if not closed by rule of convenience.

   - Does not apply to vested remainders unless subject to open

   3. Who: Identify the relevant and, if applicable, validating lives

   - Relevant life: Person who affects vesting, usually mentioned or implied by the grant (e.g., prior life tenant, the parent where a conveyance is made to a child)
   - Validating life: Person who tells us whether or not the interest vests within the perpetuities period (lifetime plus 21 years)

     - Must have been _____ when the interests were created;
     - Can validate her own interest;
     - If no validating life, then the interest is _____ and we strike it from the grant; if there is a validating life, the interest is good.

   4. "When, What, Who?" Application

   > **Example 38:** Oliver conveys Blackacre "to Anna, but if the land is ever used as a business during Anna's lifetime, to Ben."
   >
   > **When:** Interests created _____; inter vivos.
   >
   > **What:** Interest subject to RAP is _____.
   >
   > **Who:** Lives in being at the creation of the interest are _____, _____, and _____.
   >
   > **Validating life?** Will we know 21 years after their lives whether this interest will vest or not? Yes, at _____ death we will know whether she used the land for business purposes. So _____ is the validating life.
   >
   > **Result:** RAP is not violated. Ben's executory interest is valid.

Example 39: Professor Kramer conveys "$1000 to my Themis students who are admitted to the bar." (Not a binding contract!)

When: Interests created _____.

What: Interest subject to RAP is students' _____.

Who: Lives in being at the creation of the interest are _____ and _____.

Validating life? Will we know 21 years after someone's death whether this interest vests or not? _____, we will know whether it vested or failed.

Result: No violation. Students' executory interests are valid.

Note 10: RAP is not about whether an interest vests or fails. It is about whether we will **know** if it vests or fails. Cannot have uncertainty.

CHAPTER 6: RAP VIOLATIONS

We ~~strike out~~ the violating interest, as if the interest was never created in the first place.

Example 40: Oliver conveys "to Anna for life, then to Anna's first child who reaches the age of 22." This conveyance violates RAP. It is a contingent remainder, and possible for the contingent remainder in Anna's first child to vest more than 21 years after Anna's life. Anna's first child, even if alive, is not a validating life because the child could die.

Result—strike the offending interest: Oliver conveys to Anna for life, ~~then to Anna's first child who reaches the age of 22~~.

Anna's interest: A _____.

Anna's first child's interest: _____.

Oliver interest: A _____.

Example 41: Oliver conveys, "to Anna so long as the property is used as a farm, then to Ben." Anna has a fee simple subject to an executory interest and Ben has an executory interest. This conveyance violates RAP. It is possible that Ben's executory interest will vest more than 21 years after Anna's or Ben's death.

Result—strike the offending interest: Oliver conveys to Anna so long as the property is used as a farm, ~~then to Ben~~.

Anna's interest: A _____.

Ben's interest: _____.

Oliver's interest: A _____.

Example 42: *Oliver conveys "to my grandchildren who reach 21." Oliver has two children, Anna and Ben, and three grandchildren under the age of 21. This conveyance violates RAP. It is possible that Oliver could have another child—call her C—who gives birth to a grandchild after Oliver, Anna, and Ben have died. This grandchild will not reach age 21 until more than 21 years after the deaths of the measuring lives (C is not a validating life because she was not in existence when the interest was created).*

Result—strike the offending interest: ~~Oliver conveys to my grandchildren who reach 21~~*.*

Grandchildren who reach 21: _____.

Oliver's interest: A _____.

What's the key fact? Oliver is _____.

CHAPTER 7:   RAP—SPECIAL CASES

A. RAP and Class Gifts

- Special Rule: If the gift to any member of the class is void under RAP, then the gift is void as to all members of the class. The gift is "bad as to one, bad as to all." (The "all or nothing" rule.)

    Example 43: *Oliver conveys "to Anna for life, then to her children who reach 25." At the time of the conveyance, Anna's son Ben is 26 and her daughter Carmen is 18.*

    Who are members of the class? _____.

    > **Editorial Note 2:** The members of the class are Anna's children. Before they can be entitled to take the property they must satisfy the condition of reaching 25.

    Has any class member vested? _____, Ben's remainder has vested.

    Is the class closed? _____, Anna is still alive and may have more children.

- Remember: Living people have the nasty habit of breeding. Property law assumes that anyone who is alive can still have children.

    Does the gift survive RAP? _____. Anna could have another kid (call her Dana) after the conveyance. Dana can't be a validating life. Dana could vest more than 21 years after Anna, Ben, and Carmen's death.

What happens to Ben's interest? _____.

Result—strike the offending interest: Oliver conveys to Anna for life, ~~then to her children who reach 25~~.

Anna's interest: A _____.

Oliver interest: A _____.

Children, including Ben who is vested, have

_____.

B. Rule of Convenience

- An *interpretative* rule
- Can save a class gift from being _____ under RAP
- For purposes of avoiding RAP, the class closes as soon as a member of the class is entitled to _____ possession.

> *Example 44:* Oliver conveys "to Anna for life, then to Anna's grandchildren."
> *Anna has one grandchild, Ben. It is possible that other grandchildren will be*
> *born more than 21 years after Anna or Ben's death. Without the Rule of*
> *Convenience, the gift to Ben is _____ under RAP.*
> *With the Rule of Convenience, Ben will take at*
> _____. *When Anna dies, the class treated as*
> _____.

C. Exceptions to the Class Gift Rule (when the "all or nothing" rule does not apply)

Two exceptions:

- Transfers of a specific _____ to each class member, and
- Transfers to a _____ that vests at a _____ time, e.g., "to the children of B, and upon the death of each, to that child's issue"

D. Exceptions to RAP

1. Charities

- RAP does not apply to a gift from one _____ to another charity.
- The gift to the alternate charity is not subject to RAP

> *Example 45:* Oliver conveys Blackacre "to the Donald McRonald House so long
> *as the property is used to support cancer patients and their families, then to the*
> *Glaser Elizabeth Pediatric AIDS Fund."*
>
> *The AIDS Fund's executory interest, which normally would violate RAP, is valid*
> *because RAP does not apply to charity-to-charity gifts.*

2. Options

- o RAP does not apply to an _____ held by a current tenant to purchase a fee interest in the leasehold property.
- o Nor does it apply to an option (or right of first refusal) in a _____ transaction.

E. "Wait and See" Approach

- The traditional RAP has been softened by reform (e.g., Uniform Statutory Rule Against Perpetuities).
- The most common modern approach is to "wait and see" if an interest subject to RAP vests within the perpetuities period.
- Some of these states changed the vesting period to _____ years.

> **Exam Tip 3:** The bar exam still tests the traditional RAP though you should be aware of the modern "wait and see" approach.

F. Cy Pres

- An equitable doctrine (borrowed from the law of trusts) that allows a court to reform a transfer to avoid RAP.

CHAPTER 8: CONCURRENT ESTATES

A. Basics

1. Definition

- o Ownership or possession of real property by two or more persons simultaneously

    Example 46: Oliver conveys Blackacre "to Anna and Ben and their heirs." Anna and Ben are _____ owners of Blackacre.

2. Basic Rule

- o Concurrent owners each have right to use or possess the _____ property.
- o Exception: Concurrent owners can contract out of the basic rule.

3. Three Kinds of Concurrent Ownership/Concurrent Estates

- o Tenancy in _____;
- o _____ tenancy;
- o Tenancy by the _____.

B. Tenancy in Common

- Default concurrent interest

- o Any conveyance to more than one person is presumed to be a tenancy in common.

- Concurrent owners have _____ but _____ interests in the property.

> ***Example 47:*** *Oliver conveys Blackacre "in equal shares to Anna and Ben." Their interests are separate because they have _____ shares in Blackacre. Their interests are undivided because Blackacre is not physically divided; Anna and Ben each have a right to possess the _____ of Blackacre.*

- No right of survivorship
  - Each co-tenant can transfer the property freely at death as well as during life.

> ***Example 48:*** *Oliver conveys Blackacre "in equal shares to Anna, Ben, and Carmen." Anna conveys her interest to Amy. Ben dies and his will gives his entire estate to his son Brad. Who owns Blackacre? Amy has a _____ interest in Blackacre. Brad has a _____ interest in Blackacre. Carmen has a _____ interest in Blackacre.*

C. Joint Tenancy

- The defining characteristic is the right of _____, whereby the surviving joint tenant(s) automatically take the deceased tenant's interest.

> ***Example 49:*** *Oliver conveys Blackacre "to Anna and Ben as joint tenants with a right of survivorship." Anna dies in a tragic hunting accident. Anna's will leaves everything to her daughter Amy. Who owns Blackacre and why? _____, who takes under the right of survivorship.*

- How do you create a joint tenancy?
  - Grantor must make a clear expression of intent; PLUS
  - Must be survivorship language, e.g., "as joint tenants with a right of survivorship."

D. Four Unities [PITT]

To create a joint tenancy, you need four unities:

- **Possession:** Every joint tenant has an equal right to possess the whole of the property.

> **Note 11:** Tenancy in common and tenancy by the entirety also require the unity of possession. The remaining three unities set the joint tenancy apart.

- **Interest:** Joint tenants must have an _____ share of the same type of interest.

> ***Example 50:*** *Anna and Ben own Blackacre as joint tenants. Each has a 50% share and each owns the property in fee simple—equal shares, equal interests.*

- **Time:** Joint tenants must receive their interests at the same _____.

- **Title:** Joint tenants must receive their interests in the same _____ of title.

> ***Example 51:*** *Oliver's will leaves Blackacre "to Anna and Ben as joint tenants with a right of survivorship." The will further provides that Anna takes a 1/3 interest and Ben takes a 2/3 interest. Are the four unities present?*
>
> ***Possession:*** _____, *Anna and Ben have possession.*
>
> ***Interest:*** _____, *they did not receive the same interest (Anna received 1/3; Ben 2/3).*
>
> ***Time:*** _____, *they received their interests at the same time.*
>
> ***Title:*** _____, *received it by the same instrument (i.e., Oliver's will).*
>
> *This conveyance would create a _____.*

> **Note 12:** The four unities are needed to create a joint tenancy and also to maintain a joint tenancy. If one unity is lost, the joint tenancy is severed.

E. Severance

- If any of the unities are severed (i.e., _____), then the joint tenancy is terminated and turns into a _____.
- Common situations:
  - **Inter vivos transfer:** Transfer during life will destroy/sever the right of survivorship and convert the estate into a tenancy in common.

    > **Note 13:** Conveyance by only one of more than two joint tenants does not destroy the joint tenancy of the remaining joint tenants.

    > ***Example 52:*** *Anna, Ben, and Carmen own Blackacre as joint tenants. Anna transfers her share to Amy. What effect on the joint tenancy?*
    >
    > *Amy's interest: A _____.*
    >
    > *Ben and Carmen's interests: _____.*

    > **Note 14:** Any lien against a joint tenant's interest _____ upon that tenant's death, so the surviving tenants' interests are not _____.

  - **Mortgages:** A joint tenant grants a mortgage interest in the joint tenancy to a creditor. Does the mortgage sever the joint tenancy?

- **Majority:** Most jurisdictions follow a _____ theory. The mortgage is treated as a lien and does not destroy the joint tenancy.
- **Minority:** A minority of jurisdictions follows a _____ theory. The mortgage severs title and the tenancy between the joint tenants and the creditor is converted into a tenancy in common.

- **Leases:** A joint tenant leases her share in the property to a tenant. Does the lease sever the joint tenancy? Jurisdictions are split.

- Some jurisdictions hold that the lease _____ the joint tenancy.
- Other jurisdictions treat the lease as a _____ suspension of the joint tenancy.

F. Tenancy by the Entirety

- Joint tenancy between _____.

- Marriage is the fifth unity (sometimes called the unity of person).

- Has a right of _____.
- Tenants by the entirety cannot alienate or encumber their shares without the _____ of their spouse.
- Magic words: Property conveyed "as tenants by the entirety, with a right of survivorship"
- If the grant is ambiguous, courts presume property is held as joint tenants or as tenants in common.

CHAPTER 9: RIGHTS AND OBLIGATIONS OF CONCURRENT OWNERS

A. Possession and Use

- **General Rule:** Each co-tenant has right to possess _____ of the property, regardless of that co-tenant's share and regardless of the type of co-tenancy.
- **Exception:** Co-tenants have entered into an agreement to the contrary

> *Example 53:   Anna and Ben are tenants in common in Blackacre. Anna owns a 2/3 share and Ben owns a 1/3 share. Ben is in sole possession of Blackacre. They have no agreement as to possession.*
>
> *Question 1: Ben owns a 1/3 share. Can he still occupy the whole of the property? _____.*
>
> *Question 2: Is Ben an adverse possessor? _____, Ben's use is not adverse to Anna's interest.*

Question 3: Does one co-tenant owe the other a duty to pay rent?

_____, a co-tenant in possession is not required to pay rent to co-tenants out of _____.

- **Ouster:** Co-tenant in possession denies another co-tenant _____ to the property (e.g., one tenant changes the locks, or throws out the co-tenant's stuff)

  ○ Remedies for the ousted tenant:

    ▪ Get an _____ granting access to the property; and/or
    ▪ Recover _____ for the value of the use while the co-tenant was unable to access the property.

B. Third Party Rents and Operating Expenses

1. Rent

  ○ Rent received from a third party's possession of the property, minus operating expenses, are divided based on _____ interests of each co-tenant

  > *Example 54:* Anna and Ben own Blackacre as tenants in common. Anna has a 10% interest and Ben has a 90% interest in Blackacre. Carmen is renting Blackacre for $1000 a month. Each month, Anna is entitled to $_____ of Carmen's rent, while Ben is entitled to $_____ of Carmen's rent. The outcome would differ if Carmen was renting from one co-tenant and the other co-tenant was also in possession.

2. Operating Expenses

  ○ Necessary charges, such as taxes or mortgage interest payments

    ▪ Divided based on _____ interests of each co-tenant
    ▪ A co-tenant can collect _____ from the other co-tenants for payments in excess of her share of the operating expenses.

3. Repairs

  ○ There is no right to reimbursement from co-tenants for _____ repairs.

  ○ However, the co-tenant who makes the repairs can get credit in a partition action.

4. Improvements

  ○ There is no right to _____ for improvements.

  ○ However, the co-tenant who makes the improvements can get credit in a partition action.

C. Partition

1. Equitable Remedy

- o Available to all holders of a tenancy in common or a _____ tenancy
- o A _____ right
- o Tenants by the entirety **do not** have the unilateral right to partition.

2. Effect

- The court will divide the property into _____ portions.
- Courts have a preference for a _____ division (i.e., a partition in kind).

  - o Court will order a partition by sale if the physical partition is:

    - ▪ Not _____ (e.g., land has complicated terrain); or
    - ▪ Not _____ to all parties.

3. Proceeds

- o Proceeds from a partition by sale are divided among the co-tenants based on their ownership interests.

  > *Example 55:* *Anna and Ben own a condo unit as tenants in common, each with a 50% share in the property. Anna sues for partition. What kind of partition will the court order? A partition _____ because a physical partition is not feasible.*

4. Agreement

- o Co-tenants can agree not to partition. Such an agreement is enforceable, provided:

  - ▪ The agreement is _____; and
  - ▪ The time limitation is _____.

CHAPTER 10:   SPECIAL ISSUES—DISCRIMINATION & CHOICE OF LAW (CONFLICT OF LAWS)

A. Discrimination

The Fair Housing Act (FHA) prohibits discrimination in the sale, _____, and financing of dwellings (homes, apartments, etc.). It also prohibits _____ that states a discriminatory preference.

- **Who's covered?** Primary focus is on _____ residential housing
- **Who's not covered?** There are three exemptions from the FHA:

  - o Single-family housing that is sold or rented without a _____;

- o Owner-occupied buildings with _____ or fewer living units ("Ms. Murphy's Boarding House");
- o Religious organizations and private clubs.

- **Who's protected?**

  Protected traits: _____, color, religion, national origin, sex, _____, and familial status

  - o Sex refers to gender discrimination, but does not include sexual _____.

  - o Familial status means families that have children under _____ or someone who is _____.

    - ▪ Special exemptions for senior living (e.g., seniors-only communities)

  - o Disability provision mandates _____ accommodations for the disabled (e.g., ramp, elevator, etc.)

- **What's prohibited?**

  - o Refusing to rent, sell, or _____ a dwelling;
  - o Requiring different rents;
  - o Falsely _____ that a unit is available;
  - o Providing different services to facilities;

    - ▪ Exception: When making a reasonable accommodation for a disabled tenant

  - o Stating a discriminatory preference in an advertisement.

    > **Note 15:** The first two exemptions (single-family without broker and Ms. Murphy boarding house) do not apply to discriminatory advertisements. But religious organizations and private clubs can list their restrictions in their advertisements.

- **Intent:** FHA allows for both intent (disparate _____) and effect (disparate _____) cases
- **Causation:** Prohibited behavior must be linked to the protected basis

  > *Example 56:* *Larry advertises an available one-bedroom unit in one of his apartment buildings. Two applicants apply for the unit—Sally, a black woman who works as a nurse, and Tim, a white male student at Acme University. Both filled out an application and, after running credit and background checks, Larry rented the unit to Tim. Did Larry violate the Fair Housing Act?*
  > _____, *there is no evidence of causation.*

  > *Example 57:* *Jenny puts the following advertisement in the local paper: "One-bedroom unit apartment available. Perfect bachelor pad. Hot tub and other amenities. Close to bus line, bars, and grocery. Utilities not included. Call*

Jenny, 867-5309. No creepers." Does the advertisement violate the Fair
Housing Act? _____, the statement "perfect
bachelor pad" states a discriminatory preference based on sex and familial
status.

> **Note 16:** The unlawful act is the advertisement itself. Jenny has violated the Act even if she does not otherwise engage in discriminatory behavior.

B. Conflict of Laws

1. **Basic Rule:** In cases about property, the controlling law is based upon where the property is _____, (i.e., law of the situs).

2. **Why do you care about this?** Law of the situs is the baseline choice of law rule in a property dispute that involves more than one state (e.g., the parties to the suit are in different states).

3. **When do you care about this?** In many testable issues involving property:

   - _____;
   - Land contract dispute;
   - Equitable interests (e.g., trust property);
   - _____ succession;
   - Interpreting conveyances.

4. **When do you ignore the basic rule?**

   - If the instrument in question _____ an applicable jurisdiction;
   - In cases involving _____, specifically with respect to classifying property as marital or separate, the domicile of the party may override the law of the situs;
   - In mortgage cases, where the mortgage documents require repayment to be made in another state.

CHAPTER 11: LANDLORD AND TENANT—THE TENANCIES

A. Lease

- Creates both a _____ interest and a _____ interest

- Landlord-tenant law is a mix of contract law and property law.

B. Tenancies

- Four types of estates that can govern the landlord-tenant relationship (i.e., tenancies):

  - Tenancy for _____;
  - _____ tenancy;
  - Tenancy at _____;

- o Tenancy at _____.
- You want to know two things:
  - o How is each created?
  - o How is each terminated?

C. Tenancy for Years

1. **Definition:** Measured by a _____ and ascertainable amount of time

> **Example 58:** *Larry leases Blackacre to Tara for two years.*

> **Note 17:** It need not be measured in years. It can be for any length of time.

> **Example 59:** *Larry leases Blackacre to Tara for two weeks. This is a tenancy for years.*

2. **Creation:** What is required to create a tenancy for years?

   - o An agreement by the landlord and the _____;
     - ▪ Purpose is to demonstrate the intent to create a leasehold
   - o If the term is longer than one year, then the agreement must be signed and in _____ because of the Statute of Frauds.

3. **Termination:** How is a tenancy for years terminated?

   - o At the end of the term:
     - ▪ Termination occurs _____ upon the expiration of the term.
     - ▪ Is notice required to terminate? _____, unless the lease requires it.
   - o Before the term is over:
     - ▪ Tenant _____ the lease, or
     - ▪ The tenant or the landlord commits a _____ breach of the lease (e.g., the tenant fails to pay rent).

D. Periodic Tenancy

1. **Definition:** Estate that is _____ and ongoing for a set period of time (e.g., month-to-month, year-to-year)

   - o Renews _____ at the end of each period until one party gives proper notice of termination

2. **Creation:** Parties must intend to create a periodic tenancy

    o   Intent can be _____ (e.g., a signed lease) or
        _____ (e.g., payment of rent)

        > ***Example 60:*** *Larry and Tara did not execute a formal lease agreement. Every*
        > *month, however, Tara pays rent and Larry accepts the payment. This will create*
        > *a periodic tenancy by implication.*

3. **Termination:** Renews automatically until proper notice is given

    o   **Old approach:** In a year-to-year lease, you must give notice at least
        _____ months in advance.
    o   **New approach:** Shorter notice requirements; many states have lowered to a month's notice.
    o   Proper notice means the terminating party gives notice before the
        _____ of what will be the
        _____ term.
    o   Most jurisdictions require written notice of termination.
    o   Notice is effective on the _____ day of the period.

        > ***Example 61:*** *Larry leased Blackacre to Tara on a month-to-month basis. Tara*
        > *gives notice of termination on February 15. When is the termination effective?*
        > _____.

E. **Tenancy at Will**

    1. **Definition:** May be _____ by either landlord or tenant at any
        time, for any reason

    2. **Creation:** Can be created by express agreement or by implication

    3. **Termination:** Can be terminated by either party _____ notice

        o   If the agreement gives only the landlord the right to terminate at will, the tenant also gets
            the right to terminate by _____.
        o   If agreement gives only the tenant the right to terminate at will, the landlord is
            _____ given the right to terminate at will.
        o   If the landlord or tenant dies, does that terminate the tenancy at will?
            _____, but this is not true for the tenancy for years or the
            periodic tenancy.

F. **Tenancy at Sufferance**

    1. **Definition:** Created when a tenant _____ after the lease has
        ended

        o   Temporary tenancy that exists before the landlord either
            _____ the prior tenant or

_____ the property to the tenant (creates a new tenancy with the holdover tenant)

- ○ Tenant owes landlord reasonable _____ of her daily use (i.e., look to rent from prior lease), as well as reasonably _____ special damages.

2. **Creation:** Distinguish between a tenancy at will and a tenancy at sufferance:

- ○ Tenancy at will: Created by _____ of the landlord and tenant
- ○ Tenancy at sufferance: Created by _____ of the tenant alone

3. **Termination:** Consider three ways to terminate:

- ○ The tenant voluntarily _____;
- ○ The landlord _____ the tenant;
- ○ The landlord _____ to the tenant.

CHAPTER 12: LANDLORD AND TENANT—TENANT'S DUTIES

A. The Gist

The tenant has two basic duties:

- • Pay _____;
- • Avoid _____.

B. Duty to Pay Rent

- • Duty arises because of the contractual relationship between the landlord and tenant (i.e., the lease requires it)
- • Three situations when duty to pay rent is suspended:

- ○ Premises are _____, so long as the tenant didn't cause the damage;
- ○ The landlord completely or partially _____ the tenant;

- ▪ Complete eviction: Removal of tenant from the entire property
- ▪ Partial eviction: Removal of tenant from a _____ of the property

- ○ The landlord materially _____ the lease.

- • Particularly concerned with breaches of the implied covenant of quiet enjoyment and the implied warranty of habitability

- ○ **Implied Covenant of Quiet Enjoyment:** The tenant can withhold rent when the landlord takes actions that make the premises *wholly or substantially*

_____ for their intended purposes, and the tenant is _____ evicted.

- Constructive Eviction—four elements:

  - Premises were _____ for their intended purposes (i.e., breach of the covenant of quiet enjoyment);
  - The tenant _____ the landlord of the problem;
  - The landlord does not correct the problem; and
  - The tenant _____ the premises after a _____ amount of time has passed.

  Example 62: *The Scott Michael Paper Company rents office space from Landlord. Due to poor construction, the office floods whenever it rains. The first time the office floods, the Company notifies Landlord and explains that it will no longer pay rent. The next day, the Company rents a new space and moves its belongings. Is the Company liable to Landlord for rent? _____. Why? Because the Company vacated _____; it did not give Landlord the opportunity to fix the problem. Note that Landlord had breached the covenant of quiet enjoyment and the Company did give Landlord notice of the problem.*

- **Implied Warranty of Habitability ("IWH"):** The landlord has an obligation to maintain the property such that it is suitable for residential use. We are concerned with conditions that threaten the tenant's _____ and _____.

  - Background points:

    - The tenant cannot _____ habitability protection;
    - The landlord's failure to comply with applicable _____ codes constitutes a breach;
    - Applies to _____ properties, usually multi-family buildings; not to commercial leases;
    - IWH and rent: If the premises are not habitable, the tenant may:

      - _____ to pay rent;
      - _____ the defect and offset costs against the rent; or
      - _____ against eviction.

      Note 18: If the tenant chooses to withhold rent, the tenant must: (i) _____ the landlord of the problem; and (ii) give the landlord a reasonable opportunity to correct the problem.

      Note 19: Unlike quiet enjoyment and constructive eviction, IWH does not require the tenant to _____ the premises.

Example 63: *Tara rents an apartment from Larry. The apartment is in a bad state—there is no hot water, ants and roaches are getting in, there is mold growing in the bathroom, and the security light over Tara's door is inoperable. Tara has repeatedly notified Larry of the problems to no avail. Can Tara withhold rent? _____, because Larry has breached IWH and failed to correct the problems.*

C. Duty to Avoid Waste

- The duty to avoid waste is a background rule; it does not have to be _____ in a lease in order to apply.

- The tenant has a duty not to commit _____ (voluntary) waste or _____ (neglectful) waste.

- A tenant may make changes to the property that _____ the property's value ("ameliorative waste"). Landlords usually require permission before a tenant can make the change.

  > **Note 20:** A landlord can put a provision in the lease prohibiting the tenant from making improvements to the property.

- **Duty to repair:** In a residential lease, the _____ is presumed to be responsible for repairs. The tenant must _____ the landlord of any needed repairs.

  > **Note 21:** The landlord is not responsible to make repairs caused by the tenant's actions.
  >
  > **Note 22:** In a commercial lease, the landlord can place the duty to repair on the tenant.

CHAPTER 13: LANDLORD AND TENANT—LANDLORD'S DUTIES

A. Duty to Mitigate Damages

If the tenant abandons the property early or is evicted by landlord, does the landlord have an obligation to mitigate damages by re-renting the property?

1. **Majority rule:** The landlord must make _____ efforts to re-rent the property.

   - The landlord must treat leasehold as if it was _____ stock, that is, like any other property she would try to rent (e.g., advertise, allow for viewings).
   - If the landlord does not make diligent efforts to mitigate, the tenant is _____ from the obligation to continue paying rent.
   - If the landlord does seek to mitigate, the landlord is entitled to the difference between the original rent and the rent received from the _____ tenant.
   - The landlord does not have to accept an unacceptable replacement tenant.

2. **Minority rule:** The landlord does not have to mitigate damages. The minority rule is more common in cases involving _____ leases.

> *Example 64:* *Larry rents a studio apartment to Tara at $2000 per month for a one-year term. Tara abandons the apartment after a month in search of a cheaper apartment. Larry does nothing until the one-year term is up. In a majority jurisdiction, can Larry recover damages from Tara?* _____*, Larry failed to make a reasonable effort to re-rent.*

> *Example 65:* *Instead, assume Larry advertised as normal but was only able to find a tenant who was willing to pay $1000 for the studio apartment. In a majority jurisdiction, can Larry collect the remaining half from Tara?* _____*, Larry met his obligation to mitigate.*

B. Holdover Tenant

How can the landlord deal with the holdover?

- Can _____ the holdover tenant; or
- Can continue the relationship with the tenant by treating the holdover tenant as a _____ tenant.

  - The landlord will continue the relationship by accepting rent.
  - Amount of rent: Rent amount under the old lease is the amount due
  - Exception: The landlord can impose a higher rent if the landlord had informed the tenant of the increase _____ the expiration of the old lease.

C. Duty to Deliver Possession

- **Majority rule:** The landlord must deliver _____ possession of the leasehold premises. This means _____ possession of the property.
- **Minority rule:** The landlord only required to deliver _____ possession.

  > Note 23: The difference between actual and legal possession is of particular importance with holdover tenant issues and the obligation to the new tenant.

D. Conditions of Leased Premises

- The landlord cannot deny the tenant **quiet enjoyment**. In practice, quiet enjoyment is violated when the landlord, or someone connected to the landlord, renders the premises unsuitable for the intended purpose.

  - The landlord must control:

    - _____ areas, such as a lobby, hallway, or laundry room;

- _____-like behavior of other tenants (Remember: Don't touch the stinky wall!).

- ○ The landlord does not have to control:

  - Off-premises actions of _____ that are beyond the landlord's control (e.g., the noisy bar across the street);

  - In a residential lease, the landlord must provide _____ premises.

    Example 66: *Larry is the landlord for an apartment building. The lock on the front door of the building is broken and, although tenants have complained, Larry has not fixed it. Young hooligans have been vandalizing the lobby hallway of the building. Tara, a tenant in the building, is injured by a piece of debris left in the hallway by one of the hooligans. Has Larry breached his obligation to Tara? _____, because the damage took place in a _____ area, which is under Larry's control.*

- • If a tenant complains about conditions, the landlord cannot retaliate by evicting the tenant.

CHAPTER 14:   LANDLORD AND TENANT—TORT LIABILITY & TRANSFERS

A. Tort Liability

- • The tenant owes a duty of _____. This extends to invitees, licensees, and foreseeable trespassers.

- • The landlord's liability to invitees, licensees, and foreseeable trespassers is as follows:

  - ○ **Common law**

    - Responsible in negligence for _____ (hidden) defects about which the tenant has not been warned;

    - Responsible for _____ completed by the landlord (or the landlord's agent) negligently;

    - Responsible for negligence that causes injuries in _____ areas of the property.

  - ○ **Modern trend:** Landlords have a general duty of reasonable care.

    Example 67: *Larry rents a studio apartment in a large building to Tara. When Tara moved in, Larry warned her that there was a loose beam in the floor of the hallway in her apartment. Shortly after moving in, Tara tripped on the loose beam and fractured her ankle. Is Larry liable for her injuries? _____, she was warned; it's not a latent defect.*

    Example 68: *Tara noticed that the building's back door had a broken hinge, causing it to slam shut quicker than most would expect it to. Tara informed*

Larry about the door. Larry sent a handyman to fix the door, but the handyman ended up making the door worse. Tara smashed her fingers in the door. Is Larry liable for her injuries? _____, under common law, because the landlord's agent undertook to repair the door, but the repair was faulty. Under modern rule, as it violates duty of care.

B. The Basics of Transfers—Subleases and Assignments

- Who's who? Three parties:

  - Landlord: _____;
  - Tenant: Transferee/transferor;
  - Subsequent tenant: _____.

- **Assignment** is a _____ transfer of the tenant's remaining term.
- **Sublease** is a transfer for _____ the entire duration of the lease.

  > **Example 69:** *Larry rents a studio apartment to Tara and the lease is set to end on August 14. Tara decides to move to Belgium for the summer so she transfers her lease to Sally Theresa. Tara will re-take possession from Sally Theresa on August 1. Is the transfer to Sally Theresa an assignment or a sublease? It is a _____; it is less than the entire duration.*

  Exam Tip 4: If the tenant retains a reversionary interest in the leasehold, then the transfer is a sublease.

C. Responsibility for Rent

- In an **assignment**, the landlord can collect rent from:

  - The _____ (because of privity of contract); or
  - The _____ tenant (because of privity of estate).

- In a **sublease**, the landlord can collect rent from:

  - The _____ (because of privity of contract and estate)
    - The subsequent tenant only has rent obligations to the original tenant.

  > **Example 70:** *Larry rents a studio apartment to Tara and the lease is set to end on August 14. Tara decides to move to Belgium for the summer so she transfers her lease to Sally Theresa. Tara will re-take possession from Sally Theresa on August 1. Larry doesn't receive rent during the summer months. Can he try to get rent from Sally Theresa? _____, because they are not in privity. He can only collect rent from _____.*

D. Permission

- **Silent lease:** If the lease is silent on the issue, a tenant may assign or sublet freely.

- **Permission:** If the lease requires the landlord's permission to transfer, but is silent as to the applicable standard, then:
  - **Majority rule:** A landlord may deny permission to a transfer only for a _____ reasonable reason.
  - **Minority rule:** A landlord may deny permission at her _____, which means for any reason or no reason at all.

- **Transferring a landlord's interest:** A landlord does not need the tenant's permission before transferring her interest. The new landlord is bound by terms of the existing lease.

  > *Example 71:* *Larry rented a one-bedroom house to Tara at $1000 per month for a one-year term. The lease included a covenant that Larry would shovel the snow and take care of the lawn maintenance. A few months into Tara's tenancy, Larry decided to move to Tahiti, so he transferred his interest in the property to Lucy. Lucy contacted Tara to inform her that her rent would go up to $1200 per month and that Tara was now responsible for snow removal and lawn care.*

  > *Question 1:* *Did Larry need Tara's permission before transferring to Lucy?* _____, *the landlord is free to transfer.*

  > *Question 2:* *Can Lucy change the terms of Tara's lease?* _____, *she needs Tara's approval.*

CHAPTER 15: LAND SALE CONTRACTS

> **Exam Tip 5:** Expect questions on the MBE in this area. The land sale contract is one of the most heavily tested subjects in real property.

A. Who's Who?

- **Seller:** Owner looking to unload property
- **Buyer:** Sucker looking to get stuck with a money pit
- **Broker** (or real estate agent): An intermediary between buyer and seller

  - **Listing agent:** The agent who assists the seller in promoting and selling the property
  - **Seller's agent:** A sub-agent for the listing agent who helps find buyers

    > **Note 24:** In most cases, the listing and seller's agent share the commission. The agent who shows you property is, in effect, working for the seller.

  - **Buyer's agent:** The broker who serves as the representative of the buyer; will receive commission similar to seller's agent fee
  - **Dual agent:** Represents both buyer and seller (many states forbid dual agency as a conflict of interest)

B. Framework

1. Two Stages

- First: _____ (where parties negotiate terms)
- Then: _____ (where parties transfer property)

2. Liability: Determined by the stage where breach occurs

- Contract stage: Any liability must be based on a _____ provision
- Deed stage: Any liability must be based on a _____ warranty

3. Doctrine of Merger

- Covenants under the contract are _____ into the deed and any remedy will flow from the deed.

C. Statute of Frauds

> **Exam Tip 6:** Expect a Statute of Frauds question on the MBE. The bar examiners test the Statute of Frauds and its exceptions rather frequently.

- Land sale contracts are subject to the Statute of Frauds.
- Three requirements:

  - Must be in _____;
  - Must be signed by the party to be _____; and
  - Must include _____ terms:

    - The _____ (i.e., the seller and the buyer);
    - _____ of the property;
    - Price and payment info (e.g., money, financing).

D. Exceptions to the Statute of Frauds

Two main exceptions:

- Part performance;
- Detrimental reliance (also called estoppel).

1. Part Performance

- Partial performance by either the seller or the buyer is treated as evidence that the contract existed.
- Look for acts of performance, such as:

  - _____ of all or part of the purchase price;
  - _____ by the purchaser; or
  - _____ by the purchaser.

2. Detrimental Reliance

o   An estoppel doctrine that applies where a party has reasonably

_____ on the contract and would suffer hardship if the

contract were not enforced.

Example 72: *Paul orally agrees to purchase Sandy's home for $75,000. Paul sends Sandy a check for the home, then proceeds to move into the new house, sell his old house, buys new furniture, and hires a contractor to make repairs. Weeks later, Sandy returns the check and demands that Paul leave the house. Can Paul enforce the contract? _____, despite the absence of a written contract, under both the part performance and the detrimental reliance exceptions to the Statute of Frauds.*

E. Marketable Title

*   **Every** land sale contract includes an implied covenant of marketable title.

    o   What is marketable title? Title that is free from an _____ risk of litigation

    o   Examples of defects in title that would render title unmarketable:

        ▪   Title acquired by adverse possession that hasn't been

            _____;

        ▪   Private encumbrances (e.g., mortgage, _____, easement);

        ▪   Violation of a _____ ordinance.

*   In judging whether title is unmarketable, the standard is that of a

    _____ buyer.

*   If the seller cannot deliver marketable title, the buyer's remedy is

    _____ of the contract.

Example 73: *Sadie contracts to sell a condo to Benson in the Hilly Flats community. A title search on Hilly Flats reveals two covenants. The first says that condos in Hilly Flats "cannot be transferred to Non-Caucasians." The second says, "No pets can reside anywhere in Hilly Flats condos."*

Can Benson rescind the contract because of the racially restrictive covenant? _____. This covenant is not enforceable under

the Fair Housing Act or the 14th Amendment of the U.S. Constitution. Thus,
there is no risk of litigation.

What about the "no pets" covenant? _____.
The covenant is an encumbrance that would prevent Benson from having a pet
(potential enforcer of the covenant: Neighbors or HOA) or from eventually
selling to anyone with a pet.

F. Delays

- Basic rule: Unless the contract or parties notify, time is NOT of the essence.
- Why does this matter? If time is not of the essence, the failure to close on the date set for close may be a _____ of the contract, but is not grounds for rescission of the contract.
- Specific performance is still available.

G. Implied Warranty of Fitness or Suitability

Applies to defects in new construction

- In most jurisdictions, both the initial homeowner-purchaser and subsequent purchasers may recover damages.
- In a minority of jurisdictions, only the original buyer can enforce this warranty.
- Generally, suit for breach of this warranty must be brought within a reasonable time after _____ of the defect (but some jurisdictions have a statutory time period).

H. Duty to Disclose Defects

Most jurisdictions impose a duty on the seller to disclose to the buyer all known, physical and _____ defects.

- Concerned with _____ or hidden defects;
- Material defect must _____ affect the value of the home, health and safety of its occupants, or the desirability of the home;
- General disclaimers (e.g., "as is") will not satisfy the seller's duty to disclose.

I. Merger

- After closing, obligations contained in the contract are merged into the deed.
- If there was something important in the contract that is not in the deed, the cause of action is lost because the deed controls after closing.

J. Seller's Remedies on Buyer's Breach

Remedies available to the seller?

- _____: Measure is the difference between the contract price and market price

- _____ : Seller can sell the property to someone else
- Specific Performance

K. Buyer's Remedies on Seller's Breach

Remedies available to the buyer?

- Damages: Measure is the difference between contract price and _____ on the date of breach

  o What if the seller breaches but acted in good faith? The buyer can only recover out-of-pocket expenses.

- Rescission: Returns payments to the buyer and _____ the contract
- Specific performance

> **Note 27:** Buyers and sellers must choose between damages and specific performance—cannot have both remedies.

L. Equitable Conversion and Risk of Loss

1. Issue

Who bears the risk of loss if there is damage to or destruction of the property?

2. Majority rule

The _____ holds equitable title during the period between the execution of the contract and the closing and delivery of the deed.

  o Buyer is responsible for any damage to the property that happens during that period.
  o As holder of legal title, the _____ has a right to possess the property.

3. Minority rule

Places the risk of loss on the _____ until the closing and delivery of deed.

> **Example 74:** Sadie and Benson agree that Sadie will sell Benson Banana Acre. Two days before Sadie and Benson are set to close on Banana Acre, an epic storm blows through town and crushes Banana Acre, reducing it to rubble. Who is responsible for the damage to Banana Acre?
>
> In a majority jurisdiction: _____. As the holder of equitable title, he bears the risk of loss.
>
> In a minority jurisdiction: _____. As the seller, she bears the risk of loss.

CHAPTER 16:   ADVERSE POSSESSION

A. The Gist

- The doctrine of adverse possession allows a person in _____
  possession to acquire good title to a piece of property. Until the person acquires good title, the
  person is a _____.

- When a person acquires title by adverse possession, the new title relates back to the date of the
  person's entry onto the property. There is no transfer of title from the former owner.

- Property owned by the _____ cannot be adversely possessed.

- Two basic rationales for the doctrine of adverse possession:

  - _____ the true owner for sleeping on her rights; and

  - Rewarding the adverse possessor for _____ good title.

B. The Elements

Four elements:

- _____ for the statutory period;

- Open and notorious;

- _____; and

- _____.

1. Continuous

a. Three phases:

- **Entry phase:** When the adverse possessor _____ the
  land; required to trigger the applicable statute of limitations;

- **End phase:** When the statute of limitations runs out of time; now, the adverse
  possessor is the legal owner of the property by operation of law;

- **Middle phase:** When the adverse possessor makes _____
  of the property, between the entry and end phases.

b. The "continuous" requirement is not literal.

Seasonal or infrequent use may suffice if the use is _____
with the type of property being possessed (e.g., a vacation home, farmland).

c. Tacking

- If the adverse possessor cannot satisfy the continuity requirement on her own, she can
  tack on her predecessor's time on the property to satisfy the statute of limitations.

  Example 75: *Anderson takes possession of Tony's property and lives there for*
  five years. Anderson later "sells" his interest in the property to Annie, who takes
  possession and lives there for three years. The statute of limitations is seven
  years. Can Annie satisfy the continuous requirement?

_____, _by tacking on Anderson's time of_
possession.

- To tack the time of adverse possession of a prior adverse possessor, the current adverse possessor must be in _____ with the prior adverse possessor. Privity is an exchange of some sort between the adverse possessors.

  d. **Disabilities**

  - The statute of limitations will not run against a true owner who has a disability at the time the adverse possession begins (e.g., infancy, _____, or imprisonment).
  - The disability must exist when the trespasser enters the property.

  e. **Interruptions**

  A true owner can interrupt the adverse possession period by _____ the adverse possessor. This will stop the adverse possession clock.

2. **Open and Notorious**

  - An adverse possessor's use must be open and notorious.
  - Use must be such that it would put a _____ true owner on notice of the adverse use.
  - The use cannot be hidden; the trespasser must use the property as if she was the true owner.

    _**Example 76:** Tony owns Blackacre but has never visited it. Annie trespasses on Blackacre and begins living there. To conceal her trespass, Annie only goes out at night and never uses lights. Would Annie's use be open and notorious? _____, because it is designed to avoid detection._

3. **Hostile**

  "Hostile" does not mean unpleasant. Possession must be _____ to the owner's interest. It is a claim of competing title.

    _**Example 77:** I invite my friend to stay at my house while I'm out of town. Is my friend's use hostile? _____, the use is permissive._

  - **Majority rule:** Ignores the adverse possessor's state of mind
  - **Minority rule:** Inquires into the adverse possessor's state of mind

    - **Good faith:** The adverse possessor's claim is hostile if she thinks the land is unowned or that she is the rightful owner. This is adverse possession based on a _____.

- **Bad faith:** The adverse possessor knows that land is not hers and she tries to acquire title to the property by adverse possession. This is adverse possession based on an aggressive trespass.

  Example 78: Trevor buys Blackacre from Charlie for $200,000 cash. Trevor didn't know that the deed was fraudulent and Charlie didn't own the rights to Blackacre. Trevor takes possession of Blackacre and begins farming it. Was Trevor's use hostile?

  In a majority jurisdiction: _____, state of mind is irrelevant and Trevor's use is adverse to the true owner's interest.

  In a good-faith jurisdiction: _____, Trevor mistakenly believed he had acquired good title from Charlie.

  In a bad-faith jurisdiction: _____, because it was based on mistake, Trevor's possession was not an aggressive trespass.

4. **Exclusive**

- An adverse possessor cannot share _____ with the true owner.
- If two people possess the property together, can they both acquire title by adverse possession? _____, they acquire title as tenants in common.

C. Scope of Possession

- Adverse possession generally traces the legal boundaries of the property
- Exception—constructive adverse possession: Adverse possessor enters under color of title from an invalid instrument (e.g., fraudulent deed) and occupies a portion of the property described in the instrument. The adverse possessor is in actual possession of the occupied land and constructive possession of the remaining land described in the deed.

  Example 79: A fraudulent deed states that a buyer purchases all 10 acres of a piece of property. When the tenant moves onto the property, she only occupies one acre. Here, the tenant entered under color of title and occupied one acre (i.e., was in actual possession of one acre). But because 10 acres are described in the deed, the tenant is in constructive possession of the remaining nine acres.

- Includes _____ rights, unless those rights already belong to a third party
- Easements can also be acquired by adverse possession (or prescription).

  Example 80: Annie regularly crosses Tony's land to reach the main road, which she has done consistently for over 10 years. The jurisdiction has a 10-year statute of limitations. Annie can acquire an easement by adverse possession (prescription). Has Annie acquired title to Tony's land?
  _____, she has only acquired the right to

_____ *his land (use rights), not to possess it*
(ownership).

CHAPTER 17: DEEEDS (AND A TASTE OF RECORDING)

A. What's What?

- Basics: A deed is a legal instrument that transfers ownership of real property.
- For a deed to be valid, it must be _____ and
_____. The delivery requirement houses the issue of intent.

1. Delivery

The controlling question is whether the grantor had the _____
intent to transfer the property.

> Note 28: Physical transfer of a deed is not required.

> *Example 81:* *Garrett executes a deed conveying Blackacre to Barbara. Garrett*
> *learns that Barbara is out of the country when he tries to deliver the deed to*
> *her. So he calls her and says, "Great news! I conveyed you Blackacre. You're*
> *the new owner." Has the deed been delivered?*
> _____, *because the phone call manifests the*
> *necessary intent to make an immediate transfer of Blackacre.*

> Note 29: Be on the lookout for situations where delivery is incomplete or
> seemingly revocable.

> *Example 82:* *Garrett asks his attorney to transfer a deed for Blackacre to*
> *Barbara "in two months' time, unless I change my mind before then." Has the*
> *deed been delivered?* _____, *because Garrett*
> *can change his mind before the date of delivery.*

> Note 30: Remember that the grantor can make proper delivery to an agent.

> *Example 83:* *Garrett gives a deed to an escrow agent with clear instructions to*
> *deliver it to Barbara. Has proper delivery been made?*
> _____.

2. Acceptance

Acceptance is generally presumed, provided the transfer is for value.

> *Example 84:* *Garrett conveys a deed to Blackacre to Barbara. A day later,*
> *Barbara changes her mind about Blackacre and says she doesn't want it. Has*
> *Barbara accepted the deed?* _____. *What must*
> *Barbara do if she doesn't want the property anymore?*
> _____.

B. Who's Who?

Brokers can be involved in land sale contracts so long as they do not practice
_____.

- **Permissible:** Most states permit real estate agents and brokers to prepare a contract of sale.
- **Impermissible:** Real estate agents cannot usually draft a legal document like a deed or mortgage.
- **Keep in mind:** We are looking for the exercise of legal _____ and whether the broker or non-lawyer is giving legal _____.

C. Contents of a Deed

- A valid deed must identify the _____ (i.e., grantor and grantee) and it must be signed by the _____, per the Statute of Frauds.
- A valid deed must include words of _____.

  - A granting clause can include any words that evidence a _____ intent to transfer.

- A valid deed must include a sufficient _____ of the property.

  - Does the description have to be a legal description? _____.
  - Can it be based on monuments or physical attributes of the property? _____.
  - Can extrinsic evidence be admitted to clarify an ambiguous description? _____.

D. Execution

1. Signature

As a general matter, the grantor's signature is required for execution to be effective.

  - Is the grantee required to sign too? _____.
  - Must the deed be witnessed or notarized? _____.
  - What if the signature is forged? The deed is _____, even if the purchaser is a BFP.

2. Agents

  - A principal can appoint an agent to execute a deed.
  - **Equal Dignities Rule:** If the agent is required to sign (e.g., execute a deed), then the agency relationship must be created in _____.

E. Recording—The Basics

- What does it mean to record? Publicly _____ your deed.
- What is the purpose of recording? _____. Tell the world you own the property.

- Does recording affect the validity of a deed? _____, a deed is valid at delivery.
- If they do not affect validity, what's the big deal with recording statutes? We're concerned about _____.

> *Example 85:* *Garrett conveys Blackacre to Barbara. Later, Garrett conveys Blackacre to Sandy without informing her about the prior deed to Barbara. Who is the subsequent purchaser? _____. The purpose of a recording statute is to mediate conflicts between first and subsequent purchasers, in this example, Barbara and Sandy.*

F. Common-Law Recording Rule

- A deed does not have to be recorded to be valid!
- The baseline for recording problems is the common-law rule. It follows the "first in _____, first in _____" principle (i.e., under the common-law rule, the first grantee to receive a deed wins).

> **Note 31:** Every state has a recording statute that modifies the common-law rule to give priority to certain deeds when there are competing claims to title.
>
> **Note 32:** In the absence of a recording statute, the common-law rule controls.

> *Example 86:* *Garrett sells his property to three people. First to Barbara, then to Candace, and finally to Darla. All three are claiming title. Who has title at common law? _____. Why? Because she was _____.*

CHAPTER 18: RECORDING ACTS

A. Scope of Recording Acts

1. **What's What?** What types of interests are covered?

   - Deeds;
   - _____;
   - Leases;
   - _____;
   - Judgments affecting title;
   - Other instruments creating an interest in land, such as _____ or _____.

   > **Note 33:** Title by adverse possession is NOT covered. Recording statutes do not cover interests created by operation of law.

2. **Who's Protected?** Who is covered by recording acts?

   - _____ purchasers

3. **Unprotected Persons:** Who is not covered by recording acts?

   o Grantees who acquire title by _____, intestacy, or devise are not protected by recording acts.

   o The policy behind recording acts is that we want to protect those who make economic investments by _____ property.

B. **Notice**

   • The concept of _____ is crucial in applying two of the three recording acts.

   • Three kinds of notice:

     o **Actual**—when the subsequent grantee has real, _____ knowledge of a prior interest;

     o **Constructive** (i.e., record notice)—when a prior interest is _____;

     o **Inquiry**—when a reasonable _____ would have disclosed the existence of prior claims.

   • **Helpful hint** about inquiry notice: There are two common situations where a subsequent grantee will be put on inquiry notice:

     o **Dude on the land:** When there is someone else living on or _____ the land; had the subsequent grantee investigated the land, he would have discovered the person in possession;

     o **Mentioned interest:** When there is an interest mentioned in the deed to some other transaction; had the subsequent grantee _____, he would have discovered the interest.

       Example 87: *Garrett's deed to Barbara references an easement from Garrett to Jones. This is _____ notice. Any subsequent purchaser in Garrett's chain of title will be charged with knowledge of the easement.*

       Exam Tip 8: Of the three types of recording acts, **notice** statutes and **race-notice** statutes are most heavily tested on the MBE.

C. **Race Statutes**

   1. **Rule:** First to _____ wins, even if the subsequent purchaser had notice of a prior, unrecorded conveyance.

   2. **Key language:** "First recorded" or "First to record"

D. **Notice Statutes**

  1. **Rule:** A subsequent purchaser wins if she acquires without notice of a prior, _____ conveyance.

  2. **Key language:** "In good faith" or "Without notice"

E. **Race-Notice Statutes**

  1. **Rule:** A subsequent purchaser wins if two requirements are met:

     ○ Acquired _____ notice of a prior unrecorded conveyance; and

     ○ Records _____.

  2. **Key language:** "In good faith" or "Without notice" plus "First duly recorded" or "First recorded"

F. **Name that Statute**

  > *Example 88:* *"No conveyance or mortgage of real property shall be good against subsequent purchasers for value and without notice unless the same be first recorded according to law." This is a _____ statute.*

  > *Example 89:* *"No conveyance or mortgage of real property shall be good against subsequent purchasers for value unless the same be first recorded according to law." This is a _____ statute.*

  > *Example 90:* *"No conveyance or mortgage of real property shall be good against subsequent purchasers for value and without notice unless the same be recorded according to law." This is a _____ statute.*

G. **Application**

  > *Example 91:* *Oliver owns Blackacre. Oliver conveys Blackacre to Anna, who does not record. Oliver later conveys Blackacre to Benny for $200,000. Benny does not know about the deed to Anna. Benny records. Then Anna records.*

  > *Who wins in a "race" state? _____. He recorded first.*

  > *Who wins in a "notice" state? _____. He bought without knowledge of Anna's prior interest.*

  > *Who wins in a "race-notice" state? _____. He recorded first and didn't have knowledge.*

  > *Example 92:* *Blackacre is located in a state that has the following statute: "No conveyance or mortgage of real property shall be good against subsequent purchasers for value unless first duly recorded in good faith." Oliver sold Blackacre to Anna, who did not record. Later, Oliver conveyed Blackacre to*

Benny for valuable consideration. Benny did not know of the prior conveyance.
Anna recorded. Then Benny recorded.

What kind of recording act is it? _____.

Who owns Blackacre? _____. Why?
_____. Benny lost the race.

Example 93:   Oliver owns Blackacre, which he conveys to Anna for $100,000.
Anna does not record. Weeks later, Oliver offers Benny Blackacre for $15,000.
Before buying it, Benny inspects Blackacre and sees Anna working in the garden
on the property. Benny goes ahead with the purchase and records his deed.

Who wins in a "race" state? _____. He recorded
first.

Who wins in a "notice" state? _____. Benny had
inquiry notice of Anna's interest.

Who wins in a "race-notice" state? _____.
Again, Benny had inquiry notice; he is not protected by the recording statute.

Example 94:   Oliver owns Blackacre. Oliver conveys Blackacre to Anna for
$100,000. Anna does not record. Weeks later, Oliver makes a gift of Blackacre
to his nephew Benny. Benny does not know about the prior conveyance to
Anna. Benny does not record. Anna records.

Is Benny covered by the recording act? _____.
Gift recipients are not covered by a recording statute.

What rule controls? The _____ rule controls—
first in time.

Who wins? _____. She was first in time.

H. Special Rules

1. Shelter Rule

A person who takes from a bona fide purchaser protected by the recording act has the same
rights as her grantor.

Example 95:   Oliver sells Blackacre to Anna, who does not record. Later, Oliver
sells Blackacre to Benny. Benny has no knowledge of the prior conveyance.
Carter is interested in buying Blackacre from Benny, though Carter is aware of
the prior transfer to Anna. Benny sells to Carter. The state is a "notice" state.

Does Carter have good title? _____. Even
though Carter had notice of the prior conveyance, Carter stands in Benny's
place, and Benny did not have notice of the conveyance to Anna.

2. **Estoppel by Deed**

- o Arises when a grantor conveys land the grantor does not own
- o If a grantor subsequently acquires title to the land, the grantor is _____ from trying to repossess on grounds that he didn't have title when he made the original conveyance.

CHAPTER 19:   DEEDS; WILLS & TRUSTS; RESTRAINTS ON ALIENATION

A. Deed

- • Reminder: After closing, the land sale contract is merged into the deed. Any liability must arise out of the _____, not the contract.
- • Three kinds of deeds:

    - o _____ warranty deed;
    - o _____ warranty deed;
    - o _____ deed.

    > **Note 35:** The list is a hierarchy from best to worst based upon the type of protection that is provided (i.e., how many warranties are built into the deed).

B. Particulars

1. General Warranty Deed

- o Provides the _____ amount of title protection; the grantor warrants title against _____ defects, even if the grantor did not cause the defects.

    a. Six implied covenants in the general warranty deed

    1) Present covenants

        - • **Covenant of seisin:** Warrants that the deed _____ the land in question;
        - • **Covenant of the right to convey:** Warrants that the grantor (i.e., the seller) has the _____ to convey the property;
        - • **Covenant against encumbrances:** Warrants that there are no _____ encumbrances on the property that could limit its value.

    2) Future covenants

        - • **Covenant of quiet enjoyment:** Grantor promises that the grantee's possession will not be _____ by a third-party claim;
        - • **Covenant of warranty:** Grantor promises to defend against future claims of _____ by a third party;

- **Covenant of further assurances:** Grantor promises to fix future title problems.

2. Special Warranty Deed

- o The grantor warrants against defects only caused by the

  _____.

- o This type of deed provides a lesser amount of title protection than a general warranty deed.
- o It includes the same six covenants as a general warranty deed, but they only apply to the acts (or omissions) of the _____.

3. Quitclaim Deed

- o The grantor makes _____ as to the health of the title.
- o This type of deed provides the least amount of title protection.
- o Often used in tax sales and intra-family disputes (e.g., divorces)

    Example 96: Sadie transfers a quitclaim deed for Banana Acre to Benson for $25,000. After taking possession, Benson discovers a bunch of his neighbors using paths on his property. He learns from them that Sadie had granted a right-of-way easement across Banana Acre, which she did not disclose to Benson. Does Benson have a claim against Sadie for failing to disclose the easements? _____. Because she used a quitclaim deed, Sadie made no warranties as to the state of the title.

    Example 97: Instead, assume that Sadie had transferred a special warranty deed. Would Benson have a claim against Sadie for failing to disclose the easements? _____. Sadie breached the covenant against _____.

    Example 98: Instead, assume that Benson discovered that a prior owner, rather than Sadie, had granted the easements across Banana Acre. Sadie still conveyed a special warranty deed. Would Benson have a claim against Sadie for failing to disclose the easements? _____.
    Sadie only warranted against defects that she herself created.

C. Breach and Remedies

- Breach of the present covenants occurs at the _____.
- Breach of the future covenants occurs _____ the conveyance, once there is interference with possession.
- Remedies: Damages

D. Wills

- Real property can be transferred by _____.
- The guiding principle in the interpretation of wills is the testator's

  _____.

- If a person dies without a will, her estate is distributed by _____ succession. This is a default estate plan created by the legislature.

1. **Who's Who?**

   o **Heirs:** People who take a decedent's _____ estate. In order to be an heir you have to survive the dead person who dies without a will;

   o **Devisee:** A person who takes a devise by will (alternative term: Legatee);

   o **Decedent:** Dead guy;

   o **Testator:** Dead guy who made a _____.

2. **What's What?**

   o **Escheat:** If a decedent dies without a will and without heirs, the decedent's property goes to the state.

   o **Ademption:** A devise of property that fails (or "adeems") because it is not in the testator's estate at _____:

     ▪ **Basic rule:** The gift _____ and the intended recipient gets nothing;

     ▪ **Satisfaction:** If the testator gives the intended beneficiary the promised gift during _____, then the beneficiary keeps the gift ("ademption by satisfaction").

   o **Lapse & Anti-Lapse**

     ▪ **Lapse:** The intended beneficiary predeceases (i.e., dies before) the testator. Traditionally, the gift fails (i.e., lapses) and would fall to the residuary gift.

     ▪ **Anti-Lapse:** Every state has an anti-lapse statute to prevent a gift from failing because an intended recipient predeceased the testator.

       - In most states, to qualify under an anti-lapse statute, the predeceasing beneficiary must be a _____ of the testator who dies leaving issue.

       - The statute replaces the intended beneficiary with a family member (e.g., the children of the beneficiary) who stands in the shoes of their parent and takes the gift on their behalf.

       - Why? More consistent with the testator's _____. Rather go to family than the residuary.

E. **Trusts**

1. **Definition**

   A device for managing property with bifurcated ownership. One person (the _____) owns property (legal title) for the benefit of another person (the _____) who holds equitable title.

- o **Charitable Trust:** Trust designed to benefit the public and is charitable in nature
- o **Private Trust:** Trust designed to satisfy some legal purpose by giving property to a person or group for the benefit of another person or group.

2. **Who's Who?**

- o **Settlor:** Person who _____ the trust
- o **Beneficiary:** Person who _____ from the trust

    - Holds equitable title (no obligations and all of the benefit);
    - Has standing to enforce the trust.

- o **Trustee:** Person (can be an entity) who _____ the trust property and holds legal title

3. **What's What?**

- o **Res:** Property that is subject to the trust. Generally, a trust must contain property.
- o **Bifurcated transfer:** Ownership is divided:

    - Giving someone _____ title to act as the owner (trustee)
    - Giving someone _____ title to benefit from that ownership (beneficiary)

        Example 99: *Sam wants to save money to pay for his son Ben's education. Sam executes the following deed: "I convey $100,000 to my friend Todd for the benefit of Ben's education." The deed creates a trust.*

        Who is the settlor? _____.

        Who is the trustee? _____.

        Who is the beneficiary? _____.

        Who has legal title? _____, as trustee.

        Who has equitable title? _____, as beneficiary.

F. Restraints on Alienation

A restriction on _____ property

1. **Where do we see these restrictions?**

    - o Inter vivos grant of an estate smaller than a fee simple;
    - o Devise of an estate smaller than a fee simple;
    - o Co-tenant agreement;
    - o Covenants that _____ with the land;
    - o Easements.

2. **Rules about restraints**

   o An absolute restraint on alienation is _____;

   o A partial restraint is valid if it is for a limited time and a _____ purpose;

   o A restriction on the **use** of property is generally permissible (e.g., covenants).

3. **What's the effect of the restraint on alienation?**

   o If the restraint is valid: Any attempt to alienate the property will be null and void.

   o If the restraint is invalid: The restraint is rejected and the property can be _____ in violation of the restraint.

CHAPTER 20:   MORTGAGES

A. Basics

What is a mortgage? A _____ device used to secure payment of a _____.

1. **Two Component Parts**

   o **The note:** Borrower's promise to repay the loan/debt;

   o **The _____:** Instrument that provides security for the note.

   Put it together: If the borrower defaults on the loan, then the lender can force a _____ sale to satisfy the outstanding debt.

2. **Big Picture**

   o Lender lends money (with interest) to someone who wants to purchase a home;

   o Lender takes an interest in the home as _____;

   o When the loan is paid, everybody benefits;

   o If payments are not made, the lender will foreclose on its interest and force a sale of the home to satisfy the debt.

3. **Who's Who?**

   o **Mortgagor:** The borrower

   o **Mortgagee:** The lender

4. **Two Kinds of Mortgages**

   o **Purchase money mortgage:** A person takes out a loan for the purpose of _____ property

   o **Future advance mortgage:** A line of credit used for home _____, construction, business, and commercial loans (often referred to as a "second mortgage")

Example 100: *Bonnie takes out a $100,000 mortgage from America's Bank to buy a home. Years later, she takes out a $25,000 second mortgage from Village Bank to renovate her kitchen. Now both America's Bank and Village Bank have an interest in Bonnie's home. She now has two separate mortgages to pay. Two different lenders have an interest in her property that could be foreclosed upon.*

B. Lien States v. Title States

- **Majority** ("lien state"): Treats a mortgage as a lien that does not _____ a joint tenancy

- **Minority** ("title state"): A mortgage does sever a joint tenancy and converts it into a tenancy in common

> **Exam Tip 9:** This is an ideal exam question. Encompasses two areas of study: Concurrent ownership and security devices (mortgages).

C. Alternatives to Mortgages—Equitable Mortgages

1. Deed of Trust

- Operates like a mortgage but uses a _____ to hold title for the benefit of the lender (i.e., the beneficiary of the trust receiving the payments)

2. Installment Land Contract

- The seller finances the purchase; the seller retains _____ until the buyer makes the final payment on an installment plan.
- **Traditional rule:** If the buyer breaches (i.e., misses a payment), the seller keeps the installment payments made and the property.
- **Modern approaches:** States are trying to assist defaulting buyers:

  - Some treat installment contracts as a _____, requiring the seller to foreclose;
  - Some give the buyer the equitable right of _____ to stop a foreclosure sale;
  - Some allow the seller to retain ownership, but require some _____ for what's been paid.

3. Absolute Deed

The mortgagor (borrower) transfers the _____ to the property instead of conveying a security interest in exchange for the loan.

- If this is a mortgage disguised as a sale, the borrower must prove a mortgage-like agreement by _____ evidence (i.e., that there was an obligation created prior to or contemporaneously with the transfer);
- Parol evidence is admissible to make this showing;

- Statute of Frauds does not bar _____ evidence about the agreement.

4. **Conditional Sale and Repurchase**

   - The owner sells property to the lender who leases the property back to the owner in exchange for a loan.
   - The lender gives the owner the option to repurchase after the loan is paid off.

D. **Transfers**

1. **By Mortgagor/Borrower**

   a. **Liability of mortgagor/borrower**

      - Mortgagor may transfer the property by deed (sale), by will, or by intestate succession.
      - Mortgagor remains _____ liable after the transfer unless:

        - Lender/mortgagee _____ mortgagor; or
        - Lender _____ the transferee's (buyer/new owner) obligation.

      - **Due-on-sale clause:** Lender has the option to demand immediate full payment upon transfer. Think of this as an _____ clause that allows the lender to speed up the payment when the property is

        _____.

      - **Due-on-encumbrance clause:** An acceleration clause when the mortgagor obtains a _____ mortgage or otherwise encumbers the property.

   b. **Liability of subsequent transferee**

      1) "Assumes" the mortgage

         - Upon default, if the buyer/transferee assumes the mortgage, the transferee is _____ liable for the mortgage.
         - Note: **Both** the original mortgagor **and** the transferee are liable upon default.
         - In most jurisdictions, the assumption agreement does **not** need to be in writing.

      2) Takes "subject to" the mortgage

         - Transferee is **not** personally liable upon default.
         - If the deed is silent or ambiguous as to liability, the transferee/buyer is considered to have taken title _____ to the mortgage.

2. **By Mortgagee/Lender**

   Example 101: Bonnie takes out a $250,000 loan from Local Bank to buy a home. Local Bank assigns the note and mortgage to America's Bank. Despite this

transfer, Bonnie still must make her mortgage payments. The payments will go
to America's Bank.

Special Situation #1: *Local Bank transfers the note but not the mortgage. The*
rule is that the mortgage _____ the note.

Special Situation #2: *Local Bank transfers the mortgage but not the note. The*
transfer is either (i) _____ because the note is
the evidence of the debt, or (ii) the note and mortgage are considered a single
entity, thus the note follows the mortgage.

CHAPTER 21:   FORECLOSURE

A. Pre-Foreclosure Rights and Duties

1.   **When Can the Mortgagee/Lender Take Possession?**

   a.   **Lien theory state**

   - The mortgagee/lender cannot take possession prior to foreclosure because lender has a _____ until foreclosure is complete.
   - The mortgagor is the owner up until foreclosure.

   b.   **Title theory state**

   - The lender technically has the right, as the holder of title, to _____ the property at any time.

   c.   **Intermediate title theory state**

   - A minority of jurisdictions modify the title theory.
   - The mortgagor retains title until _____, at which point the lender can take possession.

2.   **Waste**

   o   A homeowner cannot commit waste that will impair the lender's security interest.

   o   Affirmative waste, _____ waste, and permissive waste are more of a concern than ameliorative waste (improvements).

3.   **Equity of Redemption**

   o   A common law right held by the mortgagor to reclaim _____ and prevent foreclosure upon the full payment of the debt.

   o   The mortgagor must exercise this right _____ the foreclosure sale.

   > ***Example 102:*** *Bonnie takes out a $350,000 mortgage to buy a condo. She*
   > *misses a considerable number of payments and the bank initiates a foreclosure*

sale on account of Bonnie's default. Bonnie can

_____ the foreclosure under the equity of

redemption if she can repay the debt in full

_____ the foreclosure sale.

- o **Deed in lieu of foreclosure:** Rather than face foreclosure, the mortgagor can convey the property to the lender in exchange for releasing her from any outstanding debt.
- o **"Clogging" the equity of redemption**
  - ▪ To "clog" is to create terms that make it _____ for a borrower to exercise her equity of redemption.
  - ▪ Courts will intervene to prevent clogging.
  - ▪ For instance, a borrower may waive the right to redeem in exchange for consideration. A court is going to be very skeptical of this provision, as it will prevent the borrower from recovering before foreclosure.

B. Foreclosure Methods

1. What's What?

A foreclosure is a _____ sale of an asset to pay off a debt.

2. Notice

The mortgagee must give notice _____ foreclosing.

3. Two Methods

- ▪ **Judicial sale:** Sale under the _____ of a court
- ▪ **Power of sale** (private sale): Sale held by the mortgagee/lender
- o Either way, the proceeds of the sale are used to pay off the debt.
- o Excess proceeds will be used to satisfy other _____.

4. Deficiency

Is the mortgagor responsible if the sale produces less than the mortgagor owes? _____. In that situation, the court can issue a deficiency judgment for the remaining balance.

> **Example 103:** *Bonnie takes out a $200,000 mortgage from America's Bank to buy a home. She defaults on the loan and the home is foreclosed upon and sold for $100,000. The remaining debt, including principal and interest, is $175,000. What happens to the proceeds of the sale? The bank will take the $100,000 and get a deficiency judgment against Bonnie for the remaining $_____.*

C. Priorities

Now imagine more than one interest in the property is being foreclosed. How do we reconcile the competing interests? Which survive, which melt away?

1. **General Rule**

   ○ **Senior interests:** Interests acquired _____ the interest that is being foreclosed. They _____ the foreclosure.

   ○ **Junior interests:** Interests acquired _____ the interest that is being foreclosed. They are _____ by the foreclosure.

   ○ **First in time rule:** Surviving debts are satisfied _____.

   Classify the interest as either senior or junior and then apply the rule to determine whether the interest survives foreclosure.

2. **Exceptions to the Chronological "First in Time" Rule**

   a. **Purchase-money mortgage exception**

      ▪ Mortgage given to a lender in exchange for a loan to buy real property

      ▪ The purchase money mortgage has priority over mortgages and liens created by or against the purchaser/mortgagor _____ the purchaser/mortgagor's acquisition of the property.

      Example 104: *Bernard took out a $200,000 mortgage from America's Bank to purchase a home. After failing to make payments, he is in default. He is likewise in default on an earlier judgment lien from a traffic accident. America's Bank forecloses. Although it is junior to the judgment lien, the America's Bank mortgage would take priority.*

   b. **Recording act exception**

      ▪ A senior mortgage may sometimes not get recorded.

      ▪ A junior mortgage that satisfies the requirements of the state recording act may take _____ over the unrecorded senior mortgage.

      Example 105: *America's Bank is foreclosing on its mortgage on Blueberry Acre. America's Bank never recorded its mortgage interest. Village Bank has a later (junior) mortgage on Blueberry Acre. At the time of the execution, Village Bank was not aware of the earlier interest. The jurisdiction follows a notice rule for recording. Because it took its interest without knowledge (notice) of the senior interest, Village Bank's junior interest will take priority.*

   c. **Subordination agreement between mortgagees**

      A senior mortgagee can _____ to subordinate its interest to a junior interest.

d. Mortgage modifications

- A senior mortgagee who enters into an agreement with the mortgagor/landowner to modify the mortgage by making it _____ burdensome subordinates its interest, but only as to the modification. The original mortgage will otherwise remain superior.
- Likewise, if a senior mortgagee releases a mortgage and, at the same time, replaces it with a new mortgage, the new mortgage retains the same priority as the former mortgage, except to the extent a change is materially _____ to a junior mortgage holder.

e. Future-advances mortgages

A line of credit; *see* MBE Real Property outline at V.E.2.D.

f. After-acquired property

- A mortgagor/borrower may grant a mortgagee/lender rights to property that the mortgagor/borrower acquires in the future.
- The mortgage must _____ state that it applies to after-acquired property.
- Upon foreclosure, an interest in after-acquired property is _____ to a purchase-money mortgage.

D. Effects of Foreclosure

1. Mortgagor

- Foreclosure _____ the mortgagor's interest in the property.
- Exception: Statutory redemption:

    - Some states allow the mortgagor to redeem the property even _____ the foreclosure sale.
    - A statute enables the homeowner to _____ the foreclosure.
      It ends the purchaser's title and restores title to the homeowner.

    Example 106: Bonnie purchased a home for $350,000. Bonnie can't afford to make payments and defaults. Polly purchases the home at a foreclosure sale. Normally, at that point, Polly would become the rightful owner of the house and Bonnie's interest would be extinguished. In a state with statutory redemption, however, Bonnie can _____ the subsequent sale to Polly, provided she satisfies the statute.

    Note 36: Absent statutory redemption, the purchaser of property at a foreclosure sale takes the property **free and clear** of any junior mortgage and subject to any senior mortgage.

2. **Purchaser**

   o The purchaser of property at a foreclosure sale takes the property
   _____ and _____ of any junior
   mortgage and subject to any senior mortgage; BUT

   o The purchase may be subject to the mortgagor's statutory right of
   _____, if one exists.

3. **Senior interests**

   The rights of senior interests are generally not affected by the foreclosure sale.

4. **Junior interests**

   The rights of junior interests are generally _____.

CHAPTER 22:   EASEMENTS, PART I

A. Basics

1. **Definition:** Right held by one person to make _____ of another
   person's land

2. **Servient Estate:** Land _____ by the easement

3. **Dominant Estate:** Land _____ by the easement

   > *Example 107: Sissy has an easement to cross Dominic's property to reach the*
   > *highway. Who has the dominant estate? _____.*
   > *Who has the servient estate? _____.*

4. **Affirmative Easement:** The holder has the right to _____ on
   someone else's property.

   > *Example 108: Eddie has an easement to cross Sue's land to reach the highway.*

5. **Negative Easement:** The holder has the right to _____ someone
   from doing something on her land.

   > *Example 109: Eddie has an easement that entitles him to prevent Sue from*
   > *growing her bamboo to a height that blocks Eddie's view of the mountains.*

6. **Easement Appurtenant:** The easement is tied to the _____ of the
   land.

   > *Example 110: Eddie and Sue are neighbors. Eddie has the right to cross Sue's*
   > *land to reach the highway. Who has the dominant estate?*
   > *_____. Who has the servient estate?*
   > *_____.*

Note 37: An easement appurtenant is fully transferable; it goes with the land.

7. **Easement in Gross:** The easement benefits the holder _____.

> **Example 111:** *Sue has a lovely pool. Eddie is an avid swimmer but doesn't have a pool. Sue gives Eddie an easement so he can use her pool. It does not matter where Eddie lives. It benefits him personally.*

Note 38: In an easement in gross, there is no dominant estate, only a servient estate.

Note 39: Traditionally, easements in gross were not transferable, but now courts allow the easement to be transferred if there is intent for it to be transferable.

B. Creating an Easement

Two methods:

- _____ easement
- _____ easement

C. Express Easements

- An express easement is subject to the Statute of Frauds. Thus, it must be in _____.

- It can be created by a _____.

- It can also be created by _____. An easement by reservation is created when a grantor conveys land but reserves an easement right in the land for the grantor's use and benefit.

> **Example 112:** *Eddie conveys Yellowacre to Sue. In the deed, Eddie "reserves the right to cross Yellowacre to reach the lake."*

- Remember:

  o Express easements are subject to _____ statutes.

  o A _____ easement must be express; it cannot be created by implication. Why? Implied easements arise out of circumstances and a negative right will rarely be created by circumstances.

D. Implied Easements (Easements by Operation of Law; Non-Express Easements)

Exam Tip 10: Expect a question on the MBE on implied easements.

- Implied easements are informal; they arise out of factual circumstances.
- They are _____.
- They are not subject to the Statute of Frauds.
- They are not subject to recording statutes, unless the subsequent purchaser had _____ of the easement.

- Four kinds:
  - Easement by _____;
  - Easement by _____ (easement by prior use);
  - Easement by _____;
  - Easement by _____.

E. Implied Easement by Necessity

- An easement by necessity is created only when property is virtually _____ (e.g., when the property is landlocked; there is no road or access without crossing another's land).
- Conditions that must be met:
  - **Common ownership:** Dominant and servient estates were owned in _____ by one person; and
  - **Necessity at severance:** When the estates were severed into two separate estates (severance), one of the properties became virtually useless without an easement.
- "Necessity" in a strict sense
- Ends when it is no longer necessary

> **Example 113:** Donna owns Brownacre. She divides the property, selling the west portion to Wayne, and keeping the east portion for herself. When he purchased the property, Wayne asked Donna if he could cross her land because it was more convenient than using the road that abuts the north side of his property. Does Wayne have an easement by necessity?
> _____, because inconvenience is not enough.

CHAPTER 23: EASEMENTS, PART II

A. Implied Easement by Implication

1. What Is It?

An easement by implication is created by an existing use on a property.

2. Conditions that Must be Met

- **Common ownership:** A large estate owned by one owner
- **Before severance:** The owner of the large tract uses the land as if there's an easement on it. We call this a quasi-easement. It's "quasi" because an owner can't have an easement over her own land.

> **Example 114:** Olivia owns Cherryacre. Her house is on the west side of the tract and she crosses the east side of the tract to reach the highway.

- ○ **After severance:** Use must be _____ and apparent at the time of severance.
- ○ **Necessity:** Use must be reasonably _____ to the dominant estate's use and enjoyment.

>
> *Example 115: Olivia owns Purple Acre. She lived on the west side of the property and regularly crossed to the east side to reach the well. She did not have indoor plumbing in her home. She sold the east half (with the well) to Sam, but the deed did not reserve an express easement over Sam's property for Olivia to access the well. Olivia kept crossing Sam's property to fetch water until Sam demanded that she stop. Has Olivia acquired an easement by implication? _____ .*

B. Implied Easement by Prescription

1. What Is It?

It's like acquiring an easement by _____ possession.

2. Important Differences

- ○ Adverse possession is about possession, whereas an easement by prescription concerns _____ .
- ○ Elements are the same as adverse possession, except exclusivity. Do you see why?

C. Implied Easement by Estoppel

1. Creation

- ○ **Permission:** Starts with a _____ use (e.g., the first neighbor permits the second neighbor to use her land). This is a **license**.
- ○ **Reliance:** Continues when the second neighbor _____ on the first neighbor's promise
  - ▪ Reliance must be reasonable and in good faith;
  - ▪ Look for facts where the second neighbor invested money in reliance on the first neighbor's promise (e.g., made improvements to the easement).
- ○ **Permission withdrawn:** Finally, the first neighbor withdraws permission.

2. Result

If reliance was _____ to the second neighbor, the first neighbor is estopped from withdrawing permission, in effect creating an easement.

> *Example 116: Olivia and Sam are neighbors. Olivia gives Sam permission to use the roadway across her property to reach Sam's property. Based on this promise, Sam uses the roadway to construct a cabin on his property. After*

building the cabin and paving the roadway, Olivia blocks the roadway and tells Sam he is trespassing. Can Olivia prevent Sam from using the road?

_____, because he has acquired an easement by estoppel.

D. Scope

Depends on the type of easement

1. Express Easements

Determined by the terms of the easement when it was created

- **Ambiguous terms:** If the terms are ambiguous, the court considers the _____ of the original parties as to the purpose of the easement.
- **Changes in use:** Changes in use of an easement are tested under a _____ standard. Presume the parties contemplated both its current use and its future use, which means the future use of an easement must be reasonably foreseeable.
- **Trespass:** If the use exceeds the scope, the dominant tenant is _____ on the servient estate.

    Example 117: Oliver gave Mary an easement to take walks along the forest on his property. After years of strolling on the property, Mary has begun riding her motorcycle on the path across Oliver's property. Can Oliver eject her from the path? _____, because Mary's current use was not reasonably foreseeable when they created the easement. Her current use burdens the scope.

- **Watch out!** Be on the lookout for fact patterns where a person has an easement to cross another's land and the holder of the easement seeks to redevelop or _____ the property to add many new holders.

    - Considerations:
        - Can the easement be transferred to the new holders of the estate?
        - Was the new use an ordinary foreseeable development?

- **Also note:** The holder of the dominant estate is not entitled to use the easement to access property acquired after the easement is created.

2. Implied Easements

Determined by the _____ of the prior use or necessity

E. Duty to Maintain

- Who has the duty to maintain the property subject to an easement? The
  _____ of the easement.
- **Exception:** Parties can otherwise contract.

F. Termination

1. Release

- ○ The holder of the easement _____ releases it.
- ○ The release must be in _____, because it is subject to the
  Statute of Frauds.

2. Merger

- ○ An easement is terminated if the owner of the easement acquires fee title to the underlying
  estate.
- ○ The easement _____ into the title.

  *Example 118: Jose has an easement that gives him a right to cross Jenny's land
  to reach the river. Later Jose purchases Jenny's land. Is Jose's easement
  terminated? _____, the dominant and servient
  estates have merged. Jose cannot have an easement on his own property.*

3. Abandonment

The owner acts in an affirmative way that shows a clear intent to relinquish the right.

- ○ Requires more than non-use or statements;
- ○ Usually need _____ plus an act demonstrating an
  _____ to abandon.

  *Example 119: Rancher gives Shepherd an easement to use a path on his
  property so that Shepherd's sheep can get to the river to drink. Fed up with
  country living, Shepherd sells his flock and moves to New York City with plans
  never to return. Has Shepherd abandoned his easement?
  _____, because Shepherd no longer uses the
  path and has taken acts (i.e., selling his sheep, moving to New York City) that
  demonstrate his intent to abandon the easement.*

4. Prescription

The holder fails to protect against a _____ for the statutory
period.

  *Example 120: Millhouse has an easement to use the path along Lulu's property.
  Lulu hates Millhouse and no longer wants him on her property. She puts up a
  fence to block Millhouse's access to the path. If the path is blocked for the*

statutory period, will Millhouse's easement be terminated?

_____, Lulu's action prevented Millhouse from

exercising his easement rights.

5. **Sale to a Bona Fide Purchaser**

6. **Estoppel**

The servient owner changes position to his _____ in reliance on statements or conduct of the easement holder that the easement is abandoned.

> ***Example 121:*** *Horace has an easement to use the road on Grace's property.*
> *Horace tells Grace that he is not going to use the road anymore. Grace hires a*
> *landscape designer who begins work to turn the path into a giant topiary*
> *garden. After the garden is half built, Horace demands that Grace reinstate the*
> *path for his use. Was the easement terminated?*
> *_____, Grace reasonably relied on Horace's*
> *statement.*

7. **End of Necessity**

An easement by necessity lasts as long as the easement is _____. If it is no longer necessary, the easement ends.

G. Not Easements

Distinguish an easement from two other interests:

1. **Profit**

   o Right to enter another's land and remove a specific natural _____ (e.g., oil, gas, timber)

   o Note: Operates similarly to an easement, but profits cannot be created by _____.

2. **License**

   o A revocable _____ to use another's land (e.g., a ticket to a sporting event; the permission you give to a plumber to come into your house)

- Remember: Easements are not revocable but licenses are revocable.
- Remember: An easement binds _____, whereas a license only binds the _____.

CHAPTER 24: REAL COVENANTS

Exam Tip 11: Nearly every MBE has tested real covenants.

A. The Gist

- What is it? A promise concerning the use of the land that runs to successors to the promise

    > *Example 122:* Oliver conveys a neighboring property to Caleb. In the deed, Oliver and Caleb agree to paint their houses white. This agreement is governed by contract law.

    > *Example 123: Compare:* Caleb later conveys his property to Gertrude, who intends to paint her house yellow. Contract law cannot resolve the issue of whether Oliver can enforce the agreement against Gertrude, but property law does.

- When an agreement binds a successor, it "runs with the land."
    - The **benefit** of the covenant is the ability to _____ the covenant.
    - The **burden** of the covenant is being _____ to it (i.e., bound by it).

    > *Example 124:* Oliver conveyed property to Caleb and they both agreed to paint their houses white. When Caleb conveys to Gertrude, who intends to paint her house yellow, Oliver wants to stop Gertrude from breaching the covenant. Are we running the benefit or the burden to Gertrude? The _____. The burden running from Caleb to Gertrude will prevent her from breaching the covenant.

B. Requirements to Run

Five elements:

- _____;
- _____;
- Touch and concern;
- _____;
- _____.

C. Writing

A real covenant is subject to the Statute of Frauds, so it must be in writing.

> **Note 41:** Real covenants can be recorded. Are they subject to recording acts? _____.

D. Intent

To bind a successor, the original parties must intend for the covenant to run with the land.

E. Touch and Concern

- A real covenant must touch and concern the land in order to run.
- The benefit or burden of the covenant must affect _____ parties as owners of the land.

  - **Negative covenant:** A restriction on use will usually touch and concern because they restrict what you can do with your land. Watch out for promises that are unenforceable such as _____ covenants, as these do not touch and concern.
  - **Affirmative covenant:** A covenant to pay money (e.g., homeowners' association fees). Traditionally, such fees did not touch and concern, but the modern trend is to say that these fees **do** touch and concern.

F. Notice

- What kind of notice is required to run a real covenant? Either _____ notice or _____ (i.e., record) notice;
- _____ notice may also suffice for an equitable servitude.

G. Horizontal Privity

- To run the burden to a successor, the _____ parties to the promise must have been in horizontal privity.
- Horizontal privity refers to privity of _____, where the estate and covenant are contained in the same instrument (e.g., the deed).

  - **Helpful Hint:** Look for a transfer of property between the original parties that contains a covenant in it. (Key for horizontal privity: Look for the original parties to the agreement.)

    Example 125: Oliver owns Blackacre and Whiteacre. He conveys Whiteacre to Caleb. The deed says "Oliver and Caleb promise to use their property for residential purposes only." Are Caleb and Oliver in horizontal privity? _____. Why? There was a transfer and the covenant was included in the transfer.

    Note 42: You do not need horizontal privity to run a **benefit**.

H. Vertical Privity

- Vertical privity refers to the relationship between the original party to the agreement and his/her _____ to the property.
- To run the **burden** of the covenant to the successor, the successor must take the original party's _____ interest. This is called **strict** vertical privity.

- To run the **benefit** of the covenant to the successor, the successor need only take an interest that is _____ of the original party's estate. This is called **relaxed** vertical privity.

> *Example 126: Oliver and Caleb have in their deeds to Blackacre and Whiteacre a promise not to build a shed on their properties. Oliver conveys his fee simple interest to Marsha, who plans to build a shed on the property. Can Caleb recover against Marsha? Ask first if you're running the benefit or the burden and then what kind of vertical privity is needed. Here we're running the _____. To run the burden, you need _____ vertical privity. So here, because Marsha took Oliver's fee simple interest (strict vertical privity), we have enough to run the burden, provided there is horizontal privity.*

> *Example 127: Would there still have been vertical privity if Oliver had conveyed a life estate to Marsha? _____, because she took an interest carved out of the fee simple interest rather than the whole fee simple interest.*

> **Exam Tip 13: Ask yourself a series of questions:**
>
> (i) Identify whether you are running the benefit or the burden;
>
> (ii) If it is the **benefit**, you need **relaxed** vertical privity and you don't care about horizontal privity;
>
> (iii) If it is the **burden**, you need horizontal privity and **strict** vertical privity.

I. Remedy

The remedy for a breach of a real covenant is _____.

CHAPTER 25: EQUITABLE SERVITUDES

- Two ways to bind a successor to an original party's promise: (i) real covenant; (ii) equitable servitude;
- An equitable servitude has an easier standard to meet and the remedy differs.

A. The Gist

- Operates like a real covenant but with easier requirements;
- To bind a successor:
  - It must be in _____;
  - Must have been _____ to run with the land (same standard as a real covenant);
  - Must _____ the land (same standard as a real covenant);
  - Successor must have _____ (actual, record, or inquiry).

- No privity requirement.
- The remedy for a breach is _____ relief.

B. Implied Reciprocal Servitude

- It is a kind of equitable servitude that is implied and need NOT be in writing.
- Usually comes up in _____ communities (e.g., condo, subdivision);
- How are they created?
  - Developer must _____ to create a covenant (i.e., promise) on all plots in the subdivision;
  - Promises must be _____ (i.e., benefits and burdens each and every parcel equally);
  - Must be _____ rather than positive (i.e., it must be a restriction on the owner's use);
  - A successor must be on _____ of the restriction (at least inquiry notice); and
  - Must be a _____ plan or scheme.

    Example 128: Developer Joe Schmo has an idea for a community. He buys the land and writes up a master plan for the community. He begins conveying the property, including a restriction that your house must be painted white. However, some of the later transfers do not include a "white house" covenant. One of the new owners does not have the "white house" covenant expressed in her deed and this owner wants to paint her house turquoise. This owner will not find a "white house" covenant in her chain of title.

    Should the owner be bound by a restriction that wasn't in her deed? Though the owner had neither record nor actual notice, the owner may be on _____ notice. Why? Looking around, every house is painted white. Even though the restriction is not in the deed, it may be implied—an exception to the requirement that the promise needs to be in writing. It is an implied reciprocal servitude.

  - To prove there is a common plan, look for:
    - A (recorded) map of the community showing the common scheme;
    - Marketing or _____ of the community;
    - Oral or written mention that the lots are burdened by common restriction.

C. Termination

Terminates as an easement does (i.e., merger, release, etc.)

D. Changed Circumstances Doctrine

- Look for situations where the restriction no longer makes _____ due to _____ changes in the surrounding area since the restriction was put in place.

- **Critical question:** Does the property subject to the restriction still retain some benefit from the restriction?

  > *Example 129: The houses in the Hilly Flats subdivision all have restrictions against commercial use. When Hilly Flats was developed, the surrounding neighborhoods were exclusively residential. In the following years, commercial properties developed adjacent to Hilly Flats, though there are no commercial properties within the subdivision itself. Henry wants to open a business on his property within Hilly Flats. His neighbor opposes it, seeking to have the servitude enforced.*
  >
  > *Will the court continue to enforce it? _____.*
  > *Although there is change outside the community, there have not been changed circumstances inside the community, so residents still benefit from the restriction (e.g., noise, traffic). Change outside the community is not sufficient to terminate.*

E. Equitable Defenses

Equitable defenses are available, including unclean hands (the plaintiff not acting in good faith) and laches (unreasonable _____).

F. Common Interest Communities

- **What are we talking about?**

  o Real estate development in which individual units/lots are burdened by a covenant to pay dues to an association;

  o The association:

    ▪ **Services:** Maintains grounds, provides facilities, etc.

    ▪ **Enforces the covenants:** The association is the "heavy" when your neighbor breaks the rules.

- **Three types**

  o **Owners' Associations:** Where property owners belong and pay _____ to an association or board;

  o **Condominiums:** Where individual units are owned outright, but common areas are owned _____ as tenants in common;

  o **Cooperatives:** Property is owned by a corporation (made up of residents/shareholders) that leases individual units to shareholders (residents).

- **Governance**
  - **Declaration:** The governing documents that outline the controlling covenants and restrictions, as well as the particulars about the association or board.

    Note 43: Rules laid out in a declaration are valid so long as they are not illegal, against public policy, or _____.

  - **Powers:** The board has general powers to manage the common property and administer the residents. For example:
    - Assessments/fees;
    - Manage and maintain the common property (e.g., clubhouse, gym);
    - Enforce rules;
    - Create new rules.
      - Basic test: A new rule must be reasonably related to further a _____ purpose of the association (think: rational basis test).

- **Duties**

  To the community: The association must deal _____ with members of the community.

  - Good faith;
  - _____;
  - Ordinary care;
  - Business Judgment Rule controls (the board is shielded from honest but mistaken business decisions).

G. Fixtures

1. What Is It?

Tangible personal property that is _____ to real property in a manner that is treated as part of the real property (e.g., a wall or a bridge; the materials used to make a wall or a bridge)

2. Making Improvements

- A fee simple owner of property is free to make improvements to the property, including fixtures, subject to governmental land use regulations.
- Holders of a life estate or tenants, by contrast, are limited by the doctrine of _____.

  Example 130: Anita is the fee simple owner of Apple Acre. Sick of buying eggs every week, Anita decides to build a large chicken coop in her backyard. The municipality has no restrictions against landowners keeping farm animals on their property. Can Anita make the improvement?

_____, *she is a fee simple owner and there are no governmental restrictions against her doing so.*

Example 131: *Ray is the life tenant on Iowa Acre, a corn farm. After hearing a mysterious voice, Ray plows under his cornfield and builds a baseball field. Should Ray be worried about a claim by the future interest holder?*

_____, *Ray's action could be considered waste.*

3. Removal

- o The _____ of real property is generally entitled to the chattel, unless the seller reserves in the _____ the right to keep the chattel.
- o **Life tenants and tenants:** Presumption is that they can remove fixtures unless doing so would _____ damage the property

4. Trespassers

- o **Old rule:** Trespassers could never remove any fixtures or improvements that they installed.
- o **New rule:** Trespassers can remove an improvement, or at least recover the value added to the property, so long as they acted in _____.

Example 132: *Terry rents an apartment from Leo. Terry installs special lights that she uses to grow orchids. The lights, which hang on a stand and are not permanently affixed to the property, can be removed with ease. The lease does not contain a provision about improvements or fixtures. Leo is eager to keep the lights on the property, hoping to repurpose them to as fancy patio lights. Can Terry remove the lights at the end of the lease?*

_____. *Removing the lights will not cause permanent damage to the property.*

Example 133: *Archibald takes possession of Cotton Acre, thinking he is the rightful owner. During his three-year stay on Cotton Acre, Archibald repaired the barn and built a shed for farm equipment. Butch, the rightful owner of Cotton Acre, discovers Archibald and demands that he leave Cotton Acre at once. Archibald agrees, but insists that Butch pay him the value of the shed Archibald built. Will Archibald recover the value of the shed?*

_____, *(in a modern jurisdiction) because Archibald improved Cotton Acre in good faith.*

CHAPTER 26: LAND USE

A. Zoning Basics

1. What are We Talking About?

- State and local governments may regulate the use of land through zoning laws.
- Zoning laws are enacted for the _____ and _____ of the community.

    - States have authority to zone through police powers.
    - Local governments get power to zone through specific enabling acts.

2. Objective

- Segregate _____ uses from being developed in the same area (e.g., residential v. commercial and industrial)
- **Cumulative zoning:** The traditional approach in which residential use is permitted everywhere, commercial use is restricted to some areas, and industrial use is allowed in the fewest areas.
- **Mutually exclusive zoning:** Some jurisdictions have developed an approach where only one type of use is permitted by zone.

B. Nonconforming Uses

Two situations:

1. Existing Nonconforming Properties

When zoning is changed and a structure does not satisfy the zone's requirements, it is called a "nonconforming use."

- The goal of the property owner is to get the nonconforming use _____ in.
- **Vested rights:** If the project is in process when the change happens, the developer must have the proper building permits by the time the ordinance takes effect. The developer must also demonstrate the project was in _____.
- What if...?

    - Owner wants to expand the nonconforming use? This is generally _____.
    - The nonconforming owner switches to another nonconforming use? _____.
    - The nonconforming owner transfers the property to a new owner? _____.

2. Post-Ordinance Nonconforming Properties

When the property owner requests a change **after** the zoning ordinance is in place.

a. **Variance**

Owner applies for a variance, essentially permission to violate the zoning rules.

1) **Use variance:** Obtain the right to use property in a manner not permitted by zoning

Example 134: Otis wants to open a café in a residential neighborhood. To support his case, he argues that there is already a smattering of small businesses in the neighborhood, that his cafe won't increase the burden on the neighborhood traffic patterns, and that his café will make the neighborhood more desirable. The argument is about the use and trying to make it consistent with the existing neighborhood.

2) **Area variance:** Focuses on restrictions concerning property development.

Example 135: Amanda wants to build a fence around her property. Her plan is to follow the natural tree line surrounding her property. One spot of the proposed fence, on the west side of her property, will slightly encroach on the City's utility right of way. Amanda argues that the encroachment is slight and that diverting from the tree line will be unsightly.

b. **Standard**

The person applying for a variance must show ALL of the following:

- Compliance would create unnecessary _____;
- The hardship arises from circumstances _____ to the property;
- The owner did not create the hardship;
- The variance is in keeping with the overall _____ of the ordinance; and
- The variance will not cause substantial _____ to the general welfare.

C. **Nuisance**

1. **Private nuisance**

   o A _____ and _____ interference with another individual's use or enjoyment of his property.
   o **Substantial:** One that would be offensive, inconvenient, or _____ to an average person in the community.
   o **Unreasonable:** The injury outweighs the _____ of the defendant's actions.

2. **Public nuisance**

   o Unreasonable interference with the health, _____, or property rights of the community.

- **Private party:** Must show that she suffered a _____ kind of harm than the rest of the community.

3. **Remedies**

   - Usual remedy is damages;
   - If money damages are inadequate or unavailable, the court can impose _____ relief.

D. Water Rights

Two basic approaches:

1. **Riparian Rights**

   - Doctrine of riparian rights holds that landowners who _____ a waterway own the rights to the waterway. The right depends upon whether the landowner is located near the water.
   - Riparians share the right to _____ use of the water, such that one riparian is liable to another for interference with the other's use.

2. **Prior Appropriation**

   - **First in time, first in right:** The _____ person to use the water, regardless of where their land is located, has the rights to the water.
   - **Beneficial use:** In a prior appropriation jurisdiction, the user must put the water to a _____ use. Any productive use satisfies this standard.

E. Support Rights

1. **Lateral Support Rights**

   - A neighboring landowner cannot _____ so as to cause a cave in (i.e., subsidence) on an adjacent owner's land.
   - Applicable standards:

     - Did the neighbor's buildings (structures) contribute to the cave in? If so, the standard to apply to the one excavating is _____.
     - What if the neighbor's buildings did not contribute to cave in? The standard to apply is _____.

2. **Subjacent Support**

   - Think _____ rights.
   - The surface landowners have the right not to have their land subside from the activities of the owners of _____ rights.

STUDY HARD, GOOD LUCK ON THE EXAM, AND THANKS FOR YOUR TIME.

[END OF HANDOUT]

Torts

TORTS

PROFESSOR LESLIE KENDRICK
UNIVERSITY OF VIRGINIA SCHOOL OF LAW

CHAPTER 1:   **INTENTIONAL TORTS INVOLVING PHYSICAL INJURY**

A. Generally

1. **Three Elements**—to prove an intentional tort, the plaintiff must prove:

    ○ _____;

    ○ _____; and

    ○ _____.

2. **Intent**

    ○ The actor acts with the _____ of causing the consequence; or

    ○ The actor knows that the consequence is _____
       to follow.

    a. **Children and** _____ **persons**—can
        be held liable for intentional torts if they act with the requisite intent

    b. **Transferred intent**—when the intent to commit one tort satisfies the required intent for a
        different tort; this applies when a person commits:

        ▪ A _____ intentional tort against the _____ person
           that he intended to harm;

        ▪ The _____ intentional tort against a _____person; or

        ▪ A _____ intentional tort against a _____ person.

        Example 1:   *Tom, Gatsby, and Nick are drinking mint juleps at a hotel. Tom
        throws a punch at Gatsby, intending to hit him. If he hits him, that's a battery.*

        *Different tort/same person: Tom misses Gatsby, but he puts him in reasonable
        apprehension of imminent harm. Under the doctrine of transferred intent, the
        intent to commit a battery satisfies the intent requirement for assault.*

        *Same tort/different person: If the punch misses Gatsby and hits Nick, Tom
        commits battery against Nick.*

        *Different tort/different person: Tom intends to punch Gatsby, misses Gatsby,
        misses Nick, but puts Nick in reasonable apprehension of being hit. The intent
        to commit battery against Gatsby will transfer to the intentional tort of assault
        against Nick.*

B. Battery

   1. Definition

      1) Defendant causes a _____ or _____ contact with the person of another; and

      2) Acts with the _____ to cause that contact or the apprehension of that contact.

   2. Causation—act must result in _____ of a harmful or offensive nature

   3. Harmful or Offensive Contact

      a. Harmful—causes an _____, pain, or illness

      b. Offensive

- A person of ordinary sensibilities would find the contact offensive.

  Example 2: *Spitting on somebody; groping somebody*

- Victim need not be _____ of the touching to be offensive.

  Example 3: *An operating room attendant inappropriately touches a patient under anesthesia. This is a battery even though the patient is not aware of it because it is objectively offensive.*

- If the victim is _____, and the defendant knows that about the victim, the defendant may still be liable

      c. Contact—the contact can be direct, but need not be

  Example 4: *Setting a bucket above a door, such that ice water falls on a person's head when the door is opened. Pulling a chair out from under someone who's about to sit down, so that they fall on the ground.*

      d. With the Person of Another—includes anything _____ to the plaintiff's person

  Example 5: *Contact with the hat on your head, the book in your hand, the bike you're sitting on, the pet you have on a leash.*

   4. Intent

      ○ ***What has to be intended is the _____, not the offense

  Example 6: *Tom intentionally shakes Myrtle by the shoulders. It doesn't matter whether he intended to cause offense; if he intended the contact and the contact is objectively offensive, he's liable for battery.*

      ○ The doctrine of **transferred intent** _____ to battery.

5. **Damages**

   o No proof of actual harm is required; the plaintiff can recover _____ damages.

   o The plaintiff can also recover damages from physical harm flowing from the battery.

     ▪ "_____-plaintiff" rule—a defendant is liable for all harm that flows from a battery, even if it is much worse than the defendant expected it to be.

   o Many states allow _____ damages if the defendant acted:

     ▪ Outrageously; or

     ▪ With _____.

6. **Consent Defense**—there is no battery if there is express or implied consent.

   > *Example 7:* Tom and Nick enter a boxing contest. If Tom punches Nick and injures him while boxing, Nick's suit for battery will not succeed because of the defense of consent.

C. Assault

1. **Definition**—defendant engages in an act that:

   o Causes reasonable _____ of an imminent harmful or offensive bodily contact; and

   o The defendant _____ to cause apprehension of such contact or to cause such contact itself.

2. **Bodily Contact**—not required

3. **Plaintiff's Apprehension**

   o Must be reasonable

   o Plaintiff must be _____ of the defendant's action

   > *Example 8:* If you are sleeping and someone gropes you, that person commits battery even though you are not aware of it. If you are sleeping and someone pretends to hit you, there is no assault because assault requires awareness.

4. **Imminent**

   o Must be without significant _____

   o Threats of future harm or hypothetical harm are not sufficient.

5. **Mere Words**

   o Generally, "mere words do not constitute an assault."

   o Words can suffice in certain circumstances. If the defendant is able to carry out the threat imminently and takes action designed to put the victim in a state of apprehension, then there may be an assault.

> *Example 9:* The defendant comes up behind the plaintiff in a dark alley and says, "Your money or your life." These words in this context can constitute an assault.

6. **Intent**—may be present in one of two ways:

   o The defendant must intend to cause either:

   - An apprehension of imminent harmful or offensive contact; or
   - The contact itself.

     > *Example 10:* Tom intends to punch Nick, but he misses. He does, however, put Nick in reasonable apprehension of imminent harmful contact. Nick can make out a claim of assault.

7. **Damages**

   o No proof of _____ damages is required; the plaintiff can recover nominal damages.

   o The plaintiff can also recover damages from physical harm flowing from the assault.

   o In appropriate cases, _____ damages may be available.

CHAPTER 2: INTENTIONAL TORTS: IIED, FALSE IMPRISONMENT, AND DEFENSES

A. Intentional Infliction of Emotional Distress (IIED)

1. **Definition**—defendant intentionally or recklessly engages in extreme and _____ conduct that causes the plaintiff severe emotional distress

2. **Intent**—The defendant must:

   o Intend to cause severe emotional distress; or

   o Act with _____ as to the risk of causing severe emotional distress.

3. **Extreme and Outrageous Conduct**—Conduct that exceeds the possible limits of human decency, so as to be entirely _____ in a civilized society.

   > *Example 11:* As a practical joke, the defendant tells the plaintiff that his wife has been killed in an accident.

   o Courts are more likely to find conduct or language to be extreme and outrageous if:

   - The defendant is in a position of _____ or _____ over the plaintiff; or
   - The plaintiff is a member of a group that has a heightened _____ (such as young children or the elderly).

4. **Public Figures—Constitutional Limitations**

  o Public figures and public officials cannot recover unless they can show that the words
    contain a _____ statement of fact that was made with "actual _____."

    ▪ Actual malice—with knowledge that the statement was false or with
      _____ disregard of its potential falsity.

  o The Supreme Court has suggested that even private plaintiffs cannot recover if the conduct
    at issue is speech on a matter of _____. (*Snyder v. Phelps*)

5. **Conduct Toward Third Parties**

  If the defendant directed extreme and outrageous conduct toward one party and ended up
  causing severe emotional distress to another party, the doctrine of transferred intent *may* make
  him liable for IIED, but only in certain circumstances.

  a. **Immediate family member**

    An immediate family member of the victim who is present at the time of the conduct and
    perceives the conduct may recover for IIED regardless of whether that family member
    suffers bodily injury as a result of the distress.

    > *Example 12:* *A defendant acted outrageously toward a young child and the
    > child's mother is present at the time. If the mother experiences emotional
    > distress, she may be able to recover under the tort of IIED.*

  b. **Bystander**

    Can recover for IIED if present at the time of the conduct, perceives the conduct, and suffers
    distress that results in _____ (i.e., physical
    manifestation of the distress).

  c. **Different intentional tort**

    If the defendant commits a different intentional tort toward one victim, thereby causing
    severe emotional distress to another, the same rules apply.

    > *Example 13:* *The defendant threatens a battery against the mother's child in
    > the mother's presence.*

6. **Causation**—defendant's actions must be a cause in fact of the plaintiff's harm.

7. **Damages**—plaintiff must prove severe emotional distress beyond what a reasonable person
   should endure.

  o Often, the outrageous nature of the conduct is evidence of the plaintiff's distress.
  o **Hypersensitivity**—if the plaintiff experiences an unreasonable level of emotional distress,
    then the defendant is only liable if aware of the plaintiff's hypersensitivity.
  o Physical injury is not required (except in the case of a bystander, discussed above).

B. False Imprisonment

1. Definition—three elements:

o   Defendant intends to _____ or _____ another within fixed boundaries;

o   The actions directly or indirectly result in confinement; and

o   Plaintiff is _____ of the confinement or _____ by it

> *Example 14: Locking a person in a closet*

2. Confined Within Bounded Area

o   Area can be large

o   Area need not be _____

> *Example 15: The van may be moving, but if the person cannot leave the van, that is confinement.*

3. Methods of Confinement

o   Use of physical _____, physical force, threats, invalid invocation of legal _____, duress, or refusing to provide a safe means of escape

o   A court may find false imprisonment when the defendant has refused to perform a _____ to help a person escape

> *Example 16: A store clerk refuses to unlock a dressing room in which someone is locked.*

o   **Shopkeeper's privilege**—a shopkeeper can, for a _____ time and in a reasonable _____, detain a suspected shoplifter.

4. Time of Confinement—immaterial to the tort

5. Intent

o   Defendant must act:

▪   With the _____ of confining the plaintiff; or

▪   _____ that the plaintiff's confinement is substantially certain to result.

o   **Confinement due to defendant's negligence**—defendant will not be liable under the intentional tort of false imprisonment

o   Transferred intent applies.

> *Example 17: If Gatsby intends to confine Tom but confines Nick, he is liable to Nick for false imprisonment.*

>*Example 18:* *If Gatsby intends to hit Nick with a log but instead blocks him into a corner with it, such that he is confined, Gatsby is liable to Nick for false imprisonment.*

6. **Damages**—plaintiff can recover _____ damages; actual damages are also compensable.

C. Defenses to Intentional Torts Involving Personal Injury

1. Consent

a. **Express consent**—the plaintiff, by words or actions, manifests the willingness to submit to the defendant's conduct.

- The defendant's conduct may not exceed the scope of the consent.
- Consent by **mistake**—a _____ defense unless the defendant caused the mistake or knew of it and took advantage of it
- Consent by **fraud**—invalid if it goes to an _____ matter. If the fraud only goes to a collateral matter, consent is still a valid defense.

b. **Implied consent**—the plaintiff is silent (or otherwise nonresponsive) where their silence and continued participation can reasonably be construed as consent

- **Emergencies**—it is fair to assume that someone in need of rescuing would allow a rescuer to touch him absent explicit consent
- **Injuries arising from athletic contests**—consent within the scope of the sport
  - A defendant could be liable if the conduct is reckless
- **Mutual consent to combat**

c. **Capacity**—Lack of capacity may undermine the validity of consent (e.g., youth, intoxication, incompetency).

2. Self-Defense

a. **Use of reasonable force**—force that is _____ to defend against an offensive contact or bodily harm (i.e., not excessive).

b. **Duty to retreat**

- Traditionally, most courts required retreat before one could use deadly force.
- Most jurisdictions state that you need not retreat before using reasonable, proportionate force.

  Note 1: These are called "stand your ground" laws.

c. **Initial aggressor**—NOT permitted to claim self-defense unless the other party has responded to nondeadly force with deadly force

      d. Injuries to bystanders—A person acting in self-defense is not liable for injury to bystanders as long as the injury was _____ and the actor was not negligent toward the bystander.

3. **Defense of Others**—may use reasonable force in defense of others, if the others would be entitled to use self-defense

4. **Defense of Property**

    a. Reasonable force—may be used if the person reasonably believes it is necessary to prevent tortious harm to the property

    b. Deadly force—cannot be used

    A person may never use **deadly mechanical devices** to defend property (e.g., a spring gun).

    c. Recapture of chattels (personal property)

      ■ Reasonable force may be used to reclaim _____ property that has been wrongfully taken, but only if you first request its return, unless that would be futile.

      ■ If the original taking was lawful (like a bailment) then only _____ means may be used.

    d. Force to regain possession of land

      ■ **Common law**—reasonable force permitted

      ■ **Modern rule**—use of force is no longer permitted; only legal process

5. **Parental Discipline**—parents may use reasonable force as necessary to discipline children.

6. **Privilege of Arrest**

    a. Private citizen

      ■ Permitted to use reasonable force to make an arrest in the case of a _____ IF:

        • The felony has actually been committed; and

        • The arresting party has _____ to suspect that the person being arrested has committed the felony.

      ■ It _____ a defense to make a reasonable mistake as to the identity of the felon.

      ■ It _____ a defense to make a mistake as to whether the felony was actually committed.

    b. Police

      ■ Must reasonably believe that a felony has been committed and that the person arrested committed it

- An officer who makes a mistake as to whether a felony has been committed is _____ to tort liability.

   c. **Misdemeanor**

- An arrest by a police officer may only be made if the misdemeanor was committed in the officer's _____.
- An arrest by a private person may only be made if there is a "_____ _____."

CHAPTER 3: HARMS TO PERSONAL PROPERTY AND LAND

A. Trespass to Chattels

1. **Definition**—an intentional interference with the plaintiff's right to _____ personal property either by:

   o _____ the plaintiff of the chattel;
   o _____ or _____ with the plaintiff's chattel; or
   o Damaging the chattel.

2. **Intent**

   o Only the intent to do the interfering act is necessary; need not intend to interfere
   o _____ about the legality of the action is not a defense.

3. **Damages**

   o May recover actual damages, damages resulting from the loss of use, or the cost of repair
   o In cases involving use or intermeddling, plaintiff may only recover actual damages.

B. Conversion

1. **Definition**—intentionally committing an act depriving the plaintiff of possession of his chattel or interfering with the plaintiff's chattel in a manner so serious as to deprive the plaintiff entirely of the use of the chattel.

2. **Intent**

   o Defendant must only intend to commit _____that interferes.
   o Mistake of law or fact _____ a defense.

3. **Damages**—plaintiff can recover the chattel's full value at the time of conversion

4. **Trespass to Chattels vs. Conversion**—Courts consider the following factors:

   o The _____ and extent of the interference;
   o Defendant's intent to assert a right inconsistent with the rightful possessor;
   o Defendant's _____;

- o Expense or inconvenience to the plaintiff; and
- o Extent of the harm

> **Note 2:** The more extreme the interference, the more likely the court will find conversion.

C. Trespass to Land

1. **Definition**—defendant intentionally causes a _____ invasion of someone's land

2. **Intent**

   - o Defendant need only have the intent to enter the land or cause the physical invasion
   - o Intent to commit a wrongful trespass is NOT required.
   - o Mistake of _____ is not a defense.

3. **Physical Invasion**—includes causing objects to invade the land

4. **Trespass vs. Nuisance**

   - o **Nuisance**—may or may not involve a physical invasion or intrusion
   - o **Trespass**—_____ involves an actual physical invasion or intrusion upon the land

5. **Rightful Plaintiff**—anyone in _____ can bring an action, not just the owner.

6. **Damages**—no proof of _____ damages is required.

7. **Necessity as a Defense to Trespass**

   a. **In general**—available to a person who enters onto the land of another or interferes with that individual's personal property to prevent an _____ or other severe _____

   b. **Private necessity** (partial or qualified privilege)

      - The defendant must pay for _____ damages she has caused.
      - The defendant is not liable for _____ damages.
      - The landowner may not use force to exclude the person.

   c. **Public necessity**

      - Private property is intruded upon or destroyed when necessary to protect a large number of people from public calamities.

        Example 19: *A fire breaks out in town. Gatsby's swimming pool can be utilized and even damaged to protect the public from the fire.*

      - NOT liable for damages to the property

D. Nuisance

Exam Tip 2: The law of nuisance is tested frequently on the MBE.

1. Private Nuisance

a. **Definition**—an activity that **substantially** and _____ interferes with another's _____ and _____ of land

> **Example 20:** _Loud noises or foul odors_

b. **Interference**

- Courts are vague regarding what constitutes an **unreasonable** interference.

  - Must be annoying to an ordinary, _____ person
  - Someone hypersensitive may not have a cause of action for nuisance.
  - Someone who is not actually bothered may still have a cause of action for nuisance if it would bother an ordinary, reasonable person.

- Courts will also balance the interference with the _____ of the nuisance.

c. **Not a nuisance**

- Courts have refused to find the blocking of sunlight or the obstruction of _____ to be nuisances.
- **Exception**: The spite fence or spite wall

  - If a person puts up a fence or wall with no _____ except to block a neighbor's view or sunlight, then courts will sometimes find that to be a nuisance.

d. **Defenses to private nuisance**

- Compliance with state or local administrative _____

  - Evidence as to whether the activity is reasonable
  - Not a complete defense

- **"Coming to the nuisance"**

  - Courts are hesitant to find a nuisance if you moved somewhere knowing about that conduct.
  - But NOT a complete defense—one factor considered by the court

  > **Example 21:** _If you knowingly locate your vacation home next to my cement plant, your "coming to the nuisance" will be a factor in your nuisance suit against me. It will not be dispositive._

2. Public Nuisance

o An unreasonable interference with a right common to the _____ as a whole

> *Example 22:* Old examples: blocking a public highway or waterway.

> *Example 23:* New examples: pollution, claims in tobacco litigation, claims in opioid litigation.

- o **Public official**—can bring an action on behalf of the public to abate the nuisance—e.g., a state attorney general can sue to enjoin polluting activity that harms public health
- o **Private individual**—generally cannot recover unless the individual has been harmed in a special or _____ way, different from the general public

CHAPTER 4:   NEGLIGENCE: OVERVIEW AND DUTY

A. Elements

1. _____—an obligation toward another party

2. _____—the failure to meet that obligation

3. _____—cause in fact (actual cause) and proximate cause (legal cause)

4. _____—the loss suffered

> **Exam Tip 3:** Approximately half of the Torts questions on the MBE test the topic of negligence.
>
> **Exam Tip 4:** When analyzing answer choices to negligence questions, look for the elements. For instance, if there is no duty, then you can dismiss answer choices involving breach, causation, or damages.

B. Duty

- A _____ obligation to act a certain way (as opposed to a social or moral one); two aspects:
  - o Is there a duty or not? (like a light switch, on or off)
  - o What is the nature of that duty—what is the standard of care?
    - ▪ In most cases, the standard is reasonable care.
    - ▪ There are some exceptional standards, such as utmost care for common carriers.

1. Is There a Duty? General Principles

- o In general, a duty of care is owed to all persons who may _____ be injured by the defendant's course of conduct.
- o In general, there is no duty to act _____, even if the failure to act appears to be unreasonable.

a. Duty and Foreseeability

- ▪ In many jurisdictions, courts refer to foreseeability in deciding whether there is a duty.

- There is some overlap with the concept of proximate cause.

  Exam Tip 5: If you see a problem and you think, this is an unforeseeable plaintiff, look for an answer that says, "No liability because this is an unforeseeable plaintiff," and know that it might be described as a duty problem or a proximate cause problem.

b. **Scope of Duty—Foreseeability of Harm**

  - Foreseeability of harm alone does not create a duty.
  - Most courts emphasize the foreseeability of harm to the plaintiff when evaluating the existence of a duty.

c. **Scope of Duty—Foreseeability of Plaintiff**

  - No liability to an _____ plaintiff.

    Note 3: Some courts make this a duty issue, some make it a proximate cause issue.

  - Majority view—Cardozo approach
    - A duty is owed to a plaintiff only if the plaintiff is a member of the class of persons who might be foreseeably harmed by the conduct.

  - Minority view (the Restatement view)—Andrews approach
    - Anytime conduct could harm someone, there is a duty to everyone; whether this particular plaintiff was foreseeable is a proximate cause issue

    Note 4: Whether it is analyzed as duty or proximate cause, there is no liability toward an unforeseeable plaintiff.

d. **Categories of plaintiffs:**

  - **Rescuers**—a person who comes to the aid of another is a _____ victim.
    - Cardozo: "Danger invites rescue."
  - **Crime Victims**—considered foreseeable plaintiffs in certain circumstances

    Example 24: A train negligently takes a passenger past his stop and drops him in a high-crime area. The railroad may be liable in tort if that passenger becomes a victim of a crime.

2. **Affirmative Duty to Act**

   In general, there is no affirmative duty to help others, but there are exceptions:

   a. **Assumption of duty**—Voluntary Undertaking: a person who voluntarily aids or rescues another has a duty of _____ in the performance of that aid or rescue.

> *Example 25:* *At a party, the defendant sees the plaintiff hit his head and offers to take him to the hospital. She then gets distracted by the party and forgets about him in the car. If the plaintiff suffers further injury because of the failure to follow through, the defendant could be liable for her failure to use reasonable care in the rescue she undertook.*

    b. Placing another in _____

> *Example 26:* *If Tom sees Nick drowning in a pool, he does not have a duty to rescue him. However, if Tom is the one who knocked Nick into the water, then he does have a duty.*

    c. By authority—a person with the ability and actual authority to _____ another has a duty to exercise reasonable control.

> *Example 27:* *A warden's control over a prisoner; a parent's control over a child*

    d. By relationship—defendant has a special relationship with the plaintiff

> *Example 28:* *Common carrier-passenger; innkeeper-guest*

> **Note 5:** These affirmative duties are not a Superman duty. It is a duty of _____ care to aid or assist those persons and prevent reasonably foreseeable injuries.

CHAPTER 5:   NEGLIGENCE: STANDARD OF CARE

A. Standard of Care

- Reasonably prudent person under the circumstances—generally an _____ standard

1. Mental and emotional characteristics

Objective standard—defendant is presumed to have _____ mental abilities and knowledge

2. Physical characteristics

_____ standard—particular physical characteristics are taken into account; defendant is compared with a reasonably prudent person with like characteristics

> *Example 29:* *A blind defendant will be evaluated in comparison with a reasonably prudent blind person.*

3. Intoxication

Objective standard—held to the same standard as sober people unless the intoxication was

_____

4. **Children**

   o _____ standard—reasonable child of similar _____,
     intelligence, and experience

   o **Adult activities**—Children engaged in high-risk adult activities (e.g., driving a car) are held to
     the objective standard for adults.

B. **Standards of Care for Specific Situations**

   1. **Common Carriers and Innkeepers**

      o **Traditional rule:** _____ care—highest duty of care consistent with the
        practical operation of the business

      o **Many courts today:** liable only for ordinary negligence (not a higher standard)

      > **Editorial Note 1:** A majority of courts continue to hold common carriers to the
      > higher standard of care, but now hold innkeepers to the ordinary
      > negligence standard.

   2. **Automobile Drivers**

      o **Guests and friends in a car**—drivers were traditionally liable only for _____
        negligent, wanton, or willful misconduct (often under "guest statutes").

      o Most jurisdictions apply a general duty of _____
        standard to the driver of a car.

   3. **Bailors and Bailees**

      o **Bailment**—a bailee temporarily takes _____ of another's
        (the bailor's) property.

        > ***Example 30:*** *A driver leaves a car with a valet.*

      o **Common law:** Complicated rules regarding the standard of care in a bailment; for example:

        ▪ Bailor must warn a gratuitous bailee of known _____ conditions
        ▪ If the bailor receives the sole benefit, then the bailee has a lesser duty.
        ▪ If the bailee receives a benefit, then he has a higher duty of care; even slight negligence
          can result in liability.

   4. **Emergency Situations**—standard of care is that of a reasonable person under the
      _____ circumstances.

C. **Possessors of Land**—relates to negligence in the maintenance of property (e.g., artificial or natural
   conditions on the land)

   1. **Two Approaches**

      o **Traditional tripartite structure**—one-half of jurisdictions continue to follow this approach

- The standard of care depends on the status of the entrant as a trespasser (lowest standard of care), a licensee (intermediate standard of care), or an invitee (highest standard of care).
  - **Modern (California) way**—one-half of jurisdictions follow this approach
    - Reasonable standard of care under the circumstances, with the status of the entrant as one of the relevant circumstances

2. **Trespassers**

Someone on the land without consent or _____

a. **Traditional Approach**
  - **Duty**: refrain from _____, _____, intentional, or reckless misconduct
    - Use of a _____ or trap will result in liability
  - **Undiscovered trespassers**—no duty owed
  - **Discovered or anticipated trespassers**—must warn or protect them from hidden dangers
  - **"Attractive nuisance" doctrine**—may be liable for injuries to children trespassing on the land if:
    a) An _____ condition exists in a place where the owner _____ or has reason to know that children are likely to trespass;
    b) The land possessor knows or has reason to know that the artificial condition poses an unreasonable risk of _____ or serious _____ _____;
    c) The children, because of their age, do not discover or cannot appreciate the danger;
    d) The utility of maintaining the condition is slight compared to the risk of injury; and
    e) The land possessor fails to exercise reasonable care
  - **"Flagrant trespassers"**—in some jurisdictions, owed an even lesser duty of care

3. **Licensees**
  - Enters the land with express or implied permission

    Example 31: Social guests; allowing neighborhood children to walk across the property on their way to school

  - **Traditional rule:** Land possessor has a duty to either make the property reasonably safe or warn licensees of _____ dangers.
    - No duty to _____ for dangers

- Must exercise reasonable care in conducting activities on the land

4. **Invitees**
   o Someone who comes onto the land for a material or _____ purpose
      - **Public invitee**—the land is held open to the public

        Example 32: *State fair*

      - **Business visitor**—for a purpose connected to business dealings with the possessor

        Example 33: *A customer in the owner's business*

   o Land possessor owes a duty of _____—the duty to use reasonable care to _____ the property, discover unreasonably dangerous conditions, and take reasonable steps to protect the invitee from them.
   o **Non-delegable duty**—cannot avoid the duty by assigning care of the property to an independent contractor

5. **California Way (Minority and Third Restatement approach)**
   o Some states—reasonable standard of care under all the circumstances for all entrants
      - The fact that the land entrant is trespassing is one fact that the jury may consider in deciding whether the land possessor has exercised reasonable care
   o The Third Restatement § 52—reasonable care under the circumstances, except "flagrant trespassers"
      - The only duty to flagrant trespassers is to not act in an intentional, willful, or wanton manner to cause physical harm.

        Example 34: *A burglar in a home would be a flagrant trespasser; but someone injured while walking in a public park at midnight, despite the presence of a posted notice that the park was closed after dusk, would not be.*

        Note 6: This distinction has not been widely adopted by the courts.

6. **Landlord and Tenant**
   o Landlord must:
      - Maintain safe _____ areas;
      - Warn of _____ dangers (especially for premises that are leased for public use); and
      - Repair hazardous conditions

        Note 7: As an occupier of land, the tenant continues to be liable for injuries arising from conditions within the tenant's control.

7. **Off-Premises Victim**

   o Land possessor is generally not liable for injuries resulting from _____ conditions

      ▪ Exception: Trees in urban areas

   o **Artificial conditions**—must prevent _____ risk of harm to persons not on the premises

   o Must exercise reasonable care in conducting activities on the land

CHAPTER 6: NEGLIGENCE: BREACH

A. Breach of Duty—Generally

- Definition—a violation of the _____

1. **Traditional Approach**—Reasonable person standard. Focuses on a common-sense approach of what the reasonably prudent person would do under the circumstances.

2. **Cost-Benefit Analysis**—Hand Formula (B < PL) (Burden v. Probability of harm x severity of Loss)

   > **Exam Tip 6:** Do not get hung up on the difference here; it's really just two ways of getting to the same result.

B. Breach of Duty—Specific Rules

1. **Custom**—majority practice within an industry or profession

   a. **Generally**—evidence of custom _____, but not dispositive

      > **Example 35:** Imagine that most tugboats have radios on board. This fact is relevant and therefore admissible in a case where the jury must determine if it was negligent for a tugboat not to have a radio. But it is NOT dispositive.

   b. **Professionals**—lawyers, doctors, accountants, electricians

      ▪ Custom is admissible and _____

         • Compliance with custom is a shield = _____
         • Deviation from custom is a sword = _____

   c. **Physicians**

      ▪ **Traditional rule**—physician in the "same or similar" locality
      ▪ **Modern trend**—national standard
      ▪ **Informed consent**—Patients must give informed _____:

         • Doctors must explain _____ of medical procedures.
         • Doctors are not required to inform the patient if:

            o The risks are commonly _____;

- The patient is unconscious;
- The patient waives/refuses the information;
- The patient is incompetent; or
- The patient would be harmed by disclosure (e.g., it would cause a heart attack).

2. **Statutes**—when a law or statute establishes a particular standard of care, violation of the law constitutes a breach; unexcused statutory violations constitute negligence _____.

   a. **Elements:**

      1) A criminal law or regulatory statute imposes a particular _____ for the protection or benefit of others;

      2) Defendant _____ the statute;

      3) Plaintiff must be in the _____ of people intended to be protected by the statute;

      4) The accident must be the _____ that the statute was intended to protect against; and

      5) The harm was _____ by a violation of the statute

         Example 36: Daisy is speeding and hits Myrtle with the car. The speeding law imposes a duty for the protection of others; Daisy violated it; Myrtle is in the intended class of protected persons; this is exactly the type of harm the statute is meant to protect against; and let's stipulate that the harm was caused by the statutory violation—absent the speeding, Myrtle would not have been hit. Negligence per se applies.

         Example 37: A law states that sheep must be in pens on a ship. The law is designed to protect livestock from contagious diseases. Some sheep on a ship are not in pens, and they are washed overboard. The violation of the statute does not constitute negligence per se, because the harm that occurred is not the type that the statute was intended to protect against.

         Exam Tip 7: At the heart of a negligence per se analysis is the question: is this the type of harm that the statute was intended to prevent?

   b. **Violation by plaintiff**—counts as comparative or contributory negligence

   c. **Compliance with a statute**—generally does not constitute reasonable care; does not mean the person was NOT negligent

         Example 38: I could be observing the speed limit, but that does not mean I was driving carefully. Maybe I was doing something else negligent, maybe I should have been driving even more slowly given road conditions.

d. Defenses—Excuse

- Defendant may show that complying with the statute would be even more dangerous than violating the statute
- Compliance was _____ or an emergency justified violation of the statute
- Incapacity (physical disability), exercised reasonable care in trying to comply, vagueness

Example 39: *A brother and sister are walking along the shoulder of the highway with their backs to traffic. They are hit by a car. A statute says that pedestrians on the shoulder should walk facing traffic, but they claim breaking the statute was not negligent per se because the side of the road they were supposed to walk on had very heavy traffic, and they were walking on the safer side. An excuse may be available.*

CHAPTER 7:   NEGLIGENCE: BREACH (CONT.)

A. Res Ipsa Loquitur

1. **General Principle**—in some cases, circumstantial evidence of negligence is sufficient evidence of negligence.

    Example 40: *A barrel rolls out of a building and injures a passerby. A jury could reasonably conclude that some type of negligence was the most likely cause of that injury.*

2. **Traditional Elements:**

    1) The accident was of a kind that does not ordinarily _____ in the absence of negligence;

    2) It was caused by an agent or instrumentality within the _____ _____ of the defendant; and

    3) It was not due to any action on the part of the _____

3. **Modern Trends**

    a. **Medical malpractice**—in cases in which medical personnel acted negligently to harm a patient, a small number of jurisdictions shift the burden by holding ALL defendants jointly and severally liable unless they can exonerate themselves.

    b. **Products liability**—many courts ignore the exclusivity requirement when it is clear that the defect originated upstream of the package's wrapping.

    c. **Comparative-fault jurisdictions**—many comparative-fault jurisdictions (discussed later) loosely apply the third element (i.e., that the harm was not caused by any action by the plaintiff).

4. **Third Restatement**—applies the elements generously:

   o The accident is a type of accident that _____ happens as a result of negligence of a class of actors; and

   o The defendant is a member of that class.

   > **Exam Tip 8:** Res ipsa loquitur just reminds the trier of fact that circumstantial evidence can be sufficient to infer negligence.

5. **Procedural Effect—in most jurisdictions**

   o Allows the case to go to the jury

   o Avoids a _____ in favor of the defendant (allows the plaintiff to make a prima facie case of negligence without direct evidence of negligence)

   o Jury can infer negligence, but need not

CHAPTER 8: NEGLIGENCE: CAUSATION—CAUSE IN FACT

A. **Causation—has two components:**

- Cause in fact, or actual cause
- Proximate cause, or legal cause

B. **Cause in Fact**

1. **"But-for" test**—plaintiff must show that the injury would not have occurred "but for" the defendant's negligence

   > **Example 41:** The brakes on a car are negligently repaired. The car is struck by a meteorite, injuring the driver. The person who repaired the brakes is not liable, because his negligence is not the but-for cause of the injury.

2. **Multiple or indeterminate causes**—the "but-for" test can be problematic in some cases

   a. **Common problematic circumstances:**

      ▪ **Multiple** _____—it cannot be said that any of the defendant's tortious conduct necessarily was required to produce the harm;

      > **Example 42:** Several partygoers throw a piano off a roof, damaging a car. The plaintiff will have difficulty showing that the conduct of any defendant was necessary to cause the plaintiff's harm.

      ▪ **Multiple possible** _____—the plaintiff cannot prove which of various possible causes actually caused the harm; or

      ▪ **Loss of chance**—patient is misdiagnosed due to the defendant's negligence but cannot show that the misdiagnosis actually caused the harm

b. **"Substantial factor" test**

- Used when there are conceptual problems with causation due to multiple causes
- The test is whether the defendant's tortious conduct was a "substantial factor" in causing the harm.
- Third Restatement refers to this as "multiple sufficient causes" doctrine

   Example 43: *There are two separate fires, which merge and consume the plaintiff's home. Either fire alone could have destroyed the home, so the plaintiff cannot show which fire was the actual cause. The plaintiff can show that each fire was a substantial factor in causing the harm.*

c. **Alternative causation**

- Plaintiff's harm was caused by only one of a few defendants (usually two) and each was negligent, and it cannot be determined which one caused the harm.

   Example 44: *Three friends were hunting, and two of them negligently fired their guns toward the third friend. The third friend is hit by one of the bullets, but he cannot show which gun it came from.*

- Courts will **shift the burden of proof to the defendants**—will impose joint and several liability on both unless one can show he did not cause the harm

d. **Concert of action**—if two or more tortfeasors were acting together _____ and that causes the plaintiff's harm, then all defendants will be jointly and severally liable.

3. **Loss of chance of recovery (medical misdiagnosis)**

- Under the traditional but-for analysis, a patient with less than a 50% chance of survival could not recover for negligent misdiagnosis because they were likely to die anyway; the doctor's negligence was not a "but-for" cause of the patient's death.

   Example 45: *A patient has a 20% chance of survival. The doctor negligently misdiagnoses the patient's condition, reducing the patient's chance of survival even further. The patient then dies.*

- Loss of chance doctrine—if a physician negligently reduces the plaintiff's chance of survival, then that plaintiff can recover for the lost chance of recovery.

   - Plaintiff cannot recover the entire amount of damages; but can recover the portion that represents their lost chance of survival

Example 46: *Plaintiff was misdiagnosed by defendant doctor. The plaintiff's chances of survival were 40% without the negligent misdiagnosis and 25% after the misdiagnosis. Plaintiff's total damages were $1,000,000.*

Patient's lost chance = _____

*Defendant's liability = $*_____

CHAPTER 9: NEGLIGENCE: CAUSATION—PROXIMATE CAUSE (LEGAL CAUSE)

Note 8: Recall that there is no liability to an unforeseeable plaintiff whether that rule is characterized as a duty issue or a proximate cause issue.

A. Scope of Liability

- Person is liable for the _____ that made her conduct negligent. The issue is whether the injury that occurred was within the scope of the defendant's breach.

  Example 47: *A speeding trolley is hit by a falling tree. Although speeding is negligent, being hit by a tree is not within the scope of liability—it is not one of the risks that makes speeding negligent in the first place.*

  Example 48: *An adult gives a handgun to a child. The child drops the gun on his foot, injuring himself. While it is foreseeable that a child might drop a heavy object, the heaviness of the gun is not what makes giving a gun to a child negligent in the first place. This injury could be outside the scope of liability.*

  Example 49: *The defendant fails to put a barricade around an open shaft at a construction site. Barricades are supposed to be used to protect people from falling down the shaft, but in this case a radiator falls down the shaft and injures a person at the bottom. The judge would have to decide if this particular harm was within the scope of what made the conduct negligent in the first place. (Cardozo said yes, this is within the scope of liability.)*

  Exam Tip 9: When asking whether a particular consequence of negligence is too remote, ask "is this what made the conduct negligent to begin with?"

B. Foreseeability of Harm

- Majority rule is no liability for an unforeseeable type of harm

  Example 50: *If Daisy speeds down a street and causes a pedestrian to jump out of the way and sprain an ankle, then Daisy is liable. If the sound of the car reminds a passerby of a car the passerby used to own, and the sound makes the passerby want to go for a drive, and the passerby is later in a car accident while driving, then Daisy is not liable.*

C. **Intervening vs. Superseding Causes**

- Courts used to distinguish between "intervening" causes, which do not break the chain of causation, and "superseding" causes, which do. Some courts still make this distinction.
- The real issue is whether the injury is within the _____ of what made the conduct negligent in the first place.
- Third-party criminal acts may or may not break the chain of causation.

> **Example 51:** *A train negligently takes a passenger past his stop and drops him in a high-crime area. The passenger is assaulted on the way home. The railroad may be liable in tort. The assault is an intervening criminal act, but that does not relieve the railroad of liability. It is entirely foreseeable that such an assault would happen—that's exactly the kind of risk that made the railroad's behavior negligent in the first place.*

> **Example 52:** *Daisy speeds down a street and causes a pedestrian to jump out of the way. While standing there on the sidewalk, the person is mugged by a third party. Daisy is not liable: it is not foreseeable that speeding will cause someone to get mugged. It's not one of the risks that made this conduct negligent in the first place.*

D. **Extent of Damages**

- The defendant is liable for the full extent of the plaintiff's injuries, even if the extent is unusual or unforeseeable (Eggshell plaintiff rule).

> **Example 53:** *Jordan is not watching where she is going and rear ends another car. Most people would not experience major injury, but the driver of the other car has a bone condition that leads her to have a serious injury. Jordan is liable for the full extent of the damages, even if she could not foresee them.*

> **Exam Tip 10:** The TYPE of damages must be foreseeable, but not the EXTENT.

CHAPTER 10:   NEGLIGENCE: DAMAGES

A. **Compensatory Damages**

1. **Actual (Compensatory) Damages**

   - Purpose is to make the plaintiff whole again
   - Sometimes, a plaintiff who suffers a _____ injury can also recover for _____ damages (i.e., "parasitic damages").

2. **Mitigation of Damages**

   - Plaintiff must take steps to mitigate damages
   - Can be considered a duty, but it's more of a limitation on recovery

3. **Personal Injury—Categories of Compensatory Damages**

   o _____, both past and future
   o Lost income and reduced _____
   o Pain and suffering, both past and future

4. **Property Damage**

   a. **General rule**—plaintiff may recover the difference in the _____ _____ of the property before and after the injury

   b. **Cost of repair** or **replacement value** often allowed as an alternative measure of damages

B. Collateral-Source Rule

1. **Traditional rule**

   o Benefits or payments to the plaintiff from outside sources are not credited against the liability of any tortfeasor.

   > *Example 54:* *The plaintiff's healthcare costs were covered by the plaintiff's health insurance, not the plaintiff. Under the collateral source rule, the defendant cannot claim that his damages should be reduced by that amount.*

   o Evidence of such payments is not admissible at trial.

   > **Note 9:** Typical insurance plans include a provision that any amounts recovered by the plaintiff would first reimburse the insurance company for payments made to cover the plaintiff's expenses.

2. **Modern trend**

   Most states have passed statutes that eliminate or substantially modify the collateral source rule to avoid double recovery.

C. Punitive Damages

   • Purpose is to punish and deter future conduct
   • May be available if the defendant acted _____, _____, recklessly, or with _____, or if an inherently malicious tort is involved
   • Availability may be limited by statute
   • The U.S. Supreme Court has held that as a matter of due process punitive damages must be within a single-digit ratio of any compensatory damages.

   > *Example 55:* *A punitive damages award that is ten times higher than the compensatory award would be constitutionally suspect. A punitive award that is nine times the amount of the compensatory award would not raise as much of a red flag because it stays within the single-digit ratio.*

CHAPTER 11: NEGLIGENCE: SPECIAL RULES OF LIABILITY

A. Pure Emotional Harm—Negligent Infliction of Emotional Distress (NIED)

- At common law, plaintiffs could not recover for NIED absent a physical injury.
- Now, plaintiffs can recover for NIED in specific circumstances:

1. **Zone of danger**—a plaintiff can recover for NIED if:
   - The plaintiff was within the "zone of danger" of the threatened physical impact; and
   - The threat of physical impact caused emotional distress.

     Example 56: A pedestrian is on the sidewalk and a car is being driven right at them. They are in the zone of danger of this negligent car, but the car does not actually hit the pedestrian. If the pedestrian experiences emotional distress from this event, they can recover for NIED.

     Exam Tip 11: Think of this as analogous to assault (apprehension of contact).

2. **Bystander recovery**—a bystander can recover for NIED if the bystander:

   1) Is _____ to the person injured by the defendant;

   2) Was present at the scene of the injury; and

   3) _____ the injury.

   - These are proximity requirements—relational, geographic, and temporal

3. **Special relationship**
   - Negligent mishandling of a _____
   - Negligent medical information (e.g., a negligent misdiagnosis)

4. **Physical manifestation**—most jurisdictions require some physical manifestation of distress (such as nausea, insomnia, or miscarriage).

B. Pure Economic Loss

- A plaintiff who suffers only economic loss without any related personal injury or property damage cannot recover in negligence.

     Example 57: Someone negligently damages a road. A business owner loses business due to the damage to the road. The owner cannot recover for that economic loss because the business owner has not suffered any personal injury or property damage.

     Note 10: If the plaintiff can prove personal injury or property damage, then the plaintiff can recover those damages and also economic damages.

C. Wrongful Death and Survival Actions

1. Wrongful death

- o Brought by the decedent's _____ or representative to recover losses **suffered by the spouse or representative** as a result of the decedent's death
- o Can include loss of economic support and loss of consortium

2. Survival action

- o Brought by a representative of the decedent's estate **on behalf of the** _____ for claims that the decedent would have had at the time of the decedent's death
- o Claims include damages resulting from personal injury or property damage

D. Recovery for Loss Arising from Injury to Family Members

- Family members (typically a spouse) can claim loss of consortium or companionship.

E. "Wrongful Life" and "Wrongful Birth" Claims

1. Wrongful life

- o Claim by _____ for defendant's negligent failure to properly perform a contraceptive procedure or diagnose a congenital defect
- o A few states permit a "wrongful life" action, but they limit the child's recovery to special damages attributable to the disability.

2. Wrongful birth

- o Claim by _____ for defendant's negligent failure to properly perform a contraceptive procedure or diagnose a congenital defect
- o Many states do permit recovery for the medical expenses of labor as well as for pain and suffering.
- o In the case of a child with a disability, may be able to recover damages for the additional medical expenses of caring for that child, and, in some states, may recover for emotional distress as well

CHAPTER 12: NEGLIGENCE: VICARIOUS LIABILITY AND IMMUNITIES

A. Vicarious Liability—when one person is held liable for another person's negligence

> ***Example 58:*** *An employer being held liable for an employee's torts*

- **Joint and Several Liability**—The responsible party can still be held liable for his negligence, but the employer is also liable.

  - o Sometimes the individual employee cannot be identified; the employer would be still be liable under joint and several liability.

- **Indemnification**—The party held vicariously liable may seek indemnification from the party who was directly responsible.

1. **Respondeat Superior**

   o The employer is held vicariously liable for the negligence of an employee, if it occurred within the _____.

   o **Distinction:** Employer's own negligence v. vicarious liability for an employee's conduct

     - **Direct negligence**—the employer is liable for the employer's own negligence.
     - **Vicarious liability**—the employer is liable for the employee's actions.

       Example 59: A pizza company hires bad drivers or provides them with alcohol before their shift. The employer's actions are negligent in their own right.

       Example 60: The pizza company is as careful as possible in the hiring, training, and supervising of its employees, yet one employee decides, on his own, contrary to instructions, and without the employer's knowledge, to consume alcohol while delivering pizzas, and he negligently gets into an accident. Vicarious liability applies.

   a. **Intentional torts**—employers are generally not liable for the intentional torts of employees

     - Exception: when the employee's conduct is within the _____ _____ (e.g., force is inherent in the employee's work)

       Example 61: A bar bouncer beats up a customer thinking he is serving the employer's interests.

   b. **Scope of employment—Frolic and detour**

     - **Detour** (_____ deviation from the scope of employment)—the employer _____ liable.
     - **Frolic** (_____ deviation from the scope of employment)—the employer _____ liable.

       Example 62: A pizza driver stops by the cleaners to get his dry cleaning while delivering pizzas and injures someone in the parking lot. This could be considered a detour. On the other hand, a pizza driver who skips out on work for a couple hours to have a picnic is likely to be on a frolic.

2. **Torts Committed by Independent Contractors**

   o Employers are generally _____ for torts committed by independent contractors.

       Example 63: You hire someone to paint your house while you are on vacation. The painter is negligent in the process and injures someone. You are not liable, because the painter is an independent contractor.

a. **Independent contractor v. employee**

If the employer retains a right of _____ over the way that employee does the work, then the courts will treat that person as an employee.

b. **Vicarious liability for an independent contractor's torts**

- **Non-delegable duties**:

    - Inherently _____ activities;
    - Duties to the public or specific plaintiffs for certain types of work, such as construction work by a roadway;
    - Shopkeepers have a duty to keep the premises safe for the public

- **Apparent agency doctrine**—general agency doctrine; an independent contractor (IC) will be treated as an employee if:

    - The injured person accepted the IC's services based on a reasonable belief that the IC was an employee, based on manifestations from the putative employer; and
    - The IC's negligence is a factual cause of harm to one who receives the services, and such harm is within the scope of liability.

    Example 64: *You accept medical services from a doctor wearing a name tag with the hospital logo. If the doctor commits malpractice, you may be able use apparent agency doctrine to establish the hospital's vicarious liability, even if the hospital says the doctor was an IC, if you can show you reasonably relied on the hospital's representation, as manifested in the name tag.*

3. **Business Partners**—can be liable for the torts of other business partners committed _____ of the business's purpose.

4. **Automobile Owners**

a. **Negligent entrustment**—an owner can be **directly liable** for negligently entrusting a vehicle (or any other dangerous object) to someone who is not in the position to care for it.

b. **Family-purpose doctrine**—the owner of an automobile may be vicariously liable for the tortious acts of **any family member** driving the car with permission.

c. **Owner liability statutes**—the owner of an automobile may be vicariously liable for the tortious acts of **anyone** driving the car with permission.

> **Editorial Note 2:** The Professor misspoke with regard to owner liability statutes. The owner can be vicariously liable for torts committed by anyone driving <u>with</u> permission.

5. **Parents and Children**

a. **General rule**—parents generally _____ vicariously liable for their minor children's torts.

b. **Negligence of parents**—parents can be liable for their own negligence with respect to their children's conduct (e.g., negligent supervision)

6. **"Dram Shop" Liability**

   o Holds bar owners, bartenders, and even _____ liable for injuries caused when people drink too much alcohol and injure third parties

   o Liability is based on statute and varies by state, especially liability for social hosts.

   o **Direct liability** for the server's own negligence in serving the person

   > **Exam Tip 12:** These laws hold the bar or social host liable IN ADDITION to the drunk driver, not INSTEAD OF the drunk driver.

B. **Immunities**

   1. **Federal and State Governments**

      o Traditionally, state and federal governments were immune from tort liability.

      o Immunity has been _____ by statutes.

      a. **Federal Tort Claims Act**

         ▪ Expressly _____ immunity and allows the federal government to be sued for certain kinds of torts

         ▪ There are exceptions (i.e., situations in which the federal government **maintains** immunity), including certain enumerated torts, _____ functions, and traditional governmental activities.

      b. **State governments and municipalities**

         ▪ Most states have waived immunity to some extent.

         ▪ Municipalities are generally governed by the state tort claims statute.

         ▪ **Governmental v. proprietary functions**

            • **Governmental functions** (e.g., police, court system)—immunity _____

            • **Proprietary functions** (often performed by a private company, e.g., utilities, parking lots)—immunity _____

      c. **Government officials**

         ▪ _____ **functions**—immunity applies

         ▪ _____ **functions**—no immunity

         ▪ **Westfall Act**—precludes any personal liability on the part of a federal employee under state tort law.

   2. **Intra-Family Immunities**—largely eliminated; a family member can be sued for negligently injuring another family member

      o **Core parenting activities**—immunity still applies

3. **Charitable Immunity**—_____ in most states, though some states still limit recovery

CHAPTER 13: NEGLIGENCE: SHARING LIABILITY AMONG MULTIPLE DEFENDANTS

A. Joint and Several Liability

- Two or more defendants are each liable for a single and indivisible harm to the plaintiff; each defendant is subject to liability to the plaintiff for **the entire harm**.
- Plaintiff can recover **all** of his damages from any negligent party.
- **Applications:**

  o Two or more tortfeasors;

  o Tortfeasors acting in _____;

  o Alternative liability;

  o Res ipsa loquitur used against multiple defendants;

  o Both _____ and _____ are liable

    Example 65: *Defendant 1 and Defendant 2 have been found jointly and severally liable for a judgment. However, Defendant 2 is cannot be found to enforce the judgment. Defendant 1 will be liable for the entire amount of damages.*

    Example 66: *Contribution: Following the above example, Defendant 1 pays the entire judgment to the plaintiff. Defendant 1 now has a right of contribution against Defendant 2 for paying more than his share of the total liability.*

    Example 67: *Indemnification: Defendant 1 is an employer and Defendant 2 is the negligent employee. Defendant 1 pays the full amount of the judgment and seeks full reimbursement for payment pursuant to the employee's duty of indemnification.*

- Multiple defendants can be held jointly and severally liable, even if a jury apportions each defendant a different percentage of fault.

    Note 11: Some jurisdictions limit a defendant's joint liability if he is less than 10% at fault. The defendant will be liable only for his share of fault.

CHAPTER 14: NEGLIGENCE: DEFENSES

A. Contributory Negligence

- If the plaintiff was negligent in some way, that negligence completely _____ the plaintiff's recovery.

Example 68: *Jordan and Daisy are both driving negligently. Owing to both their negligence, they hit each other. Jordan tries to sue Daisy for negligently causing her injuries, but Daisy has a defense of contributory negligence that is a complete bar to recovery.*

- This is the old common-law rule and is still the rule in only a handful of states.

1. **"Last clear chance" doctrine**

   o Allows a negligent plaintiff to recover upon showing that the defendant had the last clear chance to avoid injuring the plaintiff but failed to do so.

   Example 69: *Daisy is speeding and sees Myrtle negligently walk into the street. She should not feel free to run her over on the theory that Myrtle's contributory negligence will relieve her of liability. If Daisy has the last clear chance to avoid the injury, then contributory negligence will not be a bar.*

B. **Comparative Fault**

- Plaintiff's negligence does not completely bar recovery; it _____ the plaintiff's ability to recover
- Most jurisdictions have adopted a comparative fault approach.

1. **Pure comparative negligence**—plaintiff's recovery is reduced by plaintiff's percentage of fault

   Example 70: *Jordan and Daisy negligently collide, and Jordan sues Daisy. If the jury finds that the plaintiff (Jordan) is 10% at fault and Daisy is 90 % at fault. Jordan will recover only 90% of the judgment that she was not at fault for.*

   Example 71: *Alternatively, If the jury finds that the Jordan (the plaintiff) is 90% at fault, then she can recover only 10% of her damages.*

2. **Modified comparative negligence**

   o If the plaintiff is **MORE at fault** than the defendant, then the plaintiff's recovery is

   _____.

   Example 72: *Jordan and Daisy negligently collide, and Jordan sues Daisy. If the jury determines that Jordan is more at fault than Daisy, she cannot recover.*

   o **Some jurisdictions:** If the plaintiff and defendant are **EQUALLY at fault**, then the plaintiff's recovery is barred.

   Example 73: *Jordan and Daisy negligently collide, and Jordan sues Daisy. If the jury determines that Jordan is 50% at fault, she cannot recover.*

a. Multiple defendants

> *Example 74:* Jordan, Daisy, and Gatsby are all driving negligently and end up in a collision. Jordan sues Daisy and Gatsby in a modified comparative negligence jurisdiction.

- If there is more than one defendant, the plaintiff's negligence is compared with the total negligence of all defendants combined.

> *Example 75:* Jordan is 40% at fault and Daisy and Gatsby are each 30% liable (60% liable together). Jordan can recover because her percent of fault is less than Daisy and Gatsby combined.

> *Example 76:* Jordan is 60% at fault and Daisy and Gatsby are each 20% at fault. Jordan cannot recover because she is more at fault than the defendants combined.

3. Relationship to other defenses

- Most courts no longer use the last clear chance doctrine in a comparative negligence jurisdiction.
- Comparative fault is not a defense to _____ torts
- Will reduce the plaintiff's recovery even if the defendant's conduct is willful, wanton, or reckless

C. Imputed Contributory Negligence

- One party's negligence is imputed to another party

> *Example 77:* An employee is negligently driving during the scope of employment and is in a car accident with another negligent driver. The negligence of the employee might be imputed to the employer in the employer's suit against the third party who negligently damaged the employer's vehicle.

> *Example 78:* Can also apply to business partners

- Imputed contributory negligence is generally disfavored. It does NOT apply to:

- A child plaintiff whose parent's negligence was a contributing cause of her harm, in a suit against a third party.
- A married plaintiff whose spouse was contributorily negligent in causing the harm, in a suit against a third party.

D. Assumption of the Risk

- Applies when a party _____ and _____ embraces a risk for some purpose of his own
- Analogous to the defense of _____ in intentional torts
- Can be express or implied

1. **Express assumption of risk**

   o Typically a writing, such as an exculpatory clause in a contract

   o In general, parties can contract to disclaim liability for negligence.

   o Courts will ask two questions:

      1) Is the waiver _____?

      2) Is the waiver _____?

   o Courts might not enforce exculpatory provisions in certain situations:

      ▪ The waiver disclaims liability for _____ or _____ misconduct;

      ▪ There is a gross disparity of _____ between the two parties;

      ▪ The party seeking to enforce the provision offers services of great importance to the public (e.g., medical services);

      ▪ The provision is subject to contract defenses (e.g., fraud or duress);

      ▪ The enforcement would be against public _____

2. **Implied assumption of risk**

   a. **Participants in and spectators of athletic events**

      ▪ Courts often hold that a participant or spectator cannot recover because the party knew of the risks and chose to accept those risks.

   b. **Unreasonably proceeding in the face of known, specific risk**

      ▪ Occurs when the plaintiff voluntarily encounters a known, specific risk

      ▪ **Contributory negligence jurisdictions** and a minority of comparative-fault jurisdictions—this form of assumption of the risk remains a total bar to recovery.

      ▪ **Most comparative fault jurisdictions**—this form of assumption of the risk has been merged into the comparative-fault analysis and merely reduces recovery.

         • The issue is whether the plaintiff reasonably or unreasonably encountered the risk

CHAPTER 15: STRICT LIABILITY

A. In General

   • Under strict liability, defendant will be liable no matter how _____ they were

   • Three general categories:

      o Abnormally _____ activities;

      o _____; and

      o Defective products

B. Abnormally Dangerous Activities

1. **Basic Rule**—a defendant engaged in an abnormally dangerous activity will be held strictly liable for personal injuries and property damage caused by the activity, regardless of _____ to prevent the harm.

2. **"Abnormally Dangerous" Activity factors:**

   ○ Whether it creates a foreseeable and highly _____ risk of harm even when the actor takes due care;

   ○ The _____ of the harm resulting from the activity;

   ○ The appropriateness of the _____ for the activity;

   ○ Whether it has great value to the community

   > *Example 79:* *Blasting is the classic example.*

3. **Scope of Liability**—defendant is liable for the harm that _____ from the risk that made the activity abnormally dangerous

   > *Example 80:* *If your truck is full of explosives and it blows up, then you may be strictly liable.*

   > *Example 81:* *If your truck is full of explosives and you run over a pedestrian, then you are liable only if you were negligent, because that is not the risk that made explosives abnormally dangerous.*

C. Animals

1. **Wild Animals**—animals that, as a _____ or _____, are not customarily kept in the service of humankind

   a. **Dangerous propensity**—owners are strictly liable for the harm arising from the animal's dangerous propensities.

   b. **Liability to trespassers**

      ▪ Injuries caused to _____ or _____—strictly liable

      ▪ _____—not strictly liable

         • **Exception** in some jurisdictions: injuries caused by a _____ _____

2. **Domestic Animals**

   a. **Known to be dangerous**—if the owner _____ or has reason to know that the particular animal has _____, the owner is strictly liable.

   b. **"Dog-bite" statutes**—many states hold dog owners strictly liable for injuries caused by dogs

      > **Note 12:** "Dog-bite" statutes vary widely from state to state.

3. **Trespassing Animals**—the owner of any animal is strictly liable for reasonably
_____ damage caused by his animal while trespassing on
another's land.

> *Example 82:* *The cows get out and trample a neighbor's property.*

a. **Exceptions:**

- **Household pets**, unless the owner knows or has reason to know that the pet is
_____ on another's property in a harmful way
- **Animals on public roads**—a _____ standard applies

D. **Defenses to Strict Liability**

1. **Contributory Negligence**—the plaintiff's contributory negligence _____
bar recovery.

2. **Comparative Negligence**—jurisdictions vary:

o   In some, the plaintiff's negligence does not bar recovery;
o   In others, and under the Third Restatement, the plaintiff's negligence will diminish her
recovery.

3. **Assumption of the Risk**—the plaintiff's assumption of the risk is a _____
_____ to recovery.

CHAPTER 16:   PRODUCTS LIABILITY

A. **Overview**—a plaintiff can bring different types of claims for products liability:

- Negligence—plaintiff must prove duty, breach, causation, and damages
- Strict Liability for Defective Products
- Breach of Warranty Claim

B. **Strict Products Liability**

- There are three types of product defects: manufacturing defects, design defects, and failure to
warn.

> *Example 83:* *A motorcycle may be defective in different ways:*
>
> *Manufacture: The motorcycle has plastic bolts where there are supposed to be metal bolts; the motorcycle was defectively manufactured.*
>
> *Design: The motorcycle was built as designed, but it is unstable when carrying a passenger or heavy rider; the motorcycle's design is defective.*
>
> *Failure to warn: The manufacturer should have warned riders that the motorcycle cannot accommodate passengers.*

1. **Elements of a Claim**—the plaintiff must show:

   o The product was _____ (in manufacture, design, or failure to warn);

   o The defect existed when the product left the defendant's _____; and

   o The defect caused the plaintiff's injury when the product was used in a
   _____ way.

   > **Note 13:** Strict liability can apply to multiple parties in the chain of producing and selling the product. Potential defendants are discussed more below.

2. **Defective Product**

   a. **Manufacturing defect**

      ▪ The product deviated from its intended _____.

      ▪ The product does not conform to the manufacturer's own
      _____.

   b. **Design defect**—two tests:

      ▪ **Consumer expectation test**—the product is defective in design if it is less safe than the
      _____ would expect.

      ▪ **Risk-utility test**—the product is defective in design if the risks outweigh its benefits;
      must show that there is a reasonable _____ design

      > **Note 14:** The more technical the product is, the more likely it is that experts will be required and the risk-utility test will apply.

   c. **Failure to warn**—of a foreseeable risk that is not _____ to an ordinary user

      ▪ **Learned Intermediary rule (Often applies to prescription drugs):**

        • Manufacturers of prescription drugs must warn the prescribing
        _____.

        • **Exception:** drugs marketed directly to consumers

   d. **Inference of defect**—courts may allow proof of a defect by _____
   evidence, especially when the defect causes the product to be destroyed.

3. **Plaintiffs**

   o No privity requirement—can sue up and down the chain of production or distribution

   o Anyone foreseeably injured by a defective product, including purchasers, other users, and bystanders

4. **Defendants**

   o Anyone who _____ the product when it is defective is potentially strictly liable.

   o Must be in the chain of distribution and in the _____ of selling

      ▪ **Casual sellers**—not strictly liable, but may be liable for negligence

Example 84: *Selling something to a friend or neighbor.*

o The seller may seek indemnification from another party (e.g., the manufacturer).

CHAPTER 17: PRODUCTS LIABILITY (CONT.)

A. Strict Products Liability (Cont.)

1. **Damages**

   o Plaintiff can recover for _____ or
   _____

   o **Purely economic loss**—generally not permissible under a strict-liability theory

   Note 15: May be brought as a breach of warranty claim (discussed below).

2. **Defenses**

   a. **Comparative fault**—the plaintiff's own _____ will reduce his recovery in a strict-products-liability action.

   b. **Contributory negligence**—courts hesitate to allow the plaintiff's negligence to completely bar the plaintiff's recovery against the defendant for a defective product.

   c. **Assumption of the risk**—if the risk is one that the plaintiff knew about and voluntarily chose, then the plaintiff will not be allowed to recover.

   d. **Product misuse, modification, or alteration**

      ▪ Generally, the manufacturer (or seller) will be liable as long as the misuse, modification, or alteration was _____.

      Example 85: *A manufacturer makes a car that explodes at speeds over 80 mph. Drivers are not supposed to speed, but it is foreseeable that drivers exceed the speed limit at times. The manufacturer will be liable for the defect.*

      ▪ Foreseeable misuses, modifications, and alterations are viewed as examples of comparative negligence.

   e. **Substantial change in the product**—_____ recovery

      Example 86: *Using a ceiling fan as an airplane propeller*

   f. **Compliance with governmental standards**

      ▪ Compliance with safety standards is _____ that the product is not defective, but it is not _____ evidence.

      ▪ **Exception: federal preemption**—when Congress has preempted regulation in a particular area (expressly by statute or impliedly by regulating the field)

g. **"State of the art" defense**

- In some jurisdictions, the relevant state of the art at the time of manufacture or warning is evidence that the product is not defective.
- In other jurisdictions, compliance with the state of the art is a _____ _____ to recovery.

h. **Disclaimers, limitations, and waivers**—generally _____ strict-liability claims for defective products

B. Warranties

- Warranty claims may generally be brought up and down the distribution chain.
- Privity is not required.

1. **Implied warranties—Two types:**

   o **Merchantability**—the product is suitable for the _____ purposes for which it is sold.

   o **Fitness for a particular purpose**—the seller knows the particular purpose for which the product is being sold, and the buyer _____ on the seller's skill or judgment.

2. **Express Warranties**—an affirmation of fact or a promise by the seller that is part of the basis of the bargain

3. **Defenses**

   a. **Disclaimers**

   > **Note 16:** Disclaimers are covered in the Contracts materials.

   b. **Tort Defenses**

   - Assumption of the risk
   - Comparative fault
   - Contributory negligence
   - Product misuse

C. Review

1. **Three types of suits:**

   o Negligence
   o Strict liability for defective product
   o Breach of implied warranty

2. **Three ways a product may be defective:**

   o Manufacture
   o Design
   o Warning

CHAPTER 18: DEFAMATION

A. In General

- In a defamation action, a plaintiff must prove that the defendant:
    - Made a defamatory statement;
    - That is _____ the plaintiff;
    - The statement was _____ to a third party who understood its defamatory nature; and
    - _____ to the plaintiff's reputation results.

B. Defamatory Language

- Language that diminishes respect, esteem, or _____ toward the plaintiff, or _____ others from associating with the plaintiff
- **Falsity**—defamatory statements must be false in order to be actionable
- An _____ is not actionable as defamation. An opinion that implies a basis in fact is.

    > *Example 87:* *If the defendant said, "In my opinion, John Jones is a terrible artist," cannot be the basis for a defamation action because people can disagree regarding the quality of an artist's paintings.*

    > *Example 88:* *The statement, "In my opinion, John Jones is a thief," could be regarded as defamatory because it implies the fact that John Jones stole something.*

C. "Of or Concerning" the Plaintiff

- A reasonable person must believe that the defamatory language referred to this particular plaintiff.
- **Statements referring to a group**—a member of the group can bring an action only if the group is so small or the context is such that the matter can _____ be understood to refer to that member.

D. Publication

- The statement must be communicated to a third party.
- A person who _____ a defamatory statement may be liable for defamation.
- Federal statute provides that internet service providers and platforms are _____ for the purposes of defamation.

E. Constitutional Requirements—constitutional limitations will depend on the type of plaintiff and the content of the statement.

1. **Types of plaintiffs**

   a. **Public official**—a person who has substantial responsibility or control over a
   _____ office, including a political candidate

   b. **Public figure**

      ▪ **General purpose public figure**—a person of persuasive power and
      _____ in society

      ▪ **Limited purpose public figure**—a person who thrusts himself into a particular
      _____

   c. **Private individuals**

2. **Constitutional limitations**

   a. **Public official/public figure**—the plaintiff must prove that the person who made the
   statement either _____ that it was false or acted with _____
   _____ for the truth

      ▪ Also called the "actual malice" standard

      > **Note 17:** Malice here does not mean motive, just that the defendant either
      > knew that the statement was false or was reckless with regard to the truth.

   b. **Private individual**

      ▪ **Matter of public concern**—plaintiff must prove that the statement is _____
      and that the person who made the statement was _____
      with respect to the falsehood (should have known the statement was false)

      ▪ **Not a matter of public concern**—it is unclear whether constitutional limitations apply; a
      state need not require a plaintiff to prove negligence

      > **Exam Tip 13:** In most jurisdictions, a plaintiff must show that the defendant
      > was at least negligent as to the falsity of the statement.

F. **Libel and Slander**

   • **Libel**—a written, _____, or recorded statement (including TV/radio
   broadcasts, e-mail, and electronic communications)

   • **Slander**—a statement that is _____

   • **Damages:**

      ○ **Libel**—plaintiff may recover _____ damages (i.e., recovery without
      _____ of measurable harm)

      ○ **Slander**—the plaintiff must prove _____ damages (requires a
      showing of economic loss); exceptions include statements communicating **slander per se**:

         ▪ Commission of a serious _____

         ▪ Unfitness for a trade or profession

- ▪ Having a loathsome _____
- ▪ Severe _____ misconduct

G. Constitutional Limitations on Damages

1. **Private individual and matter of public concern**—plaintiff can recover only _____ damages unless she shows _____

2. **Private individual but NOT a matter of public concern**—plaintiff may recover _____ damages, including presumed damages, without proving actual malice.

CHAPTER 19:   DEFENSES TO DEFAMATION; PRIVACY TORTS

A. Defenses to Defamation

1. **Truth**—absolute defense; a truthful statement cannot be _____ as defamation.

2. **Consent**—if you consent to the defamation, you cannot sue.

3. **Privileges**

   a. **Absolute privileges**—the speaker is completely _____ from liability for defamation; includes statements made:

      - ▪ In the course of judicial proceedings;
      - ▪ In the course of _____ proceedings;
      - ▪ Between _____; and
      - ▪ In required publications by radio and TV (e.g., statements by a political candidate that a station must carry and may not censor)

   b. **Conditional privilege**—the statement is made in _____ pursuant to some duty or responsibility; includes statements made:

      - ▪ In the interest of the defendant (e.g., defending your reputation);
      - ▪ In the interest of the recipient of the statement; or
      - ▪ Affecting some important public interest

        Example 89: Your company is about to hire someone. You tell the HR department that you think the potential candidate has embezzled money from another company. If your statement turns out to be false, you may be protected by the conditional privilege.

B. Invasion of Privacy

- • Right of privacy applies to _____, not _____
- • Typically terminates upon the _____ of the plaintiff
- • Invasion of privacy includes _____ separate causes of action

1. **Intrusion Upon Seclusion**—defendant intrudes upon the plaintiff's private affairs, in a manner that is objectionable to a _____ person

    Example 90: *Phone tapping; hacking into medical records; peeping Toms*

2. **False Light**—defendant (1) makes public facts about the plaintiff, (2) that place the plaintiff in a false light, (3) which would be highly _____ to a reasonable person

    Example 91: *Writing a story about one person and including a mug shot of someone else.*

3. **Appropriation of the Right to Publicity**—a property-like cause of action when someone (1) appropriates another's _____ or _____ (2) for the defendant's advantage (3) without _____, and (4) causes injury

    Note 19: The appropriation must be exploitative, but it need not be commercial.

    Example 92: *Utilizing someone's voice in a commercial*

4. **Public Disclosure of Private Facts**

    o (1) Defendant _____ a matter concerning the private life of another; and

    o (2) The matter publicized:

    ▪ (a) Is _____ to a reasonable person; and

    ▪ (b) Is not of _____ concern to the public.

    o This tort is difficult to prove because courts broadly define "legitimate public concern"

5. **Damages**—plaintiff need not prove special damages; emotional or mental distress is sufficient

6. **Defenses**

    o **Qualified and absolute privilege**—applicable to "false light" and "public disclosure" claims

    o **Consent**—applicable to invasion of privacy torts

    o **Truth**—NOT a defense to privacy torts, as opposed to defamation

CHAPTER 20:   MISREPRESENTATION AND BUSINESS TORTS

A. **Intentional Misrepresentation (Fraud)**—established by proof of the following six elements:

1. **False Representation**

    o Must be about a _____ fact

    o Can involve deceptive or misleading statements

    o Can arise through _____ a material fact

- Generally, no duty to _____ material facts to other parties; may be an affirmative duty if:
  - There is a _____ relationship;
  - The other party is likely to be misled by statements the defendant made earlier; or
  - The defendant is aware that the other party is _____ about the basic facts of the transaction, and custom suggests that disclosure should be made.

2. **Scienter**—defendant _____ that the representation is false or acted with _____ for its falsehood

3. **Intent**—defendant must intend to _____ the plaintiff to act in _____ on the misrepresentation

4. **Causation**—the misrepresentation must have caused the plaintiff to act or refrain from acting

5. **Justifiable Reliance**—reliance is NOT justifiable if the facts are _____ false or it is clear that the defendant was stating an _____.

6. **Damages**
   - Plaintiff must prove actual, economic, pecuniary loss
   - _____ damages are NOT available.
   - **Most jurisdictions**—recovery is the "benefit of the _____": the difference between the actual value received in the transaction and the value that would have been received if the misrepresentation were true (contract-like damages)
   - **Some jurisdictions**—allow only out-of-pocket losses (tort-like damages)

     Example 93: *Max persuades Herman to invest in a new aquarium by knowingly misrepresenting that all the permits have cleared. In fact, Max has not filed for any permits. Max intended to induce Herman to rely on his false statement, and Herman did so. Max will be liable to Herman for intentional misrepresentation.*

B. **Negligent Misrepresentation**—failure to take due care in providing information

   1. **Elements**
      - The defendant provided _____ information to a plaintiff;
      - As a result of the defendant's _____ in preparing the information;
      - During the course of a _____ or profession;
      - Causing justifiable reliance; and
      - The plaintiff is either:
        - In a _____ relationship with the defendant; or
        - The plaintiff is a third party known by the defendant to be a member of the limited group for whose benefit the information is supplied

Example 94: A defendant real estate agent knows the buyer wants a quiet home. He says that a particular home is surrounded by peace and quiet, when in fact an extremely noisy long-term project is taking place next door. The agent did not know about the project but should have known with reasonable care.

2. **Defenses**—negligence defenses _____ raised

3. **Damages**—plaintiff can recover reliance (out-of-pocket) and _____ damages if the negligent representation is proven with sufficient certainty

> **Exam Tip 14:** Do not confuse this with the tort of negligence. Negligence generally applies when there is physical bodily injury or damage to property.

C. Intentional Interference with Business Relations

1. Intentional Interference with a Contract

a. Elements:

- A valid _____ existed between the plaintiff and a third party;
- Defendant knew of the contractual relationship;
- Defendant **intentionally interfered** with the contract, resulting in a _____; and
- The breach caused damages to the plaintiff

b. Nature of the contract

- Must be a valid contract
- Cannot be terminable _____

c. Interference with performance other than inducing breach

- Defendant may be liable when he prevents a party from fulfilling its contractual obligations or substantially adds to the _____ of performance
- Defendant's conduct must exceed _____ and free expression

2. Interference with a Prospective Economic Advantage

- Defendant intentionally interferes with a prospective business relationship or benefit between the plaintiff and a third party, in the absence of a contract
- The elements are the same as for intentional interference with a contract (without the contract), but the conduct must be _____.

3. Misappropriation of Trade Secrets

- Plaintiff owns information that is not _____ (a valid trade secret);
- Plaintiff has taken reasonable precautions to protect it; and
- Defendant acquires the secret by _____

D. Injurious Falsehoods

1. Trade Libel—need not necessarily damage the business's reputation

- o Publication;
- o Of a false or _____ statement;
- o With malice;
- o Relating to the plaintiff's title to his business, the quality of his business, or the quality of its products; and
- o Causing _____ damages as a result of interference with or damage to business relationships

  > **Example 95:** *You publish an article in the paper stating, "I would like to congratulate my long-time friend and competitor who retired, closed his business, and moved to Florida. I look forward to serving all of his customers." If this statement is false and damages the business, then it can be actionable.*

2. Slander of Title

- o Publication;
- o Of a _____ statement;
- o Derogatory to the plaintiff's title;
- o With _____;
- o Causing special damages; and
- o Diminishes value in the eyes of third parties.

E. Wrongful Use of the Legal System

1. Malicious Prosecution

A person intentionally and maliciously institutes or pursues a legal action for an _____ _____, without _____, and the action is dismissed in favor of the person against whom it was brought.

2. Abuse of Process

- o The defendant sets in motion a legal procedure in the proper form but has abused it to achieve some _____ motive.
- o Some willful act perpetrated in the use of the process that is not proper in the regular conduct of that proceeding

  > **Example 96:** *A local board of education sued a teachers' union and subpoenaed 87 teachers for a hearing in order to prevent the teachers from walking a picket line during a labor dispute between the union and the board.*

- o The conduct must also cause damages.

[END OF HANDOUT]